The Good Tourist

Katie Wood is a name many travellers are familiar with. As a well established travel writer and journalist, she has tackled everything from backpacking in Europe, in her bestseller *Europe by Train*, to the deluxe world of country houses in *The Best of British Country House Hotels*. With twenty-three successful guidebooks to her name, and a string of freelance commissions, from the *Scotsman* and *Guardian* to the BBC, she is well qualified to comment on all aspects of the travel industry.

The perfect marriage of minds, from this series' point of view, has resulted from her marriage to Syd House. Syd is a graduate of ecological sciences and has considerable experience of practical management in conservation. Working as a Conservator for the Forestry Commission, he is responsible for encouraging the management and conservation of the woods and forests of East Central Scotland. He has travelled the world in his own right, before combining his skills with those of his wife and looking at the impact of tourism on the environment. Together they bring you the definitive work on 'green travel', examined from both the tourist and the environmental point of view.

Syd and Katie are both graduates of Edinburgh University and share a Scottish background. Katie was born in Edinburgh. After graduation she worked in journalism, and following an eighteen-month spell backpacking in Europe, her first travel guide was published in 1983. A Fellowship from the Royal Geographical Society, several travel consultancies and sixty-three countries later she is still writing and travelling full-time. Syd, originally from Gourock, travelled the world before returning to Scotland, where he became immersed in conservation matters and resumed managerial work within the Forestry Commission. He too is a Fellow of the Royal Geographical Society.

The couple married in 1984. They have two young sons, Andrew and Euan, live in Perth, Scotland, and lead a lifestyle punctuated with foreign travel, midnight writing, and an active involvement in conservation matters. They have recently completed consultancy work on the environmental impact of tourism for, among others, the English Tourist Board, the Scottish Tourist Board and British Airways.

By the same author

Europe by Train
The Best of British Country House Hotels
Ireland
Scotland
The Cheap Sleep Guide to Europe
The 100 Greatest Holidays in the World*
The 1992 Business Travel Guide*
The Good Tourist*
The Good Tourist in France*
The Good Tourist in the UK*

Also available from Mandarin Paperbacks

The Good Tourist in Turkey

KATIE WOOD
& SYD HOUSE

Mandarin

In memory of my mother, Mariette,
without whose practical help and
support this, like all my books,
could not have been written.

A Mandarin Paperback
THE GOOD TOURIST IN TURKEY

First published in Great Britain 1993
by Mandarin Paperbacks
an imprint of Reed Consumer Books Ltd
Michelin House, 81 Fulham Road, London SW3 6RB
and Auckland, Melbourne, Singapore and Toronto

Copyright © 1993 by Katie Wood and Syd House
The authors have asserted their moral rights.

A CIP catalogue record for this title
is available from the British Library
ISBN 0 7493 0809 5

Printed and bound in Great Britain
by Cox & Wyman Ltd, Reading, Berks

The Good Tourist Series

This book is aimed at the educated, probably well travelled, but most importantly environmentally-aware person. The person who loves travel but doesn't want to spoil what he or she sets out to see. It is quite different from any other guide you are likely to have seen. It is not written for the extremist Green fringe. We don't advocate everyone cycles everywhere, eats vegan and sleeps in communes. It's a soft but effective green message you'll get from this guide, and indeed any book in the *Good Tourist* series. But it works and is practical.

This series aims to show you how to visit a country in a way that gives you the most pleasure and also does the least harm (and often does actual good) for the region you are holidaying in. So, for example, we recommend you to try alternative routes rather than the crowded, well-documented ones; suggest you stay in a family-run B&B, rather than check in to the sanitised chain-hotel down the road; and we encourage you to meet the locals, giving practical suggestions on where to do this, and to learn about the impact that tourism has (and therefore the impact YOU will have) in that region. It's amazing to think that no other guidebook in the bookshop will actually tell you, the tourist, things like how many other tourists go to that area; how much money you and other visitors bring to the region in the form of tourism, and where tourism is having a detrimental impact on the environment or society, and what you can do to help.

There is a new breed of tourist; keep to learn as much as possible about where they're travelling, not just have run-of-the-mill info regurgitated in a bland style. We give you the sort of info only the locals will tell you. **Because we've asked the locals:** we've asked them to tell us where the best places to go, stay and eat are; we've asked them how tourists can be more sensitive in their area; we've asked for their opinions. Everyone from the local Ecological Group to the regional tourist councils have been canvassed and have had their say where tourists should go, and what they should know about their region. Not exactly earth shattering stuff, you might think. But, believe it or not, it's not been done before, and you'll soon see the difference it makes. Now you really can experience a genuine slice of local culture, not one put on for the tourist hordes.

Our contributors and researchers all know and have travelled extensively in (and in 99 per cent of cases, actually lived in) the regions on which they comment. Syd House and I have laid our thoughts on tourism out in the guide which launched this series – *The Good Tourist – a worldwide guide for the green traveller* (Mandarin Paperbacks £5.99). We believe that whilst immense problems are created by mass tourism and its associated developments, there are ways in which tourism can be developed which bring benefits not only to tourists, but also to the host countries and the natural environment. We hope through this series to encourage the tourist to be aware of the issues, and by following the practical guidelines found in the books, to enjoy being what until recently has been called a contradiction in terms – a 'good tourist'.

Katie Wood

We welcome comments. Please write to us care of the publishers:

Katie Wood & Syd House
Mandarin Paperbacks
Michelin House
81 Fulham Road
London SW3 6RB

Contents

Acknowledgements

The authors wish gratefully to acknowledge the support of the Kathleen Blundell Trust in the researching and writing of this work. Thanks are also due to Exodus Expeditions, Explore Worldwide, Simply Turkey and Turkish Delight.

Our thanks are owed to the following people who worked long and hard on this project:

Editorial Assistant: Vicky Lewis
Vicky Lewis first came to travel writing through membership of Tourism Concern and has been involved with the *Good Tourist* series since early days. After working on *The Good Tourist in France*, she became Katie Wood's editorial assistant, contributing to various travel guides and newspaper articles, as well as being involved in consultancy work for tourist boards on green tourism issues. Her contributions to *The Good Tourist in Turkey* are the fruits of an in-depth exploration of the western part of the country.

Researchers:
Vicky Lewis: Istanbul; Thrace & Marmara; The Aegean.

Pat Yale: The Mediterranean; Central Anatolia; The Black Sea; Eastern Turkey. Pat Yale is a freelance travel journalist, and author of *The Budget Travel Handbook* and *From Tourist Attraction to Heritage Tourism*, a study of the tourist attractions business. An ex-travel agent, she has travelled widely, mainly in non-European countries. She has made several trips to Turkey, the first in 1974 before the tourism boom, the most recent in 1991 after the Gulf War.

Caroline Upton: Introduction. Caroline Upton is a graduate of geological and environmental sciences. She works full time for an environmental consultancy in Sheffield, combining this with travelling and writing. Prior to taking up her current post she travelled and worked abroad for a year, spending much of this time in Turkey, India and Nepal.

Introduction

Highlights of Turkey

First-time visitors to Turkey are often attracted by the contrasts inherent in a country which is part Asia and part Europe. While offering the excitement of the unknown, the western aspects of the culture afford an element of the familiar, which is important to many tourists. This mix of the east and west is undoubtedly one of the highlights of Turkey. It is frequently described in the travel literature as a 'land of contrasts' – a phrase that has been overused to the point of becoming a cliché by the tourist industry in its endeavours to sell the latest destination to the prospective traveller, but it has rarely been more appropriately applied than in the case of Turkey. The physical extent and variety of the landscape is fully matched by the cultural variations between east and west, city and village. The major cities of the west, such as Istanbul and Bursa, afford many of the facilities and entertainments of the main European centres, while the resorts offer the beautiful extensive beaches combined with summer sunshine and ancient ruins which originally attracted so many tourists to Greece. But in Turkey it is still possible to find such areas relatively unspoilt. The poverty and squalor which may deter tourists from visiting other parts of Asia are not so apparent, at least in the west of Turkey, although they do, of course, exist.

In contrast to the western aspects of the culture, the way of life in the countryside and small towns, particularly in central and eastern Anatolia, has all the fascination for the visitor of a lifestyle which has changed little over the centuries. Fifty-seven per cent of the population are still country dwellers and several million people retain a semi-nomadic lifestyle. While Istanbul is a major centre for the Armenian and Greek minorities, the less well-known Muhacir minority group are important members of these farming communities of central Anatolia and also Thrace. Literally translated, 'Muhacir' means 'refugee', the original refugees being Tartars from Crimea, who were later joined by Circassian people in the late 1800s and Balkan Muslims in the late nineteenth and early twentieth centuries. Their villages, along the edge of the Anatolian plateau, are still recognisable today by the traditions which the inhabitants have kept alive. The arrival of the Muhacirs was also an important impetus for the indigenous population to change from a semi-nomadic to a settled lifestyle, originally in order to retain their land. This process of change is still continuing, as government policy and foreign aid programmes since the 1950s have favoured more intensive agriculture.

Turkey's rich cultural heritage is expressed in a number of ways, perhaps most notably through its art and architecture. Of the numerous people who have invaded or conquered the country throughout its turbulent history, the greatest artistic legacy comes from periods of occupation of the Hittites, Greeks and Romans, the Byzantines and the Seljuk and Ottoman Turks. The treasures derived from these periods can be viewed today in the fine museums of Ankara and Istanbul, of which the Turks are commendably proud, and even more impressively in the wealth of vast archaeological sites. Of particular note are the remains of Pergamon, which tower above the modern town of Bergama and are a wonderful example of Greek Hellenistic architecture. Other ancient cities show a combination of influences, with one city often built on the site of another. At Aphrodisias, south-east of Izmir, which was originally settled in the third millenium BC, the Greek city was added to and modified by the Romans and excavations have revealed a complex of stunning buildings including Roman baths, theatre and stadium. Similarly the Temple of Apollo at Didyma is an original Greek structure which was completed by the Romans. The city of Ephesus, perhaps the most famous archaeological site in Turkey, was an established port by the sixth century BC and its ruins include Byzantine structures and, nearby at Selcuk, the Ionic Temple of Artemis, one of the Seven Wonders of the Ancient World, in addition to a wealth of Hellenistic and Roman remains. Lesser known Xanthos, on the Mediterranean, is a World Heritage Site.

Byzantine art is most impressively displayed in the frescoes of the unique rock-cut churches of Cappadocia, while the Aya Sofya basilica in Istanbul is the finest example in Turkey of Byzantine grandeur in its combination of Greek and Roman styles with Oriental influences.

Turkey's position on a number of important caravan routes in the tenth to thirteenth centuries brought artists and craftsmen to the Seljuk capital at Konya, where the distinctive architectural style which reflected these Asian influences developed. Few Seljuk palaces remain today, but their styles were later incorporated into Ottoman (also called Osmanli) art which gave Turkey some of its most important tourist attractions including the Ulu Cami and Green Mosque at Bursa and the Aya Sofya in Istanbul. The age of Sultan Suleyman the Magnificent (1520–1566) also produced Istanbul's beautiful Blue Mosque, with its soaring minarets, so characteristic of the Ottoman style. This Ottoman tradition is now enjoying a resurgence in popularity following a period of European influence, while the Hittite style, which characterised many of the buildings of the new capital Ankara, is on the wane.

This cosmopolitan range of people and cultural influences has given Turkey the artistic and architectural heritage of which it is justifiably proud, but in spite of the diversity there is undoubtedly a strong and growing sense of national unity and pride in the new state of Turkey. The visitor cannot hope to avoid the reminders of Ataturk, the great national hero. Statues seem to adorn every open space in the main cities and it is a rare town which does not have its Ataturk road or street! For a country with such a turbulent past it is impossible to overemphasise the importance of this new found sense of identity and purpose. In the space of a few decades the revolutionary changes instigated by Ataturk did much to change the outlook and image of a country which, as recently as 1920, appeared set to disappear from the world map altogether, as the spoils of the First World War were divided amongst the victorious Allies. Ataturk's famous phrase 'How happy is he who can say he is a Turk' finds an echo in the attitude of many Turks today, for whom the worst insult is a slight against their country. However, while this growing sense of national identity does exist, political unrest amongst minority groups is no less of a reality, most notably among the Kurds in the south-east of the country. Their case was sharply highlighted by the Gulf War and subsequent events. To date the Turkish government has failed to offer any viable solution to their plight and they continue to resist any integration into their adoptive country. The rather idealised view of the new nation of Turkey which the government and tourist industry is, not surprisingly, at pains to promote has also suffered from the view of the country depicted in such films as *Midnight Express* and Yilmaz Guney's *Yol*, which portray a brutal, corrupt regime, dealing with problems through suppression and violence. This view is still in the minds of many potential visitors and has certainly done very little by way of enhancing the country's appeal as a holiday destination. But just how much truth is there in such a portrayal? While there is a certain amount of exaggeration, cases of individuals being tortured in places like Diyarbakir are still occurring. One of Turkey's major tasks in the years to come is to improve its very poor human rights record. It is, however, easy to allow such negative characteristics to be eclipsed. It's difficult to think of another popular holiday destination which can offer landscapes of the sheer variety and beauty of those awaiting discovery by the traveller to Turkey. From the lush Black Sea coast to the snow-capped heights of the eastern mountains, the visual delights are seemingly endless. Turkey is a paradise for both the botanist and birdwatcher with its wealth of unusual flora, springtime displays of colour and diverse bird life, while for the more energetic the remote volcanic peaks and mountain ranges offer a considerable challenge and a solitude not always to be found among the popular peaks of Europe.

In addition to such attractions, Turkey also offers considerable gratification for the palate through its cuisine, which has been described as among the finest in the world, after that of the French and Chinese. While the large international hotels of Istanbul and Ankara offer good approximations of more typical European cooking (at a price!), elsewhere local dishes are the norm and indeed any tourist who does not make the most of the opportunity to sample the range of appetizing and original dishes will be missing one of the highlights of a visit to Turkey. While the food tends to be simple, it benefits from the use of the freshest produce and the time and care taken in its preparation, as befits its standing as an art form in this country. Among the bewildering variety of dishes, prepared for local people as much as tourists, fish, lamb and the ubiquitous aubergine are always prominent and feature in kebabs and casseroles as well as less familiar meals. Imaginative use of ingredients is a striking characteristic of typical Turkish cooking and affords a wide choice for the vegetarian – though be aware that meat stock is often used in vegetable dishes. An added bonus for the visitor is the widespread practice of inviting customers into the kitchen to make their selection, a great help in overcoming language barriers, as well as an interesting experience in itself! Outside the cities, coastal resorts and larger towns, choices are somewhat more limited, but most tourists should have little difficulty in finding something appetizing, especially if they are prepared to be just a little adventurous. The variety of regional dishes also adds to the culinary interest, with the Mediterranean-influenced fish dishes of the south-west and the Arabian-influenced spicy kebabs and meatballs of the south-east reflecting the two main components of Turkish cuisine.

The range of spices for sale in Turkey's markets and bazaars is staggering. Indeed, these places, along with the numerous family-run shops, are good hunting grounds for all types of souvenir: from onyx vases and brass tea services, to traditional water pipes and colourful kilims or carpets.

With so many reasons for a visit, travellers to Turkey are faced with the difficult decision of exactly where to go and which of the many attractions to see in their limited holiday time. The sheer size of the country makes any attempt to cover all, or even a majority, of these attractions doomed to failure. Each geographical region is of sufficient size and interest to occupy the tourist for far longer than the traditional two-week break, while certain destinations such as Istanbul are in themselves more than enough for a shorter visit. Rather than spend valuable time on coaches and trains, rushing from one destination to another, only to end up with a series of shallow impressions, the visitor to Turkey is well advised to select a particular region or theme for the holiday: anything from a lazy fortnight at a coastal resort, to visits to some of the main archaeological sights or a trek in the mountains. Clearly, it is possible to combine some of these options, i.e. by selecting a resort near to such sights as Aphrodisias and Ephesus and arranging day trips. Unusual festivals still take place all over Turkey. Among numerous others, a handicraft festival takes place in August at Avanos; the grape harvest is celebrated at Urgup in September; and you can watch camel wrestling at Selcuk in January. The golden rule to get the most from a visit is to select an appropriate destination or area, based on some research before leaving home, and not to try and cover too much ground!

For the botanist, birdwatcher and archaeologist a number of special interest tours are available from British companies, or travellers may prefer to put together their own itinerary. Options are discussed in **Where Are The Positive Holidays?**. Options for trekkers and mountaineers are also considered in this section.

For the less specific traveller **Istanbul** is, understandably, a very popular destination. Not only does it offer some of the finest mosques, palaces and museums in Turkey, but also the excitement of haggling in the Grand Bazaar and, for the romantically inclined, the incomparable sight of sunrise over the Bosphorus. It is also a good centre for visiting the resorts of both the Bosphorus and the Sea of Marmara. The city of **Bursa**, to the south of Istanbul, is less well known as a tourist destination, but has much to offer, most notably its magnificent mosques and Museum of Turkish and Islamic Antiquities. It is well situated for exploring the National Park at Mount Uludag to the south-west of the city and also for visits to the battlefields and memorials of Gallipoli, near Canakkale, and the legendary city of Troy. The resorts of the Sea of Marmara are also within easy reach. The **Aegean** coastline is of particular interest not only to the sun seeker, but also to anyone with an interest in historical sites, as the great sites of Ephesus, Pergamon, Miletus and Aphrodisias are all located in this vicinity. The very different ports of **Izmir** and **Kusadasi** are both good bases from which to explore the area. A most unusual attraction can be found at **Pamukkale**, where hot springs cascade down famous cliffs known as the 'Cotton Castle'. **Thrace**, the European area of the Turkish landmass, is often neglected by tourists as it lacks the famous monuments and attractions of Asian Turkey. However, its major city, **Edirne**, has a wealth of fine buildings, which are a legacy of its time as the Ottoman capital prior to the conquest of Istanbul. The great mosques of Edirne include the Selimiye Cami, which is considered by many to be one of the finest Ottoman mosques still existing. It is a pleasant town, characterised by cobbled streets and ancient timber houses, with the added attraction of the annual wrestling championships, held in June every year. **Konya**, situated on the south-east margin of the Anatolian plateau is another city often neglected by travellers in the rush between Cappadocia and the coastal resorts of the **Mediterranean**. This ancient capital of the Seljuk Turks is near the site of one of the world's oldest cities, Catal Hoyuk. It also houses the finest collection of Seljuk buildings in Turkey, together with a number of interesting and unusual museums, including that of the Whirling Dervish sect whose founder, Mevlana Rumi, lived in Konya in the thirteenth century. Although the order was disbanded by Ataturk in 1925, an annual Dervish Festival is held in December. This attractive city is well situated for access to the popular area of **Cappadocia**, with its famous rock-cut churches, underground cities and the 'fairy chimneys', which give its landscape an almost lunar aspect. Sumela Monastery, near the **Black Sea** port of Trabzon, is another popular attraction. For the more adventurous traveller **Eastern Turkey** offers the dramatic statues of the gods at Nemrut Dagi and the beauty of Lake Van, as well as the Seljuk monuments of Ezurum and Kars.

With the great wealth of attractions awaiting the traveller to Turkey, any discussion of the 'Highlights of Turkey' can only be cursory but, without doubt, the people themselves are one of these highlights. Any traveller who takes time to get to know a little of the people and their lifestyle can hardly fail to enjoy their open-spirited hospitality and generosity. While the country has something to appeal to most tourists, the visitor who makes the effort to learn something of the country's past and appreciate its present, through interest in its people and culture, will undoubtedly get the most from a trip to Turkey.

Natural History

The great variations in climate and topography which characterise Turkey are reflected in the diversity of native flora and fauna. Habitats range from the rocky, arid Mediterranean shore through the gentler, more temperate conditions of the Black Sea coast to the harsh central plateau and inhospitable mountains of the east.

Turkey has always attracted the serious botanist with its rich plant life and high proportion of unique species. Of its 8500 native species nearly thirty-one per cent are endemic. Turkey's location, as a meeting place of European, Mediterranean and Iranian floras, is responsible for this diversity and many endemic species flourish at the boundaries of these three floristic regions. While evergreen, deciduous and coniferous forests were once widespread over the country, today only twenty-six per cent of the land is under forest cover and over half of this total is degraded and unproductive. These forested areas usually occur as strips and isolated pockets, especially along the Mediterranean and Black Sea coasts. Beech dominates the remaining deciduous forests in the latter area, with coniferous pine forests at higher altitudes. East of Trabzon, oak, birch and rowan species of Asian origin occur, while oak species of central European origin increase in abundance towards Istanbul. Extensive clearance of the native forest has led to the invasion of scrub vegetation, often with deciduous oak and rhododendron species, across much of the area.

The Mediterranean coastline and southern slopes of the Taurus mountains have also lost much of their original forest cover. The area is now typified by low growing, spiny shrubs and aromatic herbs scattered across thin, rocky soils. Plants such as wild iris, geranium, poppy and a number of orchid species flourish in this environment. The Lycian region of the western Mediterranean is particularly rich in endemic species such as *Iris xanthospuria*. It owes much of its floristic richness to having escaped the most extreme effects of the last ice age, which obliterated so many native British species. The carob and judas tree, which have survived from Tertiary times, are still present in this area. This garrigue and maquis scrub is found throughout the Mediterranean and gives the area its characteristic, colourful spring landscape. The evergreen holm and kermes oak, with aleppo pine in more arid areas, are the dominant tree species. Above 500 metres this evergreen forest zone gives way to deciduous forests of sweet chestnut, oak and beech and ultimately to coniferous forests dominated by silver fir and pine above 1500 metres. Cypress and cedar, with juniper species, are also extensive in the Taurus mountains and southern Anatolia. Above the tree line at around 1700 metres spiny shrubs such as *Astralagus* dominate. Mediterranean-type vegetation is also found locally on thin soils along the Black Sea coast.

The plateau of central and eastern Anatolia is especially rich in herbaceous species, but the records of the flora of this region are still incomplete. While this vast area exhibits great variety in its vegetation, the flora is generally of Iranian origin and largely comprises deciduous oak scrub where original forest cover has been degraded, or treeless steppe vegetation. The steppes of central Anatolia are dominated by herbs, grasses and spiny shrubs, but much of the native plant cover has been lost and vast areas converted to agricultural land. Halophytic (salt tolerant) vegetation occurs locally e.g. around Tuz Golu.

Turkey's forests have suffered a great deal in the past from illegal cutting and overgrazing. Current attempts by the forest service to replant 250,000 acres per year have been generally successful to date, but have led to the widespread planting of conifers and the introduction of exotic species such as eucalyptus, which have limited value as wildlife habitats. Eucalyptus are perceived as beneficial by foresters, both for their speed of growth and their drying effect on waterlogged soils. However, many marsh areas are important for wildlife and may be adversely affected by the planting of such species. Many of Turkey's wetlands have already been damaged by drainage or irrigation programmes, particularly those associated with the major river deltas such as the Seyhan and Buyuk Menderes, where large areas have been converted to agricultural land. Important inland wetlands, such as the Sultansazligi marshes near Kayseri, have also been affected, but some relatively untouched wetland habitats still persist, e.g. in the east, near Lake Van (Van Golu).

The wildlife of Turkey is as rich and varied as its flora. The Mediterranean and Aegean coastlines abound with tortoises, lizards and butterflies. Among the larger mammals jackals and wild boar are important, while leopards, wolves and bears still occur in the mountains, especially in the east of the country. Turkey is particularly noted for its birdlife, again largely due to its central position between Europe, Asia and Africa. It lies on the major migration routes for a number of waterfowl species and also for birds of prey and soaring birds, such as storks and pelicans. Many migratory species which are becoming increasingly rare in Europe are common in Turkey, while the country's wetlands are of global importance as breeding sites for such species as the pygmy cormorant. 'Bottleneck' areas for migratory birds include the Bosphorus, which makes Istanbul and its surroundings an unlikely haven for bird watchers. Other important sites include Lake Manyas (Kus) and Lake Apolyont (Uluabat), to the south of the Sea of Marmara, which are noted as breeding sites for the globally rare dalmation pelican. Further east, the coniferous forests of Mount Uludag near Bursa provide habitats for such species as Kruper's nuthatch, the black woodpecker and the goldcrest and hunting grounds for golden eagles and the rare lammergeier. Inland, the marshes of the Lake Van area are important breeding grounds for many species including the little egret and avocet.

The marine fauna of Turkey includes three endangered Mediterranean species: the Mediterranean monk seal and the green and loggerhead turtles. Dalyan is the site of one of the two remaining breeding beaches for the loggerhead turtle in the Mediterranean. The recent controversy over tourist developments at this location was responsible to a large extent for providing a timely reminder of Turkey's ecological importance and the threat posed by the rapid growth of tourism and related development.

Intensive agriculture is another factor which has displaced the native flora and fauna of the country. Thirty-six per cent of land is now devoted to agricultural production, especially in the wheat-growing areas of the central Anatolian steppe, the fertile deltas of the Aegean and the plains of Adana. However, in spite of the ever-increasing pressure from other, often conflicting, land-uses and the loss or degradation of valuable habitats, the importance of Turkey's natural heritage is beyond question and is undoubtedly one of the country's most attractive features. It is important for visitors to the country to encourage local efforts to conserve and protect this natural heritage.

The Geography of Turkey

The modern day republic of Turkey covers an area of some 781,000 square kilometres: almost three times the size of Great Britain or nearly equivalent to the total area of France and Germany. On maps it appears to form a natural rectangular unit linking East and West. The division between Europe and Asia is in fact uneven, with Asiatic Turkey, commonly known as Anatolia, comprising ninety-seven per cent of the total area. From north to south up to 684 kilometres of land separate the Black Sea in the north from the shores of the Mediterranean, while the remainder of Turkey's 7240 kilometre-coastline faces the Aegean to the west. Turkey shares its European borders with Bulgaria and Greece in the north-west, with the former Soviet Union to the north-east, while its Asiatic neighbours comprise Syria and Iraq to the south, and Iran to the east. Its boundaries are predominantly natural and are defined by seas or mountains.

The great Pontus and Taurus mountain ranges run through the country from east to west, parallel to the Black Sea and Mediterranean coasts, before coalescing into a complex of plateaux and peaks, which form the country's eastern boundary. These eastern mountains, with heights in excess of 3000 metres, constitute a formidable barrier to travel, as do the Taurus mountains in the south. Glacial activity is still occurring in Turkey, but is confined to the permanent snow patches of these mountains.

Within the boundaries of the Turkish Republic the variety of natural characteristics is immense; the arid central plateau, the fertile plains of the south-east, the temperate Black Sea and semi-tropical Mediterranean coastlines and the towering mountain ranges. Geologically, the region is unstable and prone to earthquakes (such as that at Erzincan in 1992) due to the existence of three major fracture zones where the Turkish and Aegean landmasses meet.

Asiatic Turkey, or Anatolia, is essentially a high, undulating plateau of 1000 metres, rising to 1500 metres in the east and isolated from the coastal belts by mountains. While the Pontus mountains are discontinuous and dissected by river systems, the Taurus mountains are less easily crossed. Access to the fertile plain to the south-east and to the Mediterranean coast is largely confined to passes such as the Cilician Gates, near Adana. The western edge of the plateau, as it falls towards the Aegean, is less clearly defined.

The plateau itself is characterised by its extreme continental climate of hot dry summers and cold winters. Its soils, which are developed on limestone bedrock, are of generally low fertility unless irrigated, and much of the area is used for cereal production and sheep breeding. Parts of the Central Anatolian plateau were once forested and remnants of this forest still remain, particularly around Konya. In the most arid areas, such as the southern Konya basin, calcareous semi-desert type soils occur. These have, however, proved productive under irrigation. The basaltic peaks of extinct volcanoes are features of the plateau landscape, most notably at Erciyes Dagi, south of Kayseri, whose outpouring of lava and ash in the Tertiary, up to 65 million years ago, gave rise to the stunning landscape of Cappadocia. Mount Ararat to the east is another example of an extinct volcanic peak. Salt and freshwater lakes also constitute major features of the Central Plateau, the largest of which are Tuz Golu south of Ankara and Lake Van in eastern Anatolia. Further to the east, in the Eastern Highlands, remnants of once extensive forests characterise some areas, while these highlands are also noted for apricot and grape production.

Anatolia is drained by a number of rivers; to the east primarily by the Gediz and Greater and Lesser Menderes, whose valleys afford access from coast to plateau. The drainage pattern to north and south is controlled by the Pontus and Taurus ranges. Numerous streams rise in these mountains and flow down to the coastal plains, while rivers rising further inland, i.e. the Kizilirmak (Red River), Yesilirmak (Green River), the Sakarya and the Coruh rivers make their way to the Black Sea through gaps in the Pontus mountains. To the south, the Ceyhan and Seyhan are the main rivers, which drain to the fertile plains around Adana. The two major rivers of Turkey, the Tigris (Dicle) and Euphrates (Firat), rise at the eastern edge of the plateau, from where they drain to the South. The Taurus and Pontus ranges are themselves forested, although little remains of the forest of Taurus. In the Pontus mountains deciduous trees give way to conifers with increasing height. Apples are grown on the south side of these mountains, while to the north, along the Black Sea coast, fruits, cereals, tobacco and hazelnuts are the main crops. This coast is temperate and receives abundant rainfall, particularly at its eastern end. Such a climate affords the region one of its greatest attractions – a lush green forested landscape gradually giving way to towering mountains.

The coastal regions of Turkey are very different in character. The Aegean coast is lined with fertile outwash plains of the Gediz and Menderes rivers. A variety of cereal crops thrive here in addition to cotton, tobacco, olives and figs. Further inland, towards the Pontus Mountains, these arable plains are overtaken by the coniferous forests on the foothills of the Anatolian Plateau.

The Mediterranean or Turquoise coast, in addition to being an important holiday centre, is the main citrus fruit-, banana- and date-growing area. Its wide sandy beaches line the coast, while inland the arable areas give way to the remaining forests of the Taurus mountains.

Two other distinct regions are worthy of note: the fertile plains around Adana to the south-east of the Taurus mountains, and 'European Turkey', or Thrace. The plains around Adana are important cereal-growing areas, while Thrace, which forms the hinterland of Istanbul to the north-west of the Sea of Marmara, is characterised by grazing land and cereals in the south and centre. In the north of Thrace and around Istanbul are some of the best remaining wooded areas in Turkey. The Sea of Marmara separates Thrace from 'Asian Turkey'. Its southern shore is particularly fertile and the humid climate makes it an important area for fruit production, particularly peaches, apricots and grapes.

Turkey is a relatively sparsely populated country and its 56 million people are still mainly country dwellers though there is now much migration to the cities. Rural densities of population are usually within the range of 2–20 per square kilometre depending on physical factors, most notably the availability of water. The country's average population density is around seventy per square kilometre (in southern Britain a population density in excess of one hundred per square kilometre is common). Istanbul, with nearly ten million people, is Turkey's most populous city, followed by the capital, Ankara, and Izmir. The other major cities and towns have much smaller populations, usually numbered in the hundreds of thousands. Of this group, Adana and Bursa are the largest, with populations of 600,000–2 million.

Since the constitution of 1921 the country has been divided into sixty-seven provinces, which are further subdivided into districts and townships. These townships or communities enjoy a high degree of autonomy, although their leaders are appointed by central government in Ankara. Local government in towns is through a council body headed by a mayor.

Climate

Turkey is not under the influence of a single climatic regime, rather its climate varies greatly over its 781,000 square kilometres of land area. The main control over the country's climate is exerted through the succession of cyclones or atmospheric disturbances which develop over the North Atlantic and travel westwards over Turkey and other Middle Eastern countries.

The most extreme conditions are experienced on the Central Anatolian plateau and in the mountain regions. During the winter months, very cold air masses develop over the plateau, which bring cold, generally dry weather, as moist air is displaced to the north and south. The first snows are usually experienced in this region by early October and persist through until mid to late spring. Cold air movement from the plateau down river valleys such as the Gediz can decrease winter temperatures in the Izmir area to the west. The situation is similar in the mountain regions, although these experience greater precipitation, usually in the form of snow. During the summer months, stable low pressure systems become established over Anatolia, bringing hot, arid conditions. Average daily temperatures are well in excess of 30°C and temperatures of up to 43°C have been noted on the plateau. Mean rainfall on the plateau is 300mm per annum.

The climate of the Black Sea coast is more temperate, due to the proximity of the ocean, which acts as a major moisture source and causes increased rainfall. This relatively cool water body also has a moderating effect on summer temperatures. Precipitation occurs throughout the year along this coast, as it lies in the path of major cyclonic disturbances.

The Mediterranean coast is subject to higher average temperatures than the Black Sea coast, with less annual precipitation. The temperature differences reflect both the relatively high temperature of the Mediterranean, as compared to the Black Sea, and the more southerly location of the Mediterranean coastal belt. This coast is not affected by the passage of a continuous series of cyclones in the same way as the Black Sea coast and rainfall levels are lower as a result. The moderating influence of these two water bodies on the temperature persists for only a few miles inland. Beyond this point temperatures increase rapidly.

The greatest temperature variations between regions occur in the winter, with mean temperatures decreasing generally towards the north and east of the country. In January the average daily maximum temperature at Izmir on the west coast is 12°C, rising to a daily maximum of 15°C at the Mediterranean resorts, while Ankara's maximum is only 4°C and Erzurum's is 5°C. Summer temperatures are less variable between regions, e.g. an average daily maximum of 33°C in Izmir, 26°C at Trabzon on the Black Sea coast and 25°C at Erzurum in the east. Greatest overall temperature ranges are experienced on the plateau and in the east, where temperatures vary by up to 25°C between the summer and winter months.

Climatic variations are reflected in sea temperatures – the swimming season runs from June to September on the Black Sea coast, when water temperatures are between 20 and 24°C, and from April to October along the Mediterranean coast, where sea temperatures remain above 18°C for a longer period.

Industry

The early 1980s marked a period of economic growth for Turkey, as it made a deliberate move away from public sector dependence and market intervention towards free trade and reliance on market forces. However, by the late 1980s Turkey, in common with many Middle Eastern countries, was suffering from high levels of inflation combined with decreased output, particularly in the agricultural sector.

The situation today shows some improvement, with revenues from tourism playing an important part in this economic recovery. Nonetheless, inflation remains high as does unemployment. Reduced public investment in manufacturing and mining industries has affected growth in these sectors, while private investment is only just recovering from the slump. The sixth Five Year Plan (1990–1994) aims to improve the economic position by increasing reliance on market forces, reducing unemployment to below 10 per cent by the end of the period, cutting inflation and increasing annual growth in Gross National Product (GNP) from around 5 per cent to over 8 per cent by 1994. This plan also aims to emphasise the importance of Turkey's industrial development. Today, agriculture accounts for some 17 per cent of Turkey's Gross Domestic Product (GDP) and employs around half the workforce. The country is virtually self-sufficient in agricultural produce and exports are worth in excess of $2000 million p.a. Nuts, fruit and vegetables are the main export crops. Tobacco is also significant as an export crop, while fishery products constitute a minor source of income.

Asiatic Turkey is also rich in mineral deposits, although these resources have not been heavily exploited to date. The chromite deposits of the east make Turkey one of the world's principal chrome producers. Other important mineral and hydrocarbon deposits are boron, coal, copper, oil and iron. However, Turkey is still dependent on imports for much of its mineral requirements. It also imports $3000 million worth of oil each year. The principal manufacturing industries are the textile industry, which produces mainly cotton, woollen and silk cloth, and the glass, ceramics, iron and steel industries. Bursa is the main centre for silk production. Chemicals have become an increasingly important export since the early 1980s. Although industries such as the textile industry, which are traditionally associated with Turkey, still dominate the export markets, recent trends indicate that high-tech industries, such as the manufacture of electrical equipment and products, are playing an increasingly important role in this market.

Tourism is the great economic success story of Turkey in recent years. It brought over $3300 million into the country in 1990 and was largely responsible for the return to a positive balance of payments in 1988. Of the current annual influx of foreign tourists, which is in excess of 5 million, the majority are German, with 970,000 Germans having visited Turkey in 1990. British tourists formed the second largest group of 350,000 in the same year. 1991 figures were down on those of 1990, as a result of the Gulf War and widespread recession.

The History of Turkey

The perception of Turkey as a meeting place of East and West, the bridge between widely differing if not necessarily antagonistic cultures, is so widespread and frequently quoted as to have become a cliché. Indeed, its cosmopolitan mix of European and Asian influences is one of the country's main attractions to the more intrepid tourist. How did this view of Turkey evolve? The location of Turkey, the geographical accident of its position between East and West, is surely only part of the story. To achieve some insight and understanding into the culture of modern Turkey it is necessary to trace the forces that shaped it throughout its long and colourful history.

Anatolia, as Turkey was known, has the distinction of being the site of the world's second oldest known city – Catal Hoyuk (up to 7000 BC). Only Jericho (8000 BC) shows signs of an earlier urban civilisation. Prior to this, evidence of the presence of mankind in Anatolia dates back one million years, as shown by the oldest human remains outside Africa which were discovered within the last decade in a cave outside Istanbul. While these earliest people left little behind except their bones, the cave dwellers of Beldibu, Belbasi and the Kara In (Black Cave), near modern day Antalya on the Mediterranean coast, bequeathed us a wealth of paintings and engravings. This decorative tradition is also much in evidence at Catal Hoyuk. The earliest known paintings on plastered walls were discovered in the remains of this city. They depict hunting and religious subjects and show that the worship of the Mother Goddess and the bull, which persisted in the region until the arrival of Christianity, had already begun. The remains of this earliest city can still be viewed as a mound in Konya and in the Ankara museum, where the simple yet finely wrought tools and decorative objects give evidence of a relatively sophisticated civilisation, in which textiles were woven and the black glassy mineral, obsidian, used and exported.

Catal Hoyuk was abandoned for unknown reasons around 5000 BC, but city-based civilisations continued to spread throughout Anatolia, as shown by the numerous Bronze Age mounds discovered across the country. The most famous city is, without a doubt, the legendary city of Troy. This gives evidence not only of increasingly sophisticated civilisation, but also of the arrival of organised warfare, which required the construction of defensive city walls. Troy's most famous treasures – the hoards of gold unearthed by Schliemann in the late nineteenth century – show Troy II (dated around 3000 BC), the Trojan city of Homer, to have housed a civilisation of considerable wealth.

The next landmark in Turkey's history, following the sacking of Troy in the Trojan War by Greek invaders, was the destruction of the Hittite culture. The Hittites, a people of Middle Eastern origin, who moved into Anatolia around 2000 BC and subsequently expanded their empire into Syria, fell before the combined might of the Greek invasion. While the Achaean Greeks became established on the Aegean coast, the 'Sea Peoples', including the Phrygians, moved in from the north and west to establish domination in Central and Western Turkey and found the city of Ankara. King Midas, surely the most famous Phrygian, established a capital at Gordion. However, the domination of the Phrygians was relatively short-lived and Midas later committed suicide after his defeat by the European Cimmerians around 695 BC.

The Hellenic influence continued with the establishment of the Lydian empire in Western Turkey around 650 BC. An account of this is given in the *Histories* of Herodotus, which also states that the Lydians were the inventors not only of coinage, but also of dice and ball games, when famine forced them to devise a distraction from hunger! The wealth of their culture was embodied by King Croesus, whose name is still synonymous with great riches today.

In 546 BC the Persian culture came to challenge the Greek and add to the racial diversity of Anatolia, through the invasion of the conquering Persian forces under King Cyrus. Their influence, which persisted for two centuries, reduced the power of the Greek coastal city states, but this period was generally one of stability and prosperity. It ended only with the appearance of one of the greatest leaders the world has ever known.

It is impossible to overemphasise the historical importance or influence of Alexander the Great. Through him, the dream of his father

King Phillip of Macedonia to liberate Asia Minor from the Persian yoke was realised. He crossed the Dardanelles into Anatolia in 334 BC and in eleven years swept victoriously through the entire Middle East, liberating the city states of Anatolia en route and aiding the spread of the Hellenistic influence throughout the country. His untimely death in 323 BC put an end to his vision of the eventual fusion of European and Asiatic races, and left a potentially explosive racial mix in Anatolia. He also died without any clear successor, which resulted in the subdivision of his great Empire between his three generals and set the scene for a time of discord between the several small kingdoms which subsequently flourished.

The expanding might of the Roman Empire was the force which finally resolved this particular strife. By 190 BC the Aegean coast was in Roman hands and when Attalus III, the last king of Pergamon and most powerful of Anatolian rulers, bequeathed his kingdom to these invaders, the fate of Anatolia was sealed. At least for several centuries. The contributions of the Roman Empire to Anatolia are many and varied. Primarily the Romans brought a period of peace and prosperity. Great cities grew and flourished and the previously less-developed interior shared in these benefits. Under the Romans the prevailing classical civilisation was challenged by the growth of a new religion – Christianity. Not least as a result of St Paul's journeys in Anatolia, the new creed grew rapidly. Unfortunately the era of peace ended. Religious persecution erupted and was only checked in AD 324 by the new Emperor, Constantine, who declared all religions to be equal. The attacks on the Roman Empire by the European Goths and the subsequent split of the Empire into East and West marked the onset of a new era. The great city of Byzantium was founded in AD 324. This demonstrated the growing strength of this eastern part of the Empire, while the western lands struggled under the onslaught of invaders. The Byzantine Empire flourished, especially under Justinian, until the birth of Islam in the seventh century AD and the Arab invasion of Anatolia in AD 654. The early years of Byzantium also marked the gradual rise of Greek over Roman civilisation, with Greek replacing Latin as the official language.

The heritage of the Islamic invasion and the eventual victory of the Arab invaders is clearly evident in the modern republic of Turkey, where Islam is the religion of over 90 per cent of the inhabitants. Byzantium finally fell to Islam in AD 1453, after centuries of internal division and unrest within Anatolia. However, it was the Turks, not the Arabs, who finally conquered this great city. The Seljuk Turks, who had come from North East Asia to rout the Byzantines in 1071, captured much of Anatolia from the Arabs. However, as the Mongol hordes under Genghis Khan swept across the region in the late thirteenth century the Seljuks were under threat. They were saved, as legend has it, by the intervention of one Ertugral, father of Osman, who turned the tide of battle against the advancing Mongols. In subsequent years this Ottoman clan succeeded in uniting the disparate tribes of Anatolia and in so doing laid the foundations of the mighty Ottoman Empire. Constantinople became the new capital of the Empire under its new name – Istanbul – the City of Islam. Under the reign of Suleyman the Magnificent (1520–1566), the Ottoman Empire achieved its greatest glory and influence. Yugoslavia, Hungary and much of North Africa came under its domination. However, the extravagant opulence of Suleyman's court held within it the seeds of its own destruction.

By the nineteenth century much of the Empire's strength had been dissipated, as internal and external strife took their toll on the by now moribund empire. As the decline continued and Turkey became known as 'The Sick Man of Europe', a new movement, which called for the end of the Sultan's absolute power and the adoption of a democratic constitution, emerged. The growing strength and influence of these 'Young Turks' forced the last Ottoman sultan to proclaim a constitution in 1876. It also allowed them to reimpose the constitution and depose this same sultan in 1908 after he revoked the 1876 agreement. The efforts of this early constitutional government were interrupted in 1914 by the First World War. This, more than anything else, sealed the fate of the once great Ottoman Empire. The days of glory were over. As a result of the German Kaiser's persuasive abilities, Turkey entered the war on the side of the Axis powers. It achieved only one notable victory in the war. At Gallipoli in 1915 the Turkish forces, under the command of one Mustafa Kemal, successfully defended the Dardanelles against the combined forces of the Australians and New Zealanders (the ANZACS), the French and the British. From this campaign a man who was to become one of the most influential leaders of the century – Mustafa Kemal, later to be known as Ataturk or Father of the Turks – emerged. Indeed, he was the true Father of the Turkish nation as we know it today. However, in November 1918, when Turkey signed an armistice with the Allies and the once great Ottoman Empire was brought to its knees, the prospects for the country appeared overwhelmingly bleak. As the Allies divided the spoils between themselves, it seemed that Turkey would disappear from the world map altogether. The Treaty of Sèvres, signed in 1920, appeared to be the death knell. Former Ottoman provinces, such as Iraq and Palestine, came under British influence and Syria under the French, while the Italians were promised several of the Southern provinces.

However, there was one fact the Allies had failed to reckon with. The final humiliation came for the Turks when Greece, a one-time subject, was promised territory on the Aegean coast by the British and subsequently invaded Izmir. This was the final spur needed for the nationalist movement, under Kemal Ataturk, to make its influence felt. Thus began the Turkish War of Independence, which lasted until 1922 and ended with Ataturk a national hero. After this victory and the successful expulsion of Greek forces, Turkey became a republic in 1923. Inevitably the first president was none other than Mustafa Kemal Ataturk. The following years saw some of the most radical changes in Turkey's long and turbulent history. In the short space of fifteen years prior to his death, Ataturk succeeded in changing the face of the country. A great believer in western-style culture as the way forward, he began by reducing the power of Islamic religious leaders through replacing the religious courts with the Swiss-style legal code. He then proceeded to forbid the study of the *Koran* in schools, replace the Arabic with the western-style script, give women the vote and ban the wearing of the fez. Ataturk's impact on his country was immeasurable. In less than twenty years following the decline of the Ottoman Empire and its post-war dismantling by the Allies, Turkey emerged from the wreckage as a forward-looking, confident and, in many ways, westernised nation.

Soviet influence was also an important factor in this early post-war development, especially after the financial crisis of 1929. Turkey's first Five Year Plan was instigated from 1934–1939, with Soviet assistance.

Since Ataturk's death in 1938 and the loss of his inspirational leadership, the divisions within the country have been highlighted. In the late 1940s after the Second World War, in which Turkey remained effectively neutral in spite of having declared on the side of the Allies, the country became a democracy with the formation of the Democratic Party, who subsequently took office in 1950. Turkey's involvement with the West increased from this time. The United States in particular offered economic assistance – although at a price. The military base facilities which Turkey still affords the US – as evident in the 1991 Gulf War – date from this time. Further military integration with the West came about through Turkey's membership of NATO from 1952.

After a brief honeymoon period of economic expansion and growth of free trade, the Democratic government, led by Menderes, hit trouble. As a result of foreign trade and subsequent economic problems, Menderes found himself increasingly unpopular and responded in a progressively more extreme fashion. Repressive measures, ranging from the imprisoning of opponents to press censorship, became commonplace. The situation culminated in the ignominious end of the Democratic Party in 1960, when Menderes was deposed by a popularly-supported military coup. He was later sentenced and hanged. The army, unusually, did not attempt to retain power. Under their guidance a new constitution was drafted in 1961 and subsequently adopted. This constitution retained democracy and indeed appeared remarkably liberal, especially after the repressive Menderes years. This new liberalism was evident in the formation of Turkey's first Socialist Party. It was, however, the newly-created Justice Party, heirs to the tradition of the Democratic Party, who took the lead in the new Turkey. After an initial coalition period, the Justice Party assumed complete control of the government in 1965, under Demirel. It was in 1964, under the coalition government, that the Cyprus crisis initially blew up and almost provoked war with Greece. The situation was resolved temporarily by American intervention, which succeeded in dissuading Turkey from this course of action.

As the economic situation worsened in subsequent years, unrest among extreme political groups of both left and right grew. Assailed from both sides, the government fell to another military coup in 1971.

On the restoration of Parliament in 1972, after the widespread imposition of martial law and severe measures particularly against the left, the RRP – the party originally formed by Ataturk – was restored to power in an historic agreement with the Islamic fundamentalists. This allowed religion to assume a high-profile role in the country for the first time since Ataturk. However, the political turmoil of Turkey was far from resolved. This and subsequent weak coalition governments were unable to achieve political consensus between the extreme left and right political wings in the country. The situation was exacerbated by Turkey's invasion of Cyprus in 1974 and its subsequent isolation from the West, as they expressed their disapproval of this action. By 1980 the army was moved to intervene again to stop almost certain civil war. This time the measures imposed by the army were more severe than in the past and clearly aimed at preventing any future relapse into a comparable state of economic and civil disorder. It was not until 1983 that elections were held again in the country, after a new constitution was drawn up in 1982. This 1983 election was very tightly controlled, with only three parties allowed to participate. It resulted in victory for the conservative Motherland Party under Turgut Ozal.

The following years have been ones of relative stability for Turkey, as major efforts have been made to amend Turkey's human rights record and bring an end to the political isolation of the Seventies. However, the Gulf War in 1991 and the subsequent plight of Kurdish refugees in the south-east of the country have brought it some unwelcome publicity. Today Ozal is still the President (his term ends in 1996), but November 1991 saw the election of his political foe, Demirel, who was ousted by the army in 1980, as Prime Minister. Turkey has clearly not yet done enough in certain areas to amend the more negative aspects of its image in the eyes of the world. It was recently refused EC membership, for a number of reasons including both economic and human rights considerations. However, the great strides Turkey has made this century towards fully acceptable democracy and complete integration with Europe cannot be denied. The pace of change has been rapid and many obstacles have been tackled and overcome. Today Turkey still finds itself a bridge between East and West, but with a greater sense of stability and a more positive outlook, as its diverse people increasingly find a common sense of identity and purpose within Ataturk's nation.

The Real Turkey

Turkey is portrayed by its own tourist board as 'a paradise preserved'. They present an image of unspoilt golden beaches and cosmopolitan resort towns set in a landscape steeped in centuries of history and culture. This image is widely echoed in the tourist literature, which dwells on the attractions of the Black Sea, Aegean and Mediterranean coastlines, the vast archaeological sites and the glories of Istanbul, Turkey's 'crowning work of art', with brief mention of the natural beauty of the rugged interior. This is clearly a somewhat idealised portrait of the country and visitors to Turkey whose expectations are based solely on travel brochures and official government literature can expect a number of surprises as they discover the land and people for themselves.

An aspect of any country which is often given scant attention by such literature is the characteristics of its native population. The diverse mix of peoples and cultures who constitute the inhabitants of modern Turkey reflect the country's turbulent history. Over the centuries this land area has been invaded and settled by races as different as the Hittites, the Greeks, the Romans and the Persians. While the Turks comprise over 90 per cent of the present population, minority groups, who have preserved their own culture to differing extents, are found throughout the country. The Kurds in particular still retain their traditional way of life along the eastern border and refuse to be integrated into mainstream Turkish life at any cost, as evidenced by recent events. Armenian Christians are a major non-Islamic group, while Greeks, Arabs and Jews are other important racial minorities.

In spite of this racial mix, the overriding impression of prospective visitors is based on the Islamic aspects of the culture and the Muslim beliefs of 98 per cent of the population. Many have a stereotyped view of the traditional Muslim, centred on the idea of a very strict code of religious beliefs, inflexible attitudes towards women and an element of hostility towards western culture, all of which may provoke a certain uneasiness in the potential traveller. This image in itself is at odds with the rather quaint, picturesque rural characters who feature in much travel literature. The reality is rather more complex, but undoubtedly the people themselves are one of the most pleasant surprises in store for the visitor. In all areas accustomed to tourists and even in those where outsiders are a relatively new phenomenon the traveller can expect a warm welcome and overwhelming hospitality. The 'Terrible Turk' image finds little echo in the friendly, helpful nature of the Turkish people. This hospitality to strangers has its roots in the Muslim tradition, which, to quote one researcher, views travel as 'an exercise in reflective endurance for which travellers need every assistance that can be offered'. This tradition also promotes the idea that 'the guest comes from God' and should be treated accordingly! Elements of this attitude still persist and extend even to non-Muslims. Visitors may find themselves the recipients of free glasses of tea at one of the numerous roadside tea houses, much friendly curiosity concerning their own homes and families and requests for impromptu English lessons. For attitudes towards women travellers, see **The Art of Being a Good Tourist**. While the Turks are well aware of the economic potential of tourism, the 'hard sell' is rare, except in the tourist areas of Istanbul, and souvenir salesmen appear to favour good-humoured persuasion and bartering over a more persistent approach. Although tourists may find the gregarious nature of the people rather overwhelming, they will not, as a rule, be seriously hassled to buy goods and services, or to give money to beggars.

Since the sweeping reforms initiated by Ataturk in the 1920s, the drive to become a modern, industrialised, western society and to lose the slightly 'backward' image has continued and is reflected in a variety of ways in the modern Turkey. Ataturk is still regarded as the national hero and is virtually idolised by many Turks for his work in almost single-handedly building the new Turkey. The extent to which the traditional culture and ways of life persist varies significantly between the rural and urban areas and across the country. In the major cities of Ankara and Istanbul young Turkish women dressed in the latest, revealing European-style clothing, often accompanied by boyfriends, are not uncommon sights, while the denim-clad occupants of the university campus could easily be mistaken for their British counterparts. Women often occupy professional positions in the civil service, banks and the tourist industry, while female science and technology students are an accepted feature of university life. However, in spite of these signs of emancipation, Turkish society is still very much a male-dominated one, even in the major cities. In the East, women are virtually invisible. Arranged marriages are the norm and account for 90 per cent of all liaisons among the rural population, where the unmarried state is still seen as shameful for women. One tradition is the placing of a bottle on top of the chimney to signify that there is a girl in the household who is waiting for a husband. Considerable importance is attached to the number of carpets and quilts a girl can accumulate in the form of dowry.

While the state provides compulsory, free, secular education at the primary level, only 25 per cent of young people continue their schooling beyond this point. In the villages and especially in the more remote areas of central and eastern Turkey, education is still viewed as less important for girls than the traditional domestic and agricultural skills. In such small rural communities it is often the women who do most of the work in the fields, in addition to their household responsibilities. However, any woman who is having problems with her husband (or her mother-in-law) can indicate this by wearing a black headscarf with red trimmings!

Internal migration is growing, although family ties and the responsibility to care for elderly relatives are important factors for the comparatively poor, rural-based sector of the population. However an increasing willingness to accept change is shown in movement from the country to the cities and even abroad. West Germany has always been a favoured destination for this latter group which accounts for the position of German as the second foreign language in Turkey, after English.

In common with so many aspects of the culture, leisure and entertainment are a curious mix of the traditional and the modern. Football, as a spectator and participation sport, is a passion for many men and also the major outlet for gambling through the football pools, while volleyball is enjoyed by both sexes. The ancient sport of oiled wrestling is still popular and the annual championships at Edirne regularly attract large crowds. In spite of the unspoilt natural beauty of the countryside, hiking as a recreational activity does not appeal to the average city-bred Turk. A more typical excursion is a family trip to a picnic site, which allows access to the country while involving the minimum of walking.

The cinema is the most popular form of entertainment and specialises in low-budget all-action epics, while theatre and opera have a growing following in the cities, especially among the wealthier people. TV soap operas also appear to have a dedicated audience! Folk music and dancing are still an important aspect of the culture and are a feature of many festive occasions and celebrations, with dances varying from region to region, although belly dancing is now performed mainly for tourists.

The tea-house (*cay bahcesi*) is still an important focus of social life for men, especially in the villages, and is a place for talk and a game of backgammon or *okey* (which is played like rummy, but with numbered tiles) – both very popular activities in Turkey. These tend to be male preserves, although unaccompanied women travellers will provoke curiosity, not hostility, if appropriately dressed. The tourist will find the glass of tea an almost ubiquitous feature of any visit to Turkey. If the numerous roadside stalls and tea-houses are not enough, free glasses of tea, often apple, orange or lemon flavoured, are usually offered even in the smartest carpet shops.

A visit to a carpet shop is in itself a fascinating experience. The tourist who shows the slightest interest is normally treated to a display of carpets and kilims from all regions of the country and a discourse on their origin and the significance of their designs. The whole process is conducted in a relaxed, leisurely fashion, without excessive pressure to buy. The purchase of a carpet is, however, made temptingly easy by the wide acceptance of credit cards. Carpet-making *is* a traditional Turkish skill, which has been practised for many years throughout the country. The designs are specific to certain areas and often relate to local traditions. In this sense they are an authentic part of the culture, although mass-produced, poor-quality imitations of the real thing do exist. It is worth doing a little research beforehand if contemplating making a purchase. The cut taken by many tour operators or guides can push up prices by 30 per cent and the profit made by a dealer on selling a carpet to a wealthy tourist is usually out of all proportion to the income received by the weaver. In addition, many weavers (usually women) suffer damage to their eyesight. However, such income is still important in some communities, so the decision as to whether to buy or not is a difficult one to make, especially as this is true for many souvenirs produced for the tourist market.

The 'hamam' or Turkish Bath is an important feature of everyday life for both men and women, with at least one in every town. It is a social occasion for most Turks and offers the opportunity for relaxation and conversation with friends, in addition to the relatively cheap luxury of steam rooms at various temperatures, a bath and a massage. The Turkish Bath originally existed as the only means for most people to enjoy a bath, as private houses seldom had such facilities, but even though this is now only the case in the east, they have retained their popularity.

One unexpected feature which will confront the first-time visitor to Turkey is the ubiquitous lemon water cologne, which is seemingly offered on all occasions, from long coach journeys to trips to the bank manager's office. This is a basic courtesy in Turkey and once tourists become accustomed to the rather pungent liquid, it is undeniably refreshing, especially on the hottest days.

Differing degrees of cultural conservatism throughout the country are expressed in attitudes to drink and religious matters in general. The Islamic ban on alcohol is widely disregarded by Turkish men in the cities and coastal resort towns, at least with respect to the national drink, *raki*, but western-style bars are unknown apart from in the major international hotels. The local equivalent is the '*gazino*' – a kind of drinking house which plays Turkish music. Otherwise, drinking is usually confined to restaurants as an accompaniment to a meal. In the more conservative villages and towns of eastern Anatolia, however, the ban on alcohol is more strictly observed as are other religious injunctions such as the fast of Ramadan.

In contrast, change is particularly marked in the coastal resort areas, where previously agricultural communities are now entirely dependent on the income from tourism. Awareness of the negative aspects of this growing industry and their potentially precarious economic position is generally absent among local populations, except where the dearth of tourism in the wake of the Gulf War has driven it home. Many areas now have a second generation of 'pansiyon' owners, brought up with the relative wealth afforded by tourism, which is increasingly becoming *the* industry which young people aspire to work in. This is reflected in the development of training centres such as OTEM, the government-built Hotel Training Centre in Kemer, Antalya.

Aspirations to the western lifestyle are also reflected in the preferred holiday destinations of the Turkish people themselves. The favoured holidays are to the resort towns of the Aegean and Mediterranean coasts patronised by the foreign tourists and the shores of the Sea of Marmara, or for the wealthier Turks, far eastern and European package tours are popular. Internal travel within the country and particularly to the east is not common, as such undeveloped destinations hold little appeal.

In its culture, as in many other aspects, Turkey shows a variety of widely differing characteristics. The fruits of the great push for westernisation are seen in the more liberal attitudes of the city dweller, the growth of industry, modern architecture and the aspirations of the university-educated youth. However, these changes have had little impact on vast areas of the country, particularly in the east and in the interior of the Anatolian plateau, where tourism has yet to make its mark. Here the traditional Muslim way of life continues almost unaltered. The real Turkey cannot, therefore, be easily defined and the oversimplifications of much travel literature only occasionally coincide with reality. Discovering the 'real' Turkey is one of the great pleasures in store for any prospective traveller.

The Tourist Industry

Since 1980, when the new Ministry of Culture and Tourism was established and began its efforts to market Turkey as a major tourist destination, the scale and style of this industry has changed almost beyond recognition. In 1970 Turkey was visited by only 446,000 tourists, as opposed to some 18 and 15 million who spent their holidays in the most popular Mediterranean countries of France and Spain respectively. At this time the package tour industry in Britain was taking off and sending thousands abroad each year to destinations which had previously been the almost exclusive domain of a wealthy élite. Turkey hardly featured in this development of mass tourism, although a Ministry of Tourism had been set up as early as 1963 and certain areas designated as tourism development areas during the 1970s. During this early phase of the industry in Turkey, British arrivals were mainly independent travellers, who perceived their trip as something of a challenge and an adventure. Numbers of British tourists grew slowly until 1985, when the figures leapt from 90,000 in the previous year to 125,000. The number of British arrivals continued to grow until 1988, with a record 465,000 noted for that year. Since 1988, the total number of international tourist arrivals has continued to increase, from 4.2 million to 5.4 million in 1990, although British arrivals have decreased by around 13 per cent.

So, what are the causes of the overall increase in Turkey's international tourist industry and the recent decline in the British share of the market? There are three main factors which have enhanced the country's popularity as a tourist destination in recent years. The first is the deliberate policy to market the country pursued by the Ministry of Culture and Tourism since 1980. By giving Turkey a higher profile as a holiday destination, the Ministry has ensured that more people consider Turkey as a serious option when planning their annual break. Unfortunately, this has been achieved in the past more through building the sort of coastal resorts that the tourist will have become accustomed to in other parts of the Mediterranean, rather than by stressing the unique history and culture of the country and its wealth of natural attractions.

A second reason must be that this increasing awareness of Turkey as a potential holiday destination has coincided with a desire for something new and different among people accustomed to the type of package tours on offer in Spain and other European destinations. This may appear to be something of a contradiction, as the Turkish tourist industry has responded largely by trying to cater exactly for this sort of package tour! However, Turkey does have a number of distinct advantages over its Mediterranean neighbours: it is relatively uncrowded and there are still many unspoilt areas of great natural beauty on the most popular Aegean and Mediterranean coastal stretch. This will come as a pleasant shock to people accustomed to environments which have been allowed to deteriorate through poorly planned and constructed developments and pollution of seas and beaches. Although facilities can be rather more basic than those on offer in some of the main resorts of the long-established holiday destinations, for many people this is more than compensated for by the predominantly clean beaches and bathing waters.

The third factor appears to be an increasing environmental awareness among certain holidaymakers and a desire to explore beyond the beach resorts. As the adventure sector of the package tour market continues to develop, with an increasing number of British tour operators offering trekking, wildlife, botanical and skiing holidays, the wealth of unspoilt land, the natural beauty and the diverse flora and fauna are enhancing Turkey's appeal as a tourist destination. This is especially true for those people in search of something other than the traditional beach holiday and who wish to enjoy a more authentic experience of the country. The Ministry of Culture and Tourism was recently split into its two separate constituents, with the Ministry of Culture now responsible for heritage conservation and the Ministry of Tourism responsible for all aspects of the development and promotion of the Turkish tourist industry. This latter ministry is beginning to recognise the potential in these alternative forms of tourism, but as yet has made no concerted effort to diversify the industry away from the established coastal resorts, the main cities and Cappadocia.

The decline in the British share of the market is more difficult to explain. For the 1991 season the Gulf War and Kurdish unrest combined to discourage many tourists of all nationalities, but the decline in numbers of British visitors prior to this may be because the tourist industry 'oversold' Turkey before its infrastructure or facilities were ready to cope, resulting in dissatisfaction among holidaymakers in the late 1980s. Tourism is now one of Turkey's biggest industries and of great importance to the economy. The annual turnover of the tourism industry is currently around $3,400 million, which makes it one of the country's largest sources of income, after the manufacturing industries. Tourism currently stands at some 3 per cent of the GNP (Gross National Product) of the country as a whole. Generally, the economic impact of tourism is greatest in the Mediterranean and Aegean coastal regions and Istanbul, with Istanbul receiving over one million foreign visitors each year, Antalya province 644,000 and Izmir province some 553,000 foreign tourists. Most of these tourists arrive in the summer months from June through to September, but there has been a marked increase in winter arrivals in recent years. Between 1989 and 1990 there was a 68 per cent increase in December arrivals. This appears to reflect changing trends in the type of holidays favoured by visitors to Turkey. While 67 per cent still declare the purpose of their visit as 'holiday/vacation', 8.7 per cent state the purpose of their visit as 'culture', while only 0.8 per cent favour active sports.

Tourism is a very important source of foreign income for Turkey and increasing the amount of foreign currency and foreign investment was the major motivation behind the 1980s marketing drive initiated by the Ministry of Culture and Tourism. It brings in more foreign cash than Turkey's agricultural exports. More than 5 million foreign tourists spend a total of $520 million annually. The 350,000 British tourists who currently visit the country each year are the second most important market, but their numbers are far outweighed by those of the 971,000 Germans. France, Greece and the USA are the other main markets, with 206,000 to 311,000 of their citizens visiting Turkey each year. The Turks themselves holiday mainly within their own country, with only around 3 million of the 56 million people taking their holidays abroad. They spend around $178 per head outside Turkey, as against the $621 spent by each of the 5.4 million foreign tourists in the country. Therefore, Turkey has an extremely healthy positive travel 'balance of payments' at around $2.8 billion, which compares very favourably with Britain's current $7 billion negative balance. Tourism accounted for a total 25.5 per cent of Turkey's 1990 export earnings.

The other major advantage of the tourist industry is the amount of employment it creates. With unemployment at around 10 per cent, the service industries, which include tourism, employ around 5 million citizens. The level of unemployment has fallen since the 1987 high of 11.6 per cent and tourism looks set to become one of the growth areas for employment in the future. However, there is potentially a negative aspect of this development – the loss of alternative sources of income in certain areas, as whole families and villages abandon traditional occupations for the more lucrative business of tourism.

The economic and social benefits of tourism account for the importance accorded to it by central government and the effort put into marketing it worldwide. The Ministry of Tourism is responsible for all aspects of the tourist industry in Turkey. Most towns or tourist destinations will have a Tourism Information Office, with full-time staff, who can advise on local accommodation, sights and events. The Ministry is also responsible for licensing accommodation facilities and domestic travel agencies. There are now information offices located throughout the country, even in such remote locations as Kars and Van. Generally speaking, staff at these offices will usually understand English to a reasonable standard. However the range of information they are able to offer will depend largely on whether they are a small regional centre, or located in a major city. In the former case, information will apply only to the immediate locality. It is also worth noting that in the particularly remote areas of eastern Turkey these offices may close outside the high season. Also worthy of note for the independent traveller is the fact that the Tourist Information Offices do not offer a book-ahead service to other areas, although they will supply accommodation lists for their own and possibly other regions. In addition to the main centrally-run office, some towns will also have an office, or '*turizm dernegi*' operated by a local tourism association.

On an international level, there are Turkish Embassy Information Counsellors' offices in fifteen countries worldwide. Their function is to offer information to anyone contemplating a visit to Turkey and generally to promote the country as an attractive tourist destination. This is achieved largely through the production of brochures, information leaflets and factsheets.

The industry itself is split between tourists who visit as part of an organised package and those who choose to travel independently. The package tour share of the market has increased in recent years and in 1989 it accounted for 51 per cent of all foreign arrivals in the country. This growth of Turkey as a mass holiday destination is reflected in recent developments within the industry. These include the movement of major hotel chains into Turkey, which indicates a growing confidence in the future of the country as a major international tourist destination in the eyes of the travel industry. Some of the major names are Sheraton, Hilton International and the giant Holiday Inn chain. Until the 1980s Turkey was not a major package tour destination. Now the number of tour companies offering holidays there is increasing annually. Some of the major companies have recently started to take an interest in the country and include it in their programmes, including Thomsons and members of the mighty Owners Abroad consortium. This has led to an outcry from locals and some of the smaller specialist companies, who have accused the large conglomerates of destroying the country. While the industry underwent its rapid expansion during the last decade, this was often unfortunately at the expense of local communities and the environment. Uncontrolled, illegal building was a feature of this early expansion, with a corresponding decrease in the perceived quality of the country as a tourist destination. The industry currently appears to be going through a period of reappraisal, with some of the larger companies pulling out of destinations they had previously favoured and the smaller companies being forced to rethink their strategies as many of their original, unspoilt discoveries succumb to the impact of mass tourism. The government is putting together a number of new strategies and building controls, which will, in theory, ameliorate the situation and prevent the worst negative impacts of the industry (See **How Green is Turkey?**).

In the meantime, Turkey is still the destination of the small-scale specialist travel operators and, to a lesser extent, the adventurous independent traveller rather than the large international tour operators. These small operators tend to favour self-catering villa-type accommodation and small-scale family-run pensions over the larger hotels. However, this type of accommodation accounts for only around 5000 of the country's total 180,000 licensed beds. The most popular type of accommodation, by visitor numbers, is hotels, which are used by 89 per cent of all arrivals. The five-star, luxury hotels are the most popular category in Istanbul, while available statistics show two-star hotels to be the next most popular accommodation type. The purpose-built holiday villages accounted for 5.3 per cent of the 1990 arrivals, with the other accommodation categories of *pansiyons*, motels, *oberj* and campsites accounting for the remaining 6 per cent.

The attitude of the Turks towards the foreign tourist is usually very positive. Tourists are much more likely to find themselves overwhelmed by the friendly response of local people than on the receiving end of any hostility. The young people especially seem to recognise the future potential of tourism in Turkey and are eager to see the industry develop further. It is true that this attitude has its disadvantages, as they may have a more competitive and business-like attitude towards tourists than the previous generation. There is no doubt that tourism has played its part in keeping certain communities alive, especially in rural areas, by encouraging young people to stay, rather than look for work elsewhere. In the more remote areas, where tourists are still something of a rarity, travellers may find themselves faced with a rather pointed curiosity, but rarely with hostility, providing some basic guidelines as to dress and behaviour are followed (See **The Art of Being a Good Tourist**). Once this initial curiosity and suspicion is overcome, the welcome is usually very friendly and helpful.

The future of Turkey's tourist industry is still very much in the balance. As more foreign tour operators offer ecological and adventure-type holidays, the Turkish government is beginning to become aware of the possibilities inherent in the wealth of wildlife and unspoilt country which Turkey has to offer. They are considering ways to diversify away from coastal tourism, in accordance with the requirements of the Mediterranean Action Plan. The likely impacts of this type of tourism depend largely on how effectively it is controlled and administered.

How Green is Turkey?

As one of the most recent recruits to the ranks of major holiday destinations Turkey is, not surprisingly, still reeling under the impact of its new-found popularity. The last ten years have seen unprecedented growth in its tourist industry as people have moved on from the more traditional destinations of Spain, Greece and France in search of somewhere fresh and relatively unspoilt. Turkey's initial response to the influx of holiday-makers gave every indication that it was only a matter of time before it succumbed to the same environmental degradation and mass commercialisation as its European neighbours. The rise of the 'concrete costas' and increasing pollution of beaches and coastal waters which have contributed so significantly to Spain's declining tourism fortunes appeared to be finding an echo in the early growth of the tourist industry in Turkey, although the vast scale of the country meant this impact was not so immediately apparent.

A Turkish Ministry of Tourism was established in 1963 and was responsible for the designation of the Aegean and Mediterranean coasts, the Sea of Marmara area and Cappadocia as Tourism Development Areas in the 1970s. However, realisation of the country's full tourism potential did not become a major part of the government's economic strategy until the early 1980s under the new Ministry of Culture and Tourism. Their initial lack of concern for the environment and ecological consequences of the rapid growth of the tourist industry was neatly summarised during the 1987/1988 controversy over the development of the Dalyan Delta. In the face of growing national and international pressure from conservationists to protect one of the few remaining sites used by the endangered loggerhead turtle, a previous Minister of Tourism was quoted as saying that the development programme 'could not be sacrificed for a few tortoises'.

This initial boom period was marked by a surge of poorly managed and planned coastal tourist developments, which relied both on internal and overseas funding. One of the stated aims of government policy was to bring in foreign currency and encourage foreign investment. Environmental considerations were apparently way down on the list of priorities. The early 1980s saw the loss of agricultural land and degradation of valuable ecological and archaeological sites as the most popular coastal towns and villages were transformed by 'concrete fields' of holiday developments. The construction of licensed hotels and guest houses was matched by that of illegal pensions and more basic beach housing, as local people rushed to cash in on tourism. Increasingly, the message from the British holiday industry was 'visit Turkey, one of the last unspoilt Mediterranean destinations, but visit now before it's too late'. Thankfully, a number of events since 1987 indicate some change in government attitude towards conservation issues, which were first brought to international attention by the Dalyan controversy. As a result of adverse publicity and widespread opposition, the area was declared a 'Special Conservation Zone' and the planned development halted. A five year tourism plan was launched which aimed at a careful, balanced approach to the expansion of tourism. This plan was intended not only to promote the growth of this economically important industry, but also to preserve and protect the environmental and cultural heritage of the country.

How successful has this been? The tourist capacity of the major resorts has continued to increase, with 180,000 licensed beds in Turkey in 1990 and a target of 369,200 set for 1992. Foreign exchange receipts have almost tripled since 1986 to $33,500 million in 1990. Both the above indicate that the economic side of the plan is very successful, but changes in attitude to conservation issues have been somewhat slower. The Ministry of Culture and Tourism has now split into two separate units. The Ministry of Tourism has taken a number of important initiatives since 1986. These include stricter licensing controls for tourism development, which demand construction of adequate sewerage facilities. The practice of awarding financial incentives for such developments is still current, but only where this condition is fulfilled. The unlicensed pensions which sprang up during the early 1980s are gradually being demolished as the government draws up new plans for major tourist areas such as Olu Deniz. On a larger scale, over 125 areas have been designated as Tourism Areas, which means planning is under central rather than local control, while twelve Specially Protected Areas of particular ecological importance have also been declared. The Ministry of Tourism stresses that environmental issues will be given prime importance in planning for such areas. The World Bank-sponsored South West Coast Environmental Project began in 1988. This aims to identify and eliminate current wastewater and sewage disposal difficulties and provide an adequate regional infrastructure for future development along the Aegean and Mediterranean Coasts. A water analysis survey was carried out along the coastline in 1990 to determine the impact of tourism on water quality and priority areas for action were identified on the basis of this. A new survey to determine the carrying capacity of the coast for tourism is nearing completion and the policy of awarding financial incentives for further development may be reviewed as a result. A new Coastal Zone Management Plan is now under discussion, which aims to draw up a coordinated approach to environmental protection and cover all areas of potential conflict between ecological issues and tourism development.

All these major projects fall under the umbrella of the Mediterranean Action Plan which was approved by sixteen Mediterranean countries in 1975. Under this plan, funded by UNEP, Turkey has signed a number of protocols and conventions to protect the Mediterranean sea against pollution from ships and land-based sources. It is also one of the countries considered in the Blue Plan which aims to promote sound environmental management in this area in the future, through analysis and prediction based on current trends. Problems identified in this component of the Mediterranean Action Plan include the concentration of tourists in particular areas over a short season, the degradation of natural sites, and competition with locals for scarce resources such as water. It recommends governments to try and diversify into different forms of tourism and spread the load throughout the country and over a longer season where possible. It also encourages the promotion of increased environmental awareness. There are signs that the Ministry of Tourism in Turkey is responding to these recommendations through its plans to promote spa towns, ski resorts and mountain tourism as alternatives to the coastal resorts. This is the cause for some concern among conservationists, who fear that poor control and management of such developments could have disastrous effects. The situation in Dalyan indicates that there is good cause for such concern. In spite of its SPA status, building is still continuing, with plans for building further facilities on the beach itself. There is little publicity regarding the ecological importance of the area and the SPA team appear to be doing little to protect the turtle population. The team is based in Ankara and does not include an ecologist, a situation which has prompted calls from conservationists for autonomous local groups.

Recent years have seen a growing awareness of ecological and environmental issues in Turkey, especially amongst young people. Conservation of resources and appreciation of the countryside have been the subject of a series of television advertisements and there is some evidence of increasing enjoyment of wildlife and rural areas in the country. However, the vast majority of Turks who can afford vacations still prefer to holiday in the coastal resorts, with the national parks as a second choice. Conservation issues are still not a matter of general concern. The Turkish Association for the Conservation of Nature and Natural Resources, one of the main conservation organisations in Turkey, is currently attempting to raise the interest of young people through education, clubs and competitions. This influential organisation, which has over 5000 members, with branches in various cities, is the representative of the council of Europe 'Centre Naturopa' body in Turkey. While outside government control, it liaises closely with government ministers on a number of issues and also receives funding for particular projects. Its president is involved in negotiations over the proposed Coastal Zone Management plan with officials from the Ministry of Tourism and other conservationists. Members are also involved in research into diversification of tourism into the interior of the country and the carrying capacities of particular areas. Possible methods of damage limitation and reducing the load on already popular areas such as Cappadocia are also under consideration. DHKD – or the Society for the Protection of Wildlife, based in Istanbul and Ankara, is the other major conservation organisation and has in previous years sent members to Dalyan to assist the local Turtle Protection Group in its work. Such small groups are a feature of the Turkish conservation scene. They often operate in isolation and as a result the conservationist voice is still a weak one. However, there is some international support from organisations such as AGA (Aktionsgemeinschaft Artenschutz e.V.), a German conservation group, who are closely involved in the battle to preserve Dalyan and have previously sent both funds and volunteers to the area. MEDASSET, the Mediterranean Association to Save the Sea Turtles, has also been active from its bases in London and Athens, most recently in a campaign to protect the beach at Patara from further uncontrolled development.

Away from the coastal zone, twenty-five of the most beautiful and ecologically important parts of the country are protected by National Park Status. The Department of National Parks has recently come under the General Directorate of Forestry, which is concerned to restore forest cover and prevent further illegal cutting and burning of this resource. However, a newly-completed holiday complex near Olu Deniz was built by foreign developers on Forestry Directorate land, with full permission from the government! Conservation bodies feel that any future attempts to pass such developments should be met with strong opposition.

Both the tourist industry and more particularly the conservation movement are relatively new to Turkey. Green politics have yet to make their mark and although there are some hopeful signs that government attitudes to Green issues are changing, this can only be judged through the extent to which they enforce the conservation legislation already passed and their willingness to sacrifice immediate economic gain for the sake of further safeguarding Turkey's natural heritage.

Sightseeing

As Turkey's tourist industry has expanded in recent years, its most popular areas and tourist attractions have become increasingly commercialised and packed with visitors in the high season. However, the sheer size of the country has done much to reduce these negative impacts and with a little careful planning it is still possible to enjoy the best of Turkey without encountering crowds of fellow tourists.

Istanbul is, not surprisingly, one of the most popular destinations away from the coastal resorts, as many visitors feel a trip to Turkey would be incomplete without experiencing this cosmopolitan city. It is at its busiest during the summer months, when tourists of all nationalities add to the noise, bustle and confusion which characterise its streets. If you want to enjoy Istanbul at a more relaxed pace with the minimum of hassles, try visiting in the autumn or the spring. As well as being less crowded, the pleasantly cool weather is also more conducive to leisurely appreciation of the great sights and buildings of the city. A number of British-based travel companies are now offering short off-season breaks which are well worth considering. (Further details are given in **Where are the Positive Holidays?**)

The most popular summer destinations overall for British tourists are, however, the coastal resort towns of the Aegean and Mediterranean. If you particularly want to avoid groups of fellow countrymen, visit the most popular resorts out of season. The peak period for some of the main resorts such as Marmaris, Bodrum and Fethiye only lasts from July through to September, outside which period these towns are relatively peaceful, while the climate is still favourable for a leisurely beach holiday. Accommodation for the independent tourist will be easier to find, possibly cheaper, and there will be a far wider choice. If visiting these coasts during the peak summer months, it is still possible to find areas which are virtually unspoilt and offer a far more relaxed holiday than the major resorts, not to mention the chance to avoid crowds of fellow tourists. Some of the smaller villages such as Gumusluk, Occakoy and Akyaka now appear in the brochures of the smaller tour operators and are well worth considering if looking for a quieter holiday on the Aegean or Mediterranean coasts during the peak season.

If you are especially keen to avoid the crowds, vast areas of Turkey are virtually untouched by the tourist industry and may well offer you the opportunity to be the only tourist for miles! However, a holiday in the remoter parts of the Taurus Mountains or eastern Turkey is obviously not everyone's idea of a relaxing break, although these regions do have many attractions to offer the traveller. Less remote regions which are least visited by the British are Thrace, the European area of the Turkish landmass and, for beach holidays, the Black Sea resorts of Akcakoca, Amasra, Unye and Sile.

Whatever time of year you choose to holiday in Turkey you are unlikely to meet large numbers of Turkish tourists away from the main coastal resorts, with the exception of the Uludag ski resort, which tends to be particularly busy during the Turkish half-term from late January to mid February. Those who can afford to take the type of two-week vacations enjoyed by their western European counterparts often favour journeys abroad to the Far East or the European culture tours to such cities as Vienna and Rome. Those who holiday within Turkey itself tend to prefer the beaches of the south and west to the less-developed areas of central and eastern Anatolia, but their numbers are relatively insignificant in the face of the million or so foreign tourists, most of whom are German or British, who flock to these areas from June through to September. Coastal resorts around Istanbul are also popular with the city's inhabitants – in particular Kumburgaz, on the shores of the sea of Marmara, where many of the wealthier Turkish people have holiday villas. Other popular tourist destinations are Lycia, in the extreme south-west of the country, and Cappadocia, with its fantastic geological formations and underground cities. The latter features in much British travel literature and experiences a great annual influx of visitors in the high season. This is starting to cause problems with respect to congestion at the major sites and erosion of the natural beauty of the area. If you want to see Cappadocia at its best, once again the advice is to travel out of season. As with so many of the most popular areas of Turkey the peak tourist influx is of a very limited extent, so it really does make sense to visit outside these peak times and enjoy the area at its best if at all possible. The famous archaeological sites of Lycia and the Aegean coastal area are popular both with foreign tourists and with Turkish people themselves. At the height of the summer season it is possible to find coachloads of schoolchildren wandering through the ruins, in addition to the seemingly ubiquitous multinational archaeological tours! Unless you really want the opportunity to 'listen in' on one of these discourses, all these sites can be enjoyed in a much more peaceful fashion at other times of the year! If out-of-season visits are impossible, the best advice is to enjoy these attractions during the relatively cool early part of the day and the late afternoon, leaving ample time for relaxation at midday.

If you want to avoid fellow tourists of any nationality, there are a number of areas worth considering at most times of the year: outside the main coastal resorts and the major cities, such as Istanbul and Ankara, there are vast areas still relatively untouched by the tourist industry. The general rule is the further east you go, the less commercialised and adapted to tourism the country becomes. The most famous sites and landmarks of eastern Turkey do now attract a steady influx of visitors. The statues of Nemrut Dagi, Lake Van and some of the ruined Armenian churches of the east are becoming better known, but Turkey has the advantage over many of its rival holiday destinations of few problems of overcrowding by tourists outside the main areas previously noted. Eastern Turkey still maintains its image as the preserve of the more adventurous traveller, by virtue of the lack of development of the tourist industry here and the scarcity of facilities. A luxury holiday is not an option in this area! The curiosity which the traveller may arouse in these regions has also effectively deterred many people, especially women, from venturing away from the well-known resort areas, except as part of an organised package tour. All this means that for those travellers prepared to forgo certain comforts, 'getting away from it all' in Turkey could not be simpler. The government is now attempting to diversify the industry away from the major resorts and a number of British companies offer special interest-type holidays to these regions, but – with the exception of Cappadocia, Trabzon, Ani and selected attractions – running into crowds of fellow holiday-makers is unlikely to be a major problem in Central Anatolia and eastern Turkey in the foreseeable future.

Communications

Turkey's transport system offers various ways of visiting the major sites and tourist attractions.

The rail network is a good option in the more developed west of the country for visiting the major towns, but this state-owned and operated system has not yet been expanded to serve the coastal resorts or certain destinations in eastern Turkey adequately. However, within its limitations the network offers the cheapest means of getting around. The services are generally reliable and second-class accommodation is reasonably clean and comfortable. The main drawbacks with this particular transport option are the need to make bookings well in advance and the often excruciatingly slow pace of the journeys. As so many Turkish people use the trains, and services (except to the main cities) are often very limited in number, they tend to fill up quickly. While offering a great chance to socialise, the hours it takes to reach a destination on anything other than express trains may seem rather excessive!

The coach network is far more comprehensive and covers all destinations of any size in Turkey. Although slightly more expensive than rail travel, many tourists find the coach a more convenient option for internal travel and costs are still very competitive, especially when compared to the British equivalent – a 550 kilometre journey from Ankara to Antalya will only set you back around £10. With so many coaches operating between the main destinations, finding a seat is rarely a problem and the hordes of ticket touts at all main bus stations are always eager to help! An additional bonus is the state of the coaches themselves – they are usually clean, modern and very comfortable.

However, any coach journey is only as comfortable as the state of the roads, which tends to be rather variable! There are some 40,000 kilometres of asphalt roads in good condition, which link the major cities and coastal resort destinations, with an additional 20,000 kilometres of secondary roads. These tend to be rather less well-maintained and enlivened by frequent potholes, while the minor local roads are often little more than tracks. Turkey has a low level of private car ownership compared to most western European holiday destinations, so the main traffic on the roads tends to be lorries and coaches. The main highways which cross the country, the E5 to Syria and Lebanon, the E24 to Iraq and the E23 to Iran are among the busiest routes, especially the former, which links Istanbul and Ankara. However, this is the only road where very heavy traffic is encountered; and elsewhere traffic moves freely outside the towns and cities. Links to Europe are also much improved since the completion of the six-lane Istanbul bypass and two bridges over the Bosphorus, which link up ultimately to the Istanbul–Izmit express route. These major roads offer the best option for anyone wanting to drive long distances in a hurry, but the motorway stretches south of Istanbul and to the east of Mersin on the Mediterranean coast are toll roads and also less than relaxing on the nerves.

Most tourists who choose to drive themselves around Turkey hire cars once they arrive, so at least do not have to cope with the problem of a left-hand drive car in addition to driving on the 'wrong' side of the road. However, the heavy lorries on the main roads can be rather stressful as can the Turkish habit of overtaking on blind corners and on the tops of hills! For those in a less desperate hurry, avoiding the three main E roads noted above in favour of the other highways will reduce stress levels slightly. Unfortunately, the secondary stabilised roads do not offer a good alternative for the driver with a less hectic schedule, as the network is poorly developed and these roads, by virtue of their condition, are something of an adventure in themselves! Avoiding driving at night is good advice for anyone wishing to keep their nerves intact! Tractors and hay carts chugging along without lights are not uncommon. The Ministry of Culture and Tourism distributes an annually updated road map, which is very helpful to tourists, although it is worth noting that these maps are sometimes somewhat optimistic with regard to the extent of completed road building projects. One very useful distinction is the practice of writing signs in black on a yellow background to denote sights of interest for tourists.

A more peaceful, although much slower, option for internal travel is the use of the Turkish Maritime Lines services between the major coastal resorts of the Black Sea, Aegean and Mediterranean. Fares are very cheap and services include a nine-day trip from Istanbul to Hopa along the Black Sea coast and a popular ten-day Mediterranean trip from Istanbul through to Antalya, which calls at all the main resort towns such as Marmaris, Bodrum and Fethiye en route. For leisurely exploration of coastal sites of interest these trips offer a worthwhile alternative to more conventional modes of travel, although accommodation tends to be slightly spartan.

For covering very long distances, the state airline Turkish Airlines (THY) offers frequent services between the main cities of Istanbul, Ankara and Izmir, in addition to flights to over fifteen other destinations at competitive prices.

The ubiquitous *dolmus* (a mini-bus with a fixed route, which you can hail at any point on that route) is a very important feature for the independent traveller and offers cheap and frequent services to all short-distance destinations likely to be of interest to tourists. Privately -organised trips to local attractions are a feature of most tourist areas, so access to the main sites is unlikely to be a problem for anyone without their own transport.

Red Tape

Turkey presents few bureaucratic problems for the holidaymaker. Anyone holding a full British passport or a UK visitor's passport is entitled to stay in the country for up to three months, with a visa. The visa costs £5, payable in Sterling, and can be obtained at the point of entry to Turkey. There is no need to apply for a visa from the Turkish Consulate prior to a visit. For trips of a longer duration, contact the Turkish Consulate General on 071 589 0360/0949 for information. Once in the country it is possible to apply to the local Police Authority for extensions of up to three months.

There are no restrictions on the amount of foreign currency or Turkish lira which a tourist can bring into the country. The lira (TL) is the basic unit of currency and is available as 500, 1000, 5000 and 10,000 notes and 10, 50, 100 and 200 coins. Exchange rates are favourable for the British visitor as inflation in Turkey is high – around 30 per cent. The major international credit cards such as American Express, Visa, Access and Diners Club are becoming more widely accepted in the main cities and resorts, but tourists who intend to travel to the more remote areas should be aware that credit cards may be refused in these regions. It is always a good idea to have a reasonable supply of traveller's cheques, Eurocheques or foreign currency, which can be changed at any bank. Many hotels in the main tourist areas will also cash traveller's cheques, but the banks usually offer the best rate. While the rate in Turkey will be better than that which can be obtained at a British bank, it is wise to take enough Turkish currency to tide you over until you reach your destination, as exchange rates at the airport are not usually particularly good. Bear in mind that exchange facilities are less common in the east of the country. Currency exchange slips are given as proof of each transaction and should be retained so that any excess Turkish lira can be reconverted at the end of the holiday and to prove that any major purchases were made with legally exchanged money. It is also worth noting that regulations against the export of antiques are very strict!

As Turkey is not yet a member of the EC, the E111 form, which entitles British visitors to use the health services of other European holiday destinations on the same basis as the locals, does not apply. A good travel insurance policy, which offers comprehensive health insurance, is a must. Most tour operators offer an insurance deal, although the tourist is perfectly free to shop around. Expect to pay around £15 for two weeks' cover, which includes medical expenses incurred. Hospital treatment is available in government-run hospitals if necessary and is usually of a good standard. The emergency number to call an ambulance is 077. Chemists stock a wide selection of drugs for minor ailments. No vaccinations are required for Turkey, although cholera, typhoid, polio and tetanus are recommended by the Department of Health and Malaria tablets may be advisable in some eastern areas. It is advisable to check with your doctor six weeks before departure if in doubt about coverage for the above. Although Turkey is a reasonably clean, hygienic country, even in the main resorts stomach upsets are commonplace. It's wise to stick to freshly cooked food and bottled water (*Hayat* is a reliable local brand). If in doubt, ask local people for their advice.

The main public holidays are 1 January, 23 April, 19 May, 30 August and 29 October. The religious festivals of Kurban Bayrami (The Feast of the Sacrifice) and Seker Bayrami (Sugar Festival), which marks the end of Ramadan, the month of fasting, are the most important of the Muslim calendar. Their dates change each year and during these times shops and government offices are closed. It is a good idea to find out when these particular religious festivals fall, as many Turks take the opportunity to flock to the Aegean and Mediterranean resorts for a three- or four-day break and finding accommodation will be extremely difficult!

Turkish post offices are easily distinguished by their yellow 'PTT' signs. Main offices are open from 8.00 until 24.00 Monday to Saturday and 9.00 to 19.00 on Sundays, while the smaller offices open from 8.30–17.00 and are closed over the weekend, as are government offices. They will exchange money and cash traveller's cheques, in addition to the usual post office services. Most shops open from 9.30 to 19.00 and are closed on Sundays. Telephone calls can be made from PTT telephone booths, using tokens (*jetons*) or phone cards. These booths are found in all towns and offer the most economic way of making a local, national or international call.

Useful phone numbers: 077 – Emergency Service, 011 – Directory Enquiries.

Budgeting

For British visitors, Turkey offers a cheap holiday, especially when compared with prices at home or at some of the main European destinations.

The cost of accommodation varies drastically according to quality, locality and time of year. Expect to pay around £10 a night for a simple, comfortable hotel room and as little as £5 in a basic pension. Food will not be a major expense on a Turkish holiday – unless of course the holidaymaker chooses to make it so! Even on a tight budget it is possible to enjoy some very good meals. The traditional breakfast of cheese, honey, jam, olives and fresh bread, accompanied by tea, will set you back around 50 pence. For a full three-course meal with wine the cost may be as little as £5. Obviously, expect to pay more in larger hotels and restaurants in the main cities, or if you choose to search out 'western-style' food. The small family-run restaurants which serve local dishes and are frequented by Turkish people as well as tourists are usually the best value – they are often called *Lokantasi*. There is normally a good choice of dishes available. Indulging in afternoon tea at one of the ubiquitous '*cay*' (pronounced 'chah-yee') shops is a similarly cheap occupation (12 pence or less for a glass of tea), but if you add European-type cakes at a tourist café in one of the main resorts, costs will increase dramatically.

Travel by public transport is very cheap. For coach travel, the cost works out at around 2p per kilometre for the longer journeys, with rail fares slightly cheaper! Petrol costs around 38 pence per litre. Car hire charges are approximately £12.50 per day, plus 13 pence per kilometre. Travel by dolmus is a very good option over short distances, but taxis can be expensive – £1.00 to £1.90 in the main cities for a cross-town journey of a few kilometres. The taxis should be metered, but the drivers do not always choose to use them.

Entry charges for monuments and museums are generally low, i.e. from around 75 pence to £1.90 at some of the major archaeological sites.

Overall it is possible to live with a reasonable degree of comfort on around £15 per day. This includes simple accommodation, sightseeing and eating out at pleasant, if not luxurious restaurants. Regional variations are, however, considerable. You should bargain on spending more than this on the Aegean and Mediterranean coasts and in Istanbul, but much less in eastern Turkey.

When To Go

The decision on when to visit Turkey depends to a large extent on just what you require from your holiday. Flights and accommodation are cheaper outside the peak season of July to September and the main sights will be blissfully quiet and peaceful. Temperatures will also be more conducive to sightseeing outside the summer months in western Turkey. Off-season short breaks to Istanbul, including special Christmas shopping trips, are on offer from a number of tour operators, or can be organised on an individual basis. For the sun-seekers, the climate is favourable for swimming and waterside relaxation from April to November along the southern Aegean and Mediterranean coasts, although those determined to cultivate a serious tan are better advised to visit between May and October, when average temperatures are above 20°C! Even in the high season it is still possible to find some quiet spots in this most popular area, or the Black Sea coast offers a good alternative. The swimming season is shorter here – from June to September – and the weather generally a shade wetter and mistier.

For the keen ornithologist, the autumn migrations will influence the decision as to when to visit, while for the botanist the spring flowers are a major attraction. The dedicated walker will also find conditions much more pleasant in the spring or autumn, as temperatures on the central Anatolian plateau can reach 24°C in August. However, anyone wishing to explore eastern Turkey may encounter heavy snow between October and April and runs the risk of certain roads being blocked if they choose to visit at this time.

Another way to decide when to visit is to plan a trip around a particular event or festival. The Information Counsellor's Office in London will supply a list of festival dates on request. Popular festivals include the Whirling Dervish Festival at Konya in December and the Camel Wrestling Festival at Selcuk in January. The range of festivals is enough to satisfy any interest. In addition to the better-known events, there are a variety of music, arts and culture festivals throughout the year. Local tourist information offices will also be able to give details of any festivals in the area.

Where Are the Positive Holidays?

The potential visitor to Turkey can be forgiven for feeling rather overwhelmed by the range of holidays on offer. Many of the large tour operators now feature Turkey in their brochures, in addition to which there are a growing number of small, specialist companies which concentrate solely on Turkey or include it in a limited range of destinations. In the face of such choice, how is it possible to select a 'green' or 'positive' holiday package? There are a number of guidelines to assist the concerned tourist in making a decision: initially the brochure itself is the first source of information. Does it give a background as to the historical, ecological and cultural significance of the holiday area? Does it attempt to describe the local people accurately and suggest guidelines as to appropriate behaviour for the tourist, or does it resort to stereotyped images to portray 'local colour'? If the travel company is making any contribution to conservation projects at local, national or even international level, these will be mentioned in the brochure, as will membership of Green Flag International. This is a private non-profit-making company working with the tourism industry to make environmental improvements at tourism destinations throughout the world, as well as encouraging its members to make their own operations as 'green' as possible. A number of companies are now supporting international initiatives such as the preservation of the rainforest and research into endangered species, which, although often of no direct benefit to Turkey as a holiday destination, are undeniably of value and show a genuine concern to protect the environment. The best type of commitment is, however, shown by those companies which make direct contributions to initiatives at the host destination.

Another point worth looking for is the style of the brochure itself. Is it a no-expense-spared glossy production or does it indicate a more responsible use of resources, possibly even recycled paper? The nature of the holiday package is a major consideration in selecting a 'green' holiday. Does it support the local economy through the use of rented local accommodation and employment of local people? If a full or half-board package, does it serve local produce? Is it small in scale and does it show a concern to preserve the character and beauty of the area and encourage interest in its history and ecology? Does it promote the use of public transport for excursions and is there any mention of opportunities to meet and talk with local people? This latter is a particularly important consideration for travellers contemplating a touring holiday and is often discounted by companies eager to rush the tourist around to the maximum number of sights in their two weeks' vacation.

General Holidays

About 86 British tour operators include Turkey in their programme for summer holidays, with 28 offering winter breaks and 25 providing sailing and yachting holidays. While the larger companies sell through most travel agents, a number of the smaller specialist companies only sell directly to the public or through selected ABTA agents. Many of the companies listed below fall into this category and you will have to contact them directly for brochures and further information.

The best tour operators can offer detailed advice on accommodation options, choice of destination, etc from personal knowledge and are therefore particularly helpful for first-time visitors to Turkey. They can also offer details of local excursions, possibly organise short cruises as part of the overall package and suggest itineraries for those who opt for a fly/drive-type holiday. As an added advantage, once at the destination local representatives of the company are available to deal with any problems or queries which might arise and generally ensure that visitors get the most from their holiday. The security of having pre-booked hotel rooms, apartments or pensions is important for many tourists, especially those with young children, or the elderly, and potentially saves hours wasted in frustrating searches for suitable accommodation. Budgeting is also much easier on a package holiday, as the bulk of the cost will have been paid prior to departure – though this might limit the amount of your money which ends up in local Turkish pockets.

For those who wish to explore a particular area of the country in detail, or merely base themselves within easy reach of an attractive beach, a self-catering package, using rented local accommodation, is a good option. Such holidays not only contribute to the local economy, but also tend to be low impact. The type of holiday properties which can be rented directly from the owners in destinations such as France and Italy are not yet a feature of the Turkish travel scene and arrangements to rent such property are best made through a reputable tour operator. **Simply Turkey** (8 Chiswick Terrace, Acton Lane, London W4 5LY, Tel. 081 747 1011) are one of the leaders in this field and have been offering a range of private villas in small unspoilt villages since 1983. They offer mainly locally-owned properties, often built in traditional style and lovingly restored to high standards, and are careful to stress their commitment to low impact, small-scale tourism and conservation through their brochure and membership of Green Flag International. Most of the properties are located on the popular southern Aegean and western Mediterranean coasts, but Simply Turkey have made it a policy to avoid the increasingly crowded resort towns of these coasts and base their programme in nearby small peaceful villages which are still untouched by mass tourism. From about £310 per person in a party of four for two weeks self-catering (with maid service) and return flight to the UK to £490 per person for the more luxurious properties in the peak season.

Ilios Island Holidays (18 Market Square, Horsham, West Sussex RH12 1EU, Tel. 0403 59788) also offer a selection of traditional style cottages and villas in the unspoilt fishing village of Akyaka on the popular Mediterranean coast. From £290 per person for two weeks in the low season to £533 in the high season.

Beach Villas (Holidays) Ltd (8 Market Passage, Cambridge CB2 3QR, Tel. 0223 31113), members of Green Flag International, offer apartments and villas for two-week holidays in the small village of Gumusluk near Bodrum. They recently demonstrated their commitment to maintaining the character of the area and to small-scale tourism through encouraging their clients to participate in a boycott campaign against bars playing loud western pop music along the otherwise peaceful beach!

Also worth considering: **Just Turkey** (13 Hillgate Street, London W8 7SP, Tel. 071 221 8686) for villas and apartments. From around £280 per person for two weeks in October to £360 in August. **Turkish Villas** (35 Hanover Gardens, London SE11 5TN, Tel. 071 735 6037) for a good selection of privately-owned villas on the Bodrum peninsula, northern Aegean and Mediterranean coasts.

Camping and caravanning holidays have yet to make their mark as a major component of the Turkish tourist industry. However a number of British-based companies do offer such holidays, while camping is often an integral feature of the trekking and adventure-type holidays on offer (see **Adventure/Activity Holidays**).

Overseas Camping Tours Ltd (181 Edward Street, Brighton BN2 2JB, Tel. 0273 655825) offer self-drive motorcaravans or estate cars with camping pack, which includes tents and sleeping bags. The company bases its vehicles at Gokcek, near Dalaman airport, and offers free route maps and advice on itineraries. The company has also produced *The Çamping Guide to Western Turkey*, which is available to their clients and also generally through selected bookshops. Fly/drive motorcaravan packages are also available, as are similar packages which include hire of small motorboats and camping equipment. Prices for hire of a 4-berth motorcaravan range from £360 per person for two weeks in May to £525 in June, inclusive of flight. Delivery and collection of vehicles from other airports can be arranged at an extra charge of up to £110.

The tourist who opts for a fly/drive package based on hotels and pensions, or single centre hotel-based holidays has far more choice available. Recent developments in this sector of the Turkish tourism market include major international chains such as Hilton International, Holiday Inn and Sheraton moving into the country. Hilton International have invested in a major development at Mersin, east of Antalya, while Holiday Inn Worldwide have signed a management agreement with a Turkish company for a seafront hotel in Istanbul. However, the 'Good Tourist' can still find many British-based companies who offer tours using small-scale, locally-owned accommodation.

The Travel Alternative (27 Park End Street, Oxford OX1 1HU, Tel. 0865 791636) offer escorted group tours based in small hotels in eastern Turkey and Cappadocia (from £949–£1160 per person for 16 to 18 days including flight). They will also put together tailor-made itineraries for the independent traveller. **Simply Turkey** (address above) also offer this service, in addition to short breaks in Istanbul and hotel-based holidays in Dalyan, using carefully selected hotels.

Turkish Delight Holidays (address above) will arrange tailor-made holidays and a fly/drive package using Dalaman airport, with advice on itineraries. In addition to their villa programme, they offer a range of hotels and pensions at resorts along the Mediterranean coast. They have shown particular care in their choice of this accommodation and their brochure stresses the opportunity to get to know the Turkish hosts and a little of the language in the smaller, family-run properties.

Orientours (Kent House, 87 Regent Street, London W1R 8LS, Tel. 071 434 1551) are specialists in pilgrimages to Biblical sites and have recently expanded their programme to include a four-night 'Classic Tours' break in Istanbul. This tour is based at selected three- and four-star hotels and the price includes guided tours of the main churches and mosques. From around £300 per person, including flight and accommodation.

Voyages Jules Verne (21 Dorset Square, London NW1 6QG, Tel. 071 723 6556) also offer short breaks in Istanbul, with the choice of either a carefully-restored eighteenth-century hotel in the old town on the European side of the city, or a modern five-star luxury hotel, near the Grand Bazaar.

Other Turkey specialists include **Metak Holidays** (70 Welbeck Street, London W1M 7HA, Tel. 071 935 6961), who make use of good, three-star hotels in well-chosen locations.

Adventure/Activity Holidays

These are a fairly recent feature of the tourist industry in Turkey, with the exception of sailing holidays which have long been popular with a British clientele. Of course, Turkey's miles of beautiful coastline have always made it an obvious destination for the yachting fraternity, but its other natural assets have only been exploited more recently, for instance through walking and skiing holidays.

Walking

Anyone wishing to explore Turkey on foot may find the lack of maps and information as to long-distance footpaths something of a disincentive. For this reason, many potential trekkers choose one of the excellent walking holidays now offered by a selection of British companies rather than opting to 'go it alone'. A number of the companies detailed below are well-known international operators of 'adventure holidays' while others are smaller, more specialised concerns.

In the former category, **Explore Worldwide Ltd** (1 Frederick Street, Aldershot, Hants GU11 1LG, Tel. 1252 319448) offer small group walking holidays in Lycia, based on the use of small pensions and villagers' homes in the more remote areas. The tours also include a short cruise and opportunities to explore Istanbul and Antalya with a local guide and Explore group leader. The basic sixteen-day tour with flight and half-board accommodation, with full board while trekking, costs from £398–£430 per person. They also offer a variety of other tours throughout Turkey, including the east, which may afford the opportunity for some leisurely hiking.

For the more energetic, **Exodus Expeditions** (9 Weir Road, London SW12 0LT, Tel. 081 675 5550) offer a range of treks graded from easy to strenuous in Lycia, the Taurus mountains and the Kackar mountains, along the Black Sea coast. Their accompanied tours make use of private village accommodation where possible, or else camp-sites and small hotels. They are usually led by bilingual staff in collaboration with local guides and luggage is transferred ahead by donkey! Treks last fifteen days and prices range from £530–£740 per person, including full board while on the trek and flight from London.

Both **Hann Overland** (201/203 Vauxhall Bridge Road, London SW1V 1ER, Tel. 071 834 7337) and **Sherpa Expeditions** (131a Heston Road, Hounslow, Middlesex TW5 0RD, Tel. 081 577 2717) offer a range of accompanied treks from seven to seventeen days. Sherpa's treks in

Cappadocia and the Taurus Mountains and their ascent of Mount Ararat in eastern Turkey afford the keen trekker the opportunity to make non-technical ascents of some of Turkey's impressive peaks. Sherpa's prices start at around £1000 per person for sixteen days, including flight and half-board accommodation in hotels, or camping.

Of the smaller companies, **Simply Turkey** (address above) is again worth a mention for its treks in the remoter parts of the Taurus mountains. These are led by an expert Turkish guide and involve an opportunity to meet and live with nomadic people. The tour costs around £735 per person for fifteen days' full board, including flight.

The Istanbul-based company **Kosmos Travel Ltd** (Bagdat Caddesi 288 181060 Caddeboston, Istanbul/Turkey, Tel. (90-1) 134 34 20) offers escorted small group treks in Lycia and the Taurus mountains, with support vehicle. Kosmos Travel affords the 'Good Tourist' the rare opportunity to support a Turkish-based company, which is promoting simple, predominantly camping holidays in some of Turkey's most beautiful, unspoilt areas. They also offer a range of exploratory tours by truck in Central and Eastern Anatolia, Cappadocia and south-west Turkey.

Another good Turkish operator, which specialises in adventure and activity holidays of all sorts, predominantly in the Lycia region but also in Eastern Turkey and Cappadocia, is **Travel Alternatif** (Bagdat Caddesi, Samnu Is Merkezi 36/8, 81030 Kiziltoprak, Istanbul/Turkey, Tel. (90-1) 345 6650). As well as being extremely knowledgeable about the regions visited, their staff are aware of environmental issues. Tailor-made holidays can be arranged. For a wide range of exciting trips, including treks in the East (culminating in one up Mount Ararat), contact **Trek Travel** (Aydede Caddesi 10, 80090 Taksim, Istanbul/Turkey, Tel. (90-1) 155 1624).

Holidays Afloat

Flotilla sailing holidays and general watersports holidays are now offered by many of the general tour operators as an alternative to, or as part of, a more traditional villa-based break. **CV Travel** (43 Cadogan Street, Chelsea, London SW3 2PR, Tel. 071 581 0851) offer *gulets* (traditional Turkish boats), with four to eight double cabins, for private charter along the Aegean coastline complete with Turkish crew. They are members of Green Flag International and are currently supporting a local conservation group in Corfu. From £120 per person per week, exclusive of food and travel.

Gulet holidays are also offered by **Simply Turkey** (address above) from £400 per person per week in the low season to £538 in peak season for ten people sharing, for Simply Turkey's 'Blue Cruises'.

Kosmos Travel Ltd (address above) run one-week sail treks in the Gulf of Gokova. Specialist cruising holidays are also offered by **Simply Turkey** and **Temple World** (13 The Avenue, Kew, Richmond, Surrey TW9 2AL, Tel. 081 940 4114), for those who wish to combine botanical or archaeological interests with sailing. The Temple World programme includes an Easter cruise, especially designed to take advantage of the spring flowers of the Mediterranean coastal region and an Aegean cruise, beginning at Bodrum, which takes in some of Turkey's most famous archaeological sites including Ephesus and Miletus. The tours cost £995 per person including flights, full-board accommodation and the services of a knowledgeable guest leader.

For the more energetic who wish to develop their own sailing skills, **Falcon Sailing** (Falcon Boutique, 13 Hillgate Street, London W8 7SP, Tel. 071 727 0232) offer flotilla sailing and independent charter around the Bodrum peninsula and dinghy sailing and windsurfing tuition from bases at the small resorts of Bitez and Yalikavak, also on the Bodrum peninsula. Prices for dinghy sailing and windsurfing from around £300–£600 per person for two weeks including half board and flight.

Aquasport Tours Ltd (181 Edward Street, Brighton, East Sussex BN2 2JB, Tel. 0273 685824) are a small company who offer waterskiing, diving and sailboarding tuition from their bases in small hotels and campsites at Marmaris and Bodrum. They arrange flights or overland departures from London. Prices from around £260 per person per week for overland travel and accommodation in village rooms or campsites.

Best Yachting and Tourism Ltd (Hillier House, 509 Upper Richmond Road, London SW14 7EE, Tel. 081 878 3227) offer sailing schools and watersports tuition, which can be combined with holidays in their range of self-catering villas and cottages, in addition to *gulet* holidays.

For the adventurous, **Travel Alternatif** (address above) offer canoeing and simple rafting holidays, as well as white-water rafting on the Euphrates and a Lycian 'sail-and-trek' holiday.

Skiing

The majority of tourists contemplating a skiing holiday will almost automatically head for the often overcrowded Alpine resorts, without pausing to consider Turkey as a possible destination. This is hardly surprising in view of the fact that there are only eight ski resorts in the country and these have a somewhat low profile compared to their European competitors. In recent years the environmental impact of skiing has been increasingly brought to public attention by conservationists concerned at the visual and ecological damage caused in fragile environments by the initial construction of ski lifts etc and the subsequent pressure of numbers in the most popular resorts. Downhill skiing is potentially particularly harmful and, if you want to book through a British-based company, it is the only option currently available in Turkey. However, for the determined downhill skier the Turkish resorts have the advantage of being relatively quiet and 'spreading the load' away from the main Alpine skiing centres.

Ski Turkey Ltd (316 Reigate Road, Bromley, Kent BR1 5JN, Tel. 081 461 5701) are the authorised agents for the country's premier ski resort of Uludag. This is set in the Uludag National Park, south of Istanbul and offers facilities especially suitable for the beginner and intermediate level skier. The village is purpose-built and comprises a variety of two-, three- and four-star modern hotels, with shops, swimming pool, bars and restaurants. The season runs from December to April.

President Holidays (542 Kingsland Road, London E8 4AH, Tel. 071 249 4002) offer the opportunity to combine a skiing holiday in Uludag with a short break in Istanbul at selected four-star hotels. Prices from around £360 per person for one week's half board at a hotel in Uludag, not inclusive of lift pass or ski hire. Ski Turkey Ltd can give details of other companies offering skiing holidays at Uludag and at the country's other resorts such as Saklikent, near Antalya and Erciyes, near Kayseri.

Turkey-based **Travel Alternatif** offer challenging ski treks in the mid Taurus mountains.

Special Interest Holidays

While the type of activity holidays available in other holiday destinations, such as organised cycling or horse-riding trips, are not yet a feature of the Turkish tourist industry there are a number of less strenuous special interest tours available by way of compensation. These range from archaeological through historical to art and music tours.

Page and Moy Ltd (136–140 London Road, Leicester LE2 1EN, Tel. 0533 552521) offer a number of tours including an 'Aegean and Lycian shores' tour with experienced lecturers in art history and architecture, which takes in some of Turkey's most important archaeological sites. Accommodation varies from hotels in the major towns to simple family accommodation in the more remote areas. While such tours may not offer as many opportunities for contact with the local people as might be wished, they do afford a valuable insight into the history and culture of the country and are suitable both for interested amateurs and the more knowledgeable. Prices for the two-week Aegean tour are £1095 per person including flight, half-board accommodation and entrance fees to sites.

Prospect Music and Art Limited (454–458 Chiswick High Road, London W4 5TT, Tel. 081 995 2151) also offer an accompanied 'Classical Turkey' tour, which includes many of these most famous archaeological sites in addition to less well-known locations, at thirteen days from £1175 per person.

For steam railway enthusiasts, **Turkish Delight** (address above) offer steam tours with the Turkish State Railways Authority from Izmir east to Malatya, which include visits to places of historical and archaeological interest. From around £1085 per person for two weeks including half-board accommodation in local hotels and flights.

Simply Turkey (address above) offer escorted archaeological and painting tours and a tour of Syrian Orthodox churches in south-western Turkey (for details of escorted tours Tel. 081 995 1121).

Regent Holidays (Regent House, 31A High Street, Shanklin, Isle of Wight PO37 6SW, Tel. 0983 864212) is a small company which can arrange special interest tours focusing on archaeology, natural history and language learning – as well as some more obscure themes. Accommodation is mainly self-catering.

Wildlife/Ecological Holidays

Turkey has a great deal to offer the wildlife and botanical enthusiast – a fact which a number of tour operators have woken up to in recent years. **Cox and Kings** (Cox and Kings Travel Ltd, St James Court, Buckingham Gate, London SW1E 6AF, Tel. 071 834 7472) are one of the companies who have declared their commitment to preservation of fragile habitats and endangered species and to small-scale responsible tourism. They back this declaration by buying an acre of Belize rainforest for every client booking on one of their wildlife holidays. They offer a botanical tour to south-western Turkey, from around £1000 per person for two weeks including flight and half-board accommodation.

Ornitholidays (1/3 Victoria Drive, Bognor Regis, West Sussex PO21 2PW, Tel. 0243 821 230) are a small specialist company who have been running tours for bird enthusiasts for twenty-seven years. They are business supporters of the RSPB and have recently implemented their own conservation fund to assist in the protection of endangered species and habitats worldwide. This is funded through clients' donations and also through Subbuteo Natural History Books Ltd, who have agreed to donate to the fund a proportion of the proceeds made from book sales to Ornitholidays clients. They offer an autumn tour to western Turkey, based in hotels at Istanbul, Bursa and the nearby Uludag National Park, to coincide with a major bird of prey migration. The tour is led by an experienced guide and costs from around £1000 per person for two weeks including flight and accommodation.

Naturetrek (Chautara, Bighton, nr Alresford, Hampshire SO24 9RB, Tel. 0962 733051) offer a seventeen-day combined botanical and bird-watching tour in Eastern Turkey, which includes a five-day trek in the Kackar Mountains. Their brochure gives the potential traveller an excellent idea of just what to expect and is at pains to stress the Naturetrek philosophy of giving their clients sufficient time not only to appreciate the natural history and beauty of the areas they visit, but also the culture and lifestyle of the local people. Prices are £1300 per person for seventeen days, including flight and accommodation.

Pingrum Specialist Tours (Woodend House, Woodend, Little Horwood, Milton Keynes MK17 0PE, Tel. 029671 2992) specialise in archaeological and natural history tours, mainly in Europe and Asia. They too offer a combined birdwatching and botanical tour, with experienced British leaders and also a Turkish guide. Their two-week tour of the Mediterranean coast and central Turkey includes many major wildlife habitats such as the Dalyan Delta and the Mount Uludag National Park. From around £800 per person.

Voyages Jules Verne (21 Dorset Square, London NW1 6QG, Tel. 071 724 6624) include a sixteen-night painting, history and botany tour of the Aegean and south coasts in their Natural World programme, while the small specialist company **Turkish Wildlife Holidays** (8 The Grange, Elmdon Park, Solihull B92 9EL, Tel. 021 742 5420) offer a range of tours including small group tours in Eastern Turkey, birdwatching tours to coincide with the major Bosphorus migration and trekking and climbing tours in the Kackar and Taurus Mountains.

Volunteer/Conservation Holidays

For those who wish to make a more direct contribution to their chosen destination while on holiday, voluntary work on projects of environmental and/or social significance are a good option.

The International Voluntary Service (162 Upper New Walk, Leicester LE1 7QA, Tel. 0533 549430) regularly recruits volunteers for its camps in Turkey. These have previously covered a number of areas and types of project, from making paths for historical sites at Mugla, to building schools and health centres at Bursa and Samsun. Many IVS camps include the opportunity for informal study of local ecology, so the volunteer does not only have the chance to learn and practise Turkish, but also to develop some appreciation and understanding of local conservation issues. Camps vary in length from two to four weeks and cost from £70, not including travel. Minimum age for volunteers is eighteen.

Archaeology Abroad (31–34 Gordon Square, London WC1H 0PY) publish an annual information bulletin, available from the secretary at the above address, which gives details of digs requiring volunteers worldwide. They will be able to advise on current projects in Turkey.

Europe Conservation (Via Fusetti 14, 20143 Milan, Italy, Tel. 010 39 2 5810 3135) is a new environmental organisation, which has previously organised archaeological camps in Turkey. Information on current projects is available from the above address.

Earthwatch is an international organisation, which recruits volunteers to assist in scientific research projects worldwide. Volunteers are expected to contribute, sometimes quite substantially, towards the cost of the expedition, but do have the opportunity to work alongside experts in a particular field. Projects cover a wide variety of topics in ecology, archaeology, sociology and geology. There are over a hundred projects each year, which are regularly updated. Information on current and proposed future projects can be gained initially from Sally Moys, Earthwatch Europe, Belsyre Court, 57 Woodstock Road, Oxford, OX2 6HU. Tel. 0865 311600.

Istanbul-based tour operator **Genctur Turizm** (Yerebatan Caddesi 15/3, Sultanahmet, Istanbul/Turkey, Tel. (90-1) 528 0734 or 526 5409) offers some working holidays, and there's also the possibility of joining the Turkish conservation organisation **DHKD** (PO Box 18, 80810 Bebek, Istanbul/Turkey) on one of its summer campaigns in an area of environmental concern.

Travelling Independently

Turkey has long been seen as the domain of the more adventurous independent traveller and it has only become a major destination since its discovery by the package tour operators. It has become increasingly popular with the independent visitor too since its transformation into a mainstream holiday destination, although package tours still comprise the lion's share of the market. For those wanting the freedom of independent travel and prepared to use that little extra initiative, an independent holiday in Turkey is a perfectly feasible option and with many of the tour operators listed in the previous section offering flight-only deals, in addition to those offered by the major airlines, arriving at the holiday destination is unlikely to pose a problem. Nor is the search for accommodation, although the search for suitable accommodation may prove somewhat more difficult! The popular resorts will almost inevitably have their hotel touts at the bus stations, but the better accommodation will be difficult to find. The villas discussed in the previous section can really only be booked through the listed tour companies before leaving home, so the independent traveller in the high season may be forced to fall back on a room in one of the many hotels which have recently sprung up to cater for the mass tourist trade.

Sustainable tourism programmes are generally rather difficult to track down and fit into once in Turkey. Local Tourist Information offices will be able to help with general accommodation queries and advice as to local attractions, but this rarely includes information as to local walks or guides, except in the main mountaineering areas (see below). As noted in the previous section, the general policy appears to be to discourage independent travellers from venturing off the major tourist routes and trekking away into the wilderness. Certain Turkish-based travel companies do however offer small group tours to the more remote areas, e.g. Kosmos Travel, Trek Travel and Travel Alternatif. The Turkish Embassy Information Counsellor's Office in London produces a useful guide for the independent traveller which lists all the registered tour operators in Turkey, in addition to the yacht marinas and yacht operators. The types of service offered by these companies is variable, from those licensed only to operate tours for the benefit of Turkish citizens, to those such as Kosmos who organise tours throughout the country for foreign visitors. While it is relatively simple to find companies who offer coach tours to the main tourist attractions, trips of a more exploratory, adventurous nature and those which highlight areas of ecological interest are more difficult to find.

The London-based information office also produces very useful lists of licensed accommodation throughout Turkey, of all categories from luxury hotels through to pensions and a list of camp-sites. Once in Turkey, the local Tourist Information office will be able to help with accommodation, local maps and advice as to sights and attractions in the vicinity. However, it is worth noting that the standard of the service is highly variable. While the offices in the main cities such as Istanbul and Ankara will be able to supply comprehensive information on their own region and the country as a whole, the smaller offices will only be able to offer much more limited information related to the particular town or region.

For independent tourists who wish to pursue a particular activity, such as trekking or climbing, offices in the relevant towns near the main mountaineering areas, such as the Munzur Mountains near Erzincan, or the Kackar mountain chain along the Black Sea coast, should be able to supply route plans and put the tourist in touch with local guides. Permits are required for foreign mountaineers in certain areas, e.g. for Mount Ararat, Mount Agri – the highest mountain in Anatolia – and the Hakkari range, south-east of Lake Van. Due to Kurdish guerrilla activity the latter area was forbidden to climbers during the late 1980s. Anyone planning a climbing trip should contact the information office in London initially for up-to-date information regarding requirements for permits, routes, the availability of local guides and the current status of the Hakkari range. The Turkish Mountaineering Club will also be able to offer information and put the traveller in touch with local climbers – contact address from the Information Counsellor's Office in London, who can supply information regarding arrangements for any particular activity or interest in Turkey.

Transport Options

Travel to Turkey by **coach** is not an option used by many people due to the length and the rather gruelling nature of the journey. Most tourists prefer to pay that little bit extra, travel in comfort by air and spend their valuable holiday time exploring their destination, rather than sitting in a bus crossing Europe! However, coach travel is a cheap transport option and may be attractive for those who are on an extended tour rather than a traditional one- or two-week break, providing they are prepared to put up with a little discomfort. **Supabus** operate a service from London to

Istanbul, but a much greater choice of services is available from France, Germany and Italy; even in these cases the journey still takes two to three days.

By **rail**: As an option for getting to Turkey, this is really no more attractive than coach travel. Services leave daily from London's Victoria Station under normal conditions and connect with services to Istanbul at Paris, Venice and Munich. The journey takes roughly two days and costs from £170 single, £293 return. However, the route goes through Yugoslavia and the service is not running at the time of writing. Up-to-date information on the situation is available from **British Rail European Travel Centre** (Victoria Station, PO Box 303, London SW1V 1JY, Tel. 071 834 2345). Another option is to travel to Turkey as part of an InterRail trip. InterRail tickets cost around £260 (or £180 if you're under 26) for a month's unlimited travel throughout Europe, including Turkey and Morocco. Again, direct access to Turkey would be difficult given the current situation in Yugoslavia, but alternative routes are available, e.g. by ferry from Italy or the Greek Islands (see below).

By private **car** it will take at least four days to cover the 3000 kilometres between London and Istanbul. The usual routes of Calais or Ostend to Brussels, Cologne and Frankfurt, then on through Zagreb and Belgrade to Istanbul are, however, impracticable at the time of writing, as they pass through Yugoslavia. Driving south from Germany to the Italian port of Ancona and taking the car ferry to one of the Aegean or Mediterranean ports would appear to be the safest and most feasible option. Driving to Turkey is really only a cost-effective option if there are enough people to share petrol costs. Even then, the long and exhausting journey will be sufficient to deter many people, unless they have the time to explore the attractions en route at leisure. Taking a charter flight, then arranging car hire once in Turkey may prove both cheaper and considerably less effort!

By **air**: Scheduled flights serve mainly Istanbul and Ankara. **Turkish Airlines** (THY) operate regular services from all main European cities to the major international airports of Istanbul, Ankara, Izmir, Adana, Dalaman and Antalya. From Britain they operate daily airbus services to Istanbul, with discounts of 60 per cent for holders of an International Student Identity Card who are under twenty-two. **British Airways** offer daily 'Poundstretcher Flights' to Istanbul from Heathrow for £349 return up to £466 in the peak season, from July to the end of September. These PEX fares do not require an advance booking period, but full payment is required at the time of booking, if this is within eight weeks of the proposed departure date. Charter flights offer a great deal more flexibility in terms of which Turkish airport they serve and are now widely available. Tour operators who offer flight-only deals include **Simply Turkey,** (through 'Simply Travel', Tel. 081 995 3883), **Beach Villas, First Resort Holidays,** (73 South Audley Street, London W1Y 5FF, Tel. 071 355 2321), **Just Turkey, Orientours, President Holidays, The Travel Alternative, UK Express** (Whitehall House, 41 Whitehall, London SW1A 2BY, Tel. 071 839 2702) and **USIT Charters** (52 Grosvenor Gardens, London SW1W 0AG, Tel. 071 823 5151). USIT Charters specialise in cheap summer flights to Istanbul for students and young people. The other companies listed above use mainly Monarch Airways, British Airways, Dan Air, Caledonian Airways and Britannia Airways for flights to all Turkey's main airports from a number of locations in the UK. Dalaman airport is widely used by charter flights, as it serves the main Mediterranean coastal resorts. Most charter flights are from Heathrow and Gatwick, but a wider choice of departure points is becoming available. **Just Turkey,** for example, offer flights to Dalaman from Manchester and Glasgow, in addition to Gatwick. Flights to Antalya are available from the London airports, Manchester, Birmingham and Cardiff, and flights to Izmir from Glasgow. Britannia Airways now also depart from East Midlands, Bristol and Newcastle airports for Turkish destinations. Prices range from around £200 return in the low season to £300 peak season from major UK to Turkish airports. Advertisements in Sunday newspapers and magazines such as *Time Out* also offer cheap flights to Turkey, but are unlikely to offer a better deal than the companies listed above.

By **sea**: There are no direct boat or ferry services, with the exception of cruises, between Britain and Turkey, but at least part of the journey can be accomplished on the water through use of Turkish Maritime Lines services from Ancona and Venice in Italy, or from the Greek Islands. Routes available include Rhodes to Marmaris, Samos to Kusadasi, Kos to Bodrum and Chios to Cesme. From the Greek islands, services take from one to three and a half hours. From Italy, journeys from Ancona to Izmir take three days and are certainly not a cheap option – a one-way trip, including cabin, starts from around £150 per person, with an additional charge of around £100 for transport of a car. **Libra Maritime**, (54 Corso Garibaldi, Brindisi), a Greek company, run a ferry service from Brindisi and Piraeus to Izmir, which takes around forty hours. If you have bought a cheap charter flight to Greece, then travel onwards to Turkey, you may find the return flight is invalidated by doing so. Check carefully in advance.

Accommodation Options

The independent traveller has a number of options which are not open to the package tourist. **Servas International** (Bankside Cottage, Welton-Le-Wold, nr Louth, Lincs N11 0QT) is an organisation which seeks to promote international friendship and hospitality, through putting families and individuals willing to act as hosts for one or two days in touch with travellers who would like the opportunity to live with local people for a short period. A membership fee is required and the traveller is also required to pay a fee for a 'host list' of the country of interest. Arranging short stays is then left to the individual, who is not expected to pay for any subsequent hospitality. Send an SAE to the above address for further details.

The Experiment in International Living ('Otesaga', Upper Wyche, Malvern, Worcs WR14 4EN, Tel. 0684 562577) is another non-religious, non-political and non-profit-making organisation which operates a home-stay programme worldwide. Individual homestays are arranged in all areas of Turkey, for one to four weeks, with prices from £160 per week, not including travel to Turkey. The cost goes towards paying host families and administration charges. The organisation, which was founded in 1932, declares its aims as enhancing understanding and world peace. To this end it also offers a number of youth exchanges, organised study programmes which have previously included conservation topics, language schools and tailor-made trips for youth groups, clubs and societies, companies etc. Full details of all current projects are available from the above address. The organisation also has a travel service, which will assist with travel arrangements even for people not participating in one of their programmes.

There is a range of other options for those going it alone, depending on time of year, size of budget available and which areas of the country the traveller wishes to visit. As already noted, renting private villas is difficult within Turkey and all but impossible in the popular areas during the high season. Similarly, although local information offices may have details of some rooms to let in local houses, this type of informal homestay is not a major feature of the Turkish travel scene and anyone desiring this type of holiday is best advised to go through the organisations listed above. For the budget traveller, youth hostels are one possible option for an overnight stay. However, they are often inconveniently located away from tourist attractions and do not offer much of a saving over the cheaper hotels and pensions. Further details of hostels in Turkey can be obtained from the **Youth Hostels Association**, (Trevelyan House, St Stephen's Hill, St Albans, Herts AL1 2DY, Tel. 0727 55215), or the **Scottish Youth Hostels Association**, (7 Glebe Crescent, Stirling FK8 2JA, Tel. 0786 51181). Camping is another possibility worth considering. Although the network of registered camp-sites is fairly sparse, they do tend to be located along the main tourist routes. The best sites in Turkey are those run by the **Mocamp Kervansaray** chain, which often have restaurants and even simple rooms in addition to the more basic facilities of electricity and running water. The Information Counsellor's Office in London produces a leaflet on camping in Turkey, which details registered sites around the country. **Overseas Camping Tours Ltd** (address above) produce a very useful book *The Camping Guide to Western Turkey*, which was originally intended as an information sheet for their clients, but has recently been published and is now available directly from their offices for £4.50 or from specialist bookshops at £3.95. Camping on unregistered sites is possible, but not advisable!

The list of licensed accommodation, which is also available from the London office, covers all categories of hotel from luxury five-star establishments down to Class 4, one-star accommodation. Registered pensions, motels and *oberj* are also listed. These lists are in no way an infallible guide, but they are a useful starting point in the hunt for accommodation. Many perfectly reasonable establishments are not registered, as criteria for inclusion in the list are necessarily somewhat subjective and arbitrary. The independent traveller arriving at a tourist destination is unlikely to have problems finding accommodation – the touts will usually come to you! For the unregistered facilities, the only possible means of assessment is by going to have a good look! This is probably advisable for the listed establishments as well if possible, as standards can be rather variable. **Turban** is a reliable Turkish chain with high standards of comfort.

As a general guide, at the top end of the scale the luxury hotels will cost from upwards of £60 per night and are only found in the main cities. Standards of comfort and available facilities decrease down the scale to the one-star, basic hotels and pensions and the no-star establishments. Pensions are generally small, basic, family-run establishments with shared facilities. One-star and pension accommodation can be only £5 per night, or even less with some determined bartering in the low season, but the traveller cannot expect too much in the way of luxury for this sort of price. However, the room should at least be clean and indeed it is possible to find perfectly adequate, if simple, accommodation at this end of the market. Women travellers and families should look out for the word 'Aile' in hotel names, as this indicates the establishment is suitable for them. The better-class hotels will not be an option in the more remote areas and travellers in these regions must be prepared to 'rough it' a little. Certain areas of eastern Turkey which experience a significant influx of tourists such as Van and Urfa do now have some good hotels, but beware of coinciding with coach tours who may have pre-booked the better accommodation. The rule is book ahead where possible!

If booking ahead it is probably wise to opt for the more expensive accommodation, as standards are more likely to live up to expectations. It is possible to correspond directly with the hotel itself. Alternatively, a number of British-based companies offer an accommodation-only service: **Small World** (13 Hillgate Street, London W8 7SP, Tel. 071 221 1121), **Orientours**, **Intra Travel** (44 Maple Street, London W1P 5GD, Tel. 071 323 3303), **Best Yachting and Tourism Ltd, Stepaway Ltd** (1 Highfield, Dudbridge Hill, Stroud, Glos. GL5 3HN, Tel. 0453 752214) and **President Holidays** are among the companies offering this service. A wide range of accommodation types is offered and the tourist choosing to book through one of these agents will at least have a little more idea what to expect than someone corresponding directly with the hotel. However, this kind of forward planning necessitates a fairly rigid schedule and involves a certain loss of spontaneity for the independent traveller. It also means less of your money ends up in the local economy. The third option is available through a Turkey-based organisation called **Turistik Ev Pansiyonculugunu Gelistirme Dernegi** (Cumhuriyet Bulvari 84/803, Izmir/Turkey, Tel. (90-51) 257273 or 214295 or 212528). They offer information on and reservations for family-run guest-houses in twenty-five (predominantly coastal) locations throughout Turkey.

The tourist offices in London and Turkey itself can offer advice regarding accommodation, but do not provide a booking-ahead service.

Accommodation

The 'Good Tourist' has a number of options when selecting accommodation in Turkey. This choice is partly determined by the initial decision between independent travel or a package tour. House letting is not yet an available option for the potential visitor to Turkey. The nearest option is to rent a locally-owned traditional cottage or villa through one of the tour companies based in Britain which offers this service. This type of property varies greatly in size, style and standard of comfort, but is almost invariably located in a relatively unspoilt village or small town along the popular western stretch of the Mediterranean coast and the Bodrum peninsula. Some are relatively remote, others in the centre of the village. Some are old properties which have been carefully-restored, while others are modern, but have been built in traditional styles. As one travel operator points out in their brochure, it is important not to confuse the term 'villa' with the type of luxurious property which might be described in such a way in the south of France. The Turkish villa varies from a splendid Ottoman-style house to a simple stone cottage. The only real drawback with these properties is that they are only available along the main coastal resort stretch at present and cannot be booked through local tourist offices within the country.

A good option, open to both the package tourist and the independent traveller, are the small family-run pensions, which are available in all main tourist areas, both coastal and inland, although their character and quality may vary rather drastically between Istanbul, Marmaris and Van for example! Both the Ministry of Tourism-listed pensions and the unlisted properties are worth consideration. With a basic, simple, clean pension, the owner and family will often be the factor that makes all the difference for the traveller. The better companies who offer holidays based in this type of accommodation tend to use properties carefully selected for their facilities and style, but also the friendly, welcoming nature of their owners. It is stressed as a positive point in the brochures that travellers may find themselves giving informal English lessons, or learning the art of backgammon! For the independent traveller, the best way to judge a pension is really to go and have a look and meet the owner. The list of registered properties put out by the Ministry of Tourism is useful, but hardly comprehensive. Pensions can be very cheap – especially out of season. This time of year has the added advantage that the owner will have more leisure to talk to guests. Prices generally range from £5 to £10 per night for rooms with shared facilities, but will vary with the facilities available and also the time of year.

Camping is another good option – in certain areas of the country. Unfortunately, the number of registered camp-sites is still less than significant. Standards can be very high in the best sites (see **Travelling**

Independently). The best initial source of information is the London information office – address above.

Holiday villages are a fairly recent phenomenon in Turkey. Again the London information office will be able to supply details of localities and facilities. Some of these, such as the Belek Holiday Village near Antalya, rely to varying extents on international finance and management. They are, arguably, a good way of 'containing' tourist activity and therefore limiting the damage it may cause to the surrounding area. Unfortunately, they may also limit financial input from the development to the local population. For the tourist staying at a Holiday Village, facilities are provided on site and there is little incentive to venture further afield and see some real Turkish life. A number of British-based companies use this type of accommodation, which is best suited to those looking for a week's sunbathing and not much more! Anyone contemplating this type of holiday should ask a few searching questions of the tour operators (see **Checklist for the Good Tourist**). It *is* difficult to generalise, as obviously standards vary between the different villages, and in some cases these holidays may prove less damaging than a poorly-run botanical holiday, where rare plants may be picked or trampled underfoot!

For those requiring a better idea of real Turkish life, some adventure and walking holidays offer the tourist the opportunity to live for a few days in the more remote parts of the country in villagers' homes or tents. Homestays can provide a real insight into Turkish life. Addresses of companies offering this type of service are given in **Travelling Independently**.

Turkish hotels range all the way from basic through to luxury, in the major cities. International hotel chains such as Hilton and Sheraton International are now a feature of the Turkish tourist industry. However, some of the more luxurious properties used by the tour companies listed in **Where are the Positive Holidays?** are carefully-restored historic buildings, which still retain their traditional character and are relatively low impact and therefore not at odds with the 'Good Tourist' ethos. For the independent traveller, the hotels which feature in the brochures of the 'positive' tour companies are worth considering, as some can be booked independently. Local Tourist Information offices in Turkey will be able to offer advice regarding listed local accommodation. To book ahead, write directly to the hotels themselves, allowing plenty of time for confirmation of the booking, or go through one of the British operators who offer an accommodation-only service (see **Travelling Independently**). This latter option will obviously be more expensive than arranging accommodation in person once in the country, but the extra expense has to be weighed against the security of having pre-booked accommodation, especially in popular resorts in the high season. As a rough guide to the likely cost of low-impact, family-run accommodation and restaurants: for a first class establishment you can expect to pay from around £25 per double room (with en-suite facilities), and around £20 for a meal for two. Obviously, prices can be far above this for the very luxurious, modern international hotels! Middle-range establishments will cost around £15 per double room, often only with shared facilities, while a meal for two at this type of establishment will cost around £12. At the economy end of the range, basic, clean accommodation for two can be found for as little as £5 to £10 per night, with the cost of a full meal for two at around £8–£10.

The Art of Being a Good Tourist

To be a 'Good Tourist' in Turkey requires not only consideration of local people and customs while in the country, but also a degree of planning before embarking on a visit. A number of factors require some thought prior to departure in order to fulfil the 'Good Tourist' ethos – the choice of destination and accommodation, means of transport and the best time for a holiday.

With the rapid growth of tourism in Turkey, the popular coastal resorts and a number of destinations of particular historical or archaeological interest are now overcrowded in the high season. Such areas may already have been spoiled by tourism or be in imminent danger of such a fate. Should the considerate traveller avoid these in favour of areas relatively untouched by tourism at the risk of spreading the negative impacts, visit out of season, or confine holidays to these honeypots to peak times as the most effective way of halting further damage? The choice of mode of travel and the type of accommodation most in keeping with the country and of greatest benefit to the host population are also important considerations.

When considering the options for transport, many tourists and local people find coach travel, as opposed to rail travel, to be the most convenient option. While the railways are marginally cheaper, the state-owned rail network connects the major cities, but is poorly developed around the popular resorts of the Aegean and Mediterranean coasts (see **Sightseeing**). **Coach** travel is the option used by many Turkish people and the coaches are surprisingly clean and comfortable. Long journeys can often be accomplished at night, which leaves more time for sightseeing, and they usually include a refreshment stop. They also offer ample opportunity to talk to the locals! Competition between the hundreds of private bus companies ensures frequent services and cheap fares.

Car hire is easily arranged either prior to arrival or once in Turkey, through international firms such as Avis and Hertz, or local companies. However a private car is the most expensive option for internal travel and the unwary tourist may find the condition of minor roads and the driving style of the locals somewhat alarming. International statistics show Turkey has a very high accident rate in relation to the number of cars on the roads. Obviously a private car affords the visitor far more freedom, particularly when exploring the more remote areas, but these benefits have to be weighed against environmental considerations such as increased pollution. Lead-free petrol is generally unavailable and hire cars will not, in any case, be adapted for it.

For covering very long distances in a limited time there is really no alternative to the state-owned **Turkish Airlines**, which serves the larger cities and the main coastal resorts of the Black Sea, Aegean and Mediterranean. This is particularly useful for tourists wishing to visit the east, as international flights from Britain mainly arrive and depart from Istanbul, Ankara and Dalaman.

Accommodation options in Turkey range from the luxury hotels of Istanbul, through to the simpler hotels and family-owned *pansiyons* of many coastal resorts and government-listed camp-sites. These have been considered in greater detail in **Accommodation**.

The purpose-built **tourist complexes** do have the advantage of confining tourist development to particular areas with adequate infrastructure, such as water supply and sewerage facilities. However, opportunities to experience the 'Real Turkey' are minimised and at present only a proportion of the income generated by such developments remains in Turkey and even the Turkish-owned hotels are run through companies based in Ankara or Istanbul. Therefore although the locals may receive some benefit from this form of tourism through increased job opportunities and possible sale of local produce, these benefits can be minimal.

Family **homestays** are one of the best ways of experiencing the real Turkey and also one of the most effective methods of contributing to the local economy. These usually need to be arranged prior to departure and are organised in Britain through the Experiment in International Living (see **Travelling Independently** and **Accommodation**). Small family-run

hotels and **pansiyons** are common in all the most popular tourist areas. These vary tremendously in cost, quality and the extent to which they fit in with the local environment. Since the tourist boom began in the 1960s, the concrete eyesores common in parts of Spain and France have also sprung up in Turkey, particularly along the Aegean and Mediterranean coasts. While some of the smaller hotels and pensions are listed by the Ministry of Culture and Tourism and further details will be available at local information offices, in many cases the tourist will have to be the ultimate judge of these establishments.

A number of British tour operators offer **self-catering** or half-board accommodation in locally-owned villas and houses, which they rent during the season. Such accommodation tends to be in the local style and located in small, unspoilt villages. (Further details of all the above options are under **Accommodation**.) **Camping** is still not widespread in Turkey and is effectively limited to the government-registered camp-sites, which are located along the main tourist routes. The standards of such camp-sites are variable, with the Mocamp Kervansaray chain offering good facilities including electricity and running water. Other camp-sites may not be so well-appointed and it is advisable to check against the Ministry of Tourism list, which details available facilities. The sites on the Mediterranean coast receive the highest concentration of holidaymakers in the peak season and the 'Good Tourist' is well advised to think twice before adding to the pressure on such sites. It is not possible to generalise about the environmental impacts of these developments, as the infrastructure and level of use of individual camping grounds are so variable. The Ministry has commissioned a survey to determine the carrying capacity of the coast with respect to tourism, which will assist the 'Good Tourist' in making an informed decision as to which areas to visit or avoid. Until the result of this survey becomes available, the rule is to look at individual sites and avoid those obviously contributing to pollution, unacceptable loss of natural vegetation and other environmental problems.

This approach can be applied to all types of holiday, not only camping. The Mediterranean and Aegean coasts receive the greatest influx of holidaymakers during the high season, in July and August, but the swimming season extends from April through to November in the southern Aegean and Mediterranean regions. Therefore the attractions of the coastline can still be experienced to the full by those visiting outside the peak season, with the added benefit of greater contact with local people, who will have more time for conversation with tourists outside the busiest periods. Alternatively, it is still possible to find quiet, relatively unspoilt destinations in this coastal strip, outside such main resorts as Marmaris, Fethiye and Bodrum. The 'Good Tourist' should also consider the quieter Black Sea coast or the northern Aegean as the base for a beach-type holiday, although here the season is shorter and the weather less predictable.

For the traveller more interested in historical and archaeological sites than summer sunshine, **off-peak visits** are definitely recommended, especially for the more popular destinations such as Ephesus. A number of tour companies are now offering out of season special interest holidays to such sites, which are well worth considering. One of the great attractions of the major archaeological sites in Turkey is the absence of the restrictions which operate at so many similar locations in other countries. Visitors to Ephesus and Aphrodisias are still free to wander among the ruins at their leisure rather than forced to view them from a distance. By visiting out of season, the 'Good Tourist' can help spread the load and minimise damage, thus hopefully preserving this freedom for as long as possible.

Destinations for activity holidays leave the tourist little choice. Trekking is a relatively new pastime for travellers to Turkey and such trips are offered by a number of British companies, e.g. Exodus and Explore. Independent trekking is not encouraged by the Turkish authorities and there are few detailed maps available to assist such travellers. Tourist information offices are also generally unhelpful in this respect. Therefore, the prospective trekker is confined to the destinations offered by the tour companies. A number of ski resorts now exist, but these are relatively underdeveloped and overuse of these facilities is not a problem yet!

There is remarkably little resentment of tourists, even in the most overcrowded destinations, in spite of the flagrant breaches of 'Good Tourist' behaviour evident in many resort towns. The British visitor arriving in these beach resorts may be forgiven for assuming that behaviour acceptable in similar towns in Spain and France is also acceptable in Turkey. However, a little consideration is necessary to avoid giving offence, particularly with regard to questions of **dress**. While the residents of such resorts have become accustomed to a certain extent to seeing scantily-clad holiday-makers on the beach, this may still come as something of a shock to older people at the beginning of the season and this type of dress is best confined to the immediate area of the beach. Wandering around the local shops in beach attire or very skimpy clothing may cause offence or, alternatively, provoke unwanted attention. Topless sunbathing is another sensitive area and should really be restricted only to very isolated locations. Appropriate dress, particularly for women, i.e. no bare shoulders or skimpy shorts, will not only avoid upsetting local people, but will also make life much easier for the tourists themselves throughout the country. This is particularly important when visiting mosques and other sites of religious worship. While the average church in Britain is often only occupied during formal services, a typical mosque will have someone praying there at almost all times. It is vital to respect the religious as well as the architectural or historical significance of the place.

On a simple level, learning and using some basic Turkish **greetings** will be much appreciated, even in the westernised resort areas. Even a simple *'Merhaba'* ('Hello'), or the more formal *'Gunaydin'* ('Good Day') are effective. (For further phrases, see p.72.) Polite greetings are a very important part of Turkish social behaviour, rather than the British-style handshake. Although most people in resort towns will have at least a smattering of English, French or German, making an effort to learn a little of the language will be well received, particularly by older residents who can be sensitive to the loss of character of their home towns as a result of the growth of the tourist industry. Impromptu English lessons will also be valued (and often asked for!) by local people who are trying to improve their English.

While the tourist may feel rather overawed by the exuberant selling style of carpet and other souvenir salesmen and the crowds of hotel representatives at bus stations, a polite 'no' (*'hayir'*) is preferable to the blank silence adopted by many travellers and will usually have the desired effect – eventually! While shopping for souvenirs it is worth noting that although **haggling** is generally an acceptable and enjoyable part of the process, outside the tourist shops and markets goods may have a fixed price and attempts to haggle will not be appreciated. In such situations it is always a good idea, where possible, to follow the lead of local people.

Photography of residents is another area where some care is necessary. The golden rule is always ask before photographing that quaint group of old men drinking tea or women working in the fields. While some people are eager to be photographed and may even approach and ask for a picture to be taken, others, especially in the more remote areas, will be upset by such an invasion of privacy. Where photos are requested the subjects often ask for copies to be sent to them. While it's very easy to forget on returning home, if it is possible to fulfil such requests this can only have a positive effect on local attitudes to tourists. Photography in mosques is generally not advisable, unless it is specifically stated that this is allowed. Similarly, taking pictures of groups praying in the streets is to be avoided.

Women travelling alone in Turkey may encounter some problems, especially in remote areas, as the Turks are still unused to seeing unaccompanied women travellers. However, these problems are usually confined to calls, whistles and possibly some over-persistent male attention. Providing skimpy clothes are avoided, especially away from the main resort areas, such difficulties should be minimal in the more developed west of the country. In the east the difficulties encountered by some women tourists may be more serious and women would be well advised to consider joining up with other single travellers for visits to the remoter regions.

Finally, the 'Good Tourist' should always be aware of the damage certain actions may cause to the environment and take steps to minimise this where possible, i.e. through conservation of water resources, obeying all rules in protected areas and even expressing appreciation of the natural environment to the local people, who may be surprised that this is just as important to the tourist as swimming pools and discotheques!

By following the above suggestions as far as possible, the 'Good Tourist' will not only help to preserve the character of the country, but will also ensure the maintenance of good relations between the tourist and local populations and, incidentally, have a more enjoyable holiday too!

Checklist for the Good Tourist

1. Have I learned enough about my destination to be able to appreciate it properly and understand the issues facing this area when I arrive?

2. Can I go out of season to avoid further tourist congestion?

3. Can I use local tour operators, local transport and stay with local people?

4. If going with a tour operator, check the company:

   * works with the local community and ensures their operations are as environmentally friendly and socially acceptable as possible;

* contributes to local initiatives to keep the destination in good condition;

* creates local employment;

* uses local guides and locally-owned accommodation and transport;

* integrates tourists with locals and teaches you, prior to departure, about the destination.

5. When there, consume local produce; use public transport.

6. Remove all excess packaging before packing your case, and take biodegradable sunscreens and toiletries.

7. Buy souvenirs that are locally made and reflect the indigenous culture. Avoid all produce made from endangered species. Help conserve the native fauna and flora.

8. Be sensitive to the local customs regarding photography, begging and tipping.

All these and many more positive ideas on how to be a Good Tourist and get more fun out of your holiday are found in *The Good Tourist – a worldwide guide for the green traveller* (Mandarin Paperbacks. £5.99)

Useful Turkish Words

Pronunciation Guide

Most letters are pronounced as in English. The following are ones for which you may need guidance:

a   as in car
e   as in bed
i   as in see
o   as in dog
ö   as in German Goering, or French deux
u   as in true
ü   as in French tu, or English few
c   as in jet
ç   as in chat
g   as in girl

ğ	silent – lengthens preceding vowel; if between two vowels, as in loyal
h	as in half
j	as in French je, or English leisure
s	as in class
ş	as in shop
v	somewhere between very and worry

Simple Phrases

hello	*merhaba*
good day	*günaydin*
yes	*evet*
no	*hayir*
none	*yok*
please	*lütfen*
thank you	*teşekkür ederim* or *mersi*
goodbye (said by guest)	*allaha ismarladik*
goodbye (said by host)	*güle güle*
excuse me	*affedersiniz*
what time is it?	*saat kaç?*
how much is it?	*kaç para?*
I don't understand	*anlamadim*
what is your name?	*nedir adiniz?*
do you speak English?	*ingilizçe biliyor musunuz?*
today	*bugün*
yesterday	*dün*
tomorrow	*yarin*
beautiful	*guzel*
good	*iyi*
OK	*peki*
bad	*kötü*
big	*büyük*
small	*küçük*
hotel	*otel*
room	*oda*
bed	*yatak*
shower	*duş*
restaurant	*lokanta*
bon appetit	*afiyet olsun!*
cheers/to your health	*şerefinize!*

bill	*hesap*
toilet	*tuvalet* or *WC*
ladies	*bayanlar*
gents	*baylar*
bank	*banka*
foreign exchange	*kambiyo*
museum	*müze*
chemist	*eczane*
doctor	*doktor*
police	*polis*
bus	*otobüs*
bus station	*otogar*
train	*tren*
railway station	*istasyonu*
plane	*uçak*
airport	*hava alani*
ferry	*vapur* or *feribot*
port	*liman*
ticket	*bilet*
ticket office	*gişe*
water	*su*

Numbers

1 – *bir*; 2 – *iki*; 3 – *üç*; 4 – *dört*; 5 – *beş*; 6 – *alti*; 7 – *yedi*; 8 – *sekiz*; 9 – *dokuz*; 10 – *on*; 11 – *on bir*; 12 – *on iki*, etc; 20 – *yirmi*; 50 – *elli*; 100 – *yüz*; 1000 – *bin*; 10,000 – *on bin*; 1,000,000 – *milyon*.

Useful Terms

There are a number of Turkish terms which will just keep cropping up. This list is designed to help you with their meanings.

Architecture

covered market	*bedesten*
mosque	*cami (i)*
bazaar	*çorşi (si)*
old (as in Eski Cami)	*eski*
Turkish bath	*hamam (i)*
trading hall	*han (i)*
castle	*hisar/kale (si)*

gate	*kapi (si)*
hotel for merchants and pack animals, on trading route	*kervansaray (i)*
bridge	*köprü*
pavilion	*köşk (ü)*
tower	*kule (si)*
complex of buildings, often religious (e.g. mosque) and charitable (e.g. hospital)	*külliye (si)*
dome	*kümbet*
Islamic theological school	*medrese (si)*
prayer niche	*mihrab*
pulpit (in mosque)	*mimber*
minaret (prayer-calling tower of mosque)	*minare (si)*
palace	*saray (i)*
hall for Dervish ceremonies	*semahane*
Sufi meeting place	*tekke (si)*
tomb	*türbe (si)*
new (as in Yeni Cami)	*yeni*

People

member of a Muslim fraternity vowing poverty	*Dervish*
Muslim prayer leader	*Imam*
man who calls people to prayer	*Muezzin*
heir to throne; prince	*Şehzade*
Dervish belonging to mystical branch of Islam	*Sufi*
Sultan's mother	*Sultan Valide*

Geography

island (as in Karaada)	*ada (si)*
garden (as in çay bahçesi)	*bahçe (si)*
mount (as in Ak Dağ)	*dağ (i)*
mountains (range of)	*dağlar (i)*
sea (as in Ege Denizi)	*deniz (i)*
lake (as in Van Gölü)	*göl (ü)*

river (as in Yeşilirmak)	*irmak*

Everyday life

boulevard	*bulvar (ı)*
street	*cadde (si)*
tea	*çay*
fixed-route mini-bus which you can hail like a taxi	*dolmuş*
open-air night club with Turkish music	*gazino*
traditional wooden boat	*gulet*
coffee	*kahve*
flat-weave rug (no pile)	*kilim*
restaurant (often – though by no means always – more authentically Turkish than a 'restoran')	*lokanta (sı)*
square; plaza	*meydan (ı)*
starter; hors d'oeuvre	*meze*
hubble-bubble; water pipe	*nargile*
Turkish pizza	*pide*
post office	*PTT*
town centre	*şehir merkesi*
narrow street	*sokak*

Further Information

General Environmental Issues

Gunes Gazetesi, Cevre Servisi, Turanli Sokak No. 20, Beyazit, Istanbul, Tel. (90-1) 516 66 00. A leading Turkish daily paper which has recently started an environmental magazine.

Wildlife Protection

Society for the Protection of Wildlife–DHKD, PO Box 18, 80810 Bebek, Istanbul. One of Turkey's main conservation organisations. Has recently been involved in turtle protection work at Dalyan.

Turkish Association for the Conservation of Nature and Natural Resources, Menekse Sokak 29/4, 06440 Kizilay, Ankara, Tel. (90-4) 125 19 44. One of the largest, most influential conservation organisations in Turkey. Active across a wide range of fields including education and liaising with the government on coastal management issues.

MEDASSET (Mediterranean Association to Save the Sea Turtles), 1(c) Licavitou Street, 10672 Athens, Greece, Tel. (30-1) 36 13 572. Or c/o Daphne Corp, 24 Park Towers, 2 Brick Street, London W1Y 7DF, Tel. 071 629 0654. An organisation involved in work to save the sea turtles throughout the Mediterranean.

AGA (Aktionsgemeinschaft Artenschutz e.V.), Brigitte und Gunther Peter, Aktionsgemeinschaft Artenschutz e.V., Tubizer Strasse 1, 7015 Korntal-Munchingen, Germany. An international conservation organisation closely involved with work to protect the loggerhead turtle in Dalyan.

Heritage Conservation

Ministry of Culture, Kultur Bakanligi, Kizilay, Ankara.

Government

Undersecretariat for the Environment, Department of International Relations, Ataturk Bulvari 143, 06640 Ankara. Tel. (90-4) 1174455).

Ministry of Tourism, T.C. Turizm Bakanligi, Eskisehir Yolu, Bahcelievler, Ankara.

Ministry of Forestry and Agriculture, Tarim, Orman ve Koyisleri Bakanligi, Bakanliklar, Ankara.

British Embassy, Sehit Ersan Caddesi 46/A, Cankaya, Ankara. Tel. (90-4) 127 4310.

British Consulate, Mesrutiyet Caddesi 26, Tepebasi, Beyoglu, Istanbul. Tel. (90-1) 149 8874 or 144 7540.

Tourism Network (Britain-based)

Turkish Embassy Information Counsellor's Office, 170-173 Piccadilly, First Floor, London W1V 9DD, Tel. 071 734 8681/2.

Tourism Network (Turkey-based)

Association for the Promotion of Touristic Pensions, Turistik Ev Pansiyonculugunu Gelistirme Dernegi (TUREVS), Cumhuriyet Bulvari, Elbir Ishani No. 84–803, Izmir, Tel. (90-51) 25 72 73 or 21 42 95 or 21 57 28.

Touristic Enterprise and Hoteliers' Association, Turistik Otelciler ve Isletmeciler Birligi (TUROB), Istiklal Caddesi, Anadolu Sigorta Hani. No. 213–201, Kat 2, Galatasaray, Istanbul, Tel. (90-1) 149 51 53.

Turkish Travel Agents' Association (TURSAB), Haberler Sokak No. 15, Esentepe, Istanbul, Tel. (90-1) 175 1361 or 175 1362 or 175 1379.

Turkish Camping and Caravanning Association, Turkiye Kamp Karavan Dernegi, Nenehatun Caddesi No. 96, Gaziosmanpasa, Ankara.

Special Interests

Ministry of Foreign Affairs – Ankara Tel. (90-4) 117 27 90 – for details of mountaineering permits and local mountaineering groups. Tel. (90-4) 310 15 78 for Ankara mountaineering federation.

Sports Federations, Genclik ve Spor Mudurulugu, Federasyonu Bek., 06 050 Ulus, Ankara – for details of local sports associations.

1 Istanbul

Istanbul is a city whose very name conjures up images of the exotic – the beginning of the East and a different culture – even in those who have never been there. Picture it and you see Bosphorus steamers against a background of minarets and vast-domed mosques bathed in a hazy golden glow. It's hardly surprising we all feel we know the city, considering how frequently we are bombarded with this particular portrait of Istanbul – not just in tourist brochures and travel articles, but also in chocolate adverts, James Bond films and even nineteenth-century poetry.

Istanbul has always appealed to writers and photographers as a symbol of the 'exotic, but not *too* exotic'. Its semi-European status lends it an element of familiarity, yet there's also that first taste of Asia, complete with all its architectural, cultural and religious associations. Istanbul's claim to fame as the only city in the world with a foot in two continents has been reiterated time and again. But the divisions of the city are more complex than this.

Take the inhabitants of Istanbul. Though Muslims are in the majority, you will find members of other religions – from Greek Orthodox Christians to Sephardic Jews. The racial mix of Arabs, Kurds, Anatolians, Ottomans, White Russians and Europeans is even richer, reminding us of the city's past. After serving as capital to the Roman, Byzantine and Ottoman empires, Istanbul was subsequently delegated to the ranks of the 'provincial' under Ataturk's 1922 reforms. A more imposing provincial city is hard to imagine. Istanbul certainly retains all the pride, bustle and cosmopolitan feel of a capital.

For a supposedly secular state, Turkish devotion to Islam is unexpectedly strong – and Istanbul is no exception. The call of the muezzin resounds from the minarets; worshippers prostrate themselves in every mosque; and women cover their heads, eyes fixed shyly on the ground. Yet Istanbul is also a liberal university town. Alcohol is freely available and there are plenty of confident, jeans-clad young women pursuing education and a career. More surprising (and less obvious to the visitor) are manifestations such as transvestite singers and legal brothels.

Nor is Istanbul a stranger to cultural prostitution. New hotels are springing up with alarming rapidity; many are in the modern part, but some are incongruously built in the old town, detracting from views of its most precious architectural treasures. The 'souvenirs' hawked in the streets are not traditional Turkish crafts, but fake Lacoste T-shirts or Adidas socks.

Other worrying aspects of the city's everyday life are its litter, pollution, lack of green spaces, horrifying traffic problems and poverty, exacerbated by a steady influx of country-dwellers expecting the streets to be paved with gold. But the negative elements are – for most people – easily eclipsed by breathtaking sights like the Blue Mosque, the enormous Santa Sophia and Topkapi Palace. And it is hard to detract from such memorable experiences as losing yourself in the maze-like alleyways of the Grand Bazaar, taking a boat trip past elegant Bosphorus mansions, or being vigorously massaged amid the marble alcoves of a palatial Turkish bath-house.

The secret of an enjoyable stay in Istanbul is, without a doubt, to take your time, and to alternate visits to the classic attractions with exploration of less usual ones. It's also worth venturing out of town, whether you opt for a Bosphorus cruise, a trip to the traffic-free Princes' Islands in the Sea of Marmara, or an excursion to the Camlica Hills over in Asia. And bear in mind that you're far more likely to experience the genuine hospitality for which the Turks are renowned (a reputation deserved even in a large city like Istanbul), if you time your visit outside the peak season.

History

The history of Istanbul has been largely determined by its geography and, in particular, its strategic advantages. However, the first settlements on the Golden Horn – from around 1000 to 700 BC – were simple fishing villages. Then Greeks from Megara chose to settle at Chalcedon (now Kadikoy) on the Asian shore of the Bosphorus. This was an odd decision, as the Saray Burnu peninsula and the natural harbour of the Golden Horn, directly opposite them on the European shore, had obvious strategic superiority. But their short-sightedness was to benefit Byzas the Megarian, who was advised by the Delphic oracle to found a city opposite 'the land of the blind'. The Saray Burnu peninsula was obviously meant, so his people settled there in 657 BC, naming their city Byzantium, after its founder.

Trade flourished in this Greek city-state, which was occupied by the Persian King Darius between 512 and 478 BC, and later fell to the Romans. It continued to do well under the Pax Romana until it backed the wrong side in a civil war in AD 196 and suffered considerable damage at the hands of Emperor Septimus Severus, who later relented and rebuilt it. A further struggle for control of the Roman Empire involved Constantine defeating his rival Licinius at Chrysopolis (now Uskudar, on the Bosphorus) in AD 324. Constantine chose to expand Byzantium into the 'New Rome', capital of the Roman Empire and the western world. Its name changed to Constantinople and its size increased fivefold. This was the start of the Byzantine (or Later Roman) Empire, which was to last until 1453.

Christianity took root here after the division of the empire into East and West in 395, and Constantinople's power reached its peak (despite the Nika riots of 532) during the reign of Justinian, from 527 to 565. It was Justinian who designed and constructed the magnificent Santa Sophia church. Yet this was the point after which things started to go downhill. The lands of the empire were encroached upon first by Arabs, then by Bulgars, and, in 1204, the city of Constantinople itself was plundered by Crusaders. It no longer had the strength to resist the steadily-growing Ottoman Empire and, in 1453, Mehmet II (known as 'the Conqueror') was able to capture the city by blockading the Bosphorus with boats he had transported overland to the Golden Horn. Mehmet insisted that many churches, including Santa Sophia, became mosques and the city's name was changed to Istanbul.

New mosques were built, among them the Fatih Camii (Mosque of the Conqueror), and the city embraced Islam, becoming capital of the Ottoman Empire. This development was welcomed by the inhabitants, whose feelings are summed up in the words of a former chief minister of Constantinople: 'Who would not prefer the Turkish turban to a cardinal's hat?' Mehmet also built the lavish Topkapi Palace, completed in 1465, though Istanbul's greatest builder was probably Suleyman the Magnificent (1520–66). He was aided by Turkey's most celebrated architect, Mimar Sinan, who designed not only the famous Suleymaniye Mosque, but also a further 290 Istanbul buildings. The sixteenth century was a golden age, with arts and scholarship as vibrant as in Renaissance Italy.

However, the seventeenth century brought not only territorial losses abroad, but also increasing corruption at home, notably in Topkapi

Palace itself. A marked preference on the part of sultans for the harem as opposed to the battlefield, and a tendency to murder their advisers on the whim of their favourite harem women contributed to the empire's decline. Dissatisfaction prompted a move towards Western institutions, though Selim III, creator of a New Model Army, was assassinated in the harem by rebellious Janissaries in 1808, and the first Ottoman parliament of 1876 was extremely brief. The nineteenth century saw developments of engineering, such as the first bridge across the Golden Horn, built in 1838, and the arrival of the railway in 1870. A further link with the West was provided by the Orient Express, which connected Istanbul with Paris, and the construction of the Pera Palas hotel to welcome its first passengers in 1892.

1908 brought the occupation of the city by the revolutionary Young Turks, and Sultan Abdul Hamid II was deposed the next year. Following his exploits at Gallipoli, Mustafa Kemal (Ataturk), who had graduated as captain from the Istanbul staff college in 1905, returned to the city after the armistice. Seeing the Allied warships in the Bosphorus, he is reported to have said 'As they come, so will they go'. It was Ataturk's reforms of 1922, when he abolished the sultanate and created the Turkish Republic, which resulted in the moving of the capital to Ankara. Since then, Istanbul may have lost some of its wealth and power, but its historical and cultural riches remain.

Right up to 1973, all transport across the Bosphorus was by ferry, but Europe and Asia were finally linked by one of the longest suspension bridges in the world to celebrate the fiftieth anniversary of the Republic. Since then, two further bridges have been deemed necessary to cope with the flow of traffic. Congestion and slum clearance are two of the major problems facing the city today. Any efforts that are made seem virtually futile in the face of the massive migration of Anatolian peasants to Istanbul. Every single day of the year, around 1000 country-dwellers arrive in the city, looking for work (despite the 20 per cent unemployment rate) and, naturally, creating a certain amount of tension between established residents and the 'outsiders'.

Geography

Part of Istanbul and its suburbs belongs to the Thrace region and can be found on the European shore of the Sea of Marmara, while the rest spills over into the Marmara region on the Asian shore. The city is located at the north-eastern tip of the Sea of Marmara, just at its junction with the straits of water known as the Bosphorus (or *Istanbul Bogazi* in Turkish), which lead to the Black Sea.

Istanbul itself has a population which officially stands at 7.4 million, but is probably nearer ten. It has increased fivefold in the last thirty years and the sprawling city, which extends way beyond Theodosius's city walls, is now home to almost 20 per cent of Turkey's entire population – and still growing. The one-and-a-half-kilometre-wide Bosphorus and the narrow freshwater estuary of the Golden Horn (at right angles to the left bank of the Bosphorus) make for natural divisions in Istanbul's layout. South of the Golden Horn is the 'Old City', where you'll find most of the famous monuments; north of it (over the Galata Bridge) is the 'Modern City', including the business district; and across the Bosphorus is the more residential Asian part. Each sector is composed of various districts, whose names and natures it's worth finding out about (see **Geographical Breakdown** section).

Generally speaking, there is light industry around the Golden Horn, while the hills overlooking the Bosphorus and the shores of the Sea of Marmara are the locations of the smarter residential suburbs, and further out the vista is of dismal high-rises, interspersed with more light industry. The sprawling nature of the city means that you have to travel quite a way before you come to agricultural land. However, despite an alarmingly small amount of green space in the city itself, Istanbul and its surroundings do have some parks and sites of ecological interest.

A welcome green oasis in the city, just beyond Dolmabahce Palace, is the Yildiz Park, landscaped by the Touring Club of Turkey in 1979 and offering an ideal place for Turkish families to relax, with its gardens, lake and beautifully restored Malta Pavilion. Other central parks are the Gulhane Park surrounding Topkapi Palace, where there's a large heronry, and the Taksim Park in the more modern sector. Further up the Bosphorus there is more space, with the Emirgan and Duatepe Parks offering fabulous views of the Fatih Sultan Mehmet suspension bridge; while on the Asian shore are the Fenerbahce and Camlica Parks, and, right up near the Black Sea, the Beykoz (or Abraham Pasa) Woods. Further opportunities to 'get away from it all' are provided by the green and blissfully traffic-free Princes' Islands in the Sea of Marmara (see **Good Alternatives**).

Camlica Hill, above Beylerbeyi Palace, was re-grassed and planted with trees by the Touring Club in 1980 and is now a prime spot for viewing white storks and honey buzzards in August, and other birds of prey in autumn. In spring, you'll find flowers and a considerable number of birds at the lower Kucuk Camlica. Surprisingly, Istanbul is a rewarding place for ornithologists as it's on a major migration route for large birds such as storks and raptors, with mid-September and mid-April the peak times for the latter. The hills on either side of the northern Bosphorus (ferry stops Anodolu Kavagi and Rumeli Kavagi) are good for watching the spring migration and are also home to a number of smaller birds. The Bosphorus has a wealth of gulls and shearwaters, and Istanbul itself attracts not only swifts but also the palm dove, found nowhere else in Europe.

You will see numerous pigeons and seagulls in the city. The former are lured to places such as Eminonu by the sellers of bird seed who congregate around the Egyptian Bazaar; the seagulls are more a product of the litter which can be found almost everywhere. Istanbul certainly has major litter and pollution problems, and pollution of the Sea of Marmara is also increasing. There is a certain environmental awareness, notably among young people. A demonstration was held when it was proposed that a city square's old trees should be cut down. Yet there are curious anomalies in official attitudes. Some people sing the praises of former mayor, Dalan Berrettin, who transformed the polluted industrial and residential area of the Golden Horn by tree-planting, landscaping and creating parks. For this model achievement he was given the 1987 UNEP Global 500 award. However, it was the very same man who destroyed the woods on the banks of the Bosphorus to make way for rows and rows of cramped villas.

One organisation which does contribute a lot to restoration and maintenance of both natural and architectural heritage is the Touring Club of Turkey, much of whose work is supervised by its chairman, Celik Gulersoy, a well-known conservationist. But the general opinion is that, though the government is aware of many of the city's environmental problems, it is too weak when it comes to enforcing legislation on issues such as litter, pollution and illegal building.

Climate

Hot during the summer months, Istanbul has, nonetheless, a more varied climate than you'll find elsewhere in Turkey. It's quite possible for it to be raining in Istanbul when it's clear almost everywhere else. The city's warm periods can be interspersed with long cold spells, and there's a chance of snow in winter. Average midday temperatures range from 6°C in January and February to 24°C in July and August. They remain above 15°C from May through to October. The average water temperature ranges from 7°C in February to 24°C in August, and stays above 20°C from June to September. Watch the lights on the Galata Tower for the next day's weather forecast.

Attractions

Listing all the different elements which attract people to Istanbul would be an impossible task. Many come simply because of its exotic image; some come for the unusual architecture and culture; some for the history and museums; some for the shopping; and some for the vibrant atmosphere generated by this great city and its inhabitants.

There are four sights which most people aim to include in their visit, however short. The Sultan Ahmet Mosque, which is the only one in the world with six minarets and is usually called the Blue Mosque because of the ninety-nine shades of blue in the ceramic tiles decorating the pillars and walls of the dome; the Santa Sophia (or Aya Sofya), once the greatest church in the world, then a mosque, now a museum; Topkapi Palace, home of the Ottoman sultans and their harem, whose treasury contains the famous eighty-six-carat Spoonmaker's Diamond; and the Grand Bazaar (or Kapali Carsi), which has sixty-seven streets and a thousand shops and forms what is probably the world's largest and oldest shopping precinct.

The Suleymaniye Mosque is another popular place to visit, along with the Dolmabahce Palace, the Yeni Mosque at Eminonu, the Egyptian (or Spice) Bazaar, the underground Byzantine Cistern (supported by 336 Corinthian columns), the Hippodrome, and the Museum of Turkish Carpets near the Blue Mosque. Less famous, but equally interesting sights are the fifteenth-century Fatih Mosque, the Beylerbeyi Palace, the Museum of Turkish and Islamic Art at the Ibrahim Pass Palace, the ancient fortifications at Rumeli Hisari and the Aqueduct of Valens (or Bozdogan Kemeri). A good view of Istanbul can be had from the fourteenth-century Genoese Galata Tower, and a stroll among the mussel-sellers and milling crowds around Galata Bridge should certainly feature on any itinerary. So should a boat trip up the Golden Horn or Bosphorus (including a stop at one of its superb fish restaurants), and a visit to the Princes' Islands. You should try to experience a Turkish Bath (*Hamam*) during your visit, as well as the Beyoglu nightlife (see **Entertainments**). It's also worth noting that the area around Istanbul is good for high quality silk carpets, and there is even a spa resort, just a ferry ride away at Yalova.

Cuisine

Istanbul is the place to come if you want to sample regional specialities from all over Turkey – as well as from numerous other countries. It is also particularly good when it comes to producing certain staples of the Turkish diet. There are over 900 bakeries in Istanbul, which make for a wide variety of freshly-baked breads, and the range of jams is even more impressive. The best yoghurts come from the communities of Silivri and Kanlica, and can be consumed plain, with mountains of icing sugar or, for the brave, with salt or garlic.

Two types of soup are associated with Istanbul. The popular *Iskembeci*'s soup is a thick mixture made from lamb trotters and tripe, while another kind of trotter soup, *Beykoz Paca*, can be found only up near the Black Sea at Beykoz. *Pilavs* cooked with olive oil are an Istanbul speciality, and the Konyali restaurant at Topkapi Palace has been serving them since 1897.

Istanbul's real claim to culinary fame is, however, its seafood and fish, said to be the tastiest in the Aegean/Mediterranean region, thanks to a cross flow between the Sea of Marmara and the Black Sea. It is claimed that the Bosphorus boasts sixty varieties of fish. Mussels are popular, both fried and in rich dishes such as *pilavs*, and the freshest can be found at the village of Rumeli Kavagi. Try also the shrimp dishes up at this end of the Bosphorus. Red mullet, turbot and (in autumn) swordfish crop up frequently on menus too.

Fresh fruits such as watermelons and grapes are widely available, as are the ubiquitous grills, kebabs, *pides* (Turkish pizzas) and aubergine dishes, along with favourites like sweet sticky pastries, *lokum* (Turkish Delight) and *helva*. Spices such as cinnamon, paprika and, particularly, saffron are worth buying at the Egyptian bazaar to bring back home.

Kiosks sell fresh fruit juices (cherry and peach are delicious), and it's also advisable to buy bottled water (*Hayat* is a reliable variety, available everywhere). Tea comes in various flavours (including apple and orange), and coffee in varying degrees of sweetness. If you're looking for something stronger, *raki* is naturally a popular drink (though beware of its strength), as is the Turkish beer, *Efes*. A good idea of the sheer range of Turkish wines can be gained by a visit to Doluca on Halkali Caddesi 222 in Sefakoy.

Level of Tourism

A high proportion of foreign visitors to Turkey make Istanbul their first (or only) port of call, and most of the Marmara region's 3,640,000 foreign tourists will spend time in the city. Of those who do stay in Istanbul, the largest group chooses five-star hotels, with two-star hotels coming a close second. This shows how the city appeals to (and caters for) both wealthy business travellers and those on a tighter budget. This is borne out by the variety of districts chosen by visitors for their accommodation: in top place comes Eminonu, then Beyoglu, Fatih, Sisli and Bakirkoy (a complete mixture of the poorer and wealthier areas).

In general, the new part of Istanbul (Taksim Square and beyond) is safer at night but it is also twice as expensive as the old part. A comfortable double room plus breakfast might cost you £18–23 in Eminonu, but would be nearer £45 in Taksim. One recent development which will influence the level and type of tourism is the arrival in Istanbul of the big chain hotels. Hilton International now has two hotels here, while Sheraton is firmly ensconced and Holiday Inn has been granted a prime position on the Marmara seafront. Another foreign chain has purchased the old Ciragan Palace, a beautiful imperial building on the European shore of the Bosphorus. Until recently it was the impressive site of a public outdoor swimming pool, but it has just been converted into a £200-a-night hotel. It was of great historic interest and it's a shame that the hotel interior is unequivocally modern. It seems likely that the palace was victim of an attempt to get round awkward planning permission laws and, despite assurances that the staff will be almost exclusively local, one wonders whether this was really the best way to make use of the building.

Other recent renovations and conversions of old buildings have mostly been more sensitive. A whole row of restaurants and confectionery shops near Santa Sophia are housed in traditional wooden buildings, carefully restored by the Touring Club of Turkey and now an immensely popular Sunday afternoon haunt for local people. This was just part of the Touring Club's programme to rescue old buildings threatened by the need for more accommodation and to revitalise degraded natural spaces.

Another positive development is the idea of small, family-run hotels, which is starting to catch on in certain parts of the city (notably Sultanahmet and up in the Black Sea suburbs). Such hotels offer the ideal means to experience the natural hospitality of Turkish people and, though there is little chance of doing anything to slow the invasion of the big chains, by choosing family-run accommodation you will be sure your money's going into the right pockets. Choosing hotels which are not housed in brand new buildings may also eventually persuade the government to be tougher regarding illegal building. At the moment, new hotels are springing up left, right and centre – including on the otherwise unspoilt Princes' Islands, where building regulations regarding height are being flouted and development is leading to deforestation and pollution. The high competition, combined with loss of business as a result of the 1991 Gulf War, means that hotel prices have not increased as much as one might have expected over the last few years.

Quite apart from the issue of accommodation, tourism has a great impact on the city, both direct and indirect. Istanbul doesn't escape the problem of overcrowding at various sights in peak season, with the 'honeypots' being the Blue Mosque, Topkapi, Santa Sophia and the Grand Bazaar. Crowds are not, however, as bad as in some major cities. Istanbul is big enough to soak them up and, even at Topkapi, the result is more likely to be long queues than destruction of the atmosphere, while at the Grand Bazaar the crush of people actually contributes to the feel of the place. It is only really at the most popular mosques that you feel the nerves of worshippers must surely be wearing a little thin – though, if they are, they're too polite to show it.

Traffic congestion is a major problem in the city, though this cannot be blamed on tourists, most of whom are far too sensible to attempt to drive in Istanbul. Morning and afternoon/early evening rush hours are obviously worst, so be prepared for taxis to take a lot longer (and cost a lot more) at these times. Above all, avoid travelling on Friday afternoons, which is the worst period of the whole week. If you want to escape the traffic altogether, jump on a boat to the Princes' Islands, where there are no cars, just horse-drawn traps!

One cruel practice on the streets of Istanbul involves the use of performing bears, particularly bear cubs. Their keeper takes them around on a chain, then charges money to tourists who wish to photograph them doing elementary tricks. If the demand for this ceased (i.e. people refused to show an interest), then the practice would presumably die out.

Local people's attitudes towards tourists are generally positive. Obviously you are regarded as a potential customer by many, but usually the warm welcome is genuine and the majority of carpet-shop owners (and other traders) will serve you tea and show you their wares without insisting you make a purchase. Tourism has naturally brought in its wake a temptation for some local people to indulge in minor 'swindles' or sharp practice. The tradition of haggling for goods and services means that 'gullible' tourists *can* end up paying over the odds. But if *you're* happy that you got a reasonable deal, there's no point in agonising over whether you've been 'done' or whether you could have beat the trader down another thousand lira: he probably needs the money more than you do anyway! The most cunning rip-off merchants are not those at the bazaars or shops, but the little shoe-shine boys outside the major monuments. They'll come up to you on your first day in Istanbul and promise to clean your shoes 'free', practically wrenching your leg from its socket in an effort to make you stand still long enough for them to get going, and will promptly renege on the deal and demand extortionate sums when they've finished! If you want your shoes cleaned, it's essential to negotiate a price before you let them start.

Women visitors to Istanbul may experience some unwelcome attention, but this can usually be avoided if you dress sensibly. All too often, the simple courtesy of covering upper arms and legs is not observed. Finding unwelcome hands on you in the covered bazaar, despite the fact that you're conservatively dressed, is a profoundly annoying experience, but the chances are that the revealing attire of other western tourists has misled local men into thinking you won't object.

Good Alternatives

Meeting People

In many big cities, it's difficult to make contact with the people who actually live and work there. Istanbul is an exception: here you will have no problems getting to meet local people.

Of course, bazaars, markets, carpet shops and such like are the obvious places to go, but try the Egyptian (or Spice) bazaar as well as the Grand Bazaar, as it is here that the Turks themselves do their shopping. It sells not only spices, but many household items and, though you won't find as much in the way of souvenirs as in the Grand Bazaar, it's surprising what you can pick up. You're not nearly as likely to be pressured into buying something you don't want either.

Markets take place regularly in different parts of the city. The Cihangir flea market is in Cukurcuma Sokak and the surrounding area (next to Istiklal Caddesi). It's important you don't get carried away here and forget the law against exporting antiques, as doing so may land you in prison for ten years! Alternatively there's an open-air market on Tuesdays and Fridays at Altiyol in Kadikoy, or a crowded but fabulous waterfront art and craft market on Sundays at Ortakoy.

Among numerous carpet shops where you'll find you're welcome to sit and drink tea while the owner shows you his wares are the Cevri Kalfa Bazaar, Divanyolu Cad. 14, Sultanahmet (Tel. (1) 526 90 96 or 513 85 50), which is housed in a former school dating from the 1790s; and the Mystic Collection (Tekke), which is to be found at Corlulu Ali Pasa Medresesi (on Divanyolu Caddesi, near the Grand Bazaar). It is in a sixteenth-century Koranic school with a courtyard that serves as a tea and water-pipe garden.

If you choose to frequent the smaller, less formal restaurants and bars, you'll find it easy to strike up conversation with the waiters, who often speak good English, as many are university students helping out in the family business during the vacation. If you want to eat a simple meal with Turkish people, head for the restaurant/cafés with *Lokanta* in their name, where you can usually take your pick (by pointing at what you want) from a small selection of dishes, which often taste just as good as those served at more up-market restaurants. When Turkish families want to eat out together, they usually head for the restaurants of the Beyoglu or Galata areas.

Other popular leisure activities among Turks include excursions to parks and coffee shops on a Sunday afternoon, visiting the *Hamam* (Turkish bath), or attending a football match. Joining in one of these activities has the added advantage that you are associating with local people who are doing something they enjoy, and you're able to escape the more usual buyer/seller or client/waiter relationship.

On Sundays, Yildiz Park is always filled with those yearning for fresh air. Families picnic here or have a snack at one of the pavilions. (Emirgan Park is also pleasant; for a list of others see **Geography** section.) The coffee houses along the restored Sogukcesme Caddesi in Sultanahmet are popular at weekends. If you're looking for a Turkish bath, you'll find they vary considerably. The greatest numbers of tourists flock to the Cagaloglu Hamami, near Santa Sophia and Cagaloglu Meydani. It dates from the seventeenth century and boasts numerous famous clients, including Edward VIII and Florence Nightingale. Another one popular with foreigners is the Galatasaray Hamami, signposted from Istiklal Caddesi. This is all marble alcoves and very beautiful. Less touristy are the Mercan Oruculer Hamami at 32 Uzun Carsi Caddesi (near the Grand Bazaar); the cheap and cheerful Turistik Aga Hamami on Turnacibasi

Sokak (Beyoglu); and the Baths at Ortakoy and Beylerbeyi. If you like football, you'll automatically have something in common with most Turks as it's the national sport. The most important games are played at the Inonu Stadium and the Fenerbahce Stadium.

One way of improving your chances of getting to know local people is to learn some Turkish. Summer courses, ranging from three to eight weeks, are run by Tomer School in Gumussuyu (Tel. (1) 152 51 54); TAVA in Osmanbey (Tel. (1) 147 21 88); and Bosphorus University (Tel. (1) 163 15 00 ext 613/623).

Discovering Places

It's easy enough to get off the beaten track in Istanbul. At any of the lesser-known monuments, you may well find you're almost alone, particularly if you visit out of season.

One way of getting a new perspective on the city is to take a boat trip – up the Bosphorus, down the Golden Horn, or to the Princes' Islands in the Sea of Marmara. There are various organised trips by agencies such as Plan Tours (Cumhuriyet Cad. 131/1, 80230 Elmadag, Tel. (1) 130 22 72), ranging from 'The Bosphorus by Private Yacht' to a luxury night-time cruise. Plan Tours also do other half-day and day excursions both within the Istanbul area and to neighbouring destinations like Bursa and Troy. You can even join them for a two- to five-day tour to Cappadocia.

But perhaps the best kind of boat trip is a 'freelance' one. You can either work out an itinerary using the Turkish Maritime Organisation's ferry timetable or just stop off wherever you fancy. If you go as far as the Black Sea, you'll find it both cheap and relatively empty during the week (but prices escalate and Istanbul residents make a beeline for it on summer weekends). There are fine fish restaurants on both sides of the Bosphorus, where you can eat in more attractive and relaxed settings than in Istanbul itself. The Goksu and Beylerbeyi Palaces, plus the Rumeli and Anadolu fortresses are also all too often ignored. At the end of the Golden Horn is the Eyup mosque, the fourth most sacred pilgrimage site in the world for Muslims. The Princes' Islands can offer a particularly welcome break from the traffic and pollution of Istanbul, but (once again) they are better outside the peak season and weekends. Remember to bargain down to a reasonable price for your horse-drawn carriage ride before you get in!

As well as these out-of-town attractions, there are plenty within the city walls which do not always get the attention they deserve. Near Edirnekapi, the quarter around the Kariye Camii (formerly the Church of St Saviour in Chora) is well-preserved and historically fascinating. The Municipal Museum (Belediye Muzesi), at the foot of the impressive Aqueduct of Valens, offers a display of Istanbul daily life. The immense Fatih Mosque, the Column of Marcian and the Byzantine church of Pantocrator are all worth visiting too.

If you happen to be looking for an Istanbul-based tour operator who can offer you interesting trips to different parts of Turkey, the following are recommended: Kosmos Travel; Travel Alternatif; Trek Travel (for addresses and details, see **Introduction** p. 50).

Communications

How to Get There

Turkish Airlines (THY) operates daily **flights** to Istanbul's Ataturk Airport, as does British Airways. Students are likely to be eligible for considerable (up to 50 per cent) discounts on THY, but it may still be cheaper to go for either one of the smaller scheduled airlines (such as Istanbul Airlines or Noble Air), or a charter available through one of the package tour operators listed in the **Introduction** (p. 45). Air travel options will almost always beat other modes of transport, both financially and in terms of time and hassle, unless you're approaching Istanbul from half way across Europe.

Rail travel from Britain is not a good idea as it takes 72 hours and is gruelling. If you're approaching Istanbul from Venice, Munich, Athens, Vienna, or Belgrade, you could consider taking the express train, which takes 48 hours, 39 hours, 35 hours, 30 hours, and 26 hours respectively. All trains from Europe terminate at Sirkeci station.

Bus services to Istanbul are fairly limited from Britain, though more comprehensive from other parts of Europe. Eurolines' (Tel. 071 730 0202) London–Istanbul run lasts 70 hours. If you're travelling from Paris, Munich or Vienna, you could try Bosfor Turizm; from Zurich, try Varan Turizm. Neither of these companies has representatives in Britain.

If you are determined to **drive** all the way, bargain on the 3000 kilometres taking at least four days' pretty solid driving, though some relief can be gained by using the car **ferry** service from Venice to Istanbul (via Athens). It is run by Turkish Maritime Lines weekly from the beginning of April to the end of October and offers the only means to avoid Yugoslavia, as well as a romantic way to arrive in Istanbul.

When You're There

Bus – this is the cheapest way of getting around Istanbul. Tickets must be purchased in advance at one of the designated kiosks (marked *Plantonluk*) and a flat fare of around 10 pence (with a reduction for students) is in operation. Expect a 50 per cent mark-up on tickets offered by unofficial sellers. If your bus is marked *Cift Bilet*, it requires two tickets (those marked *Tel Bilet* need only one). The system is to drop the ticket(s) in the box as you enter the bus, and to press the button above the door just before your chosen stop. If you're not sure where to get off, local people are invariably extremely helpful. Likewise, people waiting at the bus stops will tell you which bus you need, though destinations and routes are shown on the front or side of the bus so this shouldn't be a problem. The main bus lines start from Taksim Square, Eminonu (near Galata Bridge), Beyazit (near Grand Bazaar), and Uskudar and Kadikoy on the Asian side.

Dolmus – this shared taxi comes either in the form of a minibus or a spacious old car (if it's the latter, remember to check that it's a *dolmus* and not a taxi!). Fares vary according to the destination but are fixed by the municipality (an average journey might cost around 15 to 20 pence), and the route is also fixed. It usually runs between the main bus stops in the area, but the driver will almost certainly let you get off wherever you want. The main *dolmus* stations are Taksim, Eminonu, Sirkeci, Besiktas, Aksaray, Uskudar and Kadikoy, though you can hail them from the street.

Taxi – taxis are yellow, with a 'taxi' sign on top, but are a fairly expensive option, purely because the traffic conditions are so atrocious it takes ages to get anywhere and, meanwhile, the meter is ticking happily on! Bridge-crossing tolls are also the responsibility of taxi passengers. Between midnight and 7 a.m. the fares go up. You can tell you're being charged 'night rate' as there are two red lights lit on the meter, rather than one. So if you see two during the day, it means the driver is trying to 'diddle' you!

Boat – ferries are practical, pleasant and, mile for mile, about as cheap as buses. The Turkish Maritime Organisation's Istanbul City Lines run regular services between Eminonu and Kavaklar (three hours away, at the top of the Bosphorus); Uskudar/Eminonu and

Eyup (end of Golden Horn); Eskihisar and Topcular (on the Gulf of Izmit); Sirkeci/Bostanci and the Princes' Islands; Kabatas (via Princes' Islands) and Yalova/Cinarcik (on southern coast of Sea of Marmara). There are always various stops en route and information is available at every one of these, as well as by phoning (1) 144 02 07 or calling in at their head office on Rihtim Caddesi, Karakoy. The sea-buses linking Kabatas, Bostanci and the Princes' Islands are a faster option than the ferry (for information, Tel. (1) 362 04 44). At Eminonu you can tell the destination of a ferry from the pier it is leaving from: Pier 1 for Kadikoy and Bostanci; Pier 2 for Uskudar; Pier 3 for Kuzguncuk; Pier 4 for up the Bosphorus; Pier 5 for Princes' Islands, Yalova and Cinarcik; Pier 6 for Golden Horn. The other side of the Horn, ferries leave from Karakoy's Pier 7 for Haydarpasa and Kadikoy.

Other Options – it's worth travelling the brief distance between Karakoy and Tunel (the southern end of Istiklal Caddesi) on the little underground train known as the Tunel, if only because it's the world's oldest underground railway (built in 1877). To travel from Sirkeci round to Kumkapi, Yenikapi or Yedikule, go to the station and take one of the *banliyo* commuter trains heading for Halkali. This will hug Seraglio Point, giving great views of Topkapi Palace, then follow the northern shore of the Sea of Marmara to the various destinations situated on it. Otherwise walking is a good way of getting round central Istanbul. It can even be quicker than those options which require waiting in traffic jams, though admittedly crossing main roads is a hazardous operation which can hold you up almost as badly! It also pays to look out for potholes, broken pavements etc.

Useful Local Contacts

Details of local restoration and conservation initiatives, as well as information about driving in Turkey, can be obtained from the **Turkish Touring and Automobile Association** (also known as the Touring Club), whose head office is at Halaskargazi Cad. 364, Sisli, Istanbul (Tel. (1) 131 46 31). A list of Istanbul-based tour operators can be obtained from **TURSAB** (the Union of Turkish Travel Agencies), Gazeteciler Sitesi, Haberler Sokak 15, Esentepe, Istanbul (Tel. (1) 175 13 61). The conservation organisation **DHKD** can be contacted at P.O. Box 18, 80810 Bebek, Istanbul, and the **Istanbul Turco-British Cultural Association** is based at Cumhuriyet Caddesi, Adli Han, Harbiye, Istanbul (Tel. (1) 141 05 18). Keen horse-riders could contact the **Istanbul Atlispor Kulubu**,

Binicilik Sitesi, Ucyol, Maslak, Istanbul (Tel. (1) 176 14 04).

Geographical Breakdown of Region

Istanbul – The City

Once you have mastered the basic layout of Istanbul, with its European and Asian sectors divided by the Bosphorus, and (on the European side) its Old Town and New Town divided by the Golden Horn, you'll find that the city is further broken down into numerous districts, each with its own character and reputation. The poorest districts tend to be on the outskirts of the city, at Dudullu, Umraniye and Kartal on the Asian side; and at Sirinevler, near the airport, on the European side. The central areas where poverty is most in evidence are Eminonu and Fatih, both in the Old Town south of the Golden Horn. The rich often have waterfront villas, with the most impressive old mansions situated at Bebek on the European shore of the Bosphorus. You will also find luxurious houses overlooking the Sea of Marmara between Bakirkoy and Florya.

Although most of the well-known sights are to be found south of the Golden Horn, it would be foolish not to explore further afield, so the information in the rest of this chapter is designed to give you a taste of what is on offer in each of the other major sectors, once the glories of Old Istanbul have been taken in.

Practical Tips – museums generally close on Mondays, except for the Topkapi Palace which is closed on Tuesdays instead. Exceptions to this rule are indicated in the text. The telephone code for Istanbul is 1, which means that you should omit the initial bracketed (1) from the numbers given in this chapter if phoning from within the city, but retain it if phoning from elsewhere.

South of the Golden Horn

Old Istanbul

The location of so many world-famous buildings, you will need at least two to three days exploring this part of town to do it any kind of justice. You might consider heading for the lesser-known attractions out towards the city walls before tackling the impressive offerings of Sultanahmet. This has two advantages. It means that your first impression of the city is not one of hordes of tourists battling against almost equal numbers of trinket-sellers and shoe-shine boys, but rather something gentler and more authentic. It also means you're less likely to lose momentum in your sightseeing: if you see the city's most precious treasures first, it can be easy to lapse into a blasé attitude towards the rest – despite the fact that, taken on their own terms, they are of great interest.

The Outskirts

If you head westwards along the main street (the one that turns from Divan Yolu into Yeniceriler Caddesi then Ordu Caddesi), you will find on your right, just beyond the Laleli hotel district, the Laleli Mosque. It is in Ottoman Baroque style, having been built by Sultan Mustafa III in the mid-eighteenth century. The covered market beneath it was originally constructed as a source of rent for the mosque, and now seems to act as an added incentive to pray there. If you can bear to negotiate the confusing and traffic-polluted Aksaray crossroads, you'll come to the **Valide Sultan Mosque**, an elaborate structure built in 1871 by the Sultan's mother (always known as the Valide Sultan).

In any case, you should head north up Ataturk Bulvari and, when the modern Town Hall is on your right, you'll have a splendid view of the **Aqueduct of Valens** (Bozdogan Kemeri). This was built in AD 368, almost certainly by the Emperor Valens, in order to improve the waterworks of the city. Regularly repaired, it supplied water throughout the Byzantine and Ottoman periods right up to the end of the nineteenth century. At its right-hand end is the **Sehzade Mosque**, the first important work of the famous architect Mimar Sinan. It was commissioned in 1543 by Suleyman the Magnificent, on the death of his son and heir Sehzade Mehmet (Sehzade means 'Sultan's Son').

Across the park, the other side of Ataturk Bulvari, is a **Memorial to Fatih** Sultan Mehmet (Mehmet the Conqueror), situated in a tea-garden. Just to the north of the aqueduct, you'll find the **Museum of Caricature and Humour** (Karikatur Muzesi) and the **Municipal Museum** (Belediye Muzesi). Both are housed in former religious schools (*medrese*). The first shows the popularity of cartoons as a Turkish art form and runs its own art/craft workshops. The second contains a variety of odds and ends connected with the city's past.

Continuing north-west along any of the streets running parallel to the aqueduct, you'll soon come to the Fatih district, dominated by the vast **Fatih Mosque**. Conservative dress and behaviour is advisable in this rather poor and very traditional part of the city. The mosque was first built in the late fifteenth century, but was destroyed by an earthquake in 1766 and had to be rebuilt. It contains the mausoleum of Fatih Sultan Mehmet and is surrounded by a complex of buildings including hospitals, theological schools, baths, a library and a *kervansaray*.

If you head north towards the Golden Horn, you will see the attractive **Selimiye Mosque**, named after Sultan Selim 'the Grim'. It is in a hill-top position, overlooking the Horn, and contains many yellow-coloured (i.e. early) Iznik tiles. This part of the Golden Horn is called Fener and has been the home of the **Greek Patriarchate** since around 1600. Inside the compound is the **Church of St George** which contains the patriarchal throne.

Out near the city walls is the beautiful old Kariye quarter, whose eleventh-century **Kariye Mosque** was formerly the church of St Saviour in Chora. Now a museum, the inner walls of the building are decorated with magnificent fourteenth-century frescoes (which influenced the European Renaissance) and Byzantine mosaics – the finest collection in the city. The museum is open every day except Tuesday and tea is served in the garden outside, among a collection of restored Ottoman houses. To the south-west of Kariye, right by the walls and the Edirnekapi bus station, is the **Mihrimah Mosque**. Designed by Sinan, it was commissioned by Suleyman the Magnificent's favourite daughter, Mihrimah, in the 1560s and perches on the highest of Istanbul's seven hills.

The **City Walls** (or Land Walls), which were begun in 413 and stretch from the Sea of Marmara to the Golden Horn (7 kilometres), are named after the Emperor Theodosius II. Punctuated by towers, bastions and gates, they were once described as the mightiest fortifications in Christendom. Now they provide shelter for gypsies and the extremely poor. Recently the walls and the area enclosed by them were declared a World Heritage Site by UNESCO. If you follow them north towards the Golden Horn, you'll come to the **Tefkur Sarayi**, also known as the Palace of Constantine Porphyrogenetus. The fourteenth-century Byzantine palace is somewhat dilapidated, but still in remarkable shape considering its age and a past tendency to demolish such palaces for building materials.

Where the walls end, the newly-created parkland lining the Golden Horn takes over. Once here, it would be a pity not to press on up to Eyup. If you time it right, you'll be able to catch a ferry from the Ayvansaray jetty: Eyup is the last stop on the Horn. Alternatively, it is a pleasant walk along the banks, once you've managed to get beyond the main (Cevre Yolu) road. The **Eyup Mosque** complex is where Eyup, the standard-bearer of the Prophet Mohammed, is said to have died in an attack on Constantinople in 670. The mosque was the first one to be built after the Ottoman conquest and is the fourth most important site of pilgrimage in the Islamic world. Its sacred nature means that conservative dress should be observed. The tomb of Eyup is opposite the mosque and, through a beautiful graveyard to the north of the mosque, is the **Pierre Loti Café**, named after the nineteenth-century French writer who so loved Istanbul and used it as the setting for his romantic autobiographical novel *Aziyadé*. A ferry down to the Galata Bridge at Eminonu is your most pleasant option for the journey back to the centre, but make sure you consult a ferry timetable in advance as they are not particularly frequent. If travelling in the other direction, ferries up the Golden Horn leave from Pier 6 at Eminonu.

One final area of interest on the outskirts of Old Istanbul requires a special journey. From Sirkeci station, take the *banliyo* train three stops down to **Yedikule** (The Fortress of the Seven Towers). The fortifications here are so impressive that parts of them have been turned into a museum. Look out for the **Golden Gate**, built in 390 before the walls were even started. The **Imrahor Mosque** (formerly a church) is also interesting, though little of the original structure remains. To make the trip worthwhile, you could take the train for another few stops beyond the walls and explore the wealthy (but unsafe for bathing) resorts of **Florya** and **Atakoy**, with their glossy shopping centres, or **Yesilkoy**'s Aviation Museum (Hava Muzesi), which traces the development of air flight in Turkey.

The Hub of the Old Town

Aim to arrive at **Topkapi Palace** as soon as it opens at 9.30 a.m. (every day except Tuesday). This way you'll avoid the worst of the heat, the crowds and the queues. You will also be able to book yourself on the very first Harem tour, starting at 10 a.m. Topkapi is situated on Seraglio Point (Saray Burnu) and was the centre of Ottoman intrigue from the fifteenth to the nineteenth century. The basic layout of the palace is still the same as when Mehmet the Conqueror built it in 1459, though the majority of the buildings have had to be extensively repaired (or even reconstructed) at some point, due to fire and earthquake damage. Four courtyards feed into one another: the first is the Court of the Janissaries, the second the Divan Court, the third contains the Audience Hall, and the fourth various pavilions (Kosku).

You have to have quite an imagination to divest the **Court of the**

Janissaries of its modern-day status as coach park, taxi rank and tour group gathering place. It's also where you buy your entrance ticket. The Janissaries were the Sultan's élite guards and they used to meet in the courtyard to eat *pilav*. If they overturned the vast pots of rice, this was a signal that they were dissatisfied with the Sultan's treatment of them – and revolt was not far behind! The courtyard also contains (on the left) the **Church of St Irene**. This used to be the imperial arsenal, then an artillery museum; now it is closed to the public except during the Istanbul International Festival when concerts are given there.

In order to enter the **Divan Court**, you have to go through the **Ortakapi Gate**, constructed by Suleyman in 1524, through which only the Sultan was allowed to pass on horseback. If you want to purchase a ticket for the Harem tour and to assure yourself a place on the first available one in a language you understand, the entrance is ahead of you on your left. The **Harem** consists of over 400 rooms, only a small proportion of which are open to the public, but it is nonetheless interesting to see this most private of palace areas, where the wives, concubines and children of the Sultan lived. The Sultan's Mother (Valide Sultan) reigned here – over its 400 or so residents. Also on the left of the Divan Court are the **Assembly Rooms**, where the Grand Vizier met with the imperial council, or Divan (named after the couch on which they sat), to discuss matters of state. The Sultan would often listen in through a special metal grill. On the other side of the courtyard are the **palace kitchens**, which now house a vast collection of Chinese and Japanese porcelain.

In the **third courtyard** is the Sultan's **Audience Chamber**, where he would receive important dignitaries and foreign ambassadors. The pretty grey marble building behind this is the **Library of Ahmet III**, built in 1718. The rooms to your right used to be the Turkish Baths, but now contain an impressive collection of garments, which reflect the opulent lifestyle of the Sultans. This is further corroborated by the exhibits in the **Imperial Treasury** next door, which include a solid gold throne studded with 25,000 jewels, a single uncut emerald which weighs over 3¼ kilograms, and the 86 carat Kasikci (or Spoonmaker's) Diamond.

By now you will probably need to sit down with a drink, so head for the café or restaurant in the far right-hand corner of the **fourth courtyard**. The balcony here offers superb views right across both the Golden Horn and the Bosphorus. The rest of the courtyard is taken up with gardens (once filled with tulips) and several pavilions, the **Mustafa Pasa Kosku**, **Revan Kosku** and **Bagdat Kosku**, and the Sunnet Odasi or **Circumcision Room**.

Many of the rooms surrounding the different courtyards have little exhibitions in them, ranging from clocks and watches or holy relics to weaponry – so allow time to have a look at these on your way back out.

Topkapi is set in the **Gulhane Park**, where there are open-air concerts and performances in summer, as well as a cramped little zoo and a colony of grey herons, who have chosen to make it their home. Left of the palace (as you face its entrance) is the **Archaeological Museum** complex (Arkeoloji Muzeleri). The Archaeological Museum itself was built in 1878, expressly as a museum, and houses some fascinating antiquities, the most impressive of which is the Sarcophagus of Alexander the Great (which may not actually have been his, but is certainly worthy of him!). Opposite is the smaller **Museum of Oriental Antiquities** (Eski Sark Eserler Muzesi), which contains well-preserved artefacts from the Egyptian, Assyrian, Babylonian and Hittite civilisations, including bas-reliefs, a peace treaty and law tablets. Across the courtyard is the **Cinili Kosku** (Tiled Pavilion), the oldest non-religious building in Istanbul, built by Mehmet the Conqueror in 1472 in the Seljuk style. It is now a Ceramics Museum, displaying some fine seventeenth-century Iznik tiles.

If you turn left as you leave Gulhane Park, you'll find yourself on **Sogukcesme Sokak**. This street runs along the outer walls of Topkapi and is composed of beautiful eighteenth-century Istanbul houses, restored by the Touring Club and converted into the Aya Sofya Pensions. To the right of where the street starts is a **Bazaar of Traditional Istanbul Arts** (Cafer Aga Medresesi), and at the other end of the street is the ornate **Ahmet III Fountain**, built in 1729. Follow the walls of Santa Sophia (to your right), or walk through Sultanahmet Square, a park which divides it from the Blue Mosque and contains the double-domed **Hurrem Sultan Hamam** (or Roxelana Baths), to reach the entrance of the **Santa Sophia** itself.

Usually referred to as Santa Sophia in English (meaning Church of the Divine Wisdom), the Turks call it Aya Sofya, though you will sometimes find the Greek name, Haghia Sofia, in use. The first church on this spot was probably built by the Emperor Constantine in AD 360, but it was reconstructed by Justinian in the sixth century, becoming the most important church in the Christian world, before being changed into a mosque at the Ottoman conquest, then into a museum by Ataturk. It is an architectural masterpiece, for the vast dome (31 metres wide and 55 metres high) appears to have no support at all. In fact it's held up by pillars incorporated into the thick walls. It's worth climbing up to the gallery for another perspective on this incredible building.

Nearby, in a little park on the north side of Divan Yolu Caddesi, is the **Yerebatan Sarayi** (Sunken Palace), a sixth-century Byzantine cistern. Part of a large network of city plumbing, examples of which are still being uncovered by pure chance, the massive cistern has fine brick vaulting and 336 Corinthian columns to support its roof. As you head towards the Hippodrome, you will see on your right the sixteenth-century **Ibrahim Pasa Sarayi** (restored in the nineteenth century), which now houses the **Museum of Turkish and Islamic Art** (Turk ve Islam Eserleri Muzesi). This is worth a visit as it contains one of the most impressive exhibitions of Islamic artefacts in the world, including Seljuk wall tiles, Persian miniatures, Turkish carpets and Anatolian folk art. Ibrahim Pasa was the Grand Vizier of Suleyman the Magnificent, and his palace is the ideal setting for the museum.

The strip of ground between here and the Blue Mosque is the site of the ancient **Hippodrome**, a chariot-racing track and focal point of Byzantine social life, of which little remains but some curious old monuments. The **Fountain of Kaiser Wilhelm II**, at the northern end, was a goodwill gift from the Austro-Hungarian Emperor to Sultan Abdul Hamid II in 1895; the hieroglyph-covered **Obelisk of Theodosius** was carved in Egypt around 1500 BC and transferred to Constantinople in AD 390; the spiral bronze **Serpentine Column** was brought over from the Temple of Apollo at Delphi by Constantine the Great in AD 330; and the 32-metre rough stone column at the southern end of the Hippodrome, known as the **Column of Constantine** because Constantine VII repaired it in the tenth century, is of pretty much unknown origin.

Getting from here to the **Blue Mosque** requires considerable initiative if you wish to avoid being pinned down by a shoe-shine lad or abducted by a carpet-seller! The Blue Mosque itself (whose proper name is the Sultan Ahmet Mosque) is very elegant, with its six minarets. It was built at the very beginning of the seventeenth century by the architect Mehmet and is laid out in the standard Ottoman design. At the time, its six minarets were a subject of controversy, as it seemed disrespectful to have as many as the mosque in Mecca; however, the problem was solved by Mecca adding a seventh. When you enter the mosque and see the huge 'elephant foot' pillars required to support its dome, you come to appreciate just what a feat of engineering the Santa Sophia was. The name 'blue' comes from the 20,000 Iznik tiles, in ninety-nine different shades of blue, which decorate the interior. A **Carpet and Kilim**

Museum can be approached from the north side of the mosque and offers a useful introduction to the different types of carpet woven in Turkey. Another museum which belongs to the mosque complex is the **Mosaic Museum**, created to preserve *in situ* some of the mosaics found in the palaces which had to be destroyed to build the Blue Mosque. The fifth- and sixth-century pavements from the Great Palace of the Emperor of Byzantium are particularly impressive. The entrance is at 22 Torun Sokak, just off the touristy street running behind the mosque and known as Arasta Carsisi (the Sultanahmet Bazaar).

If you continue from here down Kucuk Aya Sofya Caddesi, towards the seafront, you'll come to the **Kucuk Aya Sofya Camii** (Little Santa Sophia Mosque). A typical **Byzantine** church, constructed under Justinian's rule in AD 550, it suffered the usual fate of being converted into a mosque by the Ottomans in 1453. If you climb Mehmet Pasa Sokak, to the north, you reach the nearby **Sokullu Mehmet Pasa Mosque**, built by Mimar Sinan quite late in his career (1571), at the zenith of Ottoman architectural achievement. It is worth making the detour down Kadirga Caddesi to the waterfront district of **Kumkapi** (meaning Sand Gate), formerly an Armenian fishing village. It is known for its fish market and seafood restaurants, but is also home to the church of the Armenian Patriarchate and a colourful town square.

From here, head north up either Tiyatro Caddesi or Gedik Pasa Caddesi. When you come to Divan Yolu, unless you're running out of time, try to refrain from going straight into the Grand Bazaar, which is directly in front of you. Instead, turn up to its right along Vezirhani Caddesi, which will lead you to the **Nuruosmaniye Mosque**, built between 1748 and 1755, and one of the earliest examples of the Ottoman Baroque style.

The **Grand Bazaar** itself should be visited on at least two separate occasions. On the first, just wander through its streets getting a feel for the atmosphere and what is on offer – and don't worry about buying anything or keeping track of where you are. The second visit could be more systematic, perhaps with specific purchases in mind. The Turkish name for what we call the Grand Bazaar is Kapali Carsi, meaning 'covered market'. The bazaar dates back to the time of Mehmet the Conqueror, when it started out as a small warehouse (*bedesten*). Shops grew up around this, and caravanserais (*hans*) were set up on the edges to encourage larger-scale trade. The *hans* still provide quieter and less tourist-orientated areas to explore. The streets of the bazaar are named after trade categories (Jewellers' St, Carpetsellers' St, etc.), many of which are still accurate descriptions of their nature today, though some of the old trades have died out. The oldest part of the bazaar is the Cevahir Bedesteni (Jewellery Warehouse) at its very centre. Refreshments are available at regular intervals throughout the complex. Remember that the whole bazaar is closed on Sundays.

The exits at the western end of the Grand Bazaar will take you onto Cadircilar Caddesi, on which you will find the entrance to the Sahaflar Carsisi or **Old Book Bazaar** (it's just opposite the Fesciler Street exit). Books have been sold here off and on since Byzantine times, and the second-hand booksellers who ply their trade here nowadays are particularly colourful characters, some of whom belong to an order of dervishes. The market opens on to **Beyazit Square** and a pleasant tea-garden frequented by university students. Another feature of the square is the **Beyazit Mosque**, the oldest remaining imperial mosque in Istanbul (built in 1506), across from which is a small **Calligraphy Museum** (Bezayit Hat Sanatlari Muzesi). The impressive gateway which dominates the square is the entrance to **Istanbul University**, which used to house the Ottoman War Ministry and, before that, was the site of a home for ageing concubines. The grounds contain the **Beyazit Tower**, a fire tower which is an Istanbul landmark.

Making your way either through the university grounds (if you can get in), or along the street which hugs its walls, you will come to the **Suleymaniye Mosque**, Istanbul's largest mosque and perhaps Sinan's most impressive achievement, completed in the 1550s. The great architect's tomb can be seen in his garden, just to the north-west of the mosque. Also buried in the mosque complex, but in grander style, are Suleyman the Magnificent and his wife, Roxelana. The steep backstreets leading from behind the mosque down to the Golden Horn offer a fascinating glimpse of the small-scale light industrial workshops and storerooms of Istanbul – as well as the people who work in these dimly-lit places.

In the heart of this area is the elegant **Rustem Pasa Mosque**, built for the Grand Vizier and son-in-law of Suleyman and designed, once again, by Sinan. The interior is covered in some of the finest Iznik tiles you'll see. If you follow bustling Hasircilar Caddesi south-east, you will find yourself behind the **Egyptian Bazaar**, also known as the Spice Bazaar and, in Turkish, the Misir Carsisi. If you enter from this side, you will first come to stalls selling an incredible selection of household items, toys and clothes, before turning the corner onto a vaulted passageway of Turkish Delight, dried fruit and spice sellers. The bazaar was built in the 1660s and is part of the Yeni Mosque complex. Cafés and sellers of caged birds line the pleasantly shady square between the bazaar and the mosque. Its name, **Yeni Camii**, means New Mosque and, though it was commissioned by the mother of Sultan Mehmet III in 1597, it was only completed sixty-six years later, once Ottoman architecture had started to go downhill. The area at the front of the mosque is a mass of pigeons, encouraged by numerous sellers of birdseed.

An underpass will take you to the other side of a busy road and you will find yourself in the heart of the Galata district, where the famous **Galata Bridge** straddles the Golden Horn, always crowded. Street hawkers, fishermen and open-air barbecues line the approach to the bridge, waylaying those heading for the dirty orange and white ferries which leave from here for destinations on the Golden Horn (Pier 6), Bosphorus (Pier 4) or Princes' Islands (Pier 5).

Accommodation (Old Istanbul)

The area south of the Golden Horn is a good place to stay, in that it's close to the major sights and caters for all budgets. There's a growing number of lovely Ottoman houses, restored and converted into small hotels (often by the Touring Club), and these are ideal for those looking for first class or middle range accommodation. Those on a lower budget will also be pleasantly surprised at the hostel and hotel accommodation on offer here. If you choose to stay in Sultanahmet itself, you will, however, have to put up with being in an excessively tourist-orientated environment. Those who object to this might do better staying either in one of the hotels nearer the outskirts of the town, or else across the Golden Horn in New Istanbul.

First Class

Ramada Oteli, Ordu Cad. 226, 34470 Laleli (Tel. (1) 513 93 00): comfortable rooms in recently-restored building in busy part of town.

Yesil Ev Oteli, Kabasakal Cad. 5, Sultanahmet (Tel. (1) 511 11 50 or 528 67 64): 20 rooms in beautifully-restored old Ottoman house with traditional decor and rather old-fashioned service; the one suite comes complete with a Turkish Bath; the name means 'Green House' – and you'll soon see why it's called that (reservation essential).

Aya Sofya Pansiyonlari, Sogukcesme Sok., Sultanahmet (Tel. (1) 513 36 60): associated with the Yesil Ev Oteli, these restored houses offer a warm welcome in a central, though quiet location.

Middle Range

Turkoman Oteli, Asmalicesme Sok. 2, 34400 Sultanahmet (Tel. (1) 516 29 56 or 57): 12 rooms in restored pastel-pink nineteenth-century house, near Hippodrome; also sells carpets.

Kariye Oteli, Kariye Camii Sok. 18, 34240 Edirnekapisi (Tel. (1) 524 88 64 or 524 88 81): 24 rooms in Ottoman-style hotel and pension, in attractive setting out by city walls.

Sumengen Oteli, Mimar Mehmet Aga Cad., Amiral Tafdil S. 21, Sultanahmet (Tel. (1) 512 61 62 or 512 90 88): 36 rooms and 3 suites in beautiful old house with Turkish bath and garden.

Sokullu Pasa Oteli, Ishakpasa Mah., Mehmet Pasa Camii Sok. 10, Sultanahmet (Tel. (1) 512 37 53 or 512 37 56): 36 rooms in imposing restored Ottoman house, with indoor and outdoor restaurants, Turkish bath and relaxed atmosphere.

Economy

Hotel Ema, Yerebatan Cad., Salkim Sogut Sok. 18, Sultanahmet (Tel. (1) 511 71 66 or 512 14 63): comfortable and central, with ensuite facilities; breakfast included, and terrace bar has view of Santa Sophia.

Ipek Palas Oteli, Orhaniye Cad. 9, Sirkeci (Tel. (1) 520 97 24): 53 rooms in a faded old hotel, where silk traders stopped off in the early days of the Republic.

Hotel Nomade, Ticarethane Cad., Sultanahmet (Tel. (1) 511 12 96): a pleasant, central, family-run hotel.

Kadirga Student Hostel, Sahsuvar Mah., Comertler Sok. 6, Kumkapi (Tel. (1) 528 24 80): 500 beds in hostel behind the Blue Mosque.

Yucelt Interyouth Hostel, Caferiye Sok. 6, Sultanahmet (across from Santa Sophia) (Tel. (1) 522 4790): lively, central hostel with both dormitory and double-room accommodation.

Topkapi Ataturk Student Centre, Londra Asfalti, Cevizlibag duragi, Topkapi (Tel. (1) 582 04 55): 750 beds in hostel out near Otogar, beyond city walls.

North of the Golden Horn

New Istanbul

It is hardly accurate to call the area north of the Golden Horn 'new', as most of it goes back an impressively long way. In Byzantine times, the quarter just north of the Horn (today's Karakoy) was inhabited by Genoese traders and formed a separate city, called Galata. The Ottoman era brought the founding of a sister city called Pera by non-Muslim Europeans, just up the hill from Galata. Then, as now, these two districts were known as Beyoglu, though now, of course, the city extends far beyond this central core.

The **Karakoy** area is packed with fish restaurants, whose employees buy in their supplies from the fishing boats bobbing at the quay. If you choose to head north-west from here, along the bank of the Golden Horn, you will pass the **Arap Mosque** on your right and the larger **Azapkapi Mosque** on your left. From Sishane (the banking centre), a bus ride towards Haskoy will take you to the **Aynali Kavak Summer Palace** (closed Monday and Thursday). Built in the eighteenth century and restored many times since, the palace's name means 'mirrored poplar' and its architecture is exquisitely Turkish.

Returning to Karakoy, you can either walk up Yuksek Kaldirim Caddesi towards the Tunel quarter, passing the Galata Tower on your left, or you can take the **Tunel** itself – Istanbul's kilometre-long underground train service. The latter option is fun but means you'll have to walk back in order to visit the famous Genoese **Galata Tower**, an activity well worth the effort as a lift will take you up to enjoy a panoramic view of Istanbul from this 62-metre-high monument, built in 1348.

On the right of Galipdede Caddesi (the extension of Yuksek Kaldirim C.) is the Galata Mevlevi Tekkesi, or **Whirling Dervishes Convent**. Set in beautiful gardens, the hall now houses a **Divan Literature Museum**, and occasionally some of the few remaining practising dervishes will give a performance of their whirling. The journey from the bottom of **Istiklal Caddesi** up to Taksim Square can be made by tram or on foot. Istiklal Caddesi, once known as the Grand Rue de Pera, is an interesting street, recently pedestrianised and now targetted for a facelift intended to return it to the Istanbul equivalent of a Parisian 'grand boulevard'. This is part of a more general campaign to improve the image of the Beyoglu area, which has long been the city's sleaze centre. Istiklal itself is a respectable enough street, home to numerous embassies and consulates, some fashionable shops, and even a few churches: **St Mary Draperis**, a **Dutch Chapel**, and the Italian Gothic **San Antonio di Padua** (all on the right-hand side). Halfway along the street, where it changes direction to veer north-east, is **Galatasaray Square**. A prestigious French-influenced school, founded in the last century, is situated here.

Just beyond the Square, at number 51 on the left side of Istiklal, is the entrance to **Cicek Pasaji** (Flower Sellers' Alley). Down here, turn right into a courtyard to find a collection of lively beer taverns, at their most atmospheric in the early evening. Opinions differ as to whether recent 'improvements' to this most Turkish of haunts have sanitised it beyond recognition, or have simply made it cleaner, less raucous and more accessible to visitors. Either way, an evening here is a memorable experience in the course of which you are bound to encounter some extremely colourful characters. One of the streets leading off to the right from Istiklal, called Suterazisi Sokak, takes you to the **Galatasaray Hamami** (Turkish Bath). Though geared towards tourists nowadays, the marble men's baths are very elegant, but women could do better elsewhere.

Taksim Square, at the end of Istiklal Caddesi, is a noisy trafficky place, dominated by the vast Pullman Etap Marmara Hotel. The middle of the roundabout sports a **Monument to the Republic and Independence**, erected in 1928. At the eastern end of the square is the **Ataturk Cultural Palace**, also known as the Opera House, which hosts many performances for the Istanbul International Festival in summer. If you follow Cumhuriyet Caddesi north, in the direction of the Harbiye and Sisli districts, you will find yourself well and truly immersed in the modern, commercial side of Istanbul, as the road is lined with airline offices, travel agents and posh hotels. On the right, these back on to **Taksim Park**, at whose northern end is a cluster of modern buildings, comprising a Concert Hall, Theatre and Sports Hall. Next to these, on Valikonagi Caddesi, is Istanbul's **Military Museum** (Akseri Muzesi – closed Monday and Tuesday), which contains Ottoman military relics. At 3 p.m. on most afternoons (except Monday/Tuesday), the Janissary Band (Mehter Takimi), allegedly the first military band in the world, gives a rousing performance.

If you want to see the house where Ataturk lived, now called the **Ataturk Reforms Museum**, you'll need to take a bus up Halaskargarzi Caddesi to the Sisli district. The museum (closed at weekends) is at number 250, on the right-hand side of the street, and contains Ataturk's personal effects. If you're keen on shopping, on the way back get out of the bus halfway down Halaskargazi Caddesi, so that you can walk along Rumeli Caddesi, which is packed with fashion shops and outlets for consumer goods. From here it is not too far to the Ihlamur district, home to the nineteenth-century **Ihlamur Pavilion**, a charming palace (closed Monday and Thursday) set in a garden of lime trees.

A good walk due south from here, back on the banks of the Bosphorus, is the famous **Dolmabahce Palace**. The entrance is on the right, not far from the **Dolmabahce Mosque**. The palace itself is an ornate white building, set in pleasant gardens on the waterfront, and you will almost certainly have to queue to get in unless you arrive at 9 a.m. (closed Monday and Thursday). Built in the mid-nineteenth century by Sultan Abdulmecit, it stretches for 600 metres along the Bosphorus. The replacing of Topkapi by this much more westernised imperial palace reflected not only a rejection of the old ways, but also a desperate attempt to embrace the European in order to prop up a declining empire. The result is a lavish palace whose interior decoration can be garishly ostentatious, but can also be highly attractive in those areas where it acknowledges its Turkish inheritance. In the throne room (the largest in Europe) you will see a 4½-ton crystal chandelier (the largest in the world), a present from Queen Victoria. You can also marvel at some wonderful inlaid floors and vast Turkish carpets, several *Hamams* (one constructed of pure alabaster), a rather more austere Harem section, and the room where Ataturk died on 10 November 1938 and whose clocks are stopped at the time of his death.

At the other end of the palace (the eastern end, nearest to the Besiktas ferry stop) is the entrance to the **Fine Arts Museum** (Resim ve Heykel Muzesi). This displays Turkish paintings and sculptures from the late nineteenth century to the present day (closed Monday and Tuesday). The **Aviary**, which includes a 'bird hospital', is accessible from here, and nearby is the **Naval Museum** (Deniz Muzesi – closed Monday and Thursday). This museum is surprisingly interesting, showing imperial caiques (complete with model oarsmen), as well as offering a good insight into Turkish maritime history.

From Besiktas follow one of the steep streets running parallel to the busy Barbaros Bulvari (Serencebey Yokusu, for example) up to the **Yildiz Park**. On the edge of the park is a mosque and, next to the entrance of the Yildiz Palace Garden, is the **City Museum** (Sehir Muzesi – closed Thursday), which contains miscellaneous exhibits ranging in period from the Turkish conquest to the present day. The **Yildiz Palace** is comprised of a collection of buildings scattered around the park, many of whose pavilions were restored by the Touring Club. The most elaborate is the Swiss chalet-style **Sale Kosku** (closed Monday and Thursday), whose grand hall boasts a 400-metre-square carpet. Other pavilions have been turned into cafés and the park as a whole is a splendid place to relax, with its exotic flowers and panoramic views.

Further up the European shore of the Bosphorus, beyond the park, is the village of **Ortakoy**, situated just this side of the impressive Bogazici Koprusu suspension bridge. This is a popular area with the more trendy Istanbulites, particularly on Sundays when it has a craft market. Within a stone's throw of the ferry station you can find a Baroque imperial mosque, a Greek Orthodox Church, an Armenian Church, a synagogue and some pleasant tea-houses.

Accommodation (New Istanbul)

The accommodation in New Istanbul tends to be concentrated around Tepebasi and Taksim, and caters for those on a reasonably flexible budget. The distance from the main sights makes this a quiet, safe and prestigious area to stay, though those looking for cut-price accommodation are probably better off elsewhere.

First Class

Pera Palas Oteli, Mesrutiyet Cad. 98/100, Tepebasi (Tel. (1) 151 45 60; transport yourself back to Constantinople in this grand old hotel, built for the first Orient Express passengers; also contains a suite used by Ataturk, now a museum.

Middle Range

Buyuk Londra Oteli, Mesrutiyet Cad. 117, Tepebasi (Tel. (1) 149 10 25 or 145 06 70): more faded than the Pera Palas, and with 42 smaller rooms, this hotel still possesses an impressive *fin de siècle* atmosphere.

    Konak Oteli, Cumhuriyet Cad., Nisbet Sok. 7–9, 80230 Elmadag (Tel. (1) 148 47 44 or 45): traditional Turkish hospitality in smart hotel with highly regarded restaurant.

    Plaza Oteli, Siraselviler Cad., Aslanyatagi Sok. 19/21, Taksim (Tel. (1) 145 32 74 or 73): 33 old-fashioned rooms, many with spectacular views of the Bosphorus.

Across the Bosphorus

The Asian Side

If you wish to catch a ferry boat from Galata to the Asian shore of the Bosphorus, it's worth knowing that those leaving from pier

2 will take you to Uskudar, those from pier 7 (over at Karakoy) to Haydarpasa (where the railway station is), and those from pier 1 to Kadikoy or Bostanci. Bostanci is right on the Sea of Marmara (the closest ferry stop to the Princes' Islands). A *dolmus* ride between here and Kadikoy will reveal the upmarket shopping centres of **Bagdat Caddesi**, where Istanbul's jet set hang out. Just beyond Haydarpasa, in the Harem district, are the **Selimiye Barracks** (Selimiye Kislasi), where Florence Nightingale worked miracles of nursing. Her Crimean War hospital is now a museum in which you can see the rooms where she worked and some of her personal belongings. A guided tour of the barracks themselves, built in 1799, is also possible. Nearby are the 1805 **Selimiye Mosque** and a **British War Cemetery**.

If you continue northwards along the shore to **Uskudar**, you will pass **Leander's Tower** (Kiz Kulesi). The present tower is from the eighteenth century (though the original dates back to the twelfth), and is perched on a little island at the mouth of the harbour. Long ago, a chain between here and Seraglio Point was used to close off the Bosphorus rather effectively when so desired. The tower is best seen from the water. Uskudar itself is a very attractive suburb; there are three mosques within a stone's throw of its main square, which comes complete with a fountain. South of the square is the **Yeni Valide Mosque**, built in 1710 by Sultan Ahmet III for his mother, whose tomb can be found in its garden. On the northern side the **Mihrimah Mosque**, built by Sinan in 1547, offers good views across the square, while to the west is another slightly later Sinan mosque, the **Semsi Paša**. But perhaps the most interesting mosque is the little **Cinili Camii** (Tiled Mosque), which is quite a walk down Cavusdere Caddesi and whose interior is a mass of Iznik tiles.

Uskudar's Iskele Meydani (square) is the place to catch a bus or *dolmus* to the **Camlica Hills** (location of a huge TV mast). The bus will be marked Umraniye and you should get off at Kisikli, from where you can walk up to the top of Buyuk Camlica (Big Pine Hill). This used to be a slum area but it was turned into a park by the Touring Club.

Accommodation (Asian Side)

Accommodation on this side of the Bosphorus is fairly scarce, as few people opt to stay here. It is, however, only a ferry ride away from the main sights, so those wishing to be isolated from most other foreign visitors might consider the following recommendations.

First Class

Eysan Oteli, Rihtim Cad., Misak-i Milli Sok. 1/3, 81321 Kadikoy (Tel. (1) 346 24 40): 48 spacious rooms in hotel to the south of Haydarpasa Station.

Middle Range

Yeni Saray Oteli, Selmanipak Cad., Cesme Sok. 33, Uskudar (Tel. (1) 333 07 77 or 334 34 85): 30 rooms in slightly drab family-run hotel with Bosphorus views from terrace.

Economy

Petek Pansiyon, Alptekin Sok. 4, Fenerbahce (Tel. (1) 336 22 59): family-run pension.

Eating Out

Istanbul City

Eating out here is generally a pleasurable and remarkably inexpensive experience, unless you insist on international cuisine. However, the quality range between the cheapest *lokanta* and the priciest restaurant is not enormous so, if you're not too fussy about smart table settings and immaculate service, it's hardly worth searching out the upmarket establishments. Most of the **First Class** restaurants listed here will not break the bank, but you may well find you prefer some of the wonderful **Middle Range** or **Economy** options in any case. Surprisingly, the prime tourist area around Sultanahmet has a dearth of restaurants, but all those listed here are reasonably central. Other restaurants situated further up the Bosphorus are recommended on page 116.

First Class

Revan Restaurant, Sheraton Hotel, Asker Ocagi Caddesi 1, Taksim (Tel. (1) 131 21 21): an unusual and, by Turkish standards, pricey (around £25 a head) treat is offered at this hotel restaurant in the form of a ten-course Ottoman banquet, created from fine Turkish produce.

    Divan Hotel, Cumhuriyet Caddesi 2, Elmadag (Tel. (1) 131 41 00): first-class traditional Turkish food in a smart setting, with dancing in the evening.

Dort Mevsim (aka Four Seasons Restaurant), Istiklal Caddesi 509, Beyoglu (Tel. (1) 145 89 41): owned by a Turco-British couple who serve high quality Turkish and French cuisine; draws custom from the nearby consulates at lunchtime but closed on Sundays.

Ucler, Kumkapi Square, Kumkapi: situated in a former Greek fishing village on the Sea of Marmara, this restaurant is widely known for its seafood and aubergine dishes, but you may find the service stuffy.

Liman Lokantasi, Yolku Salonu, Rihtim Caddesi, Karakoy (Tel. (1) 144 10 33): only does weekday lunches; a friendly, old-fashioned seafood restaurant overlooking the Golden Horn and its ferries.

Pandeli, Misir Carsisi, Eminonu (Tel. (1) 522 55 34): in a guardroom just inside the Egyptian (Spice) Bazaar, this is another lunchtime-only haunt, specialising in fish and grilled meats.

Middle Range

Haci Baba, Istiklal Caddesi 49, Beyoglu (Tel. (1) 144 18 86): tasty Turkish dishes in an attractive setting with outdoor terrace.

Borsa Lokantasi, Yalikoskusku Ishani 60/62, Eminonu (Tel. (1) 522 41 73): serves filling Turkish meat dishes and is popular with local businessmen.

Kor Agup, Ordeli Bakkal Sokak 7, Kumkapi: an Istanbul institution, this atmospheric restaurant has a vast range of fresh fish dishes and many other imaginative concoctions.

Rejans, Ikuvi Geçidi 15 (a passage off Istiklal Caddesi, around no. 244), Beyoglu (Tel. (1) 144 16 10): a well-established Russian restaurant, founded in the 1930s; atmosphere best when it's crowded and the lemon vodka's flowing freely.

Cati Restaurant, 7th Floor Baro Han, Piremeci Sokak 20, Istiklal Caddesi, Beyoglu (Tel. (1) 145 16 56): excellent restaurant with views of Golden Horn, frequented by local professional people.

Konyali Restaurant, Ankara Caddesi 223, Sirkeci: long-established restaurant with *pilav* specialities (a sister Konyali restaurant is situated within the Topkapi Palace complex); lunchtime only.

Economy

Vitamin Restaurant, Divanyolu 16, Sultanahmet (Tel. (1) 526 50 86): a wide range of freshly-prepared Turkish cooking, including many vegetarian dishes.

Haci Abdullah, Sakizagaci Caddesi 19 (off Istiklal Caddesi), Beyoglu

(Tel. (1) 144 85 61): good, cheap food – popular with local people.

Han Restaurant, Kartcinar Sokak 16, Karakoy (Tel. (1) 152 54 52): good-value restaurant located in historic Genoese building, formerly a factory.

Hasir I, Kalyoncu Kullugu Caddesi 94/1, Tarlabasi, Beyoglu (Tel. (1) 150 05 57): informal restaurant with freshly-cooked vegetable and meat dishes.

Kardesler and **Merkez**, Capariz Sokak, Kumkapi: two of the great little Kumkapi seafood restaurants.

Tahta Kasik, Muallim Naci Caddesi 90, Ortakoy (Tel. (1) 161 94 43): simple dishes in restaurant with Bosphorus views.

Kanaat Lokantasi, Selmanipak Caddesi 25, Uskudar: cheap meals in pleasantly-decorated *lokanta* in Asian part of city.

Entertainments

Among daytime entertainments, one should surely include shopping, for Istanbul could justifiably be described as an Aladdin's Cave. Some recommended carpet shops and markets are listed in the **Meeting People** section; and of course there's always the Grand Bazaar. There is a list of upmarket stores in the monthly tourist guide *Istanbul Days*, available free from tourist offices and some hotels. This also contains the names of bars, cinemas, night clubs, art galleries etc, though there's no real indication as to what they're like. Ottoman military music, played on kettle drums, cymbals, clarinets and bells, is performed by the Janissary Band (Mehter Takimi) at the Military Museum (see p. 106) at 3 p.m. except Mondays and Tuesdays.

There is a free *Son et Lumière* show every night (at 8.30 or 9.00 p.m. depending on time of year) in front of the Blue Mosque in Sultanahmet Square. This offers fabulous floodlit views of the monuments and explains the rivalry between the Blue Mosque and Santa Sophia. For exact times and an indication of which language the evening's show is in, there's a board up at the tourist office and in the Square itself. Belly-dancing is a tradition known to appeal to tourists, so you will find it is part of the entertainment on offer at luxury hotels like the Pera Palas, at upmarket nightclubs like the Kervansaray, and at backstreet Beyoglu clubs, such as the Beyaz Saray Club. It is claimed that all Turkish women have the ability to belly dance 'in their blood'. *Gazinos* are a good alternative to predictable nightclubs. These are open-air restaurants with some sort of cabaret entertainment, many of which are situated on the European shore of the Bosphorus (try taking a ferry up to the Bebek Aile Gazinosu). In fact, a ferry trip up the Bosphorus can be a pleasant (and cheap) evening entertainment in itself.

Istiklal Caddesi is the place to go for the trendiest bars, but be aware that if you wander off into the backstreets around Istiklal and Taksim you'll find yourself in the red light district. A lively, beer-drinking evening, surrounded by eccentric local characters can be enjoyed at any of the taverns on the Cicek Pasaji, off Istiklal Caddesi. A more relaxing treat is a Turkish Bath and information about these is given in the **Meeting People** section.

If you time your visit to Istanbul to coincide with a festival period, you will certainly have plenty of entertainment to choose from. The Istanbul International Film Festival takes place in March/April and offers the rare opportunity to see Turkish films with English subtitles. An International Art and Culture Festival is hosted in June and July, the highlight being a performance of Mozart's *Abduction from the Seraglio* in Topkapi Palace. The tourist office should be able to give you information about current entertainments.

Useful Addresses

Istanbul's central **Tourist Office** is at Mesrutiyet Caddesi 57/6, Beyoglu (Tel. (1) 45 68 75). Other branches are to be found at: Hilton Hotel, Harbiye (Tel. (1) 33 05 92); Karakoy Limani Yolcu Salonu (Karakoy Maritime Station), Karakoy (Tel. (1) 49 57 76); Divanyolu Caddesi 3, Sultanahmet (Tel. 522 49 03); Mesrutiyet Caddesi 57, Sirkeci (Tel. (1) 43 29 28); Ataturk Hava Limani (Ataturk Airport), Yesilkoy (Tel. 573 73 99); and Iskele Meydani 5, Yalova (Tel. 121 08).

The main **Post Office** (*Buyuk Postane*) is at Yeni Postane Caddesi 25, Sirkeci. Other major branches are at Kadikoy, Galatasaray and Uskudar. You can recognise post offices by their yellow signs, marked PTT in black.

The British Consulate is at Mesrutiyet Caddesi 34, Tepebasi, Beyoglu (Tel. (1) 144 75 40). The Tourist Police are at Yerebatan Caddesi 2, Sultanahmet (Tel. (1) 527 45 03 or 528 53 69) and can help you out if you've had something stolen etc. As for **hospitals**, your best bet is either the American Admiral Bristol Hastanesi, Guzelbahce Sokak 20, Nisantasi (Tel. (1) 131 40 50); or the International Hospital, Istanbul Caddesi 82, Yesilkoy (Tel. (1) 574 78 02).

Around Istanbul

If you want to escape from the city itself, there are two main areas to explore, both of which can be managed on a day-trip from Istanbul but would be appreciated more if an overnight stay were possible. The first excursion involves exploring the villages on either side of the Bosphorus, beyond the Bogazici Koprusu suspension bridge, as the straits stretch up towards the Black Sea. The second is a visit to the quiet, though sadly rapidly-developing Princes' Islands.

Towards the Black Sea

Up the Bosphorus

Ferry is the logical way to see the villages lining the Bosphorus. They run all year, but winter sees a more commuter-orientated timetable, while in summer they go at more regular intervals and you can purchase a *buyuk tur* (Grand Tour) ticket which will allow you any number of stops. Before setting off (from Pier 4, Eminonu), you should arm yourself with a timetable, available at any ferry stop.

Along the European shore you'll see many beautiful houses, owned by Istanbul's rich and famous. Some of the prettiest Ottoman villas can be found at **Arnavutkoy**, the village just beyond Ortakoy (see p. 108) and the first suspension bridge. Like the next stop along, **Bebek**, this is probably best seen from the water. Bebek is a kind of yacht park for the very wealthy, but it's worth getting off here if you want to walk to the impressive **Rumeli Hisari** fortress (closed Mondays). The fortress was built in four months flat in 1452, an expression of Mehmet the Conqueror's impatience to take Constantinople. In summer Shakespeare plays are sometimes performed here. If you're feeling energetic, you can carry on walking up to the Duatepe Tulip Gardens at **Emirgan**, before catching the ferry again and pressing on, past the built-up bay of **Tarabya** and the villas of **Yenikoy**, to **Sariyer**.

Just south of the jetty here, you'll find the fascinating **Sadberk Hanim Museum** (closed Wednesdays). This well-laid-out display combines ethnographical exhibits with a millionaire's private art collection, some items of which date from the bronze age. To the west of Sariyer is the **Belgrade Forest**. You can get to Bahcekoy, on the edge of the forest, by *dolmus* from Cayirbasi, near Sariyer. The forest contains various reservoirs (and some aqueducts, water towers etc), as it used to supply the whole of Istanbul with water. Nowadays it provides one of the best ways of escaping the city traffic, getting a bit of exercise and drinking in the greenery. Alternatively, a thirty-kilometre *dolmus* ride from Sariyer is the Black Sea resort town of **Kilyos**, which has a very good beach. The next ferry stop up from Sariyer is **Rumeli Kavagi**, the last one on the European side of the Bosphorus and, thanks to its proximity to the Black Sea, a great place to enjoy a fresh fish meal.

Opposite here, on the Asian bank, is **Anadolu Kavagi**, a bucolic village whose hilltop Byzantine fortress offers great views of the Bosphorus opening up into the Black Sea. Further down, **Beykoz** is famed for its walnut groves and **Pasabahce** for its glassworks. On this very attractive stretch of shoreline, you will also find **Kanlica**, a village known for its yoghurts, which can be sampled at any one of the waterfront cafés. Boats can also be hired from here if you want to examine at leisure the beautiful *yali* (wooden villas) which line the shore. The oldest ones are around **Anadolu Hisari**, whose miniature fourteenth-century castle, built by Mehmet the Conqueror's grandfather, watches over a sleepy, steep-streeted village. Next stop down is **Kucuksu**, whose ornate palace (closed Mondays and Thursdays) with Rococo facade was built by the son of the Dolmabahce architect. If you think this is elaborate, head straight for the **Beylerbeyi Palace** (also closed Mondays and Thursdays), a little further on, just north of the first suspension bridge. Built for Sultan Abdul Aziz and completed in 1865, it was much admired by Princess Eugénie of France. In many ways, including the lack of crowds and a certain sense of intimacy despite all the grandeur, this makes for a much more pleasant visit than Dolmabahce. Some of the palace's intricate woodwork was actually done by the deposed Sultan Abdulhamit II, who spent the last six years of his life here. You approach the palace through a tunnel which used to carry traffic beneath the gardens, which are attractively terraced.

Accommodation (Bosphorus)

For those who would appreciate a spell out of town, some extremely pleasant accommodation can be found in the villages lining the Bosphorus; and if you want to spend some time on the Black Sea coast, it's sensible to book a night's accommodation there too.

First Class

Hidiv Kasri Oteli, Cubuklu, Beykoz (Tel. (1) 322 34 34): a friendly welcome awaits you in this attractive, palatial villa, set in its own park on the Asian side of the Bosphorus and once owned by the Egyptian royal family.

Middle Range/Economy

Bebek Oteli, Cevdetpasa Cad. 113–115, 80810 Bebek (Tel. (1) 163 30 00): 36 rooms in pleasant waterfront hotel on European side of Bosphorus.

Gurup Oteli, Kale Cad. 21/1, Kilyos, Sariyer (Tel. (1882) 11 94 or 12 51): 33 rooms in hotel with outdoor and indoor restaurants, right up on European shore of Black Sea.

Eating Out (Bosphorus)

The Bosphorus is *the* place to eat out if you're keen to sample the freshest of fish and seafood dishes. Even at the smallest village café, quality is pretty much guaranteed, though you will find that eating with a view over the Bosphorus will bump the price up. If you're trying to save money, choose less idyllically situated restaurants: the food will probably be just as good.

First Class

Urcan Restaurant, Sariyer: one of the best fish restaurants in the area, near a colourful fish market just to prove it's fresh.

Abdullah, Koru Caddesi 11, Emirgan (Tel. (1) 163 64 06): a classy restaurant with food prepared from the produce of its own kitchen garden.

Middle Range

Kamilica Karfez, Korfez Caddesi 78, Kanlica (Tel. (1) 332 01 08): an excellent fish restaurant in the village famed for its yoghurt.

Karaca, Rumeli Hisari: friendly restaurant across from disused ferry station; good for *mezes* and fish.

Economy

Kaptan, Birinci Caddesi 53, Arnavutkoy (Tel. (1) 165 84 87): simple, value-for-money fish restaurant with great atmosphere and Bosphorus views.

Metin, Rumeli Kavagi: another simple seaside restaurant with dishes such as shrin.p casserole as well as a wide variety of fresh fish.

The Sea of Marmara

Princes' Islands

These quiet islands, where no private traffic is allowed, are situated nine kilometres south-east of Istanbul and can be reached by ferry (from Bostanci or Eminonu) or by sea-bus (from Kabatas). Sadly, development restrictions are not being enforced so, although they still provide a wonderful respite from the city, their value as unspoilt havens may decrease in years to come.

The closest island to the mainland is tiny **Kinaliada** (Henna Island), which is largely Armenian in population and rather bare except for a water-sports complex, but as yet has no hotels. The next island, **Burgazada**, is mainly Jewish and Greek and has two main attractions: the church of John the Baptist, and the house of the novelist Sait Faik, now a museum. **Heybeliada** is a slightly larger island, home to the Turkish Naval Academy and a Greek Orthodox School of Theology. You can tour the island by horse and carriage or on foot, the latter option making it easier to find a deserted beach (try the northern shore) or simply enjoy a ramble through its pine woods and hills.

The largest and most popular of the Princes' Islands is **Buyukada** (Big Island), abode of the exiled Trotsky from 1929 to 1933. Again, this is the perfect place to head for the hills (there are two of them) in a search for peace and quiet. The south of the island is still quite wild and its hill boasts the Greek Monastery of St George. Horse-drawn carriage tours are available on this island too, though the shorter, more affordable one doesn't take in much more than the town itself.

Accommodation (Princes' Islands)

Finding accommodation here can be problematic, as you may find it closed in winter and booked up in summer. The summer visitors are often Turkish people taking a break from the bustle of the city and, if you want to guarantee yourself an overnight stay here, it certainly pays to get something organised in advance. If you *are* staying here, go easy on the water consumption as all fresh water must be brought from the mainland.

First Class/Middle Range

Halki Palas Oteli, Refah Sehitleri Cad. 88, Heybeliada (Tel. (1) 351

95 50 or 351 85 43): 32 rooms in converted nineteenth-century villa, with traditional restaurant and sea views.

Economy

Villa Rifat Pansiyon, Yilmaz Turk Cad., Buyukada (Tel. (1) 351 60 68): comfortable guesthouse, though not very central.

    Splendid Oteli, 23 Nisan Cad. 71, Buyukada (Tel. (1) 382 69 50): quiet little old-fashioned hotel.

2 Thrace and Marmara

Marmara and Thrace, adjacent to Istanbul and flanking the Sea of Marmara, are surprisingly unknown to foreign tourists. Forming a kind of antechamber – and a useful, undaunting introduction – to the rest of Turkey, the attractions of this part of the country are more often than not eclipsed by those of Istanbul.

Thrace, the European part of Turkey, is situated this side of the Sea of Marmara and boasts field upon field of sunflowers, roadside fruit stalls piled high with watermelons, and some very respectable vineyards. Over in Asia, Marmara is home to olive groves, lakes frequented by pelicans, and the Uludag mountain, which attempts to combine its roles as ski resort and national park.

The whole region is steeped in legend, history and tradition. This is where Paris awarded the golden apple to the most beautiful goddess, Aphrodite, on Mount Ida; it's here that Leander swam the Hellespont each night to visit his beloved Hero; and the Trojan War, immortalised by Homer, was allegedly fought here. More recently the Gallipoli Peninsula was site of the violent First World War battles during which many Australians and New Zealanders lost their lives and Ataturk proved his leadership qualities. Vast cemeteries punctuate this windswept peninsula, commemorating the dead of all nations. Less sombre reminders of the past can be found in the attractive Ottoman architecture of Edirne and Bursa. The former is a city of narrow cobbled streets and wooden houses, boasting a mosque that's arguably the masterpiece of architect Mimar Sinan. Famous greased wrestling championships take place near here in June each year. Bursa is a spa town at the foot of Mount Uludag and has a fine complex of religious Ottoman buildings. Not far from here is the traditional tile-making centre of Iznik.

Resort towns line the shores of the Sea of Marmara. Many are undergoing expansion as more and more city-bred Turks wish to acquire holiday homes, so some areas are just a mass of half-built concrete villas. But there are still some older village-style resorts to be found. On the islands in the Sea of Marmara are interesting marble quarries and a wealth of trekking possibilities, while trekking and even cycling are catered for inland from Troy. The northern reaches of the Aegean, around the Gulf of Edremit, provide pleasant sandy beaches with none of the overcrowding and loss of atmosphere associated with many of the more southerly resorts.

Though the tourism infrastructure is in place in Marmara and Thrace, it has not yet had to cope with swarms of foreign visitors, and so hasn't needed to compromise to the tastes and expectations of westerners. Instead, you may have to compromise a little yourself: the Turkish holidaymakers for whom this area caters tend to prefer rudimentary camp-sites and basic accommodation, so that's mainly what you'll find except in major towns. Any lack of comfort is, however, made up for by the chance to meet Turkish people on an equal footing, when they're in a relaxed, holiday mood, instead of in a selling or service-providing context.

History

The city of Troy, focus of Homer's Iliad, was only discovered in the nineteenth century. The site is composed of nine settlements built on top of one another, of which the sixth layer is Homer's Troy. Excavations here show that the city was an important trading centre with Greece as far back as the Bronze Age, but ultimately the Trojans became too great a rival for the Greeks and the latter sacked Troy during the Trojan War, around 1200 BC, just as the Hittite Empire was crumbling. By about the eighth century BC, the Phrygians were the dominant tribe in this part of Turkey.

During the conquest of Asia Minor by the Persians in the fifth century BC, the army of King Xerxes marched across the Dardanelles using a pontoon bridge made of ships. One of Alexander the Great's generals founded Nicaea (now Iznik) in 316 BC and shortly afterwards it became capital of the Bithynian kingdom, sharing this role, off and on, with nearby Nicomedia (now Iznik). It was a Bithynian king, Prusias I, who gave his name to Proussa (now Bursa). This was at the beginning of the second century BC, and it is thought he was aided in his choice of layout by the great Carthaginian General Hannibal, who is buried at Gebze, on the north coast of the Sea of Marmara. Roman armies gained more and more influence and, by AD 100, most of Anatolia had become part of the Roman Empire.

In AD 125 the Roman Emperor Hadrian founded the city of Hadrian-apolis (now Edirne), which became an important centre of Roman Thrace. Unfortunately, its location meant that, over the Byzantine period, it was used as a kind of punch-bag by every army with big ideas about conquering Constantinople, and as somewhere to vandalise when they retreated in failure! Meanwhile Nicaea hosted the First Ecumenical Council in AD 325, a crucial landmark in Christianity, which resulted, among other things, in the Nicaene Creed.

From the seventh century onwards, the whole area underwent numerous attacks – by Arabs, Seljuks, Greeks and the nomadic Ottoman Turks. After a long siege, Bursa was finally taken by the Ottomans and made their capital in 1326. The silk industry flourished here and new buildings were constructed. In the fourteenth century a jester named Karagoz was said to have lived in Bursa: he is now immortalised as a cheeky shadow puppet! After 1362, however, the Ottoman capital was moved to Edirne, and this city remained popular with sultans even after the conquest of Istanbul in 1453.

The sixteenth century was the height of the Iznik tile-making period: 300 kilns and factories flourished in Iznik at this time, producing tiles with floral patterns in green, red, turquoise and cobalt blue. In 1569, the eighty-year-old master architect, Mimar Sinan, designed the amazing Selimiye Mosque in Edirne. Fires and earthquakes affected Edirne and Bursa in the eighteenth and nineteenth centuries, while Edirne suffered too from Czarist occupation in the Russo-Turkish wars. But the mid-nineteenth century also brought the establishment of Hereke on the Sea of Marmara as a major carpet-producing centre, whose weavers specialised in woollen and silk carpets.

After violent Bulgarian attacks on Edirne in 1913 came the Allied naval assault on Gallipoli in 1915. The fighting lasted nine months and was extremely bloody, though the Turks, under the leadership of Mustafa Kemal (Ataturk), managed to hold their ground against the combined forces of the British, French, Australians and New Zealanders. The death toll for both sides ran into the hundreds of thousands, including 20,000 British and Australian soldiers with no known grave.

Attempts to carve up Turkey after the First World War left Greece in control of Turkish Thrace, until Turkish sovereignty was reconfirmed by the Treaty of Lausanne in 1923. Both before and since then, the region has experienced massive immigration, right up to 1989 when thousands of Turkish Bulgarians fled their own country, which was in upheaval, to seek refuge in Turkey.

There are some modern Turkish place names whose ancient equivalents might sound more familiar to you, so it's worth knowing that Canakkale Bogazi, the Dardanelles and the Hellespont are one and the same; Gelibolu is Gallipoli; and Truva is Troy.

Geography

The Marmara region covers the north-western corner of Turkey: the part surrounding Istanbul and the Sea of Marmara. It borders on Greece and Bulgaria to the north-west, the Black Sea to the north, the Aegean Sea to the west, and melts into the rest of Anatolia to the south and east. Thrace, or Trakya, is the name given to Marmara's European sector, which is situated north-west of the Sea of Marmara and comprises only three per cent of the total Turkish land mass. Thrace is made up of three provinces: Edirne; Kirklareli, and Tekirdag. Across in Asia, the rest of Marmara belongs to the provinces which flank the sea: Kocaeli in the north; then Bursa; Baliksehir, and Canakkale. By far the largest city in the region is Bursa, with a population of 1.6 million.

Thrace is a land of sunflowers, melon fields, vineyards and gentle hills, with pine woods on the Gelibolu Peninsula. The rest of the region is south-east of the Sea of Marmara, whose shore is made up of sandy beaches backed by lakes, forests and the odd mountain including, further inland, the 2543-metre-high Mount Uludag. Further south and west, near Troy, the countryside is reasonably flat and mainly agricultural, with low scrubby bushes and trees punctuating the fields. Close to the Aegean coast, around the Gulf of Edremit, the land becomes wooded and rich in olive groves. Traditionally agriculture has been the most important activity in the area, but in some spots, such as Eceabat near the Gallipoli memorials, tourism is taking over – though not too heavy-handedly as yet.

Several islands, known for their marble quarries, cluster just off the Erdek peninsula on the southern shore of the Sea of Marmara, while inland from here is Manyas Golu lake (sometimes called Kus Golu), home to the Kuscenneti bird sanctuary (literally translated: 'Bird Paradise'). This is a miniature National Park, set aside for the preservation of many of its 200 species of birds. There is a little museum and a viewing tower, from which you can see (at a distance) herons, cormorants, spoonbills and even the uncommon Dalmatian pelicans. White storks breed in the neighbouring village of Eskisigirci. The best time of year to see the birds is between March and October, particularly in spring and early summer when the breeding's going on. A little further east, the Kocabas delta forms a marshy area of flooded woodland which will also appeal to bird-watchers.

The other important place for flora and fauna is Uludag (literally: 'Great Mountain'), which is very close to Bursa. Pine-clad at the bottom, this soon gives way to beech woods, then, at around 1000 metres, alpine meadows where you'll find violets, grape hyacinths and pink primrose in springtime. Further up are fir forest and colourful crocuses. Birds you might see include the lammergeier, the golden eagle and Kruper's nuthatch, but they're more common above the tree line, around the ski resort.

Sadly, parts of the Sea of Marmara suffer from bad pollution: this is particularly true around the Gulf of Izmit, where industrial pollution is becoming a serious problem.

Climate

The climate of Thrace and Marmara varies greatly depending on which part you're in. Inland Thrace has cold and snowy winters with hot summer days but cool summer evenings, so that at Edirne the average temperature ranges from 2°C in January to 24°C in July and August. The climate at Bursa is typical of the Marmara region, with mild winters and hot, sunny summers, when temperatures are regularly as high as 28°C or 30°C. At the Uludag ski resort, however, snow can last well into early summer, though winter sports are only practicable from December to April. Meanwhile, at Canakkale, where the Dardanelles feed into the northern Aegean, winters are usually cold and rainy, with prevailing north-easterly and north-westerly winds, and summers, once again, hot. This time the temperature range is from 5°C in January to 25°C in July. The water temperature here is 24°C in August. The swimming season for the Sea of Marmara and the northern Aegean lasts from June to September, though hardy people may find the temperature acceptable from May through to November.

Attractions

Lacking in outstanding natural beauty, except perhaps on the southern shore of the Sea of Marmara, visitors are drawn to this region mainly by its historical attractions. Troy and Gallipoli are probably the most famous of these, though don't expect too much of Troy: unless you're a knowledgeable archaeologist, the legends associated with it are likely to prove more impressive than the reality. The Gallipoli peninsula has been designated a National Park of Remembrance. It can be a bleak and windswept place, but there's no denying the atmosphere: the extreme youth of the soldiers whose gravestones line the cemeteries is particularly shocking. Most tours of Gallipoli start from across the Dardanelles at Canakkale.

Some mythical events are brought to life annually through festivals: there's the Hero and Leander Festival and the Mount Ida Beauty Contest. These may sound trite, but they're arranged by and put on for local people, not simply as a tourist gimmick.

The two cities of most interest are Edirne and Bursa. Edirne's Selimiye Mosque, which has soaring minarets, a thousand windows and spectacular ceramic decoration, has been described as Sinan's 'crowning glory'. Bursa's Green Mosque complex and its therapeutic thermal baths are also impressive, while the nearby Mount Uludag offers pleasant walks and (in winter) Turkey's best skiing possibilities. Ski facilities are adequate, but no more, and it's worth taking any claims that Uludag is the 'St Moritz of Asia Minor' with a pinch of salt!

The natioinal parks at Uludag and Kuscenneti offer a focus for outdoor activity, as do the trekking possibilities of the Marmara Islands and many areas just inland from the Sea of Marmara and the Aegean coasts. Other islands, Gokceada and Bozcaada, in the Gulf of Saroz, are popular with Turkish holidaymakers, along with all the Sea of Marmara resorts and those in the northern Aegean, such as Ayvalik just south of the Gulf of Edremit.

The region is also known for its vivid ceramic tiles, still produced at Iznik; its exquisite Hereke carpets; the Trakya and Marmara Island wines; and the earthenware pots, scented soaps, straw baskets and embroidery made in the Edirne area. Other traditions you might come across are the shadow puppets of Bursa; the Sword and Shield Dance which is still a part of local culture; and the annual grease-wrestling of Edirne.

Cuisine

The Bursa area is best known for its Bursa or *Iskender* kebab, a doner kebab served on *pide* bread with a savoury tomato sauce and melted butter. Another local speciality is the *Inegol koftesi*, a grilled lamb rissole, created in the nearby town of Inegol. Bursa is also famous for its fruit, particularly peaches, and its candied chestnuts.

Over in Thrace, the Edirne area specialises in fruit too, this time water-melons, along with white feta cheese, marzipan, *helva*, and a local grape drink. The grapes also find their way into some very drinkable wines. The best Trakya wines can be found between Sarkoy and Tekirdag, on the northern shore of the Sea of Marmara, where a Festival of Wine is held each year. In addition, the Marmara Islands are known for their wines, and the whites of the northern Aegean go well with seafood.

In coastal areas, around the Sea of Marmara and, to an even greater extent, along the Aegean, fresh fish and seafood are served, both as a *meze* and a main course. The island of Alibey, just offshore from the resort of Ayvalik, has a wealth of highly-regarded fish restaurants.

One more thing: whenever you encounter sunflower oil or olives in Turkey, you can be fairly certain they came from the Marmara region. Sunflowers are ubiquitous (the symbol of Thrace is a sunflower), while the Gulf of Edremit is known as the 'Olive Riviera'.

Level of Tourism

Although the statistics show that there were over 3.5 million foreign visitors to the Marmara region in 1989, the vast majority of these would not have ventured outside Istanbul. Nonetheless, Edirne is a major Turkish entry point for those travelling overland from Europe, and 23.5 per cent of all foreign visitors to Turkey arrive at this point. It's also a popular stop-off town for many lorry-drivers travelling between Turkey and Europe, so you may find the budget hotels booked up.

Most of Bursa's foreign visitors choose to stay in four-star hotels, while most of those in Canakkale stay in two-star establishments, though this is probably more by necessity than design. The three Marmara provinces which receive most tourists are, understandably, Bursa, Canakkale and Edirne. In each case, the vast majority of tourists base themselves in the provincial capitals, though Uludag, Gelibolu and Kesan also receive some visitors.

You can hardly talk of 'honeypot' sites in connection with the Marmara region, and the provincial capitals are the only places where you're likely to meet more than a handful of foreign visitors, even at the height of the season. You will, however, meet large numbers of Turkish holidaymakers. They tend to head for the coastal resorts and the islands, usually being more interested in relaxing on the beach than in historic monuments. So this is a remarkably easy area in which to 'get away from it all'. Outside July and August the number of international tourists will be minimal; and the Turks themselves often holiday in May. So come at any other time of year and you certainly won't be complaining of overcrowding. The only thing which might bother you is a lack of top-class accommodation: just about the only city with anything above a three-star hotel is Bursa. However, if you're happy with simple accommodation, Marmara will suit you fine.

One negative development of recent years is caused by the growing desire of Istanbul inhabitants to have weekend or holiday homes on the Sea of Marmara, or even as far away as the Aegean coast. Many villa complexes are still in the process of being built and, in some parts, they form a virtually continuous concrete eyesore, blocking all views of the sea itself from the road. The European shore of the Sea of Marmara, just as you're leaving Istanbul, is a particularly afflicted stretch, and congestion on the roads is at its worst during the summer and at religious festivals, when many Istanbulites jump in the car and head for the coast. But there are plenty of areas where development hasn't taken over, though these are mostly inland.

There are only a few spots where tourism is actually taking over from agriculture as the main activity, and any tourism-related changes occurring in Marmara are a result of increased domestic tourism more than anything else. Apart from Turkish bucket-and-spade holidaymakers, there are a few 'special interest' groups of visitors who make journeys to the region. War veterans obviously tend to make a beeline for Gallipoli, as do many Australian and New Zealand tourists whose countrymen died there. Troy always used to be the preserve of keen archaeologists alone, but the last two decades have seen a great increase in general interest travellers who make a stop here. This is partly thanks to Canakkale's former tourism director, Ilhan Aksit. In 1971, he decided Troy needed a 'picture postcard' style image, with which people could identify and which could serve to draw visitors to the site. He came up with a replica of the wooden horse, which is now the most photographed part of the complex (it's certainly more photogenic than the various sets of walls!), and has proved a successful marketing strategy. Another boost to visitor numbers to Troy was recently given by the creation of an information room and panels in 1990, to coincide with the hundredth anniversary of Heinrich Schliemann's death. Schliemann was the German-American who excavated Troy in the last century, but attitudes towards him are ambivalent, with many Turks of the opinion that he plundered the site, spiriting away some of its finest treasures, including the 'Treasure of

Priam' jewellery, taken to Berlin without Turkish permission and then lost in the course of the Second World War. So don't go singing his praises too vigorously!

Good Alternatives

Meeting People

Visiting a place during its local festival is always a good way to meet Turkish people on an equal footing. And Marmara certainly has its fair share of interesting annual celebrations. The most famous is perhaps the week-long Kirkpinar Greased Wrestling Festival near Edirne in June or July. This dates back to the middle ages and involves olive oil-smothered contestants trying to pin each other's back to the ground in an effort to become the overall champion. It's very popular so you should try to purchase tickets in advance through the Edirne Tourist Office, Talat Pasa Asfalti 76/A (Tel. (181) 15260). There's also a 1915 Sea Victory Celebration at Canakkale in March; a Cherry and Culture Festival at Tekirdag in late May or early June; and an International Culture and Art Festival, known as the Bursa Fair, at Bursa in July. August brings the Troy Festival at Canakkale, as well as the Mount Ida Beauty Contest, and some colourful local fairs on Gokceada Island.

One good initiative which you might be able to visit is the DOBAG carpet-weaving project. In many villages of the Canakkale and Manisa (see **The Aegean** chapter) provinces, hundreds of women continue the age-old tradition of carpet weaving, thereby contributing to their family's income. A regional centre, run by a Fine Arts faculty member at Marmara University, has been set up at Ayvacik as part of the **DOBAG Project**, which aims to promote traditional patterns and natural dyeing methods. Carpets are produced by the Suleymankoy Regional Villages Development Cooperative, which has 340 members in thirty-two villages in the Ayvacik area. The cooperative earned nearly 1.5 billion Turkish lira in 1989. Not only does this improve the village economies, it also encourages others to make their rugs and carpets in this traditional way, so ensuring the survival of the artistic heritage for another generation.

If you want to stay at a Turkish guest-house at Canakkale or Ayvalik, you can make a reservation through either of the town tourist offices or through the central organisation, **Turistik Ev Pansiyonculugunu Gelistirme Dernegi**, Cumhuriyet Bulv. 84/803, Izmir (Tel. (51) 257273 or 214295). The other main way to meet Turkish people is by heading for some of the places described below, which are popular with Turkish rather than foreign holidaymakers.

Discovering Places

In addition to the better-known historical parts of the Marmara region, there are various lesser-known corners, which are particularly suitable for trekking or other outdoor pursuits. The largest island in the Sea of Marmara, known as Marmara Island, is home to some interesting Roman marble quarries and offers good trekking possibilities. For some useful tips about these, ask Mr Deniz of the island's Deniz Otel (Tel. (1984) 5032) or Mr Feridun of the Feriduniun Yeri Restaurant at Saraylar village (Tel. (1984) 5427).

The nearby Kapidag peninsula, where the village of Erdek is situated, is rapidly becoming a popular Turkish holiday area, though it seems as yet undiscovered by other nationalities. Mount Ida, whose Turkish name is Kaz Dagi, and the Assos area near Behramkale (both on the Biga peninsula) are good for trekking, as is Mount Uludag, where there are even a few marked trails. The islands of Gokceada and Bozcaada in the very north of the Aegean offer good sandy beaches, wine cellars and olive groves. Foreigners are generally put off going to the islands (which can be reached by ferry from Canakkale) because an application must be made through the Passport Police before a visit, since both islands are still officially military zones. The paperwork should, however, be reasonably uncomplicated and free of charge, and acts as a useful deterrent, keeping the beaches clear of all but the keenest foreign tourists! If you fancy a slightly more straightforward swim, try the Saroz gulf, north of the Gelibolu peninsula.

Turkey's first official bicycle route is along the backroads between Truva (Troy) and Kucukkuyu on the south of the Biga peninsula (i.e. the northern shore of the Edremit Gulf), offering a novel way to explore this attractive and historic area. Those who want to visit the Gallipoli sites under the auspices of an official tour could try Canakkale-based **Anatur** (Cumhuriyet Meydani Ozay Is Hani, Kat 3 No 3 (Tel. (196) 15482)), which specialises in tours of the Anzac (Australia and New Zealand Army Corp) battlefields, but also does trips to the British and French memorials and to Troy, by arrangement.

Communications

How to Get There

Most parts of the Marmara region are best reached via Istanbul, which lies at its centre and is the communications hub. A **flight** to Istanbul airport, followed by a **bus** connection to, say, Canakkale, Bursa or Edirne is probably the most frequent and efficient combination, though there are various other possibilities. If you're starting your holiday in the Ayvalik/Edremit area (northern Aegean), it would make more sense to fly to Izmir, then get a connecting bus.

Destinations on the Sea of Marmara can often be reached from Istanbul by **ferry** alone; this is the case for Canakkale, Gelibolu, Bandirma, Mudanya, the Marmara Islands, Tekirdag and Yalova, though you should enquire about the timetable in advance. If you're arriving from continental Europe by **train** and wish to explore the Thrace region, you should descend at Edirne, rather than continuing to Istanbul and having to backtrack.

When You're There

Air – internal flights are reasonably priced by British standards, though they can't compete with the Turkish coach service. They're worth the investment if you're in a hurry though, as they allow you to get from Istanbul to Bursa in just over half an hour, and to Izmir in just under an hour.

Rail – the rail network is, as usual, more limited and slower than the bus network, but you may find it of some use. Rail lines from Europe enter Turkey at Kapikule and Ispala, passing through various Thracian towns before arriving at Istanbul, and then continuing to Izmit before veering off southward to Eskisehir, eventually splitting into the Ankara and Konya lines. There's another stretch of railway between Bandirma and Balikesir, which continues south down to Manisa and Izmir; destinations between Balikesir and Kutahya (further east) are also covered. To give an idea of journey times, the trip from Istanbul to Gebze (on the north coast of the Sea of Marmara) only takes half an hour as it's on the Istanbul suburban (*banliyo*) line, but the trip to Edirne takes 5½ hours (1½ more than by bus).

Bus – to travel along the shore of the Sea of Marmara, you'll have to take the bus (or car). Apart from five major 'E' roads (the E5 between Edirne, Istanbul and Izmit; the E25 from Istanbul to

Ipsala; the E24 from Edirne, through Kesan to Canakkale, Aycavik, Edremit and Ayvalik; and the E90 from Canakkale through Bandirma to Bursa and Eskisehir), most roads are relatively minor. The main hub of the extensive bus network is obviously Istanbul, though there are a good number of services from Canakkale too. A bus journey from the north-east of the region (Istanbul) to the south-west (Ayvalik) takes around 9 hours; while it takes 8 hours from Istanbul to Balikesir; 6 hours to Bandirma; 5½ hours to Canakkale; 4½ hours to Bursa; and 4 hours to Edirne. From Canakkale it takes 6 hours to Bursa; 4½ hours to Edirne; 3½ hours to Ayvalik; and 1½ hours to Ayvacik.

Boat – destinations on the Sea of Marmara are often best reached by ferry if you're coming from Istanbul. The trip to Yalova takes 2 hours; Mudanya takes 3 hours; and Bandirma takes 4¼ hours. A faster sea-bus service serves Yalova and the Marmara Islands (information from Istanbul Central Sea Bus Office, Tel. 362 00 44). The main crossing points of the Dardanelles are between Gelibolu and Lapseki, and between Eceabat and Canakkale: crossings take 20 minutes. Ferries to Gokceada Island run from Canakkale and Kabatepe; those to Bozcaada run from Odunluk Iskelesi. Ayvalik is the starting point for boats to nearby Alibey Island as well as to the Greek island of Lesbos, known in Turkish as Midilli. The crossing to Lesbos takes two hours and you are normally limited to a rather pricey day-trip.

Other Options – for trekking possibilities and details of Turkey's first official cycle route, see **Discovering Places**. One other useful transport option is the precarious-looking cable car (*teleferik*) which will take you from Bursa 1600 metres up Mount Uludag.

Useful Local Contacts

For information about hotels and other tourism initiatives in the southern Marmara region, contact the Southern Marmara Touristic Enterprise and Hoteliers Association (**GUMTOB**), Unlu Caddesi, Camlibel Ishani Kat 2, Bursa (Tel. (24) 217406 or 181136). The **Turkish Touring and Automobile Association** (TTOK) has offices at the Greek border post (Ipsala, Tel. (1846) 1574), and at the two Bulgarian border posts (Kapikule, Tel. (1818) 1034 or 1327; and Derekoy, Tel. (187) 11431 or 11412).

Geographical Breakdown of Region

Edirne

This former capital of the Ottoman empire, which was also one of the seven largest cities in Europe at the beginning of the last century, has certainly come down in the world since its heyday. Nowadays Edirne is simply the best-known of Thrace's three provincial capitals. The city does nonetheless warrant a visit, especially if this is your first taste of Turkey: it serves as a very effective appetizer.

The most important attraction in Edirne is the **Selimiye Mosque**, situated on a hill at the northern end of Talat Pasa Caddesi and accessible from Mimar Sinan Caddesi or through the Dilaver Bey Park. It is acknowledged by many as the masterpiece of the famous Turkish architect Mimar Sinan. Sinan designed this Ottoman-style mosque in 1569 when he was eighty years old and, apparently, at his peak. Its courtyard has become commercialised, but the building itself is still very impressive. It has four elegant 71-metre-high minarets, each with three galleries, and a vast dome which contributes to a sense of lightness and space. The lightness is also due to the 999 windows which line the walls. Look out for the calligraphy and paintings on the ceiling, the sixteenth-century Iznik tiles which decorate the prayer niche (*mihrab*), and the exquisitely carved marble pulpit (*mimber*).

In the immediate vicinity of the mosque are two museums. The **Archaeological and Ethnographical Museum** is housed in a modern building and displays various archaeological remains from the region, along with some examples of local crafts, including carpets (closed on Mondays). The **Turkish Islamic Art Museum** is another provincially-orientated art and craft gallery (closed Monday afternoons), this time housed in a *medrese* which used to belong to the mosque.

Most of Edirne's other interesting buildings are even older than the Selimiye Mosque. Ten minutes' walk further out of town, still on Mimar Sinan Caddesi, is the **Muradiye Mosque**. There are good views of the surrounding countryside and river Tunca from here, while the mosque's interior boasts some of the most impressive Ottoman tile-work you'll ever see. Back in the town centre, clustered around the main square, Hurriyet Meydani, are further historic buildings. Down the hill from the Selimiye, on Talat Pasa Caddesi, is the oldest building of all, the eight-domed

Eski Mosque, which was constructed of cut stone and brick between 1403 and 1414, and is famous for the enormous calligraphic inscriptions which decorate it. Next to this is the **Bedesten**, an attractively vaulted covered market built shortly after the mosque. Across the square from here, you'll see the **Uc Serefli Mosque**, completed in 1447 by Murat I. Its tall north-west minaret, its courtyard and its low wide dome represent a radical experimentation for Ottoman architecture of the time – made possible by advances in engineering, and perfected by Sinan and others during the following century.

On the corner of Talat Pasa and Saraclar Caddesi is the **Ali Pasa Carsisi**, an extensive covered bazaar built around 1568 by the ubiquitous Sinan (who also, incidentally, built five of Edirne's Turkish bath complexes). West of here, the **Kaleici district** (meaning 'inside the fortress') is the official 'Old Town'. It's built on a grid system dating back to the middle ages and is a pleasant place to wander for a taste of everyday Turkish life.

It's also worth venturing to the outskirts of Edirne to admire the various impressive bridges that span the rivers. To the south is the **Yeni Kopru**, which crosses the Tunca and Meric rivers in one. Far older is the thirteenth-century **Gazi Mihal Kopru** over the Tunca to the west. Further north, the **Beyazit Kopru** will take you to the **Beyazit Complex**. Built by the architect Hayrettin in the late fifteenth century, this is the largest-ever Ottoman complex of religious and charitable buildings. It includes a mosque, *medrese*, kitchen, storehouse, medical school and hospital. The latter, known as a *darussifa*, is hexagonal and considered the highlight of the complex. Nowadays Beyazit is home to some of the students from Thrace University. Still further along, the river splits to form **Sarayici**, an island on which a royal palace, the now-ruined **Eski Saray**, once stood. The palace was destroyed in 1877 to save its arsenal falling into Russian hands, but this is where the stadium used for the **Kirkpinar Wrestling** is situated.

Accommodation

If you're looking for accommodation at the budget end of the market, you may find you're sharing it with assorted long-distance lorry drivers. Maarif Caddesi and Saraclar Caddesi are the best-endowed hotel areas.

First Class

Rustempasa Kervansaray Oteli, Sabuni Mah. Iki, Kapali Han Caddesi

57 (just off Talat Pasa Caddesi, near Eski Mosque) (Tel. (181) 12195). A *kervansaray* designed by Mimar Sinan and built in 1516, recently converted into Edirne's only top-range hotel.

Middle Range

Park Oteli, Maarif Caddesi 7 (Tel. (181) 14610). 61 rooms in central but fairly quiet, shabby-looking hotel.

Kervan Oteli, Kadirhane Sokak 134, Talat Pasa Caddesi (Tel. (181) 11382 or 11355). 50 rooms in an even more central, and less quiet, hotel which has been the city's 'standard' middle range option for years.

Economy

Aksarayli Pansiyon, Alipasa Ortakapi Caddesi 8, just off Maarif Caddesi (Tel. (181) 26035 or 13901). Clean rooms in attractively restored Ottoman house.

Saray Oteli, Eski Istanbul Caddesi 28 (Tel. (181) 21457). Quiet, clean, central hotel.

Fi-Fi Moteli, Demirkapi Mevkii, E5-Karayolu (Tel. (181) 11554 or 11544). 10 rooms in hotel attached to camp-site, several kilometres out of town on the Istanbul road.

Another **camp-site** is the Kervansaray Aysekadin Mocamp, Aysekadin, Istanbul Caddesi (Tel. (181) 11290).

Eating Out

Fried liver and almond dessert are Edirne's specialities. These, along with the usual kebab and rissole offerings, are served in the numerous cheap *koftecisi* and *lokantasi* on and around Saraclar Caddesi. For more upmarket dining, try the restaurant attached to the **Kervan Oteli**, or the **Deniz Restoran** at the Ali Pasa Carsisi gates. Alternatively you could head out of town towards the Yeni Bridge, where there are a number of riverside restaurants.

Entertainments

For entertainment you'll have to make do with visits to the town's bazaars (the Ali Pasa Carsisi is the biggest), or to one of its beautiful Sinan-designed Turkish baths. Try the Sokullu Pasa Hamami on Hukumet Caddesi, which dates from the late 1500s. In June or early July (depending on Ramadan), the town will be packed with people who have come to see the Kirkpinar Greased Wrestling Championships

(*Yagli Gures*), which take place at Sarayici, near the Eski Saray. Here burly men from all over Turkey smother themselves in olive oil before indulging in slippery struggles which end when one of the wrestlers has his back pinned to the grass of the stadium floor by his opponent. After numerous such bouts, an overall winner emerges. The atmosphere's exciting as betting is rife, and there are various other events such as a funfair and folk-dancing exhibitions going on at the same time.

Useful Addresses

Tourist Office: Talat Pasa Caddesi 76/A (Tel. (181) 15260); branch at Hurriyet Meydani 17 (Tel. (181) 11518). **Post Office**: Saraclar Caddesi 17. **Hospital**: just off Talat Pasa Asfalti (near Bulgarian Consulate). **Tourism Police**: Emniyet Mudurlugu (Tel. (181) 15240 or 15241 or 15242). **Greek Consulate**: Dogan Sokak 8. **Bulgarian Consulate**: Talat Pasa Caddesi 31.

Transport Options

The only public transport you're likely to need in Edirne is the *dolmus* or bus to get you into town in the first place if you're arriving by train or coach. The coach will drop you at the Otogar a couple of kilometres out of town on the Istanbul road. City buses and *dolmus* regularly run into the centre of town from here, and from the train station which is slightly further out on the same road. A second train station is located at Kapikule, the border crossing point for Bulgaria; once again, a *dolmus* will bring you to the town centre.

Rest of Thrace

Edirne, Kirklareli and Tekirdag Provinces

It must be admitted that the rest of Thrace is fairly barren when it comes to tourist attractions. The scenery – sunflowers and melon fields – is pleasant enough, but not really enough to base a holiday on. If you're interested in a simple beach holiday where you're unlikely to encounter another westerner, head for **Ibrice** or **Erikli** on the Gulf of Saroz. This most northerly part of the Aegean is attractive, sheltered for swimming, and has some inexpensive guest-house accommodation.

If you're considering staying on the northern shore of the Sea of Marmara, you'll be disappointed at all the hideous building that's going on. About the only resort with some character left (thanks to the fact that it's been a Turkish domestic holiday resort since 'way back' in the 1960s) is **Sarkoy**. It's still immensely popular with Istanbulites though, so if you want peace and quiet, time your visit outside the summer months.

Two more Thracian towns are worth a stop if you happen to be passing near them. **Uzunkopru**, a Turkish-Greek border town about sixty kilometres south of Edirne, is home to an impressive 174-arch Ottoman aqueduct, built by Murat II in 1444 and stretching 1354 metres over the Ergene river. Around eighty kilometres east of Edirne (on the E5 road to Istanbul) is **Luleburgaz**. The major attraction here is the Sokullu Mehmet Pasa Kulliyesi, a complex built between 1549 and 1569, composed of a mosque with a single minaret, a *medrese* still used as a Koranic school, and a covered bazaar.

Accommodation

Middle Range

Hongurlar Oteli, Istanbul Caddesi 73, Luleburgaz (Tel. (183) 14500). 60 rooms in one of the better hotels in the area.

Economy

Ergene Oteli, Cumhuriyet Meydani, Uzunkopru (Tel. (189) 35438). 40 rooms in nondescript but central hotel.

Erikli Oberj, Saroz Korfezi, Erikli, Kesan (Tel. (184) 11048). 21 rooms in family-run hotel near sea (Gulf of Saroz).

Cennet Motel, Sarkoy (Tel. (1868) 1057). Reasonably quiet beach-front hotel.

Eastern Marmara

Kocaeli Province

Once again, this is not the most rewarding province to holiday in, but it has the advantage that everywhere you might want to visit is within day-trip distance of Istanbul and (usually) Bursa.

Istanbul's nearest beach resort is the Black Sea town of **Sile**, a pleasant cliff-top community with the classic ingredients of a sandy bay, island and lighthouse. At weekends it's crowded to bursting point, but is usually pretty quiet at other times. For a less commercialised resort, head further along the Black Sea coast to the village of Agva. Directly opposite Sile, on the northern shore of the Sea of Marmara where it turns into the Gulf of Izmit, are **Gebze**, burial place of Hannibal, and the long-standing carpet-making area of **Hereke**. Ferries ply the highly polluted Gulf of Izmit from both these towns to their opposite numbers, **Topcular** and **Karamursel**. It's worth taking one of these boats in order to avoid the industrial provincial capital, **Izmit**, situated at the eastern end of its own Gulf.

Alternatively you could miss out on this rather unpleasant area altogether by taking a hydrofoil or ferry direct from Istanbul (Kartal) to **Yalova**. Yalova is well-known as a spa town, though it is in fact **Termal**, several kilometres inland, where you'll find the hot sulphur springs and genteel trappings associated with such places. Swimming is just about possible at **Armutlu**, on the end of the peninsula which separates the Gulfs of Izmit and Gemlik, but if you're concerned about having pristine clean water, wait till you're further west.

Accommodation

Middle Range

Club Atabay Oteli, Eskihisar, Gebze (Tel. (1991) 2611). 18 rooms and 5 suites in well-equipped hotel.

Sirin Kaptan Moteli, Kayacik Mah./Kavak Mev., Karamursel (Tel. (2181) 2473). 20 comfortable rooms.

Kumbaba Oberj, Sile (Tel. (1992) 1038). Comfortable hotel, just outside town.

Economy

For **Economy** options, try the sea-front **Ruya Moteli**, Sile (Tel. (1992) 1070); the 11-room **Ulke Oteli**, Yali Caddesi 19, at Yalova (Tel. (1938) 1680); or the **Nilgun Pansiyon**, Kuskonmaz Sokak 7, at Cinarcik (near Yalova) (Tel. (193) 51929).

Bursa

Capital of the province with the same name and first capital of the Ottoman empire, Bursa boasts a wealth of Ottoman architecture and is unusually green for a Turkish city. Its parks and gardens are partly due to the springs of its attached spa colony, Cekirge, and also to its attractive situation on the lower slopes of Mount Uludag.

Probably the best method of seeing the sights in Bursa is to work your way from east to west. The north-easternmost sight of interest is the **Yildirim Beyazit Mosque**, an early example of new Ottoman style, dating from 1391 and often seen as the model for the more famous Yesil Mosque. A long walk uphill, through a quarter of old houses, is the **Emir Sultan Mosque**, which is popular with Bursan worshippers but otherwise unremarkable. Following Yesil Caddesi westwards, you will come to Bursa's most famous cluster of attractions, and possibly the best examples of early Ottoman architecture anywhere: the **Yesil Turbe**, **Yesil Cami** and **Yesil Medrese**. The octagonal Yesil Turbe (Green Mausoleum) is covered in beautiful blue tiles, both outside and in, though the interior ones are the originals and of superior quality. The Yesil Cami (Green Mosque) was designed by the same architect, Haci Ivaz, and, though it was not quite finished when work on it stopped in 1424 and suffered earthquake damage in 1855, it is a magnificent building, described by André Gide as 'a symbol of balance, peace and clarity'. The nearby Seljuk-style *medrese* now houses the **Ethnographic Museum**, where many local crafts, including some Karagoz shadow puppets, are on display (closed Mondays).

Following the same road will take you across the narrow **Gok Dere** river, from where it's straight on to Cumhuriyet Alani, a square known by most people as **Heykel** (meaning 'statue') because of the equestrian statue of Ataturk to be found there. If you walk, ever westwards, along Ataturk Caddesi, you'll pass **Koza Parki** on your left. This pleasant garden of flowers, fountains and cafés is flanked by the ancient (1336–1413) **Orhan Gazi Mosque**, and the **Koza Han**, a former caravanserai, now part of the covered bazaar. This Han was the silk cocoon market in the days when Bursa was a leading silk centre. The silk trade is undergoing a mild revival and the Koza Han is still the place to go to purchase Bursan silk. The high points of the year are June and September, when villagers come here to sell their precious cocoons. **Emir Han** and the main **Bedesten** are also atmospheric bazaar areas, as is the picturesque **Demirciler Carsisi**, a mass of ironmongers' and blacksmiths' stands on the far side of Inonu Caddesi. In the past, if you took a picture of one of the smiths at work, promising to send him a copy was enough to ensure his cooperation, but nowadays it's more acceptable to leave him a small tip. Back near the main bazaar is the **Ulu Cami** (Great Mosque). This is built entirely in the Seljuk style of the 1390s and its roof comprises twenty domes. There is an ablutions fountain within the mosque itself, which is also impressive for its calligraphy and carved walnut pulpit.

Another old part of Bursa is the area around the **Hisar** (Fortress). On top of the ramparts a park overlooks the valley and contains not only the requisite tea-gardens, but also the **Mausoleums** of Osman, founder of the Ottoman empire, and Orhan Gazi, his son. Near the Tophane cafés is **Ressamlar Sokak** (Artists' Street), where local artists can be seen at work in a somewhat artificial environment. North-west of Bursa's second little waterway, the **Cilimboz Deresi**, is the Muradiye district. The highlight of this is the **Muradiye Kulliyesi** complex, which contains the 1426 **Mosque of Sultan Murat II** and ten very varied but mostly beautifully decorated **royal tombs**. The surrounding area, which comes to life on Tuesdays (market day), is one of lovely Ottoman houses. A restored seventeenth-century mansion, known as the **Ottoman House Museum**, is open to the public (closed Mondays) to give an idea of a wealthy Ottoman's lifestyle.

To the right of the major road, Cekirge Caddesi, is the vast **Kultur Parki**, in which can be found an **Archaeological Museum** and **Open-Air Theatre**. On the other side of Cekirge Caddesi is an **Ataturk Museum**, but you'll probably prefer to give that a miss and hop in a *dolmus* along to the spa suburb of Cekirge.

Most of the upmarket hotels are located in **Cekirge**, which is known for its warm mineral-rich springs. As you might expect, many of the hotels have their own thermal baths, but there are also a number of first-class public **hamami**. The oldest and most impressive architecturally, Eski Kaplica, were built on the site of the Roman baths. Others which can be recommended are the Yeni Kaplica (closest to Bursa) and the Karamustafa Pasa baths (reputed to have the best waters). Look out also for the **monument** to the jester Karagoz, and the **Mosque and Mausoleum of Murat I**.

Accommodation

Bursa's main hotel district is Cekirge, particularly along Cekirge Caddesi and 1. Murat Caddesi, though you should be able to find more central accommodation if you'd prefer.

First Class

Celik Palas, Cekirge Caddesi 79 (Tel. (24) 353500). 173 rooms in Bursa's best hotel, with old-fashioned (1930s) atmosphere, its own luxurious mineral baths, and a peaceful garden.

Anatolia Oteli, Cekirge Meydani (Tel. (24) 367110). 93 rooms in a four-star hotel, also with its own baths. Under the same management as the Konak Oteli in Istanbul.

Middle Range

Dikmen Oteli, Maksem Caddesi 78 (Tel. (24) 214995). 50 rooms in friendly hotel, just to the south of town centre.

Yat Oteli, Hamamlar Caddesi 31, Cekirge (Tel. (24) 363112). 42 rooms in rather bland Cekirge hotel with Turkish bath.

Economy

Adapalas Oteli, 1. Murat Caddesi 21, Cekirge (Tel. (24) 361600). 39 rooms and a thermal bath in attractive hotel with a typical health-spa appearance.

Ugur Oteli, Tahtakale Caddesi 27 (Tel. (24) 211989). Friendly, central hotel with old-fashioned Turkish courtyard.

Bilgic Oteli, Ressam Sefik Bursali (also Basak) Caddesi 30 (Tel. (24) 203190). Extremely comfortable, central hotel, recently refurbished.

Eating Out

The places to go for top-range meals are the restaurants of the best Cekirge hotels, but it would be a shame to come to Bursa without sampling the atmosphere of some of its simpler kebab or rissole restaurants.

Middle Range

Papagan Restoran, 1. Murat Caddesi 15, Cekirge. Reliable restaurant with views over river valley.

Ozkent, Kultur Parki. An open-air restaurant in Bursa's biggest park.

Canli Balik, Yeni Balik Pazari. One of Bursa's few fish restaurants, down by the fish market.

Economy

The classic recommendation, where the local speciality, Iskender kebab, is said to have originated is **Kebapci Iskenderoglu** on Ataturk Caddesi 60, with another well-known favourite being **Haci Bey** on Unlu Caddesi. Unfortunately both these have become over-commercialised, so a better option might be **Gumus Kebapci** on Gumusceken Caddesi, which is popular with local people, or the more elegant **Cicek Izgara** on Belediye Caddesi 5.

Entertainments

Those looking for a lively time in Turkish towns must be prepared to consider forms of entertainment other than the cinemas, bars and discos which western culture tries to persuade us are among the only valid ways to amuse ourselves. Even a city the size of Bursa has little 'entertainment' to offer in the conventional sense; but there's a wealth of other sources of inspiration. Bursa's Cekirge district is uniquely placed to give you the most refreshing Turkish baths in magnificent surroundings (see above for the names of recommended baths). Entrance charges can start at around £1.50, rising to up to £6 for a bath plus full massage, depending on the establishment; most baths are open until at least 10 p.m. Bear in mind that Fridays are usually very busy.

Otherwise, simply sitting at one of the town's numerous open-air cafés watching the world go by is as much entertainment as many people need. Head for the parks – Koza Parki, Tophane Parki (great views) or Kultur Parki – for the pick of the cafés. Near Tophane, you could wander down the artists' street (Ressamlar Sokak) and see if there's a bargain to be picked up. Alternatively, there's the Tuesday street market in Muradiye, the fruit and vegetable market around Inebey Caddesi (near Ulu Cami), or the halls of the covered bazaar itself to explore. If you're fortunate enough to be here in June or September, climb to the upper galleries of the Koza Hani for a bird's-eye view of the hectic silk cocoon auction.

Ask the tourist office if there are any Karagoz shadow puppet shows going on. This is the Turkish equivalent of Punch and Judy and, though it's a common form of entertainment throughout Turkey, it originated in Bursa. If you'd like to buy authentic Karagoz puppets (made from painted camel leather), go to a shop called Karagoz in the Eski Aynali Carsi part of the Bedesten. Events are often advertised in the tourist office, or in shop windows around Koza Parki. In summer, concerts, plays and other performances take place at the open-air theatre in Kultur Parki, especially during the Bursa fair in July.

Useful Addresses

Tourist Office (Central): Ulu Cami, Belediye Alt Gecit Carsisi 1 (on corner of Koza Parki) (Tel. (24) 212359); summer branch at Fevzi Cakmak Caddesi, Formara Han 75 (near Otogar) (Tel. (24) 142274 or 130411); another summer branch at Cemal Nadir Caddesi, Kizilay Karsisi, Hisar Cay Bahcesi (Tel. (24) 213368). **Post Office**: on corner of Ataturk and Maksem Caddesi. **Hospital**: Devlet Hastanesi, Hasta Yurdu Caddesi, Hisar. **Tourist Police**: Fevzi Cakmak Caddesi, Kizilay Pasaji (Tel. (24) 148300).

Transport Options

The times you'll need a bus or *dolmus* are for the uphill journey into town from the Otogar (take any vehicle marked *Heykel*); for the trip out to the cable-car for Mount Uludag (city bus number 3, marked *Teleferik*); and for the trip out to Cekirge (city bus number 1). If you want to get an idea of Bursa's layout before exploring the individual sites, you could take bus number 1 from the Emir Sultan Cami in the east of town right along the 'tourist route' to Cekirge in the west. Otherwise, despite some steep streets, the best way of getting around is on foot.

Rest of Bursa Province

The most interesting way to visit **Mount Uludag**, formerly Mount Olympus of Mysia, is by cable-car. The Teleferik starting from the eastern edge of Bursa (for directions, see **Transport Options** above) takes around half an hour one way to transport you to the Sarialan terminus and picnic area. The hotel zone is six kilometres farther on and can be reached by *dolmus* if so desired, but most people (unless they're here for the skiing) will prefer simply to take in the scenery by means of a healthy walk. Alternatively, you can take the winding road from Bursa up to the ski resort, which means passing through the Karabelen National Park gate, for which you will pay a fee if you're in your own car, but might in exchange get some leaflets on the park. The fresh air and views are worth it though, even if the few official hiking trails are rather desultorily marked out. Skiers will probably be disappointed with Turkey's foremost ski resort if they're expecting anything which can compete with the Alps, but prices are comparatively low and facilities acceptable. You can ski here from December to May, but April's blissfully uncrowded, with January and February the worst months as a result of school holidays.

Gemlik Gulf, thirty kilometres from Bursa, is rather too polluted to swim in with any peace of mind, though beaches such as those at **Armutlu** (mentioned under **Kocaeli Province**) and Kumla will do at a pinch. Unless something is done about the pollution problem here, all the hastily-built waterfront hotels will have been a total waste of resources.

The most interesting town within striking distance of Bursa is **Iznik** (ancient Nicaea), eighty-five kilometres north-east, at the tip of its own **lake**. Best-known as the source of the tiles and ceramics which grace sixteenth-century palaces and mosques throughout Turkey, Iznik also has some interesting historic buildings. The town's typically Hellenistic grid layout and some of its original walls (300 BC) can still be seen. Within the walls, the main streets, Ataturk Caddesi and Kilicaslan Caddesi, form a north-south east-west cross, intersecting at a roundabout where you'll find the Aya Sofya Museum, a church-turned-mosque-turned-museum just like its namesake in Istanbul but much less impressive. Heading east you'll come to Haci Ozbek Cami to the left of Kilicaslan Caddesi. This is one of the oldest Ottoman mosques you'll see, dating from 1332. Due south from here is the similarly ancient Suleyman Pasa Medresesi, which is still used as a Koranic school. Back north of Kilicaslan Caddesi, at its eastern end (just beyond the tourist office), is the famous 1492 green-glazed Yesil Mosque, set in its own park, but not far from the 1388 Nilufer Hatun Imareti which houses the town archaeological museum. The three remaining gates in the town walls (Lefke Kapisi, Istanbul Kapisi and Yenisehir Kapisi) are worth a look if you've got time, as is the ruined Roman amphitheatre in the south-west of the town. To round things off, a lakeside stroll is pleasant, perhaps pausing at one of the fish restaurants or tea-houses you'll find here.

The nearest town to Bursa which the tourist board dares to bill as a 'seaside resort' is **Mudanya**, but this is really just a harbour for the hydrofoil and ferry to and from Istanbul. Apparently Bursans are keen on its fish restaurants and nightclubs, but perhaps they also have a taste for ugly concrete buildings! It does boast an Armistice Museum commemorating the signing of the provisional 1922 armistice here, but that's about it. Nearby **Zeytinbagi** has more to recommend it, with its traditional Turkish architecture and Byzantine church.

Inland, just off the main E90 road between Bursa and Bandirma is **Uluabat Golu**. The best base for exploring this lake is the half-timbered island village of **Golyazi**. Roman and Byzantine ruins of ancient Apollonia can be found lying around here and there, and you may find one of the village fishermen is prepared to take you out in his boat to see some of the more remote ruins. If you prefer peace and quiet, head for this lake rather than its better-known sister, Manyas Golu, over in Balikesir province.

Accommodation

In Bursa province, the only two spots you're likely to want to over-night in, apart from Bursa itself, are Uludag (for skiers and ramblers) and Iznik (for keen sightseers). Accommodation's at a premium (and therefore slightly overpriced) in both places, on top of which a number of the Uludag hotels close in summer – so it's wise to book ahead if possible.

First Class

Beceren Oberj, 1. Gelesim Bolgesi, Uludag (Tel. (2418) 1111 or 1114). 80 rooms in rambling chalet-style hotel, considered by some to be Uludag's best.

Middle Range

Ulukardesler Oberj, 1. Gelesim Bolgesi, Uludag (Tel. (2418) 1136). 32 rooms in family-run chalet-style hotel.

    Ergun Oberj, Oteller Bolgesi, Fatintepe, Uludag (Tel. (2418) 1100). 20 rooms in another overgrown chalet.

    Camlik Moteli, Iznik (on lake road), (Tel. (252) 71631). Good value lakeside hotel, with attractive rooms and restaurant.

Economy

Uludag Tur Pansiyon, Milli Park, Uludag (Tel. (2418) 1001). Basic family-run *pansiyon*.

    Babacan Oteli, Kilicaslan Caddesi 86, Iznik (Tel. (252) 71211 or 71623). The only reasonable hotel in the town centre.

    Iznik Pansiyon, Iznik (set in from lake road), (Tel. (252) 71265). Comfortable *pansiyon* near beach; cheap and cheerful, with cooking facilities.

Western Marmara – Balikesir Province

The attractive province of Balikesir sweeps round from the Erdek peninsula and Marmara Islands to the Gulf of Edremit on the northern Aegean, an area sandwiched between the Canakkale and Izmir provinces.

One possible place to stop is **Manyas Golu**, a large shallow lake, known for its bird sanctuary, **Kuscenneti**, the smallest National Park in Turkey (only half a square kilometre). Established in 1938, the sanctuary contains a small museum and a viewing tower, but the latter is a fair way from the birds themselves and too crowded at weekends to be very effective. The spoonbills and pelicans that breed here in spring and early summer are best seen if you come during the week, armed with a powerful pair of binoculars. Just as rewarding, however, is a wander along the lakefront at the neighbouring village of **Eskisigirci**.

To get to the **Kapidagi peninsula** (also known as the **Erdek** peninsula, after its main town), you'll probably have to pass through **Bandirma**, an ugly place best ignored unless you're taking a ferry to Istanbul from here. Erdek itself is a pleasant enough town, with parks and an esplanade, expanding like mad for the domestic holiday market, but as yet hardly frequented by foreigners. The promontory beside which Erdek stretches out is wooded, with a small quarry where birds nest, so it makes a good place for a walk. Erdek is also the place to catch boats to the nearby islands, though if you're just hopping over to **Pasalimani Island**, you can get a boat as easily from the village of **Narli**, a few kilometres further up the road.

Pasalimani is the least developed island (mainly because it has fewest beaches), but is quiet and green if you want to get away from it all. The next island along, **Avsa Adasi**, is the most developed, with its beautiful vineyards and beaches. The east coast beaches are less crowded, as they're further from the main town, **Turkeli**, whose only cultural 'attraction' is a neglected church, the Aya Triada. Perhaps the most rewarding island to visit is **Marmara Adasi**, the largest at about 140 square kilometres. It owes its name (and that of its main town) to the marble quarries on its northern side. Marmara town is steep and pleasant, though the island's only respectable sandy beaches are at **Cinarli** (ferries depart for Tekirdag from here). A village which rarely gets a look-in is **Sarayler**, near the quarries. Here, Mr Feridun (owner of the Feriduniun Yeri Restaurant, Tel. (1984) 5247) will be more than happy to indicate trekking possibilities both on the goat trails of the island's interior and back on the Kapidagi peninsula.

On the mainland again, **Denizkent** sports a 1950s holiday village, the first in Turkey and fixed in an eerie time warp. Inland is the spa town of **Gonen**, whose thermal springs can be enjoyed on Banyolar Caddesi. The polluted provincial capital, **Balikesir**, should be avoided unless you're planning to catch a train from here. Much more inspiring is the pleasant northern Aegean coastal resort of **Ayvalik**. The town was built in the fifteenth century, but underwent a strange metamorphosis after the Turkish-Greek war of 1920–22, when its Greek population was expelled and all the churches converted to mosques. Tourism is understated here, taking third place to olive oil production and fishing, though there are nonetheless a few 'sights' to see. The Taksiyarhis church-turned-mosque, built in the nineteenth century, is now the town museum, containing some impressive icons and religious paintings. Most hotels are in the satellite of **Camlik** to the south, but it's worth getting a *dolmus* to take you past here to the pine-covered headland known as **Seytan Sofrasi** or the Devil's Dinner Table. From here you can enjoy a magnificent view of many of the twenty-three islands which decorate the Ayvalik gulf.

One of these islands is the Greek one, **Lesbos**, known in Turkish as Midilli, which can be reached on a day-trip from Ayvalik harbour throughout the summer (contact Ayvalik Seyahat Acentasi, Inonu Caddesi 48, Tel. (663) 11938 for details). Another day-trip from Ayvalik is the much smaller and closer island of **Alibey** (also known as Cunda), which is attached to the mainland by causeway, though it's more pleasant to take a boat. The abandoned church of St Nicholas contains a few frescoes, but a more important reason for coming here is to appreciate some freshly-cooked local fish, washed down with white Aegean wine, at one of the island's celebrated fish restaurants. Boat tours of other islands, most of which have nothing on them but beaches and the odd ruined monastery, also start from Ayvalik's harbour in summer.

North-east from Ayvalik, and important enough to have a gulf named after it, is **Edremit**. The Edremit Gulf has been dubbed the 'Olive Riviera' and it's easy to see why. This is an attractive area, once again popular with Turks but unknown to foreigners, and practically deserted outside the summer months. Edremit itself is nothing special, but is flanked by the resorts of **Oren**, **Akcay**, **Altinoluk** and **Kucukkuyu**. A ferry service operates in summer between Oren and Akcay, which is the main holiday centre. If you feel peckish when in Akcay, head for Hasan Parlakli's Narin Pide ve Kebap Salon on Ertem Pasaji, for Turkish pizzas made as you watch. Kucukkuyu has a lively market on Fridays, reasonable surfing, and is the starting point for a cycle track to Troy. Inland from the northern shore of the Edremit Gulf are the hot springs of **Gure**, at the foot of **Kaz Dagi**, the legendary Mount Ida, where Paris is said to have presented the golden apple to Aphrodite, the most beautiful goddess, in an incident which sparked off the Trojan War. Today it's possible to picnic at **Guzeloluk**, the spot where the beauty contest is alleged to have been held.

Accommodation

First Class/Middle Range

Piri Reis Oteli, Alibey Adasi, Ayvalik (Tel. (663) 71256). 38 rooms in clean, well-equipped, whitewashed hotel on Alibey Island.

Middle Range

Arteka Oteli, Ali Haydar Sari Sahil Parki 216, Erdek (Tel. (1989) 2139 or 3336). 37 rooms in hotel adjacent to sandy beach.

    Bent Oteli, Altinoluk, Edremit (Tel. (671) 61070 or 61553). 16 comfortable rooms in leafy surroundings just outside Edremit.

    Idatur Moteli, Kucukkuyu (Tel. (1969) 5056 or 5102). 68 rooms with balconies in pleasant garden setting.

    Deniz Oteli, Marmara Adasi (Tel. (1984) 5032). Hotel on Marmara Island with sea views, small private beach and very friendly English-speaking owner.

Economy

Cahit Pansiyon, Barbaros Caddesi 65, Altinoluk, Edremit (Tel. (671) 61306). 13 rooms in pleasant family-run *pansiyon*.

    Chalet Chopin Pansiyon, Cam Mah., Altinoluk, Edremit (Tel. (671) 61044). 4 rooms in charming converted mill with sea views.

    Linda Moteli, Barbaros Meydani, Akcay (Tel. (671) 43500). 16 rooms right on seafront.

Canakkale

Canakkale, somewhat scarred by the First World War, is not a terribly dynamic town, but it does serve as a good base for exploring the Canakkale province, in particular the Gallipoli peninsula. The town's name means 'pottery castle' after the rather solid pottery which used to be a major distinguishing feature, but is now found mainly in museums and souvenir shops. Its historic naval role in the First World War eclipses its pottery as a claim to fame.

    Canakkale is located at the narrowest point of the Dardanelles, having grown up around a fortress (called Cimenlik) built by Mehmet II in 1453, at the same time as its partner on the other side of the straits (Kilitbahir).

Although you can't explore the **Cimenlik fortress** in any depth, since it's still considered a military zone, it can be admired from its pleasant park, where there's a **Naval Museum**. This is worth a visit for its records of the First World War and various Ataturk memorabilia. An important role in the Gallipoli campaign was played by the **minelayer Nusrat**, a replica of which (adorned with contemporary newspaper headlines) can be visited. There's also a museum to sixteenth-century Ottoman naval hero, Piri Reis.

Canakkale's only other real attraction is situated a kilometre or so out of town on the Troy road (take bus or *dolmus* marked Guzelyali, Kepez or Intepe). Here you'll find the **Archaeological Museum**, which, arranged chronologically, includes exhibits from Troy and other nearby sites. It's unusually well laid out and therefore worth a visit.

Accommodation

Middle Range

Tusan Oteli, Guzel Yali Koyu (Tel. (196) 28210). 64 rooms in quiet situation in pine wood about 15 kilometres out of town on Troy road.

Yildiz Oteli, Kizilay Sokak 20 (Tel. (196) 11793 or 11069). 20 rooms in friendly central (English-speaking) hotel, suitable for families.

Economy

Gunul Pansiyon, Inonu Caddesi 21 (Tel. (196) 11503 or 14597). 11 rooms in family-run *pansiyon*.

Kervansaray Oteli, Fetvahane Sokak 13. Atmospheric hotel in restored eighteenth-century house with fountained garden.

Avrupa Pansiyon, Matbaa Sokak 8 (Tel. (196) 14084). Quiet, clean and family-run.

Eating Out & Entertainments

For a snack, you can't beat the stalls frying fish on the quay. The slightly pricey quayside restaurants, such as the **Bogaz**, **Rihtim**, **Canakkale**, **Entellektuel** and **Sehir**, also put out tables in summer so you can eat their fish specialities on the promenade. Cheaper fare (*pide* and *kofte*) is available inland, where the richest restaurant area is along the main street, Demircioglu Caddesi, and around the bazaar.

There's a beer garden near the waterfront, where quantities of the local beer (Efes Pilsener) are consumed, and a few bars in the Clock

Tower area. The Canakkale/Troy festival takes place in mid-August, so things will be livelier (and accommodation scarcer) then.

Useful Addresses & Transport Options

Tourist Office: Iskele Meydani 67 (Tel. (196) 11187). **Post Office**: Off Inonu Caddesi. **Hospital**: Off Demircioglu Caddesi. **Passport Police**: Fetvahane Sokak.

Tour operators running trips to the Gallipoli battlefields and memorials include **Anatur**, Cumhuriyet Meydani (Tel. (196) 15482), and **Troy Anzac Tours**, just west of the clock tower (Tel. (196) 15047). For more independent tours, ferries run regularly from Canakkale to both Eceabat and Kilitbahir on the Gallipoli peninsula, as well as to the island of Gokceada in the Aegean.

Rest of Canakkale Province

Like the Marmara region as a whole, the Canakkale province is split by the Dardanelles into two sections, the Asian and the European. The high points of the Asian side are some archaeological sites (including Troy) and a few resorts, while the European side distinguishes itself by being the Gallipoli peninsula, location of so many famous – and tragic – First World War events.

North-east of Canakkale, on the Asian shore of the Dardanelles, the only place you might want to stop is **Lapseki**, which has a medieval fortress, partner to the one opposite at Gelibolu. There is also a ferry between Lapseki and Gelibolu, to supplement the ones further down between Canakkale and Eceabat/Kilitbahir. Inland is the town of **Biga**, namesake of the whole peninsula. It is here that Alexander the Great won his first major victory over the Persians at the Battle of Granikos in 334 BC. Traditional Turkish houses can be seen here and goat-hair rugs are the speciality of the surrounding hill villages. Over on the Sea of Marmara, **Karabiga** and **Kemer** have reasonable beaches. Further south, **Can** is known for its ceramics and its therapeutic hot springs.

The market town of **Ayvacik**, in the south-west of the Biga peninsula, is at its liveliest on Fridays, when women from the surrounding villages come to town to sell their produce. These may well be the same women who participate in the DOBAG carpet-weaving project, which is run from Ayvacik and aims to promote traditional carpet designs, weaving methods and natural dyeing processes (see **Good Alternatives**). From Ayvacik one road takes you to Kucukkuyu (see **Balikesir Province**), from where cyclists can join a pleasant cycle route which follows deserted back roads past coastal olive groves and up to Troy. Heading west from Kucukkuyu, you'll come to the sleepy resort of **Kadirga**, then **Behramkale** (also known by its ancient name of **Assos**), which can be reached by *dolmus* direct from Ayvacik too. Assos not only has a harbour and beach, but also some impressive ruins and wonderful views across the Gulf of Edremit to Lesbos. The highlight is the doric Temple of Athena, built at 240 metres above sea level in the sixth century BC, and currently being restored. On the terraces between the temple and the sea is a miscellany of ruins, ranging from agoras and a gymnasium to a theatre and a necropolis.

Further up the west coast of the Biga peninsula are more ruins: those of **Alexandria Troas**, near the town of **Ezine**. Alexandria Troas was founded by a general of Alexander the Great in 300 BC, but there is little left to see now. The beaches round here are, however, sandy and relatively deserted, and there are therapeutic thermal springs nearby at **Kestanbolu**. Also nearby is **Odunluk Iskelesi**, from where you can take a boat to the island of **Bozcaada** (having first obtained a permit to do so from the Passport Police in Canakkale). Bozcaada is a charming island, covered in vineyards which produce very palatable wine. There's also an old-fashioned cobble-streeted town, some medieval mosques, a Venetian castle and several good, clean beaches.

Troy, known as Truva in Turkish, is one of Turkey's most famous archaeological sites, but it may well disappoint you. Despite claims regarding the 'nine towns' which have been discovered on the site since Heinrich Schliemann's excavations began last century, most non-archaeologists will be able to distinguish only various sets of walls. The sweeping views and a small theatre are probably the most impressive features – though the replica wooden horse may be what draws people here in the first place.

From Canakkale, only twenty kilometres north of Troy, you can take a ferry to either Eceabat or Kilitbahir (five kilometres apart) on the east of the Gallipoli peninsula, and to Gokceada island, to its west. Of the two mainland arrival points, the village of **Kilitbahir** with its vast castle is the more pleasant, though the larger **Eceabat** is a better bet if you want to catch a *dolmus* down to the main sites. Eceabat is also home to the headquarters of the Gelibolu Historical National Park (which is what the peninsula has been designated). As you take the road south between Eceabat and Kilitbahir, you'll pass the Canakkale Memorial on your right, while a few kilometres beyond the village is the Havuzlar Memorial. If you want to explore the southern cape, follow signs to **Alcitepe**, where there's a museum and a couple more memorials, before continuing to the very end of the peninsula. The French Memorial and Cemetery are here, along with the striking Turkish Memorial, whose forty-two metre-high, ochre-coloured stone monument dominates the windswept landscape for miles around. It's worth having a look into the little museum which huddles beneath it. For the very hardy, swimming is possible at **Morto Bay**.

The village of **Seddulbahir** has a fortress and is not far from the Cape Helles British Naval Memorial. You'll pass further Turkish memorials on the way back up to Alcitepe, before taking the left fork of the road past the sandy beach at **Kum Koyu** (where the sea's surprisingly warm) and on to **Kabatepe**. There are some ferries from here to the island of **Gokceada**, though they're fairly infrequent so you're probably better off travelling there from Canakkale (where you'll have to go to obtain a visitor's permit in any case).

Gokceada is the largest of the Turkish islands and the location of the prison featured in the film 'Midnight Express', but there's fortunately more to the island than that. Pine woods and olive groves cover its rolling hills and there are some reasonable beaches, a ruined castle and excellent fish restaurants on the northern shore around **Kale**. The island is sparsely populated, partly by some elderly and justifiably disgruntled Greeks whom the Turkish government did their utmost to dissuade from staying on in the early 1960s.

Back on the mainland, the north of the Gelibolu peninsula is a mass of cemeteries and memorials, details of which you can gather from the Kabatepe Information Centre and Museum. Inland a little are the Australian 'Lone Pine' memorial and cemetery, and **Conkbayiri Hill**, topped by a New Zealand Memorial, while the coast road takes you past **Anzac Cove**, site of some failed Anzac landings and, inevitably, a monument to those who lost their lives in the course of them – inscribed with some words of Ataturk. Ataturk's headquarters, further east at **Bigali**, are now a museum. The top of the peninsula is marked, on the eastern side by the town of **Gelibolu** itself. It's a pleasant enough harbour town, which prides itself in its home-caught sardines, but has little of major historic interest except a mosque in the town centre and some Ottoman tombs a little way inland. You can, however, travel across the Dardanelles to Lapseki from here, and it's also the starting place for some Gallipoli tours (ask at the tourist office, which is near the harbourside park).

Accommodation

Middle Range

Assos Kervansaray Oteli, Behramkale Koyu, Iskele, Ayvacik (Tel. (1969) 1437 or 1415). 45 rooms in attractive grey-stone mock-*kervansaray* on waterfront.

Koz Oteli, Seref S., Bozcaada (Tel. (1965) 1054 or 1189). 36 rooms in quiet hotel on Bozcaada Island.

Economy

Pansiyon Yilmaz, Liman Caddesi 1, Gelibolu (Tel. (1891) 1031). Portside *pansiyon* run by a family with contacts all over town.

Mercan Oteli, Kadirga. Small friendly family hotel.

Ece Oteli, Eceabat (Tel. (1964) 1770). Simple clean rooms.

Pansiyon Varol, Tevfikiye, Truva (Tel. (9196) 1148171). Comfortable *pansiyon* near Troy.

3 The Aegean

The Aegean region of Turkey is almost certainly the richest part of the country when it comes to ancient sites plus fabulous beaches (the prime tourist-luring combination). Some of its resorts have, however, in a few short years, developed themselves out of the market. But not before they have become dependent on the very tourists who now spurn the 'facilities' that have been built up so enthusiastically – with the dismissive comment that Aegean Turkey's become 'just like the Spanish costas'. So the Aegean resorts stand bemused, feeling the indignation of a jilted lover who's been treated like a prostitute.

As a result, the region has developed a case of schizophrenia – alongside all the other, more tangible 'developments' of its coastline. One philosophy seems to revolve around making the best of a bad job, finishing what you've started, and milking the tourist industry while you still can. This leads to the ugly concrete apartment blocks and hotels which are continuing to shoot up despite allegedly stringent planning regulations. The rest of the Aegean character is distressed at such attitudes, and frantically trying to learn from mistakes, protect unspoilt areas and come up with plans for sustainable development. The second tendency is more widespread, but the first still has the potential to undermine it.

The above picture is perhaps misleadingly negative. Aegean Turkey is still a fascinating, friendly and breathtakingly beautiful place. The preservation of its world-famous archaeological gems, Ephesus and Pergamon among them, is immaculate. And there are still ancient sites, such as the former harbour town of Miletus, parts of which can be explored without seeing another soul. Inland, the fertile soil is given over to agriculture, while some villages also specialise in carpet-weaving. The hot springs and calcareous waterfalls of Pamukkale, forming a snow-white 'cotton castle', are unique; mountainsides are home to rare flowers, and valleys turn blood-red with poppies.

Even on the coast, it's possible to find deserted sandy bays if you travel away from the resorts, perhaps by hiring a Turkish *gulet*. These traditional wooden boats were dying out, but the growth of tourism has given new life to the flagging boat-building industry and helped maintain old-fashioned skills. This is also of great benefit to the visitor, who can now spend a few memorable days ploughing the turquoise sea, perhaps accompanied by the odd dolphin but otherwise in glorious isolation. It is by approaching from the sea that you're most likely to discover one of the many remaining fishing villages which are still dusty and sleepy, and where local children will invite you round to the backyard so you can try the burning hot bread that grandmother's making on a griddle over an open fire. The famous Turkish hospitality is still in evidence, even in proximity to the discos and tacky souvenir stalls of the big resorts.

The resorts themselves also have two faces. Most superficial is usually the promenade, with its bars and clubs, but real people live in these towns too, even if they are outnumbered three to one by tourists in the peak season. The further you venture from the sea front the more likely you are to meet them – and if you visit in winter, it's guaranteed. Most resorts have grown up around ancient cities and, although Halikarnassos and Smyrna are gone forever, you'll still find historic interest in their modern-day descendants: Bodrum and Izmir.

The Aegean coast unarguably has some areas with grave problems of environmental degradation linked to thoughtless building, but in the region as a whole, these are by far outweighed by the quality of its historic sights, natural beauty, beaches, climate and welcome.

History

Throughout the third and second millenium BC, the west coast of Turkey appears to have been split into various states inhabited by sea traders of Indo-European origin. Ephesus, Miletus and other cities were built around 1000 BC, experiencing a golden age some centuries later. The cultural élite of Miletus included the mathematician Thales. In about the eighth century BC, Homer is alleged to have been born in Smyrna (now Izmir), and the Lycians occupied the south-west coast. They were probably descended from seafarers and were influenced greatly by Greek culture. Further north and inland, centred on their capital Sardis, it was the artistic Lydians who held sway – until the Persian conquest in the sixth and fifth centuries BC. It was in 485 BC that Herodotus was born in Halikarnassos (now Bodrum). This was the man who came to be known as the 'father of history', since he was the first person to write history books objectively, rather than as a source of official propaganda.

In 356 BC, on the night of Alexander the Great's birth, the temple of Artemis near Ephesus (one of the seven wonders of the ancient world) burned down and, although it was rebuilt, little remains now. By the first century AD, Ephesus was the second biggest port in Asia, with 200,000 inhabitants. Legend has it that the Virgin Mary accompanied St John the Evangelist here towards the end of her life – and even the house in which she stayed has been identified and can now be visited, having received the blessing of Pope Paul VI in 1967. It was 55 AD when St Paul visited Ephesus to preach the Gospel. At the time, his message did not go down well with the guild of jewellers who made gold and silver objects dedicated to Artemis. They staged a demonstration which forced him to leave, but Ephesus nevertheless became a major centre of early Christianity. It was in the early years of the Christian era that Mark Antony stripped the Pergamon library of books, so as to offer Cleopatra replacements for those destroyed by fire at the library of Alexandria. Cleopatra is also said to have bathed in the warm mineral waters at Hierapolis (now Pamukkale).

Western Turkey was part of the Roman, and then Byzantine empire for centuries. By the time of Basil II in the early eleventh century AD, the empire focused on the Aegean Islands, the Balkans and Anatolia, but internal instability coupled with the arrival of Turkoman tribes in the thirteenth century led to the overthrowing of the Byzantines and a period of chaos and division, with the central Aegean falling to the Aydinoglu tribe and the south-west Aegean to the Mentese. During the fifteenth century, when the Ottomans were firmly in charge, Bodrum, along with Rhodes, acted as a sanctuary for the Hospitaller Knights of St John, who used these places to control sea routes to Egypt. Suleyman the Magnificent put a stop to this by ousting them in the 1520s. The early sixteenth century was a high point of Turkish carpet-making and the results were in demand all over western Europe. One particular design, still made in Bergama as it was then, was nicknamed the Holbein carpet, due to the frequency with which it appeared in paintings by Hans Holbein the Younger.

The decline of the Ottoman empire, followed by the two Balkan wars of the early twentieth century and, ultimately, the First World War when the Turks sided with the Germans, left Turkey very much in the hands of the Allies in 1918. While the Italians occupied the south-west corner of the country, the Greeks took over control of much of the Aegean coast, which was already inhabited by many people of Greek extraction. Nationalist guerrillas, directed by Mustafa Kemal (later Ataturk) objected rather strongly to this, but the Treaty of Sèvres in May 1920 gave the majority of the Aegean to Greece. Not content with this settlement, the Greeks attempted to penetrate further inland from Izmir, until they sparked off a nationalist offensive, led by Kemal in August 1922, which forced the Greeks to retreat and flee Turkey once and for all – though not without a good deal of looting and destruction on the way. The Turkish nationalists weren't exactly blameless either, burning down most of Izmir in reprisal against Greek civilians. The 1923 Treaty of Lausanne led to an agreement between Greece and Turkey to exchange their minority populations – a thoroughly disorientating experience for many of those concerned.

Bodrum started its own trend as a 'bohemian paradise' as far back as 1923, with the arrival of Cevat Sakir Kabaagac, a young exile who chronicled local life and later came to be known as the Fisherman of Halikarnassos. Other artists were encouraged to come here and, in the 1950s, 60s and 70s, Bodrum was positively swarming with them. At this time the Aegean region was, however, still relatively untouched by tourism and it wasn't until the major road-building programmes of the late 1970s that coastal areas were opened up, while the building boom itself began, in most places, as late as the mid-1980s.

Names of modern Aegean towns which might be more familiar in their ancient forms include the obvious ones such as Efes (which used to be Ephesus); Milet (formerly Miletus or Miletos); and Bergama (formerly Pergamon). In addition there are some less self-evident ones: Geyre used to be Aphrodisias; Bodrum was Halikarnassos; Pamukkale was Hierapolis; Marmaris was Physkos, and Izmir was Smyrna.

Geography

The Aegean region of Turkey, as covered in this chapter, stretches from just below Ayvalik in the north to Koycegiz in the south (halfway between Marmaris and Dalaman, at the point where the Aegean can be said to give way to the Mediterranean). The region's most westerly spot is Cesme, to the south of the Karaburun peninsula and only ten kilometres from the Greek island of Chios. In the east, the Aegean is generally considered to extend to the Pamukkale area, just west of the Burdur lakes.

The region can be divided roughly into the northern and southern

Aegean. The former consists of the coastal province of Izmir and the inland one of Manisa; the south includes three provinces: the coastal Mugla, the inland Denizli, and Aydin which is a bit of both. Izmir is Turkey's third largest city, with a population of between two and three million, and it is the country's second most important port after Istanbul. The other provincial capitals are all a good deal smaller; Denizli tots up around 200,000, while resorts such as Bodrum and Kusadasi have only between 20,000 and 40,000 permanent residents.

The region is irrigated by many rivers, the most important being the Gediz, which flows into the Gulf of Izmir; the Kucuk Menderes (Lesser Meander), which comes out at Kusadasi; and the Buyuk Menderes (Greater Meander), which emerges at Milet and causes the coastline to shift around 6.5 metres out to sea every year. A hydroelectric power station has been built to tap the energy of the Bakir river near Bergama. All these rivers have left the coastline pleasantly serrated and the interior extremely fertile. Vineyards, cotton and tobacco fields can be found in the Denizli area, and red poppies line the lush Meander valley between Denizli and Milet. The scenery of Ancient Lycia in the south-western corner is particularly spectacular. Orange and tangerine groves line the Bodrum peninsula, while a very short way inland from Marmaris, the country becomes rugged, covered in pine forests, and seemingly littered with mountains called Ak Dagi!

The Aegean region also manages to supply 74 per cent of Turkey's olives. Bearing in mind that Turkey is the biggest olive producer in the world, with 700,000 trees yielding one million tons of olives a year, this is no mean feat. Most olive groves can be found in coastal areas, as the trees don't grow above 1000 metres. Another peculiar feature of the olive tree is that the older it gets, the heavier and tastier its yield. Unfortunately none of the Aegean coast's original forest cover remains. The Cypress trees which used to reach down to the waterfront have been replaced by the half-finished multi-storey apartment blocks you can see today. To give them due credit, however, the Turkish Forestry Authority are now making concerted efforts to redress the balance.

Inland from Izmir is the most fertile land of the Aegean, where figs, grapes, tobacco and cotton grow in abundance. This area produces 15 per cent of the national agricultural output, which explains why Izmir is such a major export harbour. Izmir's 1500 plus industrial enterprises are responsible for 15 per cent of the produce exported from Turkey. The immense extent of the industry round here has inevitably led to serious environmental problems in the Gulf of Izmir, particularly as it's not deep enough for an easy exchange of waters. This causes 'red tides', as a result of plankton bloom, which has been an increasingly frequent phenomenon, but the seriousness of the issue has now been realised and plans are underway to improve things in both the short and the long-term.

The Aegean is a great place for lovers of wildlife – as witnessed by the number of special-interest natural history holidays which take place here. Ancient sites are often good places to look for wildlife, allowing you to combine nature and culture. Orchids and the *campanula ephesia* grow at Ephesus, while storks, lizards, tortoises and various types of raptor can be spotted at Miletus, Didyma and Priene, all in the Buyuk Menderes delta. White storks nest on chimneys all over Selcuk and, at nearby Pamucak beach, migrating flamingoes can sometimes be seen. Another particularly rich area includes the saltpans of Karine and the lake of Bafa Golu, where there are carpets of flowers such as anemones and orchids and numerous types of bird, including two rare species of kingfisher. The marshy area further south around Gulluk (near Milas) is also rewarding, and botanists will enjoy the Datca peninsula.

To the east of Marmaris, at Ataturk park, you'll find what is possibly the only forest in the world of aromatic Ciga trees, used to make frankincense; fortunately it is in a protected area. If you're sailing off the coast here, you're fairly likely to see dolphins or porpoises. Just east of Marmaris, Ekincik is lucky enough to have been subjected to a temporary building ban, mainly because it's the first of the seventeen beaches along the Mediterranean coast used as a nesting site by endangered sea turtles. Other protected areas, this time honoured with National Park status, are the wild Dilek peninsula (much of which is a military zone), just south of the monstrously built-up Kusadasi resort area; and the Sipil Dagi park, which contains thermal springs and is situated near Manisa.

Climate

The climate varies a fair amount within the Aegean region, though you can be pretty certain of fine sunny weather from April to November. At Izmir, on the northern Aegean coast, the average midday temperature ranges from 9°C in January to 28°C in July and August, remaining above 15°C from April to November, but it's worth knowing that the smell from the industry in this area can get unbearable in high summer. The sea temperature here ranges from 15°C in February and March to 26°C in July and August, staying above 20°C from May to October. The southern Aegean coast is also pleasant right through from early spring to late autumn, with spring and autumn temperatures around 20–25°C, while summer ones can rise to 30–33°C. Kusadasi can grow decidedly muggy in summer. Sea temperatures here are around 18°C in spring, 24°C in summer and 20°C in autumn. Sheltered swimming and a good all-round climate are found on the coast south of Cesme. Welcome breezes occur north of Bodrum. In summer the wind (known locally as *meltem*) tends to blow in a south-easterly direction, picking up in the afternoon but virtually non-existent at night and during the early morning. The strongest winds are almost always in the gulfs. Inland, average temperatures range from around 5°C in January to 27°C in July, staying above 15°C for a slightly shorter period than on the coast (about May to October).

Attractions

One of the most compelling reasons to visit the Aegean is its wealth of ancient sites, including some of the greatest classical sites in the whole Mediterranean region. Ephesus is the second most visited place in Turkey (after the Sultanahmet quarter of Istanbul), and is breathtakingly impressive: after seeing it, you can quite comprehend St Paul's awestruck remark 'Is there a greater city?' Pergamon is another winner as a sightseeing destination – though in another sense it's a loser, having had the 200,000 books of its library pilfered by Mark Antony back in the first century, then its Temple of Zeus spirited over to Berlin at the beginning of this century. Didyma, Priene and Miletus are all different and all worth visiting; Aphrodisias, which is still being excavated, boasts a 262-metre-long stadium, with a capacity of 30,000; Hierapolis is said to have the biggest and most varied necropolis in Asia Minor, with a mixture of round, sarcophagus and house-shaped tombs. Not only are such sites memorials to the cultures of classical Anatolia, they also represent (as you'll so often hear) the cradle of western civilisation.

This claim is borne out by the fact that two of the seven wonders of the ancient world were located in the Aegean: the Temple of Artemis at Ephesus and the Tomb of King Mausolus at Halikarnassos (Bodrum), though little remains of either. Other ancient sites beckon at Sardis and Knidos, competing with more 'modern' attractions, such as the house of the Virgin Mary, near Ephesus.

One of the greatest natural wonders of the region is Pamukkale, with its calcified waterfalls where you can bathe at temperatures of 35°C – or more, if you choose to try out the Cleopatra baths, still liberally scattered with bits of ancient stonework and fallen column. Other thermal resorts are at Karahayit, Cesme and Balcova.

Bathing can, of course, also be indulged in at the numerous sandy beaches which line the Aegean coast. Izmir was once known as 'the Pearl of the Aegean', but nowadays its role as a modern port isn't really conducive to a booming tourist industry, though visitors come nonetheless. More of a pull is exerted by resort towns like Kusadasi, which has the best marina and best shopping on the coast; Bodrum, whose Halikarnassos open-air disco is known throughout Europe; and sprawling Marmaris. Each of these towns has appeal for history-lovers as well as night owls, and each is undeniably a good base for the surrounding area too. It's always worth flagging down a *dolmus* to explore inland villages, or taking a boat to a less crowded bay.

In addition to the sites, beaches and climate, the Manisa province specialises in carpet-making, so you may pick up a bargain there, and the whole region is rife with festivals all year round, including camel-wrestling in winter (see **Meeting People**).

Cuisine

As you might expect, the fish is particularly delicious in the coastal towns and villages – with grilled fish the speciality. Look out for red mullet (*barbunya*), grey mullet (*kefal*), Aegean tuna (*tranca*), bass (*levrek*) and sole (*dil baligi*). You should be able to tell what's in season from the prices. Izmir is known for its mussels, often stuffed with rice or pine nuts. There's a detectable Greek influence to Aegean cooking and you'll find many moussaka-style dishes involving aubergines, tomatoes, lamb and (not surprisingly) olives. Bulgar wheat *pilavs* are also tasty. The town of Menemen has a dish named after it, made of spicy tomatoes and egg. In dishes like this, fresh herbs such as sage (which grows in the Bodrum area) are used to advantage.

The yoghurt and water drink, *ayran*, seems particularly popular in this part of Turkey, but the less abstemious will be pleased to hear that *raki*'s widely drunk (usually on ice, with added water), as is the local beer, Efes Pilsen. For the sweet-toothed, the Cesme area's speciality is pine resin-flavoured ice cream, which tastes like the Greek wine retsina. The pine forests of the Marmaris area are the source of a delicious honey called *Cam Bali*.

Level of Tourism

There were 2,522,994 foreign visitors to the Aegean region in 1990. Of these, the different nationalities have their fixed preferences: the French head for Kusadasi, and the British for Bodrum, while the Brits and Germans hold equal sway over Marmaris, as it's around here that the Aegean, beloved of the British, gives way to the Mediterranean, preferred destination of the Germans. Ephesus is the most visited site in the region (and the second most popular in all Turkey).

In Izmir province, most people stay in the provincial capital (the majority of these choosing three-star hotels), with the next most popular destinations Cesme, then Selcuk. In Denizli province, once again most stay in the capital, though this time the majority chooses two-star hotels (there being nothing above three-star anyway); the second most popular destination in the province is Pamukkale. In the Mugla province, the top three resorts are Marmaris, Fethiye (here treated in the **Mediterranean** chapter), and Bodrum.

Just to give an idea of the strain some of the resorts are under, it's worth knowing that the population of Kusadasi more than triples in summer: a city with facilities for around 30,000 permanent residents has to cope with nearly 100,000 in peak season. It's no wonder that planning regulations go by the board and multi-storey buildings shoot up all along the coast. Kusadasi suffered particularly in the first few years after democratisation (1986), as decentralisation meant that under-educated (and sometimes downright corrupt) mayors had free rein to expand as cheaply and rapidly as possible. The resort's current problems stem from the fact that, by building so many cheap hotels and nightclubs, and by converting *kebapci* into burger-bars, it has unwittingly attracted the wrong type of clientèle. Now that the lager louts and cheapskates have descended en masse, it's become evident that no more money's being pumped into the local economy than in the days when the only visitors were the wealthy culture lovers off the big cruise ships – but the overall cost to the town is, of course, much higher. The rows of unfinished and unwanted high-rise hotels mean it has lost its authenticity – nowadays a holiday destination's most marketable asset – and no one with any money or taste wants to come any more: distinct echoes of the Costa del Sol! Fortunately, Kusadasi is the only resort which has got into such a mess; others, such as Marmaris, seem to be heading that way, but it's encouraging that every Turk you meet will quote Kusadasi as an example of a mistake from which other resorts have learned. Let's hope it's true.

Part of the problem is that development in western Turkey is all comparatively recent. The first road up to the Virgin Mary's house near Ephesus was built as recently as 1950 – and that was one of the early ones. Most road construction occurred in the 1960s and 1970s, and the building boom for tourist hotels and holiday villages followed in the 1980s, with aspiring second home owners from Istanbul and Ankara scrambling to catch up and stake their claims in the early 1990s. Today, one of the greatest eyesores on the coast is the concrete carpet of identical, half-finished villas, due to become the holiday homes of wealthy Turkish city-dwellers. And they are not just eyesores; they contribute significantly to pollution and overcrowding in certain areas. Marmaris and Bodrum have already been identified as experiencing pollution and other environmental problems by the Turkish Association for the Conservation of Nature and Natural Resources.

Though everyone admits Kusadasi is a disaster, Bodrum is a case where opinions differ. The Ministry of Tourism quotes it as an example of a municipality where the decentralisation policy, which leaves limitations on the expansion and further development of popular areas to the discretion of local authorities, has worked well. It points out that the municipality is very strict about the type of houses which may be built: they should be painted white and have a maximum of two storeys. But this regulation leads to monotonous swathes of identical 'Bodrum-style' sugar-cube houses: restrictions on the location and quantity of these dwellings seem to have been deemed unnecessary. The town is billed as a beach resort, but the water in Bodrum itself is polluted. Rumours are afoot that an 'ambitious' tourist development is to go ahead on Karaada, a quiet island half an hour by boat from Bodrum, though the tourist office insist it's only hypothetical and, in any case, years away. With any luck it will stay that way. At least the local boat-building business has been revived, thanks to the demand for *gulet* trips by some of the one million tourists who visit Bodrum each year – though presumably it's also through popular demand that many shops in Bodrum market have become hot contenders for the tackiest souvenir stall in Turkey!

It's not just the resorts which get overcrowded in peak season. The atmosphere of sites like Ephesus is definitely impaired by having to share them with thousands of other visitors. The best solution to this problem is to travel out of season. Another option is to arrive at the gate the moment the site opens in the morning. Slip in before the coach parties have had time to untangle themselves from their vehicles and it's still possible – just – to be the only person in the amphitheatre at Ephesus, which is more than enough compensation for having to get up a bit early.

Another place where the sheer volume of people can be a problem is Pamukkale, where one million hotel visitors (mainly German, British, French and Dutch) stayed in 1990. Here the beautiful white travertines, where warm waterfalls run down calcified cliffs, creating natural paddling pools, are being damaged and discoloured by the thoughtlessness of people who are too lazy to take off their shoes, as instructed, when walking across them. Sadly, the only solution to this problem would probably be to introduce on-the-spot fines, though that's extremely unlikely to happen.

So what about the success stories? There are some areas where tourism has brought undeniable benefits to the Aegean. The village of Sirince, near Selcuk, for example, was struggling to make ends meet when its main source of revenue was tobacco farming. Since it turned to fruit farming plus tourism, its fortune has changed. As a typical old hill village, with nothing much to attract people except its beautiful scenery and traditional houses, it receives about 200 visitors a day in summer, with a few peak days of around 400. This is not so many that it's totally swamped, yet it's been enough to allow new roads, a new school and a little ethnographical museum to open. Of course, the worry is that the visitor numbers will grow in future and the atmosphere of the place will be spoiled.

There are also villages along the southern Aegean coast where rural life seems to go hand in hand with small-scale tourism. Fishing and fruit farming are generally the main occupations, but in summer local people open up small restaurants to tourists who arrive on *gulet* trips. Further inland are some extremely smart holiday homes belonging to rich city-dwellers. These tend to be tasteful and hidden by fruit trees, and are only occupied between June and September. The rest of the year local people are paid to look after them and there seems genuinely to be no resentment attached to this set-up.

One British tour operator, Beach Villas, has been successful in curbing excessive tourist exploitation in this area. They specialise in the village of Gumusluk (on the Bodrum peninsula) and, when plans were afoot to alter the character of the village to suit the more lively atmosphere preferred by Thomsons, Beach Villas persuaded their clients to boycott bars which played loud music: and it worked.

Another positive development is that the Aegean coastline is now covered by a project to eliminate waste water disposal deficiencies and to prevent future ones. And Izmir, probably the worst culprit, hosted a coastline management conference in the summer of 1991.

Good Alternatives

Meeting People

Good times to meet local people are at festivals. The local speciality in this department is camel-wrestling. It sounds cruel, but Turkish people insist that no harm is done to the animals: they're far too valuable! Camel-wrestling festivals tend to take place in winter, so might offer a focus for an out-of-season holiday. There's a major one at Selcuk in mid January; one in Germencik (Aydin province) in early February; and a minor one in Saraykoy (Denizli province) in December or January. In spring (March/April), the sweet-toothed will enjoy the Mesir Macunu (or Mesir Bayrami) – a 'spiced candy' festival at Manisa. June brings the Marmaris Festival and the Bergama Fair, while the Izmir International Arts Festival takes place in June or July, and the Efes Cultural Festival in July or August. The Feast of the Assumption is on 15 August and is celebrated each year at the Virgin Mary's house near Ephesus. The Izmir International Fair is in August or September, and Manisa holds a festival in honour of the grape harvest each September.

Smaller local fairs are also held, such as the Cherry (*Kiraz*) Festival in Honaz (Denizli) in June; the Bagbozumu Festival in Cal in September; and the Apple (*Elma*) Festival in Tavas, also in September. During these, look out for *zeybek*, an Aegean dance performed by colourfully-dressed male dancers (called *efe*) and symbolising courage. A list of further festivals can be found in the Turkish Information Office's leaflet *Turkiye Travel Guide*.

Another place you can be sure of a one-to-one exchange with a local person is in his carpet shop. Pamukkale has a profusion of them, but it's worth heading for some of the hill villages around here, and in the Manisa province, where the actual weaving goes on. In Manisa, the DOBAG carpet project promotes the weaving of carpets using traditional patterns and weaving methods and natural dyes. The carpets are woven by the Yuntdagi Cooperative which has 150 members in sixteen villages, all of which benefit from the extra income brought in by the project. Another place where the women who weave the carpets work in better conditions than average is the **Tavas Hali Carpet House**, Cankurtaran Mevki, Tavas, Denizli. Here you can see the weavers at work and the management is keen to point out that they get regular tea-breaks from the eye-straining work, and only work six hours a day – the price they have to pay for this is being watched at work by the crowds of tourists being shown round. Still, it's probably better than weaving for hours on end in a badly-lit tent.

Speaking of tents, campers should bear in mind that they're not necessarily limited to the officially-designated camp-sites, which – in popular towns – are normally on the outskirts. If you want to be a bit nearer the centre of things, many *pansiyon* owners will, for a small fee, allow you to camp in their garden. If you're staying in a resort town such as Bodrum and you want to find some more 'genuine' nightlife than that offered on the seafront promenade, head for the bars and restaurants on the interior streets.

Finally, if you want to reserve a room in a locally-run guest-house in Aliaga, Bodrum, Candarli, Datca, Didim, Dikili, Foca, Karaburun, Kusadasi, Seferihisar or Soke (most of which are small- to medium-sized coastal towns), contact **Turistik Ev Pansiyonculugunu Gelistirme Dernegi**, Cumhuriyet Bulvari 84/803, Izmir (Tel. (51) 257273 or 214295 or 212528).

Discovering Places

Visiting the major sights in the Aegean region is very simple, as privately organised tours to them operate from all the main resorts. When choosing a tour, try to gauge how much time is allowed in each place; all too often you are rushed round sights too fast to appreciate them. If you're pushed for time, it's certainly worth joining a tour of, say, Priene, Miletus and Didyma from Kusadasi or Selcuk, but otherwise try visiting them under your own steam, using public transport and perhaps staying near one of them en route.

If you're looking for an off-the-beaten-track beach holiday, bear in mind that the resorts north of Izmir (for example Dikili or Foca) are far less popular as tourist destinations than the more southerly ones. Travelling to the end of the various peninsulas which adorn the coast is an option neglected by many: the Karaburun peninsula is rarely explored, and the Dilek peninsula is an unspoilt National Park, while you'll find some quiet fishing villages on the north side of the Bodrum peninsula, quite in contrast to the concrete-field resorts like Gumbet on the south side.

Exploration inland will reward you with virtual isolation from other western tourists: some old-fashioned towns to look out for are Birgi, Milas and Mugla. An 'alternative' to the overcrowded white travertines of Pamukkale might be a trip to see the less impressive, but less frequented red ones at Karahayit. The islands in the Gulf of Gokova all make pleasant retreats. One good way to see them is by boat, and *gulets* or yachts can be chartered from Bodrum or Marmaris.

For some good nature rambling suggestions, see the **Geography** section. One particular recommendation is the Bafa (or Camici) Lake region, sixty kilometres from Kusadasi. As well as rich flora and fauna, this area offers spectacular scenery, with mountains plunging right down to the lake on its eastern side, and various small islands with monasteries on them. Nearby is ruined Herakleia. Minor sites such as this one, Klaros near Ephesus, Labranda near Milas, or Alinda near Cine, can allow for a closer inspection of ancient architecture than some of the more popular crowd-pullers.

For tips on some of the lesser-known places in the Ephesus area, the person to ask is the charming Mrs Meliha Olgun, owner of the **Olgun Pansiyon** (Tel. (5467) 5751) in the seaside village of Ozdere, just west of Klaros on the Cesme headland and around thirty kilometres from Ephesus.

Communications

How to Get There

British Airways and THY have regular scheduled **flights** from London to Izmir (though you may need to change in Istanbul). Noble Air fly Stansted to Izmir once a week. Many charters fly to Izmir and to Dalaman, which is more convenient for destinations in the southernmost Aegean. The new Gulluk/Milas airport also receives charters. Turkish Airlines internal flights from Istanbul to Izmir are very frequent and take just under an hour; the daily flights to Dalaman take 1¼ hours; the twice-weekly ones to Denizli take an hour.

From Istanbul, there are two **trains** a day to Izmir and the journey takes around 11 hours; the daily train to Denizli takes 14½ hours (both leave from Haydarpasa Station). For speed and convenience, you'll do better on the **coach** which takes 9½ and 10 hours respectively – and there's one leaving Istanbul every hour. Direct coaches also serve Kusadasi (10 hours); Bodrum (12 hours); Marmaris (13 hours); and Datca (17 hours). If you're driving or hitching down from Europe, you're better off hugging the coast on the E24 (which means taking a ferry across the Dardanelles) than trying to go through Istanbul and round the Sea of Marmara.

There's a thrice-weekly **ferry** from Istanbul to Izmir, which takes about 20 hours. If you're travelling from Italy or Greece, a weekly ferry (Minoan Lines) can take you from Ancona to Kusadasi via Piraeus between May and October. Turkish Maritime Lines run weekly March to November services between Venice and Cesme (also via Piraeus, except in midsummer when they're direct). Ancona to Bodrum is another weekly possibility on TML.

When You're There

Rail – the northern Aegean is, for Turkey, reasonably well served by train. A line runs from Balikesir down through Akhisar and Manisa to Izmir. At Manisa, one branch splits off to Usak, via Salihli and Esme. The main line divides at Izmir, with a minor branch leaving Izmir-Alsancak station for Odemis and Birgi to the east, and the major one continuing from Izmir-Basmane station to Selcuk and Aydin, and along the Buyuk Menderes river valley past Nazilli and Denizli to the Burdur lakes. The southern coast is inaccessible by train: bus is the only public transport option here. Some ideas of train times within the region: from Izmir it takes 1½ hours to Manisa; 2 hours to Selcuk; 2½ hours to Odemis; 3 hours to Soke; 6 hours to Denizli. Groups are able to charter a steam train in the Aegean region, whose usual route is from Izmir to Camlik (near Selcuk): details are available on (51) 192271 or from the district chief manager at Izmir-Alsancak station.

Bus – Izmir is the transport hub of the region, with buses and *dolmus* leaving for most destinations extremely frequently. Kusadasi, Soke, Bodrum, Marmaris, Aydin and Denizli are also important interchanges. The longest journey within the region is from Bergama to Datca (on the peninsula west of Marmaris), but even this takes only around 9 hours.

Car – the major road is the E24 which hugs the west coast down as far as Selcuk, before heading off east, through Aydin, to Denizli. The other main one is the E23 from Izmir, east through Salihli, to Usak and beyond. There's no proper coast road between Bodrum and Marmaris (which is why it's so pleasant to travel this stretch by boat, stopping at small fishing villages which have been spared the building boom which inevitably follows the creation of road access).

Boat – Greek islands which can be visited by passenger ferry from Turkey are: Chios (Turkish: Sakiz), crossing time 1 hour from Cesme; Samos (Sisam), 2 hours from Kusadasi; Cos (Istankoy), 2 hours from Bodrum; and Rhodes (Rodos), 3 hours from Marmaris. Check the timetable in advance, especially in winter when services can be reduced considerably. Between April and October, the 1½ hour trip from Bodrum to Datca can be made by ferry. For those who want to make the most of their time afloat, the southern Aegean is the perfect place to hire a *gulet* or some other kind of craft. Unless you're already in a group, your best option is a 'cabin charter', which means you can hire a cabin on a boat which follows a fixed itinerary, leaving on a fixed day. If you're in a group there's much more flexibility in where you go, how long for etc. Bear in mind that prices shoot up between June and September, and boat trips are at their best value in April, May or October. Although the classic 'blue voyage' leaves from Marmaris and heads east, the area around the Bodrum peninsula and between Bodrum and Marmaris makes an equally attractive (and quieter) alternative. A good charter agency is **Yesil Marmaris**, based at Barbaros Caddesi 11, 48700 Marmaris (Tel. (612) 11033), and at Ataturk Caddesi 81, 48400 Bodrum (Tel. (6141) 3091).

Useful Local Contacts

The following addresses may prove useful for specific information about tourism in the Aegean region. The **Izmir Tourist Guides Traders' Association**, Akdeniz Caddesi, Akdeniz Ishani 51, Kat 5–514, Izmir (Tel. (51) 139957 or 141875); the **Aegean Touristic Enterprise and Accommodation Association**, Akdeniz Caddesi, 1347 Sokak 8, Amba Ishani, Kat 5–508, 35210 Izmir (Tel. (51) 194777). There is an Izmir branch of the **Turkish Touring and Automobile Association** (TTOK) at Alsancak, Ataturk Bulvari 370 (Tel. (51) 217149 or 226387).

Geographical Breakdown of Region

Izmir

The tourist board literature boasts that Izmir possesses one of the five finest natural harbours on the Mediterranean, carefully neglecting to mention that it is also one of the most polluted! Fortunately a programme to clean up the harbour is underway, though the sheer volume of industry based round here means it's unlikely that any clean-up operation will make an impression on the stench that emanates from Izmir's outskirts. The centre of town does, however, have a certain charm. The palm-lined avenues and 'velvet fortress' make up for some of the ugly modern buildings. As it is not really a tourist destination in itself, but merely a hopping-off point for so many others, it is a good place to experience Turkish workaday life as it is outside the resorts.

Though Izmir is too large to have a single 'centre', its central point is probably around the southern end of the **Kultur Parki**. This vast green park offers many activities and entertainments, from mini-golf to an outdoor theatre, and hosts the Izmir Trade Fair each August or September. North-east from here, on the west side of Ikinci Kordon near the sea-front, is the **Ataturk Museum** (closed weekends and Mondays), housed in the building Ataturk stayed in on his Izmir visits. Further up Ikinci Kordon, in the **Alsancak** district, is the **Yasar Foundation Art Museum**, housed in one of the few buildings that escaped destruction during the burning of Izmir when the Greeks were expelled in 1922. Whole terraces of eighteenth- and nineteenth-century mansions of this sort can be seen on 1480, 1481 and 1482 Sokaks, just east of Ikinci Kordon.

If you head back southwards down Birinci Kordon, which is the sea-front promenade, you'll come to Cumhuriyet Meydani where there's an **equestrian statue** of Ataturk. It is further south, and to the east of the promenade, that you'll find Izmir's **bazaar**, mainly enclosed between Fevzipasa Bulvari and Anafartalar Caddesi. Selling the usual mixture of clothing and leather goods (aimed at the tourists), along with everyday items for local people, it's an interesting place to wander, though not architecturally striking. Let your wanderings take you further east to the **Ancient Agora**, which dates from around the second century BC and includes a colonnade of Corinthian columns. Most of the other bits and pieces unearthed here are in the **Archaeological Museum**, south-west of Konak (the water-front location of the bus station, the Kutahya-tiled **Konak Mosque**, and the ornate 1901 **clock tower** which has become Izmir's logo). The museum is an interesting one, whose collections are mainly from the Izmir province. Just across the road is the attractively-housed **Ethnographic Museum**, even more fascinating, with its reconstructions of local houses and exhibitions connected with regional customs and crafts. A **Painting and Sculptural Museum** (closed Sundays) and the **Ataturk Cultural Centre** can be found near here, on Mithatpasa Caddesi.

A fair walk to the east is **Kadifekale**, the 'velvet fortress' referred to so frequently in the tourist literature. If you can't face the walk, it's possible to catch a *dolmus* from outside the Archaeological Museum. The restored third-century fortress itself is not particularly special, but the views of the city and bay are – notably at sunset. They can be enjoyed from a tea-garden in summer.

From Konak you can take a twenty-minute ferry trip across the bay to **Karsiyaka**, where the Olaf Palme Park, punctuated with ancient statues and modern cafés, graces the waterfront.

Accommodation

Being a predominantly modern city, the vast majority of Izmir's hotels are ugly high-rises. For want of recommendably small-scale four- and five-star hotels, most of the **First Class** recommendations here are three-star. At the lower end of the price range, head for the Fevzipasa Bulvari area. If you plan to visit during the Izmir Trade Fair (August/September), be sure to book accommodation in advance.

First Class

Anba Oteli, Cumhuriyet Bulvari 124 (Tel. (51) 144380). 53 comfortable rooms in central hotel with 'only' seven storeys.

Karaca Oteli, Necatibey Bulvari, 1379 Sokak 55, Alsancak (Tel. (51) 199099). 68 rooms in recently renovated hotel on palm-lined boulevard.

Atlantis Oteli, Gazi Bulvari 128 (Tel. (51) 135549). 55 rooms in smart, central hotel.

Middle Range

Billur Oteli, Anafartalar Caddesi 783 (Tel. (51) 139732). 60 airy rooms in hotel on corner of palm-lined street, near station.

Kabacam Oteli, 1364 Sokak 2/1 (Tel. (51) 123353). 28 rooms in rather drab but pleasantly small-scale hotel.

Economy

Meseret Oteli, Anafartalar Caddesi 66 (Tel. (51) 255533). Pleasant, central hotel in old building.

Ozcan Oteli, 1368 Sokak 3 (Tel. (51) 135052). Smart old-fashioned hotel.

Bilen Palas Oteli, 1369 Sokak 68 (Tel. (51) 139246). Similar to the above.

Eating Out

The cheapest and most pleasant eateries are located in the Bazaar area, notably along Anafartalar Caddesi. Try **Inci Et Lokantasi**, 1369 Sokak 51/A (Tel. (51) 198991), a cheery place specialising in kebabs. A little more upmarket is the **Sukran Lokantasi**, Anafartalar Caddesi 61, housed in an old building complete with courtyard and fountain – though the pleasant setting does rather bump up the prices. For fish specialities, try the **Halikarnass Balik Lokantasi** (corner of 870, 871 and 873 Sokaks). The waterfront restaurants along Birinci Kordon, such as the **Deniz Restaurant**, at the junction with Vasif Cinar Bulvari, offer surprisingly good value meals considering the prime location.

Entertainments

Izmir's entertainments are somewhat limited for such a large city, but this is because it is not particularly geared to tourists, so the entertainments that do exist tend to be that much more 'authentic'. Turkish families tend to amuse themselves with a Sunday afternoon out in the Kultur Parki, while older men will spend the evening puffing at a water-pipe in tea salons like the **Liman Cay Solonu** at Birinci Kordon 128. Just up the road from here starts the **Cicek Pasaji**, a collection of beer-halls serving *meze*, which tries, with limited success, to emulate its Istanbul cousin. The best *Hamam* in Izmir is the **Hosgor**, just off Mithatpasa Caddesi 10.

Except in summer, the **Ataturk Cultural Centre** is the venue for various classical music recitals, most regularly ones by the local symphony orchestra, supplemented by the wider-ranging **State Opera and Ballet**, on Milli Kutuphane Caddesi. Summer brings a changeover of venue to the Kultur Parki's open-air theatre. The Opera and Ballet ticket office can inform you of performance locations during the mid-June to mid-July **International Izmir Festival**, though many of these will be outside Izmir itself.

Useful Addresses

Tourist Office (central): Gaziosmanpasa Bulvari 1/C (next to Buyuk

Efes Oteli) (Tel. (51) 142147); (Alsancak office): Ataturk Caddesi 418 (Tel. (51) 220207); other branches at airport and harbour. **Post Office** (central): Cumhuriyet Meydani. **Hospital**: Konak Hastanesi (near Archaeological Museum). **Tourist Police**: (Tel. (51) 218652).

Transport Options

The Havas airport bus will bring you to (and collect you from) the THY office on Gaziosmanpasa Bulvari. From the Alsancak train station (suburban trains), you'll need to take the blue and white bus no. 2 into town, while long-distance trains arrive at Basmane station which is centrally situated. From the main *otogar*, you'll need a blue and white minibus marked Cankaya Mersinli, which will deposit you on Gazi Bulvari. Once in the town centre, most of the main sights can be reached on foot. For ferries across to Karsiyaka and the town bus terminal, head for Konak Meydani.

Northern Aegean – Izmir and Manisa Provinces

A good definition of the northern Aegean is the area north of the Kucuk Menderes river, and roughly coinciding with the Izmir and Manisa provinces. Though it contains only one of the Aegean's most famous sites (Pergamon), it is nonetheless a fascinating area to explore, and far less crowded than further south.

Heading north from Izmir, the first resort town you'll come to is **Foca**, founded in 600 BC as Phocaea, a member of the Ionian Federation. Though none of the ancient city remains, Foca retains considerable character thanks to its ruined Genoese fortress and attractive Ottoman houses. Its beaches are good and, despite its resort status, unspoiled; hotels and *pansiyons* are cheap, and the fish restaurants excellent. For an even better chance of escaping fellow holidaymakers, head for **Candarli**, a sheltered little fishing port with one of the best-preserved Genoese fortresses in Turkey, dating from the fourteenth century.

Half an hour further north by bus is **Dikili**, a harbour town where cruise liners and ferries from Lesbos come so that their passengers can go on day-trips inland to **Bergama**. Unbeknown to most first-time visitors, Bergama really offers two ancient sites in one: **Pergamon** itself and the equally interesting **Asklepion**. The former was a centre of culture and learning, the latter a sanctuary dedicated to Asklepios, god of health. The view from the Pergamon acropolis is magnificent, as it is set well above modern-day Bergama. As you enter the acropolis from the car park, you'll see the Heroon, an ancient temple, to your left. A path will take you past here to the Altar of Zeus, situated on a windy outcrop and shaded by pine trees. Unfortunately, all that remains now is a horseshoe-shaped remnant, the rest (including some impressive reliefs) having been transferred to Berlin in the nineteenth century. A local campaign to bring it back seems to be making little headway. It is possible to make a detour here by walking downhill to the Temple of Demeter, Gymnasium, Lower Agora and Roman Bath; as the ruins are not very well preserved and the path badly marked, few people bother coming down here. The more usual place to head next is the 10,000 seat theatre. Built into the hillside and incredibly steep, the theatre is the best spot for views.

Once you've managed to climb to the top of the eighty rows of seats (don't look down while climbing if you're prone to vertigo), you'll find yourself at the centre of the acropolis, facing the Temple of Athena. Watch out for holes in the ground here, as they're not fenced off. One of the first things you'll see after this is the impressive Library (currently under German-funded restoration), where a collection of 200,000 books was built up, under the guidance of Eumenes II, before Mark Antony took most of them to give to Cleopatra. You may notice what appears to be a mass of paper and other litter around the bushes near the library. On closer inspection, you'll see that pieces of tissue paper and white cloth have been carefully tied to the bushes: this is sometimes done by unmarried women to indicate they're on the look-out for a husband! A path will take you from here to what remains of the Temple of the Emperor Trajan, whose bust was taken to Berlin along with that of Hadrian, an action for which the Germans are trying to compensate by restoring the pillars!

Asklepion can be reached from western Bergama's aqueduct, through a military zone where photography and wandering from the road are forbidden. The function of the site was that of a health spa, and it came to its peak in the days of the famous physician Galen, who began to practise here in the second century AD. The snake you'll see carved in various places harks back to the god of medicine, Asklepios (also spelt Aesculapius), whose symbol it was. Dream analysis was often used to diagnose illnesses here, and treatment included sacred waters and mud. A sacred way (the Via Tecta) will take you through the entrance gate (Propylon) to the library and the Temple of Asklepios. The latter was built in AD 150 in the style of Rome's Pantheon. A smallish theatre overlooks an open area containing a Sacred fountain, from which it's possible to drink (unless you prefer to opt for the soft drink seller who's usually hovering nearby). Perhaps the most interesting part of the site is the vaulted underground passage, eighty metres in length, which leads to the Temple of Telesphorus, a fellow health god and father of Panacea.

A couple of sights in modern Bergama are worth a visit too. The Archaeology and Ethnography Museum houses various local finds, along with models of some of the things now in Berlin. The Red Basilica (Kizil Avlu) is a red-brick riverside ruin, part of which is now a mosque, though it was formerly a basilica and, before that, a temple to the Egyptian god Serapis. Bergama's renowned carpet shops can be found in the surrounding district. Some of their wares may originally have been woven in the pleasant carpet-weaving hill town of **Gordes**, inland and to the south-east.

The archaeological site of **Sardis** (Sart), is on the road between here and Manisa (stop at Sartmustafa), and can also be reached by train (stop at Sartmahmut) from Manisa. The two villages nestle, along with the ruins of Sardis, in an extremely fertile valley where grapes (for sultanas, not wine) grow in profusion. Capital of the Lydians until the seventh century BC, Sardis became wealthy thanks to gold in the local river, which was made into the first ever coinage in the sixth century BC, by King Croesus. But this man, whose name is still a synonym for wealth, made the fatal mistake of attacking King Cyrus of Persia, and Sardis fell to the Persians. East of Sartmustafa you can walk along the Marble Way, a Byzantine shopping street, before coming to a Synagogue with impressive mosaics (replicas, as the originals are in the Manisa Museum), and a third-century Gymnasium with restored marble court. The other site is south of the village, where the remains of the obviously vast Temple of Artemis lie in the hollow between the river and the steep red rock of the ancient citadel.

Manisa is about fifty kilometres west of here. Though little remains of the ancient town (Magnesia ad Sipylus), thanks to Greek destruction of 17,000 historic buildings at the end of the War of Independence, Manisa is a modern working town in a pleasant setting, with the odd historical gem. The Muradiye Mosque (built by Mimar Sinan) and Sultan Mosque both date from the sixteenth century, while the time-ravaged Ulu Cami goes back to the fourteenth. There are great views and, a good walk west from here, at the foot of Mount Sipylus (Sipil Dag – where there's a National Park), you can see what is known as 'the weeping rock of Niobe' (Niobe Aglayan Kaya). The town also has a museum (mainly archaeological and ethnographical), a Thursday market along Murat Caddesi, and a peculiar 'Power-Gum' festival in March or April, when sweets alleged to keep you healthy for a year are distributed to the crowd. September brings a harvest festival to celebrate the grape harvest.

Over in the Izmir province again, below Izmir itself, is the Cesme headland, extended at right angles by the Karaburun peninsula, which contributes to the Izmir Gulf's enclosed nature and thus, indirectly, to its pollution. There's one main road to take you to the tip of the headland (Cesme), but before you reach the town, it's worth taking a left turn to **Alacati**, an old Greek village whose church has been turned into a mosque-cum-meat market! Alacati is overlooked by three windmills and has excellent fishing (and therefore eating) possibilities. You can also go diving in its cave.

Cesme means 'fountain' or 'spring' in Turkish, and there are plenty of Ottoman fountains about, in addition to the Genoese fortress which is the town's highlight. The latter contains a museum and open-air theatre, and nearby a sixteenth-century *kervansaray* has been converted into a luxury hotel, while a Greek basilica awaits either conversion or restoration. 1992 saw an increase in tourism to Cesme and its headland for two reasons. Firstly, the TML service from Venice started to dock here (instead of going right on to Izmir); secondly, a new dual-carriageway opened between Cesme and Izmir, which has made access to the headland easier for both Izmir weekenders and tourists heading for the Greek island of Chios. A Cesme – Kusadasi road is also under construction. The authorities are pleased that Cesme's getting a higher profile, but it's too early to say what the consequences of the increased traffic will be.

The best beaches in the Cesme area (and indeed for hundreds of miles around) are just to the south-west at **Altinkum**, though you'll find more village-size resorts to the north, at **Dalyan** and the pleasant spa of **Ilica**. The **Karaburun** peninsula is disappointingly barren, with just a few beaches (e.g. those at Balikliova and Mordogan), which are difficult to get to without your own vehicle. More interesting is the southern side of the Cesme headland. From Seferihisar you can reach the coastal town of **Sigacik** (complete with Genoese castle), and the ancient ruins at **Teos**. Anyone interested in underwater life will be in their element around the Cesme headland, whose offshore islands offer a wealth of corals, as well as the chance to see seals and sea turtles.

A trip that's worth making if you have the time (and the inclination to escape the crowds) takes you inland along the Kucuk Menderes river valley. **Odemis** is the place to head for initially. From here you can visit the mountain lake at **Golcuk** or the small town of **Birgi**, a totally undeveloped place with traditional Ottoman houses and a splendid fourteenth-century mosque.

Accommodation

First Class

Berksoy Turizm Tesisleri, Izmir Yolu, PO Box 19, Bergama (Tel. (541) 12595). 51 rooms in hotel with garden, swimming pool and sports facilities.

Hora Oteli, Izmir Caddesi, PTT Yani 150, Ilica, Cesme (Tel. (549) 30452). 44 comfortable rooms in hotel with Turkish Bath; welcomes children.

Astoria Oteli, Bodrum Koyu Mevkii, Karaburun (Tel. (5449) 1391 or 1017). 32 rooms in new hotel.

Middle Range

Cesme Marin Oteli, Hurriyet Caddesi, Yali Sokak, Cesme (Tel. (549) 26484). 20 rooms in central, sea-front hotel.

Metay Oteli, Ataturk Caddesi 25, Dikili (Tel. (5419) 2164 or 1145). 27 rooms with ensuite facilities in small, central hotel.

Economy

Efsane Oteli, Izmir Caddesi 86, 35700 Bergama (Tel. (541) 12936). 18 rooms in central hotel.

Hanedan Oteli, Buyuk Deniz, Yali Caddesi 1, Foca (Tel. (5431) 1579). Sea-front hotel with ensuite facilities and good restaurant.

Athena Oteli, Barbaros Mahallesi, Imam Cikmazi 5, Bergama (Tel. (541) 13420). Very simple rooms in characterful Ottoman house.

Nike Pansiyon, Talatpasa Mahallesi, Tabak Kopru Cikmazi 2, Bergama. Family-run guest-house on riverbank.

Rasim Palas, Ilica (Tel. (549) 31010). Simple rooms in nineteenth-century, period-furnished spa hotel.

Kusadasi & Selcuk

Situated eighteen kilometres apart, both Kusadasi and Selcuk are 'ideal' for exploring Ephesus and the surrounding region, depending on what you want from your base. If you're looking for the kind of resort which might have been transplanted from a Spanish 'costa', Kusadasi will suit you fine. If, as is probable, you'd rather forgo the discos and tacky souvenir stalls (at least to some extent), in favour of a quieter town, head for Selcuk.

As far as sights are concerned, virtually all Kusadasi can offer are the old houses and mosque of its **Kale** district. Part of the castle on **Guvercin Adasi** (Pigeon Island – attached to the mainland by causeway) has been turned into a display area for local crafts, optimistically designated a 'museum', but that's about it. Inevitably the closest beaches are overcrowded, with the **Karova Plaji** and **Yavansu Plaji** (reachable on the Davutlar *dolmus*) the best of the bunch. If you've seen all the surrounding sights and are stuck for something to do, your best bet's a day-trip to the Greek island of Samos, or – moving upmarket – a yacht excursion to one of the sites further down the coast. Another option is to head (by *dolmus*) to the **Dilek Peninsula National Park**, nearly thirty kilometres to the south. Despite boasts in the tourist board literature that the park protects the rare Anatolian cheetah, don't get too excited. Most of the park is an inaccessible military zone – a pity for visitors, who are limited to the road and a handful of beaches, but perhaps a good thing for the wildlife. For more about Kusadasi, see **Level of Tourism** section, p. 160.

Selcuk, which used to be a centre of Christianity, is quite different. Although tourism has supplanted agriculture here, the town's location – slightly inland – has meant that it's not been subjected to cruise ship passengers or been featured in tour operators' brochures to the same extent as Kusadasi. This is despite the fact that it's actually much closer to Ephesus – and to a decent beach!

The town is dominated by the **Hill of Ayasoluk**, where St John the Evangelist was buried in the semi-reconstructed **Basilica St John**. The nearby **castle** offers good views too. Storks nest in Selcuk and the best place to see them is on the **aqueduct**, which is alongside the pedestrian precinct. One place you really must visit (along with all the tour groups heading for Ephesus) is the **Archaeological Museum**, which displays numerous finds from Ephesus, breathtakingly well-preserved. It also serves as a useful introduction to the cult of Artemis, goddess of fertility and related to the Anatolian mother-goddess Cybele. You can see why Christianity, which seems rather tame in comparison, didn't take off here at first! A short way along the road to Ephesus are the disappointing remains of the **Temple of Artemis**, one of the Seven Wonders of the Ancient World. Of its original 129 marble columns, only one remains, occasionally topped by an obliging stork. Nearby is the **Isa Bey Mosque**, a fourteenth-century Seljuk edifice.

Until recently, Selcuk boasted an amazingly unspoilt, four-kilometre-long, sandy beach, only a *dolmus* ride away. Sadly, development has started here at **Pamucak** now, so overcrowding is sure to follow swiftly, though the sheer length of the beach gives it certain advantages over other beaches in a similar predicament.

Accommodation

The top hotels of Kusadasi are all of the impersonal 200- to 350-room type, but smaller ones with perfectly acceptable standards can be tracked down, both here and in Selcuk. Kusadasi's best area for budget accommodation is around Kibris Caddesi. In Selcuk, try behind the museum.

First Class

Club Caravanserail, Okuz Mehmetpasa Kervanserai, Ataturk Bulvari 1, Kusadasi (Tel. (636) 14115). 40 rooms in restored 1618 *kervansaray*, built in golden stone and located close to harbour. Exotic and extremely luxurious – come here for a drink even if you're not staying.

Efe Oteli, Guvercin Ada Caddesi 37, PO Box 49, Kusadasi (Tel. (636) 13660). 44 rooms in imposing hotel with sea views and balconies.

Sunday Oteli, Kadinlar Denizi, Kusadasi (Tel. (636) 14525). 60 rooms in seven-storey whitewashed hotel right on sea-front.

Kalehan Oteli, Izmir Caddesi, Selcuk (Tel. (5451) 1154). 50 rooms in old-fashioned hotel decorated with traditional Turkish furnishings.

Middle Range

Stella Oteli, Haci Feyzullah Mah., Bezirgan Sokak 44, Kusadasi (Tel. (636) 11632 or 13787). 16 comfortable rooms in friendly waterfront hotel, with views of town and harbour.

Hasgul Pansiyon, Haci Feyzullah Mah., Bezirgan Sokak 51, Kusadasi (Tel. (636) 13641). 13 rooms in smart, clean *pansiyon*, quiet with bay view.

Ak Oteli, Kusadasi Caddesi 14, Selcuk (Tel. (5451) 2161 or 3143). 60 rooms in central whitewashed hotel.

Economy

Kugu Pansiyon, Ali Tepe Sitesi Yani, Kadinlar Denizi, Kusadasi

(Tel. (636) 12735). 12 rooms in attractive *pansiyon* with balconies and swimming pool, one kilometre out of town.

Ozhan Pansiyon, Kibris Caddesi 5, Kusadasi (Tel. (636) 12932). Small, clean and friendly *pansiyon*, centrally located.

Barim Pansiyon, Turgut Reis Sokak 34, Selcuk (Tel. (5451) 1927). Simple rooms in old restored house.

Suzan Pansiyon, Kallinger Caddesi 46, Selcuk (Tel. (5451) 3471). Quiet restored house with garden.

Eating Out

In Kusadasi you'll find some great fish restaurants, but the general rule is that the waterfront ones (on **Kordon Promenade**) are pricey. The further inland you go, the more reasonable they get, though the quality remains high. For delicious food in a wonderful setting, treat yourself to a meal at the **Club Caravanserail** restaurant. For **Middle Range** alternatives, head for restaurants like **Diba**, **Cam** or **Cati** on Barbaros Caddesi. The cheapest options are further inland around Kahramanlar Caddesi – try **Nazilli Doner Kebab**. One waterfront location where eating won't cost you a fortune is the **Ada Café** on Guvercin Adasi.

In Selcuk there are no real top-of-the-range restaurants. For a pleasant meal in a beautiful setting, try the **Villa Restaurant** on the left of the road out to Ephesus, just where it leaves Selcuk. Cheaper places are found around the pedestrianised Cengiz Topal Caddesi. **Bayrakli** and **Gozde** are a good bet.

Entertainments

Kusadasi's nightlife is positively 'swinging' compared with most Turkish towns. Discos are scattered around, including one in a pleasant setting on Pigeon Island. If you prefer a pub-style evening, the Kale district has its fair share. For Turkish Baths, there's a choice between touristy Kale Hamami or the slightly more authentic Belediye Hamam (Yildirim Caddesi). The area around Saglik Caddesi is alive with market stalls on Fridays. It must be admitted that Kusadasi's a good place to come for shopping (especially jewellery and leather goods), but time your shopping spree for when there isn't a cruise ship in the harbour.

The highlight of Selcuk's year comes in January, when the annual Camel-Wrestling Festival takes place on the outskirts of town. Apparently the animals (both male) are not in any way harmed, and traditional music adds to the atmosphere. Another festival, the International Efes

Culture Festival takes place in April or May, and includes traditional dancing, music and art – many performances take place at the Ephesus amphitheatre.

Useful Addresses

KUSADASI – **Tourist Office**: Iskele Meydani (Tel. (636) 11103 or 16295). **Post Office**: Barbaros Hayrettin Bulvari. **Hospital**: Ataturk Bulvari (by park – Tel. (636) 11026).

SELCUK – **Tourist Office**: intersection of Ataturk Caddesi and Sahabettindede Caddesi (formal address: Ataturk Mah., Agora Carsisi 35) (Tel. (5451) 1945 or 2712). **Post Office**: Cengiz Topal Caddesi. **Hospital**: directly across from tourist office (Tel. (5451) 1006).

Transport Options

In Kusadasi the *Otogar* is a fair way out of town, so the best place to catch your bus or *dolmus* to Selcuk or Izmir is outside the El Birlik office on Inonu Bulvari. For trips to Samos, ferry bookings are taken by agencies such as Tekin Tur (Tel. (636) 13870). You'll need to buy your ticket and leave your passport at the agency the night before if you're planning on taking the morning (8.30 a.m.) boat. If you have any queries about transport, Ekol Travel, Liman Cikmazi 3/1 (Tel. (636) 12644) are very helpful. Day-long tours to Priene, Miletus and Didyma (usually with a swim from Altinkum beach thrown in) start from both Kusadasi and Selcuk. If you want to go under your own steam, the first port of call for connections is Soke.

In Selcuk, both train and bus station are fairly central. *Dolmus* to Efes, Pamucak beach and elsewhere can be caught from opposite the tourist office – it's all very simple!

Central Aegean – Around Ephesus

This part of the Aegean is particularly rich, both for sightseers and nature lovers, yet many do not look further than Ephesus itself for their pleasures. It's worth spending an extra few days exploring all those attractions which, thanks to the proximity of the undeniably spectacular Ephesus, do not get the attention they deserve.

That's not to say you should omit **Ephesus** from your tour! There are, however, certain ways of ensuring you derive maximum enjoyment from your visit. The best option is to spend the previous night in Selcuk, which is less than four kilometres away. Do not be tempted to take a guided tour. They're expensive, far too brief and barely allow you to explore on your own. Having visited the Selcuk Museum the previous afternoon to whet your appetite, equip yourself with a water-bottle (Ephesus is very thirsty work) and catch an early *dolmus* marked Kusadasi, asking the driver to drop you at Efes. If you're feeling energetic, you can walk the pleasant tree-lined road from Selcuk to Efes in 45 minutes, but bear in mind you may need your stamina later. The site opens at 8 a.m. and you should aim to arrive as close to this as possible. If you then head directly for the **amphitheatre** (straight on, then left) and charge up to the top, you stand a fairly good chance of getting a stupendous view down the **Arcadian Way** and for miles around, without a single person visible to spoil it. Now take a deep breath, relax, and resign yourself to seeing the rest of the site in the company of numerous other visitors, consoling yourself with the thought that there's still the best part of two hours before the coach parties arrive.

The Great Theatre itself holds nearly 25,000, but has suffered from less than careful restoration in order to create more seats for the annual festival. Begun in AD 41 and completed in 117, it is nonetheless a magnificent structure, with astounding acoustics and views. It's worth pausing awhile at the top to imagine what it was like when Ephesus was a port; you can see surprisingly clearly where the line of the harbour would have been, with water practically lapping the end of the Arcadian Way. Walking along the Arcadian Way, you'll see the rather overgrown **Harbour Gymnasium** to your right. Look out, at the far end, for the **Nymphaeum**, where there used to be a fountain and pool. It's hard to imagine this being the liveliest street in Ephesus, shop-lined and equipped with street lighting. From the harbour end, there's a good view of the theatre and you can see how it is set into Mount Pion (Panayir Dagi).

Running to the right from the theatre is the marble-paved **Sacred Way**, also known as **Marble Street**. Wheel-ruts and remains of water and sewer channels are still visible. To the right is the third century BC **Agora** (marketplace). But keep checking the ground, as there's an amusing sign etched into it about halfway along the street. The woman's head indicates a **brothel**, and the footprint beside it is to show which direction it's in! You'll find the brothel at the junction with **Kuretes Way**, though its most interesting remains are some mosaic floors. Opposite is the impressive **Library of Celsus**, an elaborate early second century edifice. Goths burned its contents in AD 262, but the two-storey structure remains virtually intact. However, restoration by an Austrian team (whose name is rather crudely advertised all around the library) continues.

Heading up Kuretes Way, a path to the left takes you to what were rather obviously the **public latrines**. Further up is the Corinthian-style **Temple of Hadrian**, behind and above which are the **Baths of Scholastica** (good view of library from here). On the other side of Kuretes Way, flanked by a vast floor mosaic, is a path up to the **terrace houses**. Protected by an ugly red-brick structure, there's a small extra fee payable to view the houses, but it's well worth it, as they offer a unique opportunity to see what everyday life was like for relatively wealthy early Byzantine families.

Further along Kuretes Way, the **Fountain of Trajan** is to your left, and just above this, a side-street to the right takes you past the **Temple of Domitian** to a small **Museum of Inscriptions**. The main road continues through the **Upper Agora**, at the heart of which were the (now very ruined) **Pyrtaneum**, a town hall, and the **Temple of Hestia Boulaea**, where the eternal flame was kept. The small **Odeon** was the meeting place for the town council, as well as a theatre for musical performances. Just inside the outer gate of the site are the **Baths of Varius**.

You now have a choice of walking back down through Ephesus or trying to continue from the upper gate to Meryemana (the Virgin Mary's House), five kilometres further on. Given the difficulty of getting transport from the upper gate, you'll probably prefer to do the former. In any case, there are a couple of interesting detours to make on your way back to the *dolmus* stop opposite the Tusan Efes Motel. Just within the site's entry gate (but beyond the ticket office), a path on the left is marked 'Meryem Kilisesi'. This leads to the second- to fourth-century **Church of St Mary**. As you walk back towards the main Kusadasi – Selcuk road, the small road to your right will take you to the **Cave of the Seven Sleepers**, where seven young Christians from Ephesus were walled in around the third century AD, falling into a deep sleep and awaking only when an earthquake destroyed the wall two centuries later and Christianity was the official religion. The cave was turned into their burial place, complete with commemorative church, and a Byzantine necropolis.

If you want to visit **Meryemana**, the problem is access. Even from Selcuk, the only options are foot (it's eight kilometres uphill), taxi (quite pricey), private car, or hitching – though there **may** be the odd *dolmus* up there by summer 1993 (ask at the tourist office). The house, now a chapel, was discovered only after an eighteenth-century German nun had visions of it as the place where the Virgin Mary spent the last years of her life. It's in a pleasant setting and the nuns who run it in the summer are of various different nationalities and pleased to answer any questions you might have. The place comes alive with pilgrims on the Feast of the Assumption (15 August).

Another former stronghold of Christianity (this time Greek Orthodox) was the attractive hill village of **Sirince**, seven kilometres from Selcuk. Several *dolmus* a day make the trip from Selcuk up here, along with the odd coachload on an organised tour, though the character of the village has not yet been spoiled (except perhaps in high summer season). Sure enough, there are women selling lace in the streets, but they haven't yet discovered the 'hard-sell' techniques and wait for you to come to them. Meanwhile chickens wander unconcerned across the bus parking area and there's a fair chance someone will invite you in for tea. The surrounding hillsides, mainly covered in fruit trees, are an ideal area for gentle walks. (For more on Sirince, see **Level of Tourism**, p. 162.)

Back on the coast, to the north of Pamucak beach, just where the shore bends westwards round to form the southern edge of the Cesme headland, are two little-visited ancient sites, **Notion** and **Klaros**. The former is almost on the beach, though nowadays there's little left to see of this once-important eighth-century BC port. Klaros, 1½ kilometres inland, is more impressive. Restoration has only just started, though in Roman times the Oracle of Apollo here rivalled the one at Delphi. Other ruins include two temples, a sacred way and a monumental gate.

By taking the main road or railway inland, as it traces the course of the Buyuk Menderes river in an easterly direction, you'll come to the provincial capital, **Aydin**. Though there's not a huge amount to see in the farming town of Aydin itself (excepting perhaps the museum and the seventeenth-century Bey Mosque), it's a useful base for exploring some other neglected attractions. Thirty kilometres away to the east is the town of Sultanhisar and, three kilometres north of this, the peaceful ancient site of **Nyssa**. Much of this is overgrown with olive trees, but the Roman theatre is particularly well preserved and there's an unusual 115-metre tunnel beneath the parking area. The sculpture fragments and mosaics of the *bouleterion* (council chamber) are also of interest.

Another site rarely visited is in the valley of the river Cine, a tributary of the Meander which peels off from it in a south-easterly direction from near Aydin. The site, **Alinda**, can be reached direct from Aydin on the Karpuzlu *dolmus*. Dominating Alinda is a long market building, two of whose three storeys remain. Further up the hillside, both the theatre and the watchtower offer splendid views. House foundations, city walls and a necropolis are also in evidence. Other sites scattered along this same river valley are **Alabanda**, **Eskicine** and **Gerga**, though they are difficult to get to (Gerga involving a one-and-a-half-hour walk) and probably not worth it for the non-specialist sightseer.

If you want to explore some of the more famous sites on the coast, you'll have to head back to the transport hub of **Soke** (or, if you want a day-tour just of Priene, Miletus and Didyma, right back to Selcuk or Kusadasi). The first site to head for from here is **Priene**, magnificently situated up a winding road on the southern side of Samsun Dag. The league of Ionian cities held its congresses here around 300 BC. The most impressive building was the Temple of Athena, five of whose thirty perfect Ionic columns were re-erected in the 1960s to give some small idea of how magnificent the original must have been. Other parts of this town, built on a grid system, should also be looked out for. There's a fine *bouleterion*, a temple dedicated to Demeter, a ruined Byzantine basilica, and the inevitable theatre. You'll need to clamber down to a lower terrace if you want to examine the gymnasium and stadium.

The next site down is **Milet** (ancient Miletus). In the flood plain of the Meander, this is the least spectacularly situated of the coastal sites, but its widely scattered ruins make up for this and, being virtually flat as you would expect from a harbour town, you can gain a much better idea of its layout. It was once located on a narrow tongue of land with four different harbours, though now the silted-up Meander delta does its best to obscure this. There's a little archaeological museum on the way in, for which you pay extra. Unless you're keen to see it, you're better off heading straight for the Grand Theatre, which was once right at the water's edge. It's worth examining the exit tunnels beneath this 15,000-seater structure. Above the theatre are the remains of an eighth-century Byzantine castle which offer great views (keep imagining it's water all around). A path off to the right (as you face the theatre) leads to the well-preserved Faustina Baths, commissioned by the wife of the Emperor Marcus Aurelius. Almost hidden amongst the undergrowth south of here is, surprisingly, the early fifteenth-century Ilyas Bey Mosque. Further exploration behind the baths will reveal the Southern Agora (whose monumental gateway now resides in Berlin), beyond which is a Sacred Way, flanked on the left by the *bouleterion* and Northern Agora, and on the right by various monuments including a ruined Byzantine church, a handsome Nymphaeum (public fountain), and the Delphinion, a sixth-century temple dedicated to the patron of sailors. Miletus is one site you're better off visiting in summer; at other times the outlying areas can get marshy. Once you've finished wandering round, you could consider having a cool drink at the restored Seljuk *kervansaray* near the Theatre.

Since you may now be suffering from cultural indigestion, you might prefer to make a detour at Akkoy, instead of going straight on to the next site, Didyma. By taking the road which forks left at the village of Akkoy, you can reach the main Soke – Milas road, which skirts the beautiful and little-visited **Bafa Lake**, also known as Camici Golu. It is spectacularly situated beneath the Besparmak Mountains and is a good spot for nature rambles, sampling the delicious local fish, and (recent droughts permitting) having a swim. There are monasterial remains on many of its little islets and nearby is its very own archaeological site, **Herakleia ad Latmos**. Herakleia has a wide collection of remains from different periods, including some Hellenistic walls plus temple to Athena, some Roman baths plus theatre, and some Byzantine walls plus church. Its best feature is probably, however, its superb location. Boat trips here are sometimes arranged from Mr Ceri's Ceri'nin Yeri (see **Accommodation**).

The final one of the major coastal sites is **Didim** (ancient Didyma), which is situated towards the end of the Soke – Altinkum road. The Oracle to Apollo here is the only site to be located in the middle of a village – indeed, it's the only one compact enough for this to be feasible. The village itself is, not surprisingly, very twee and used to catering for souvenir hunters, but if you want to avoid the coach-loads you need only arrive in the morning, as they almost invariably come after midday. Look out for the cracked Medusa's head on the ground to your right as you enter the site. Only three of the shrine's 108 Ionic columns are now upright, but it is still possible to get an impression of the importance attached to it. It's worth wandering round the back to where a column lies prostrated, allowing you to see the segments of which it was made.

Beyond Didim is the beach resort of **Altinkum**, a newish place with a good beach, safe for children, but not a lot of character and some 'building-site' areas. It does offer an antidote to all the sightseeing though!

Accommodation

First Class

Holiday Oteli, Altinkum, Didim, Soke (Tel. (6353) 1842 or 2376). 27 rooms in hotel with bike hire and children's play area.

Middle Range

Ozlu Oteli, Adnan Menderes Bulvari 71, Aydin (Tel. (631) 13371. 30 rooms in central hotel on palm-tree-lined street.

Piyanci Oteli, Yunus Caddesi 13, Altinkum, Didim, Soke (Tel. (6353) 1484). 15 rooms in airy, whitewashed hotel.

Kabacam Oteli, Hukumet Bulvari 11, Sokak 2/B, Aydin (Tel. (631) 12794). Comfortable hotel, not far from train and *dolmus* stations.

Economy

Olgun Pansiyon, Ozdere, west of Klaros (Tel. (5467) 5751). Guest-house directly on the beach, owned by immensely friendly woman who'll give you all sorts of tips for exploring the region.

Nis Oteli, Altinkum Yolu, Engin Sitesi Ustu, Didim, Soke (Tel. (6353) 1688 or 1504). 20 rooms in pleasantly situated hotel.

Ceri'nin Yeri, Bafa Golu (on Soke – Milas road) (Tel. (6131) 4498). 5 rooms in simple lakeside *pansiyon* (with camp-site). Booking advisable in Turkish holiday season of May/June.

Bodrum

Bodrum, a sprawling mass of low white villas splashed with vivid bougainvillaea, is a resort popular with young people, but has so far managed to retain much of the character that earlier meccas such as Kusadasi have now lost.

It is dominated by the waterfront **Castle of St Peter**, built by the Knights of Rhodes in the fifteenth century (and best viewed from the sea). This typical crusader castle shows the influence of French, English and Italian architecture, but was actually built from the wreckage of the **Tomb of King Mausolus** (one of the Seven Wonders of the Ancient World), which had been destroyed by an earthquake a century before. Over the gates, you can even see parts of reliefs which originally belonged to the Mausoleum. Apart from one frieze, displayed inside the castle, there is little else to see of the Tomb except for its foundations (just off Turgutreis Caddesi): the other friezes ended up in the British Museum.

The Castle is home to the **Museum of Underwater Archaeology**, whose exhibits are mainly from seven shipwrecks which took place between the Bronze Age and the Byzantine Empire. Other parts of the castle (including the chapel and the four towers) house other archaeological collections.

Just to the north of the main road (Kibris Sehitler Caddesi) which heads off westwards to the Bodrum peninsula, is the town's other highlight, an ancient **amphitheatre**, begun by Mausolus and originally big enough for 13,000. It's also worth looking out for the **Haci Molla Han**, an eighteenth-century trading hall, now part of the souvenir shop and restaurant complex which forms the bazaar, just north of the castle. On the western edge of town is the **Myndos** gate, reminder of Mausolus's city wall.

Apart from the sights, Bodrum is a good place to relax, whether you stay put, take a boat trip to a nearby island or beach, or use it as a base to explore the peninsula or (by *gulet*) the Gulf of Gokova. (For more on Bodrum, see **Level of Tourism**, p. 161.)

Accommodation

Finding accommodation should not pose a problem, except in peak season and at the end of Ramadan, when Turkish people from miles around descend on the town to celebrate. The resulting atmosphere is worth booking ahead to experience – as long as you're not in search of a quiet time! At the budget end of the market, you're better off going for one of the hundreds of *pansiyons* rather than a hotel. Even better, look out for the sign *Oda Var* (Rooms to Let), which will allow you to experience a genuine Turkish home.

First Class

Halilarnas Oteli, Cumhuriyet Caddesi 128 (Tel. (6141) 1073 or 3765). This is *the* place to stay in Bodrum, but only do so if you wish to take advantage of its celebrated open-air disco. Book ahead as there are only 28 rooms.

Atrium Oteli, Fabrika Sokak 21 (Tel. (6141) 2181 or 3926). 60 rooms in smart hotel with pool and facilities for children.

Middle Range

Napa Oteli, Kiz Meslek Lisesi Karsisi (Tel. (6141) 1641 or 2583). 40 rooms in waterfront hotel with watersports facilities.

Gundem Oteli, Caferpasa Caddesi, Eckicesme Mah. (Tel. (6141) 2342). 56 rooms in quiet, overgrown *pansiyon*.

Gala Oteli, Neyzen Tevfik Caddesi 224, Yat Limani (Tel. (6141) 2216 or 1910). 15 rooms in hotel near harbour.

Angora Oteli, Cumhuriyet Caddesi, Papatya Sokak 18 (Tel. (6141) 3243 or 2193). 30 rooms in attractive hotel with restaurant and children's play area.

Dinc Pansiyon, Cumhuriyet Caddesi 123 (Tel. (6141) 1141 or 2051). 19 rooms in traditional waterfront *pansiyon*, with attractive wood interior. Can be noisy at night and you'll probably need to book in advance.

Club Princ, TMT Ustu Akcabuk Mevkii, Kumbahce (Tel. (6141) 2902 or 2933). 9 rooms in clean, comfortable *pansiyon* with restaurant and pool, two kilometres out of town.

Economy

Herodot Pansiyon, Neyzen Tevfik Caddesi 116 (Tel. (6141) 1093 or 2423). 15 rooms in clean and tidy *pansiyon* with some yacht harbour views.

Artemis Pansiyon, Cumhuriyet Caddesi 117 (Tel. (6141) 2530). 22 comfortable, sea-front rooms.

Evin Pansiyon, Kumbahce Mahallesi, Ortanca Sokak 7 (Tel. (6141) 1312. 11 rooms in good value, waterfront *pansiyon*.

Belmi Pansiyon, Yangi Sokagi 6 (turn right at Neyzen Tevfik Caddesi 56) (Tel. (6141) 1132). Old building with clean, comfortable rooms.

Eating Out

Most of the hotels listed above have reliable **Middle Range** restaurants. Bodrum is famed for its seafood – especially octopus and squid – so it's worth trying to sample it here. If it's being sold by weight, make sure you can afford what you plan to order! Some authentically Turkish food is served in authentic Turkish atmosphere at the **Mozole**, **Sakalli**, **Anfora**, **Teras** and **Han Restorans**. For directions to these, it's best to ask at the tourist office. Similarly Turkish food is on offer at lower prices from **Orhan's No 7**, off Kale Caddesi (seafood specialities) and **Og Lokanta** on Cumhuriyet Caddesi. In general, Cumhuriyet Caddesi and the area around the castle are good places to start looking for eating places, though, as usual, you pay more for a waterfront location.

Entertainments

If discos are your scene, you'll want to experience the mock-amphitheatrical **Halikarnas**, at the end of Cumhuriyet Caddesi, though the cover charge is considerable. For a more Turkish ambience, try the **Bueno Sera Bar** or the pricier **Mavi Bar**, both on Cumhuriyet Caddesi and both popular with local people and/or Turkish tourists. Eski Bankasi Sokak is lined with attractive bistros and piano bars in converted stone houses and, thanks to its inland location, neither prices nor tackiness have got too out of hand. Otherwise, just people-watching along the promenade is fun. Daytime activities popular in Bodrum include windsurfing and many other watersports. There's a *Hamam* at Dere Umurca Sokagi, and the Thursday and Friday market (up behind the bus station) is a colourful place to wander. The annual cultural festival is usually in September.

Useful Addresses

Tourist Office: Iskele (also known as 12 Eylul) Meydani (near castle) (Tel. (6141) 1091). **Post Office**: Cevat Sakir Caddesi. **Hospital**: Turgutreis Caddesi. **Turkish Airlines**: Neyzen Tevfik Caddesi 218 (Tel. (6141) 1786). **Turkish Maritime Lines**: Neyzen Tevfik Caddesi 68 (Tel. (6141) 1781).

Transport Options

The bus station is on Cevat Sakir Caddesi and it's easy enough to walk to the waterfront, tourist office etc from here. Bicycle hire is possible from **Era Turizm**, Neyzen Tevfik Caddesi 4. Boat trips are advertised all along the quay and vary little in price or content; almost all include **Kara Ada** (Black Island), which has hot springs. You can also take a ferry to the Datca peninsula or the Greek islands of Kos or Rhodes (check all the travel agents along Neyzen Tevfik Caddesi for the best price). If you're thinking of chartering a *gulet* or yacht, try **Yesil Marmaris**, Ataturk Caddesi 81 (Tel. (6141) 3091).

Southern Aegean – Mugla Province

The Mugla province stretches from the tip of the Bodrum peninsula in the west to just beyond Fethiye in the east, covering the transition of the sea from Aegean to Mediterranean (the Fethiye end of the province is therefore treated in **The Mediterranean** chapter on p. 197). This is an ideal part of the coastline to explore by boat, whether you choose day-trips or a two-week charter. Inland too, there are typical Turkish towns and the customary archaeological sites – though the ones down here are less frequented than those in the Central Aegean.

The first place to start is on the **Bodrum peninsula**, most of whose beaches are served by buses from the town. The nearest resort is **Gumbet**, which, like so many other villages on the south and west of the peninsula (where the best beaches are), has been swamped with new construction over the past three years. Along with its neighbours, **Bitez** and **Ortakent**, it is a favoured windsurfing centre, though – unless that's *all* you want to do, Ortakent probably has the edge as it boasts some fascinating turreted houses, including the 1601 Mustafa Pasa house. If you're coming by bus, bear in mind that the village itself is several kilometres inland from the beach of the same name. Further along is **Akyarlar**, a relatively unspoilt Greek village with a small beach and good fish restaurants. It is, however, rapidly becoming the 'in' place to go windsurfing, so it's doubtful whether its character will remain unchanged in the face of this new-found attention. Several other beaches are within walking distance from here.

The west of the peninsula is, with the odd exception, a mass of villas and holiday villages. The major resort is **Turgutreis** (named after a famous local Ottoman admiral who once served under Barbarossa), but it's not the place to come for peace and quiet. Much more promising are **Kadikalesi** and **Gumusluk**, just to the north. The former is a peaceful place in the heart of tangerine-growing country, while the latter has fought to maintain its character and repelled advances by the mighty Thomsons tour operator. You can visit the ancient site of Myndos here, and walk the causeway to **Tavsan Adasi** (Rabbit Island). The area around **Yalikavak** is best visited in spring, when flowers cover the hillsides, but this is an interesting village at any time of year. Its uninspiring beach means that there are few tourists and the main economic activity is sponge-diving. A 300-year-old windmill still grinds grain here. Look out also along this northern stretch for the unusual round white cisterns (*gumbetles*), used to collect water in preparation for the dry season. **Gundogan**, to the east, has a ruined monastery and some swimming possibilities, while **Golkoy** and **Turkbuku** are popular with yachtspeople but are still primarily fishing villages. The ugly purpose-built holiday village of **Torba** should, by contrast, be avoided!

North of the Bodrum peninsula is the Gulf of **Gulluk**, which used to be a pleasant enough place, but the town of Gulluk has been swamped by a multinational-sponsored holiday village and brand new international airport. Nowadays the only possible reason for coming here is so as to take a boat trip to ancient **Iassos** (modern-day Kiyikizacik), which has some rather ruined ruins and some much more appealing fish restaurants.

About thirty kilometres inland is the town of **Milas**, known for its tobacco-coloured handmade carpets and beautiful old Turkish houses (don't be put off by the high-rise blocks on the outskirts). This is a place to look out for the bottles placed on chimney-tops to indicate that there's a marriageable young woman residing within! The main specific 'sight' of the town is its Roman tomb, the *Gumuskesen*, situated uphill from the fresh-produce market and said to be a smaller version of the famous Tomb of Mausolus at Halikarnassos. The actual burial chamber now contains a wheelbarrow and other gardening equipment used to keep the surrounding lawns pretty! The network of streets off Cumhuriyet Caddesi is home to the tradesmen's bazaar, a fascinating mass of shops selling everything from pots and pans to gaudy circumcision ceremony outfits. You will also find a *kervansaray* (the Colluhani) which is still operating as it always has, as a trading hall packed with donkeys and cartloads of goods. Amidst the district of old houses is the single remaining column of a Temple of Zeus dating from the first century BC. Some fourteenth-century mosques are worth visiting too: the Firuz Bey, Orhan Bey and Ulu Cami (which is near a very small archaeological museum).

Two ruined Carian sites, **Euromos** and **Labranda**, are situated just north of Milas, though the difficulty of reaching them without either your own transport or the means to pay for a taxi successfully deters most visitors. Both boast Temples of Zeus. Although the one at Euromos is more impressive, Labranda has much more to offer as a site, including some unidentified buildings, a fourth-century tomb and a refreshing mountain location. Ten kilometres from Milas, at Pilavtepe, you can visit the vast Ildiz Carpet Farm. South of the town, on the only road between here and the south coast, is the hilltop castle at **Pecin Kale** which marks the original site of Milas (Mylasa in those days). The road hits the coast at **Oren**, whose village (which contains some attractive Ottoman houses) is a short way inland from the pine-backed beach. Amazingly, development here is at a minimum and virtually nobody visits outside the peak summer season, so this might be the perfect place to get away from it all if you don't mind the small-town atmosphere.

Another place which doesn't get the attention it deserves is the provincial capital, Mugla, accessible by very minor road from Oren or by major road from Milas. If you have your own transport and are approaching from Milas, it's worth stopping at the village of **Eskihisar**, from where you'll be able to explore the ancient site of Stratonikya, still under excavation. Though Mugla has no specific 'attractions', it is a good place to experience everyday Turkish life, with its mixture of modern buildings, pleasant avenues and fine eighteenth-century houses. If you need more excitement than this, come during its cultural festival towards the end of September.

Back on the coast, after a beautiful winding drive through pine-covered mountains, you'll be jolted back to reality by the sprawling villas which signal the growing resort of **Marmaris**. In the 'retention of character' ratings, it comes somewhere between Bodrum (five out of ten) and Kusadasi (rock bottom). Its situation, reminiscent of a Norwegian fjord, is certainly green and pleasant, and it is 'the' place to come to charter a yacht or sign up for a 'Blue Voyage', boasting the largest marina in Turkey, but it is crowded, humid and over-commercialised during the summer months. A small fortress-cum-museum and the Kaleici area which surrounds it are the only historic sights. One place to get away from the town is just east of the marina, in the Ataturk Park (part of the Gunnucek National Park), where there's a protected wood of deliciously scented Ciga (Frankincense) trees and a small beach. Much further east from here, near Kaunos, is **Ekincik**, a peaceful bay currently enjoying a temporary building ban thanks to its status as a sea turtle nesting beach. (For advice on appropriate behaviour at such beaches, see **The Mediterranean** chapter p. 197.) The other side of town, on the road which leads south-west from Marmaris, it's another story. To quote from a tourist board brochure: 'Tourists have developed the strip between Marmaris and Golenye Icmeleri into a vacation land of their own style'. Perhaps the delicate phrasing is an attempt to pass the buck regarding the ugly holiday villages which have sprung up here over the last decade!

The best use you can make of Marmaris is to take advantage of the variety of boat trips on offer. Most visit the islands or bays in the **Gokova Gulf**, including **Sedir Adasi**, or Cleopatra's Island, where meetings between said lady and Mark Antony allegedly took place. The shortest crossing from Turkey to the Greek island of Rhodes is also from Marmaris. There is little of interest on the peninsula to the south of Marmaris, which ends at Loryma, except perhaps the nautical town of **Bozburun**, a popular resort with trendy Turks.

Much more worthwhile is the narrow Datca peninsula off to the west. The scenery is breathtaking: if you're driving, you'll find it hard (but essential) to keep your eyes on the tortuous road. The peninsula forms the natural division between the Aegean of the Gokova Gulf and the Mediterranean of the Hisaronu Gulf. The town of **Datca** itself has expanded considerably recently and made concessions to the taste of the yachtspeople who come here – mostly in the shape of bars and the odd disco – but, as yet, has only done so in a half-hearted manner. The west beach is pleasant and the local boat trips worth joining. Some of the bays west of Datca are pretty much untouched. One excursion that might appeal is the one to the ancient site at **Knidos**, at the very tip of the peninsula, once known for its Aphrodite cult and resulting sacred brothels. The steep, terraced setting is more impressive than the remains, the statue of Aphrodite having been destroyed long ago by the Byzantine Christians. Only the circular foundation of her temple remains, along with two Byzantine basilicas, a Hellenistic theatre and some tacky souvenir stands.

Accommodation

First Class

Alinda Oteli, Icmeler, Marmaris (Tel. (6125) 1316 or 1403). 58 rooms in wooden-balconied hotel with pool, ten kilometres from Marmaris.

Middle Range

Tropicana Oteli, Iskele Mah., Datca (Tel. (6145) 1635 or 1930). 30 rooms in pleasantly situated hotel.

Karadeniz Oteli, Ataturk Bulvari, Marmaris (Tel. (612) 12837 or 13642). 45 rooms in plain, central, sea-front hotel.

Muratham Oteli, Kenan Evren Bulvari, Siteler Kavsagi, Marmaris (Tel. (612) 11850). 30 rooms in unobtrusive hotel on tree-backed beach, five kilometres out of town.

Begonya Oteli, Haci Mustafa Sokak 101/71, Marmaris (Tel. (612) 14095). Summer-only hotel in restored farm building.

Economy

Arslan Moteli, Uzunyali, Marmaris (Tel. (612) 16733). Long-standing favourite of Turkish families, one kilometre west of town.

Zeybek Oteli, Turgutreis Caddesi 5, Mugla (Tel. (6111) 1774). Quiet but central.

Kordon Pansiyon, 8 Kemalpasa Sokak, Marmaris (Tel. (612) 14762). Central, friendly, family-run *pansiyon*.

Sadik Pansiyon, Datca (Tel. (6145) 1196). Friendly, family-run place with sea views.

Fenerci Pansiyon, Gumusluk (Tel. (6141) 1451). Very simple waterfront guest-house with restaurant.

Inland – Pamukkale & Denizli Province

The Denizli province is best known for its two main attractions: the warm springs and calcified waterfalls of Pamukkale, and the ancient site of Aphrodisias, still under excavation. A large number of coach trips visit them, though the time allowed to explore is often minimal and other parts of the province are completely neglected.

Pamukkale, though famed for its natural phenomena, is actually also the site of **Hierapolis**, whose ruins are often undeservedly eclipsed by their unusual setting. Pamukkale Koyu, the village at the foot of the site, has become thoroughly commercialised over the last years, with numerous bars, pizza joints and souvenir shops. It can be a good place to buy a carpet though, if you bargain carefully, and some bars do try to promote a 'Turkish' atmosphere. It is worth staying overnight so that you can see the travertines at their very best, when the sun's setting on them. Next day, as you climb the hill past them, you'll appreciate their uniqueness. Warm turquoise water (which originally left the ground at 35°C) fills these basins fringed with white stalactites whose texture is most reminiscent of cauliflower. There's a booth at which you'll need to buy a ticket for the site. Six or seven years ago, the authorities tried to prevent people paddling in the pools. As you can see now, they failed miserably and resigned themselves simply to asking people to remove their shoes when on or in the travertines. Yet again, enforcement is proving difficult and this could so easily become another case of tourists destroying precisely what they set out to see.

Perhaps just as interesting as a paddle here is a swim in the pool at the Pamukkale Moteli, also known as the Cleopatra Baths. In this pleasant, garden setting, you can enjoy bath-temperature water in a pool littered with ancient columns and pieces of statuary. It's best to avoid midday though, as most tour groups come to swim here around then.

The surrounding site of Hierapolis was originally (not surprisingly) founded as a cure centre – by King Eumenes II of Pergamon in 190 BC. Part of its mineral baths are now in the Museum, which is otherwise of no great interest. Nearby is a ruined Byzantine basilica from the sixth century. The main archaeological area is just beyond the Pamukkale Moteli (also called the Turizm Moteli). Here you'll see a fourth-century Nymphaeum or monumental fountain; a third-century Temple of Apollo; the Plutonium, a pit which lets off noxious gases and used to serve as an oracle; and, most impressive of all, a Roman Theatre. This has been expertly restored by Italian stonemasons and is better preserved than most Turkish amphitheatres; performances are held here during the Pamukkale festival (May/June). Beyond the theatre are what remains of the ancient city walls and, past them, the octagonal Martyrion of St Philip. The northern city gate opens the way to a magnificent necropolis stretching several kilometres down the road to Karahayit and containing over a thousand tombs and sarcophagi of every variety, including some shaped like houses.

If you continue down this road for three or four kilometres (or go back to Pamukkale and catch a *dolmus* down it), you'll come to the village of **Karahayit**. The springs here are even hotter than those at Pamukkale and the water comes out of the ground red, thanks to an iron source, proceeding to stain the earth vivid shades of red, orange and yellow. You can bathe here, down at the camp-site, dyeing yourself and your clothes red in the process. You might consider staying at Karahayit (which has plenty of *pansiyons*) if you want a quieter base than Pamukkale.

Just off the oleander-lined road between Pamukkale and the provincial capital, Denizli, is the ancient site of **Laodikeia**, from where there are views across the Buyuk Menderes valley to the white Pamukkale cliffs. Formerly a major trading centre, known for its black wool, there is now little to see except the remains of a Roman stadium, a couple of theatres and a baths complex. A little way along the main road running north-east between Denizli and Afyon, you'll come to a sign to **Akyan**, where there's a thirteenth-century Seljuk *kervansaray*, one of whose walls is of marble, giving it the name 'White Inn'. It's pleasantly situated by a stream, near an orchard and contains a mosque and courtyard. If you're here in June and have your own transport, it might be worth trying to attend the Cherry (*Kiraz*) Festival in **Honaz** (turn right off main road, beyond Akyan turning).

The agricultural town of **Denizli** itself is large (around 200,000 inhabitants), fairly modern (thanks to earthquakes in the eighteenth and nineteenth centuries), and not a place to linger. For much more attractive surroundings, head forty-five kilometres north-west along the road to Alasehir. If you take the turning left to **Buldan**, you can visit the weaving workshops of this village, which specialises in decorative embroidery using a gold-coloured thread. Further along the main road, a turning right will take you down the pleasant road to **Guney**, lined with vineyards and a production area for the local wine.

The road to take for Aphrodisias is in the opposite direction, heading south-east from Denizli. Day-trips to Aphrodisias are arranged from Pamukkale. If you're travelling under your own steam, you'll have to look out for the **Tavas** turn-off on the right. Just before this, it's worth stopping to see the carpet-making process (not just the weaving, but also the natural dyeing processes) at the Tavas Hali Carpet House (on the left of the main road). If you don't want to succumb to temptation, leave your credit card behind! At Tavas itself, turn right at the turning to **Geyre**, the modern name for Aphrodisias.

Aphrodisias, whose name stems from the fact that this was a centre for the Aphrodite cult (also practised at Knidos), is beautifully situated on a raised plateau. Excavation is still being carried out, so rules regarding photography are a bit strict in places – though all the major buildings can be photographed with impunity. The site is certainly in the same league as Ephesus and Pergamon, but in a way is even more interesting, as so much is still being discovered. The path round the site forms a loop which (at the time of writing) can be followed in either direction. Most people head for the theatre first (which might be an argument for doing the opposite).

Behind the theatre is a mass of column bases (originally colonnades), surrounding a square called the Tetrastoon, to the south of which is a bath house. The theatre is made of white marble and virtually unscathed. The path which leads to its right offers a good view of the colonnaded Sebasteion and double *agora* on the other side. Continuing, you'll come to the Baths of Hadrian, complete with some floor mosaics. Beyond here, a narrow passageway past a grand house known as the Bishop's Palace will bring you to the exquisite little Odeon, where concerts and council meetings took place. After the fourteen remaining columns of the Temple of Aphrodite, be sure not to miss the left fork of the path, which climbs a slight incline, apparently leading nowhere, until you arrive at the edge of what – for many – is the highlight of the whole visit. The vast 30,000-seat stadium is pretty much intact, and is acknowledged to be one of the most impressive in Anatolia. It's tempting to imagine lions being let into the arena from the entrances at either end, but in fact the stadium was used for nothing more sinister than Olympic-style games. Back on the main footpath, the final building to see is the Monumental Gateway (Tetrapylon), still in the last stages of reconstruction, but nonetheless magnificent.

The city of Aphrodisias lay near some marble quarries and a famous school of Roman sculpture was located here. For this reason, the on-site museum is better than most, displaying many products of this school.

Accommodation

The bonus about staying in Pamukkale is the vast number of inexpensive family-run *pansiyons*, most of which have (or have access to) a swimming pool, usually in a nearby garden. Many *pansiyons* will also let you camp in their garden. So even those on the lowest budget can enjoy a hint of luxury.

Middle Range

Arar Oteli, Delikli Cinar Mey, 9, Denizli (Tel. (621) 37195 or 39369). 44 rooms in central hotel.

Kur-Tur Motel Karahayit Koyu, Pamukkale (Tel. (6228) 21929). 69 rooms.

Economy

Mustafa Pansiyon, Pamukkale Koyu (Tel. (6218) 1240). 32 rooms in quaint *pansiyon* with small pool.

Kervansaray Pansiyon, Pamukkale Koyu (Tel. (6218) 1209). 33 rooms in simple, friendly *pansiyon*. Pleasant setting and good restaurant.

Also in Pamukkale Koyu, try the 8-room **Arkadas Pansiyon** (Tel. (6218) 1183), or the tiny 2-room **Yalcin Pansiyon** (Tel. (6218) 1147). In Karahayit Koyu, try **Kaya Pansiyon** (Tel. (6228) 4007). There's an official camp-site at Pamukkale Girisi (Tel. (6225) 1110), the small-scale **Camtur Camping**.

4 The Mediterranean

Extending from Dalyan in the west to Dortyol in the east, Mediterranean Turkey can be divided into three main regions: the Turquoise Coast, an area of sandy beaches and popular resorts stretching from Dalyan to Antalya; the Turkish Riviera from Antalya to Alanya; and the Eastern Mediterranean, a more rugged and less accessible area sweeping from Alanya to the desolate Hatay in the east. The whole region is relentlessly mountainous, the thin strip of coastline pushed seawards by the Taurus Mountains which stretch from one end of the country to the other.

The Turquoise Coast and Turkish Riviera bear comparison with Aegean Turkey, offering visitors that same heady combination of sandy holiday resorts and ancient monuments. However the beaches here are, if anything, better and the ruins more unusual, the Lycians having stamped their mark on this coast as firmly as the Ancient Greeks did on the Aegean. Not surprisingly, tour operators have been quick to move in on erstwhile fishing villages, developing some of them at breakneck speed, and with scant regard for the environmental consequences. The new and expanding Dalaman airport and efficient Highway 400 can only accelerate this process. The beach at Dalyan has received much publicity as a breeding ground for endangered turtles, but turtles nest on other beaches in this area as well. Local residents are unlikely to point this fact out to you, but you should do your best to find out whether yours is safe or not before you go.

Antalya is the hub of mass Turkish Mediterranean tourism, with Alanya as a small but similar satellite to the east. Between the two, villages have been relentlessly transformed and you'd be hard pressed to find much left of their Turkish character. Side, in particular, lives on as a 'fishing village' only in tourist brochures.

Beyond Alanya, however, it's another story. Here the mountains creep closer to the coast, making for difficult communications and much more tentative development. There are plans for extensive tourism development around Mersin, but for the time being this stretch of coastline is well worth exploring if you're in search of peace, quiet and something more authentically Turkish. It's therefore sad that the big towns to the east, Mersin, Tarsus and Adana, are not as interesting as their evocative names might suggest.

Most of the Mediterranean is best avoided if you want to discover the 'real' Turkey, but you can nevertheless make contact with it if you drag yourself away from the beaches at least briefly. A bus ride to a small town like Elmali, north of Finike, for example, will reveal a quiet, rural lifestyle a million miles from the hectic coastal windsurfing and hang-gliding. Treks into the Taurus Mountains also take you to small villages barely touched by tourism so far. Here too you'll see the settlements of goat-rearing semi-nomads who live along the coast in winter and then herd their flocks north to the mountains each spring, setting up camp there in black woollen tents.

As elsewhere, mass tourism has tended to reduce some aspects of local culture to parodies of their former selves. Around Silifke engagements used to be celebrated with the elaborate *kasik oyunu*, or spoon dance. Nowadays you'd be lucky to see this taking place except at specially-engineered 'tourist' sessions which are unlikely to be high on authenticity.

Tourism has clearly contributed to the greater prosperity of parts of the coastline. However, the success of the textile towns further east suggests that there are viable alternative paths to development. The Turkish government has said it won't allow the rest of the coast to be concreted over as quickly as happened further west. It remains to be seen whether they're as good as their word.

History

It was the Iron Age Lycian tribe, originally a race of sailors and pirates and possibly descended from the Anatolian Luvians, who stamped their mark most firmly on the coast between Fethiye and Antalya. Not only did the Lycians have their own language and customs, but they also built distinctive rock tombs, some of them imitating wooden prototypes, others so grand they could be mini-temples cut into coastal rockfaces. The best of them can be seen at Myra where they are sadly overwhelmed by their visitors, and in Dalyan and Fethiye where sheer inaccessibility makes them more attractive to look at.

Twenty-three Lycian cities eventually formed a political alliance, the Lycian Federation, to ward off external threats. However, in 454 BC they were defeated, absorbed into the Greek Delian Confederacy and forced to pay tribute to Athens. In 404 BC the Persians, in turn, defeated them and forced them to pay tribute. In 333 BC it was Alexander the Great's turn to overwhelm the Lycians; and under Ptolemy of Egypt's government they gradually adopted the Greek language and constitution.

From 197 BC to 159 BC Lycia was governed by the Pergamene king Eumenes II. When the last Pergamene king died without heir in 133 BC, he bequeathed his lands to the Romans. Although Lycia was then absorbed into the Province of Asia with its capital at Ephesus, it stealthily regained its independence, and in 88 BC the revived Lycian League was able to ward off the encroaching Pontic king Mithridates.

However, Lycia's fate was now inextricably tied up with Rome, and in 42 BC the great city of Xanthos was destroyed by Brutus for failing to side with him in the civil war. From 43 BC Lycia was joined to Pamphylia, the Roman province east of Antalya, originally settled by Greek migrants from northern Anatolia in the thirteenth century BC.

Beyond Pamphylia lay the Roman province of Cilicia, also originally settled by the Greeks. It was here, in Tarsus, that the Christian gospel-writer St Paul was born. During his lifetime he made three great evangelical tours, the first (in AD 47–49) taking him to Antakya, Silifke, Side and Antalya. Finally in AD 59–60 St Paul was taken to Rome as a prisoner, changing ships in Myra.

In the fourth century AD the Emperor Justinian separated Lycia and Pamphylia again, and in the seventh century both provinces suffered Arab raids as the Muslims expanded from the south. From then onwards Lycia's history falls in line with the rest of Turkey's, as first the Seljuks and then the Ottomans established their hegemony.

A sad footnote to the Greek-influenced past came in the 1920s when the Greeks and Turks agreed to exchange their minority populations following the 1920–1922 Turkish War of Independence. Some of those forced to move had never seen the 'homeland' to which they were now sent. Outside Fethiye, the deserted village of Kaya Koyu stands as a permanent reminder of this episode.

Geography

Turkey's Turquoise Coast is backed by the Golgeli, Ak and Bey Mountains, parts of the limestone Taurus Mountains which extend for almost 2000 kilometres across southern Turkey. The mountainous terrain forces Highway 400 to skirt the sea, ensuring that bus passengers and drivers have fine views of the clear blue sea and many rocky coves. In spring the mountains' lower slopes are bright with asphodels, poppies and orchids. The coastline from Dalyan to Kas is particularly wrinkled and pitted, with reed-surrounded lagoons at Dalyan itself, at Olu Deniz just outside Fethiye and at Ova Golu, near Patara. Not all the resorts have particularly good beaches, although there are extensive stretches of sand at Dalyan and Patara. Just three miles south of Kas is the tiny rocky island of Meis/Kastellorizo, the smallest in the Greek Dodecanese group, while to the east is the island of Kekova.

Immediately around Fethiye the soil is very fertile, and you'll see cotton, tobacco and maize being cultivated. Olive, pomegranate, fig and Turkish oak trees also flourish alongside basil and oregano plants, and the archaeological sites are often busy with butterflies. Watch out for the occasional snake or scorpion too. Inland, however, water can be in short supply. The village of Ocakkoy was abandoned when its water supply dried up fifty years ago; its revival as a holiday village was only made possible by the sinking of an artesian well.

Between Kas and Antalya the mountains grow, if anything, more dramatic, the highest peaks being Demirkazik (3756 metres), Kizilkaya (3723 metres) and Embler (3623 metres). West of Kemer is the wooded Olympos National Park, while the ruins of Termessos also stand in a designated National Park of fine pine forest and mixed woodland where you may see wild tortoises and sombre tits. In the Bey Mountains beyond live ibex, lynx and even a few bears, but access is difficult and you'd be lucky to see them.

East of Antalya the mountains step back from the Aksu River's floodplain. The Koprulu, Irmagi and Manavgat rivers flow down from the mountains to the sea here, and there's a newly-designated National Park around the spectacular Koprulu Canyon, north of Aspendos. If you search hard you might find small orchids and irises growing in the hills. However, beyond Manavgat the Taurus Mountains sweep right down to the coast again, with innumerable minor rivers pouring through them to the sea. Here there's barely space for any road, which explains why this stretch of the coast has remained relatively undeveloped. The coastal flatlands are healthily fertile, and banana plantations flourish around Alanya.

Silifke stands in the Goksu river delta, where lagoons provide homes for gallinules and pelicans, and brightly-coloured bee-eaters can often be seen. Behind it, the Mut and Karaman road follows a dramatic route along the top of the strawberry-tree-lined Goksu Gorge.

Beyond Mersin the mountains recede again and the towns of Mersin, Tarsus, Adana, Ceyhan and Osmaniye all stand in the flat floodplain of the Seyhan and Ceyhan rivers where cereal crops are grown. They are separated from the Hatay by the Gulf of Iskenderun, a vast Mediterranean inlet used by migrating storks, pelicans and birds of prey in late August.

The mountains act as a barrier to exploration of the interior. However, if you do bus inland you'll discover dramatic mountain scenery interwoven with a patchwork of farmland, apple orchards and dense olive groves, as around Elmali. Turkey's Lake District, a cluster of reed and mountain-ringed salt and freshwater lakes, the largest being Salda, Burdur, Egirdir, Beysehir and Sugla Golus, is also inland. The lakes attract white storks, pygmy cormorants and migrating ducks, while the surrounding reeds provide homes for herons, egrets and spoonbills.

The sea may be unremittingly blue, but in reality it's becoming more polluted by the year. Consequently there are fewer fish than you might expect, and even fewer seabirds. The Eastern Mediterranean is home to most of the remaining monk seals which are also threatened by the increased pollution; in 1992 when dying seals were found scientists thought their immune systems could have been weakened by the pollution.

Dalyan's Istuzu beach shot to international fame in 1988 when the naturalist David Bellamy took up the cause of the loggerhead turtles (*Caretta caretta*) which nested there. The turtles come ashore at night between May and October, digging vast holes in the sand in which to lay their eggs before returning to the sea. Eventually the eggs hatch out and the young turtles swim towards the sea, drawn by the light of the moon shining on it. Unfortunately, with tourism's expansion came plans to build a beach hotel, with the risk that its lights would cause the babies to move in the wrong direction. The attention drawn to their plight caused that particular plan to be shelved, and Dalyan is now designated a Special Conservation Zone. However, by 1991 permanent café structures had appeared on the beach, and despite notices asking tourists to abide by simple rules to protect the nests, people didn't seem to be taking much notice. When asked about the structures, one tour operator's representative said sadly 'it's the beginning of the end'.

Endangered sea turtles (both loggerhead and green turtles) also nest at Dalaman, Fethiye, Patara, Kumluca, Belek, Kizilot, Demirtas,

Gazipasa, Goksu, Kazanli, Akyatan, Kale, Tekirova and Anamur. The site at Akyatan has now been accepted as an official nature reserve. If you're planning to visit any of these beaches you should follow the same guidelines for protecting the nests as apply at Dalyan (see below). You might also like to write to the Worldwide Fund for Nature for their free sea turtles leaflet which gives further information. Alternatively you could write to the DHKD for their guidelines. Finally if you're travelling with a tour operator who features any of these beaches, why not write and ask them if they know about the turtle nests and whether they offer advice to their clients on how to protect them?

Climate

The Mediterranean coast has a pleasant year-round climate, with temperatures only falling to an average of 11 or 12°C even in January and February, when most of the rain falls. Inevitably it can get very hot in summer, with Antalya experiencing temperatures as high as 35°C in July and August. Since this is also the height of the tourist season, better months to visit might be May, June or September.

Sea temperatures in Antalya range from around 17°C between January and March, to about 28°C in August. Sea swimming should be pleasant from May right through to November.

Things get more extreme as you travel further east; by the time you reach Mersin, Tarsus and Adana, you'll be experiencing climatic conditions typical of Eastern Turkey, the summer heat made more oppressive by the high humidity. Inland, too, extreme temperatures are common. Regular snow in the Taurus Mountains makes them difficult to explore in winter; it can also get very hot in summer, so the best time to visit is probably spring when it's cool and the mountain slopes are covered with flowers.

Attractions

Undoubtedly what lures most tourists, particularly the British, to this part of Turkey is the glorious climate and the beaches. These pleasures can be experienced in a series of pretty and fairly upmarket ex-fishing villages like Kalkan and Kas. That said, the Mediterranean coast, especially its western reaches, also offers marvellous sightseeing opportunities. The Lycian sites at Kaunos, Fethiye, Xanthos, Myra and Olympos are highlights, often combining historical interest with spectacular settings. Luckily all these sites are easily accessible from Highway 400 by public transport. Only Termessos to the north of Antalya is tricky to get to unless you take an organised tour.

East of Antalya the sightseeing options are just as impressive, with the ruins of the three great Pamphylian cities, Perge, Aspendos and Side, all boasting impressive theatres in varying states of disrepair. Once again the sites are easily accessible by public transport. Beyond Alanya, the Greek site at Anemurium is also worth visiting, although getting to it is much more of an adventure.

Perhaps the best way to combine sightseeing with soaking up the sun and appreciating the more isolated beaches is to embark on a *Mavi Yolculuk*, or 'Blue Voyage', aboard a *gulet* or Turkish yacht. Tours lasting for anything from three days to two weeks can be organised from many points along the coast.

Despite its touristy surroundings, Antalya itself has a fascinating town centre, full of attractively-restored wooden Ottoman houses. Even Alanya has an impressive fortress, high up on a hill above the over-developed tourist tat along the coast.

In a class of its own is the ruined Byzantine church of St Nicholas at Myra, which is linked to the legend of Father Christmas of whom there is a fine statue in the grounds.

Inland the easily accessible town of Elmali lets you sample something more authentically Turkish. Alternatively, small eastern towns like Silifke preserve something of the old Turkey.

Spectacular scenery can be enjoyed all over the Taurus Mountains, but the Lake District around Egridir and Beysehir is particularly lovely. The National Parks of Olympos, Termessos and Koprulu are also ideal for those who want to trek in beautiful, unspoilt surroundings.

Cuisine

Because the Mediterranean coast has so many tourists, real Turkish food is that much harder to find. What's more, despite the closeness of the sea, pollution has reduced the quantity of fish available, and prices are consequently higher than you might expect, although the quality is usually excellent. Some of the fish available has actually been bred in fish farms, as at Dalyan. If you head inland to the Lakes freshwater fish, including trout, is easier to find at reasonable prices.

Meat-lovers should look out for *tandir kebap*, mutton roasted in clay pots, a speciality of Antalya. Restaurants sell this by weight and it's not particularly cheap; watch closely or else you may end up with a bowl full of fat and gristle. Adana is, of course, the original home of the popular Adana kebab, a spicier version of the standard meat dish, using lots of red pepper.

The hinterland villages are where you'll find the more interesting culinary possibilities. In Uzuncaburc, for example, you can sample *pekmez*, or grape molasses washed down with *kenger kahvesi*, a coffee made from acanthus leaves. Locally-grown apples are ubiquitous, and peaches, plums, apricots, figs and melons commonplace breakfast foods. Aubergines turn up in more guises than you would think possible, often accompanied by delicious yoghurt.

Level of Tourism

In 1989, the Mediterranean region of Turkey as a whole received just over four and a half million foreign visitors. In 1990 the Antalya region alone received about two million tourists, almost four times as many as in 1989, indicating the speed of development in this area. In fact, in 1990 15.33 per cent of all foreign visitors to Turkey arrived in Antalya. The number of visitors from Germany fell quite sharply but was more than compensated for by the increase in the number of visiting Austrians, Scandinavians and British. The contrast with the Eastern Mediterranean region couldn't be sharper; in 1990 Adana received a mere 27,000 tourists, 2000 fewer than in 1989, perhaps reflecting worry in the latter part of the year about going anywhere near the Middle East after the Kuwait invasion.

The area's geography means that all these tourists are tightly packed into the thin strip of land between the mountains and the sea, ensuring that their impact is even greater on places like Fethiye, Antalya, Side and Alanya; Side, in particular, is swamped with tourists from June to September, and Olu Deniz is unrecognisable as the quiet and pretty resort it was just a few years ago. Not surprisingly the coastal infrastructure is hard pushed to cope with all this, with stomach upsets a common consequence of sea pollution; some of the World Bank's $200 million loan (part of the South-West Coast Environmental project) to improve the coastal sewage systems may help alleviate the problem. Temporary building bans at the Specially Protected Areas of Fethiye, Patara, Dalyan and Goksu (all turtle nesting beaches) have not always been adhered to rigidly. Huge inappropriate hotels have also gone up at Belek and Kemer.

Given all this, it's perhaps surprising that not even the easily accessible archaeological sites are completely overrun with visitors; even at Xanthos and Perge it's possible to escape the crowds if you venture beyond the main structures. Coach parties tend to visit on the same days and at the same times; those ready to make an early start can easily get the sites to themselves.

There are exceptions, of course. At Myra, for example, the site's attraction should lie in the beauty of the honey-hued rock-cut tombs, but the number of tourists in multi-coloured clothing crawling all over them completely detracts from what they've come to see. Even coming early or late in the day can't guarantee you get this site to yourself since people will already be there snapping the sunrise or sunset. In contrast, although plenty of tourists make it down to Istuzu beach at Dalyan, they are unable to get close to the rock-cut tombs which are therefore easier to appreciate than those at Myra.

The archaeological site at Patara is protected from overcrowding by the greater pull of the 16-kilometre-long sandy beach (where, once again, turtles nest), while Termessos is protected from the hordes by the greater difficulty of reaching it. However, as roads in the area are improved at breakneck speed, sites that were until recently difficult to get to and rarely visited are experiencing an upsurge of tourists. Olympos used to be tricky to get to but can now be reached by organised excursions. The same applies to the area round Kekova, until recently accessible only by boat but now connected by road to the main highway and therefore within day-trip reach of Kas.

In the mountainous hinterland, of course, it's a completely different story. Towns like Elmali are lucky to receive half a dozen tourists a day, even though they're linked to the main centres by easy bus rides. Similarly, beyond Alanya tourists fade away, and you can have the Ancient Greek site at Anemurium, and the castles near Iskele and in Silifke to yourself.

Plans exist to improve the eastbound coastal road. Should that happen the rest of the coast is likely to go the same way as the west.

Good Alternatives

Meeting People

Inevitably, given the sudden swell in tourist numbers, traditional

Turkish hospitality to strangers is harder to find in the resorts along the Turquoise Coast and Turkish Riviera. Some of the *hamams* have become extensions of the tourist experience, with male masseurs tending to women as well and mixed bathing acceptable. The carpet-sellers are still keen to talk, but there's an edge to their patter and the *cay* flows less freely. Sadly you can even encounter petty dishonesty among traders in places like Kas.

If you want to meet people as you would have done in pre-tourist Turkey, you really need to head east or inland. As soon as you do so, you'll find yourself making easy contact with people in the baths and over glasses of tea again. In particular if you become one of the very few visitors to Mersin, Tarsus or Adana you'll have ample opportunity to find out about present day Turkey, away from the distraction of historical monuments.

Another possibility is to time your visit to coincide with one of the many festivals, making sure that you book accommodation well ahead to avoid problems. Festivals to visit include: the International Music and Folklore Festival in Silifke (May), Tourism Festival in Alanya (June), Insuyu Festival in Burdur (August), Carnival in Kemer (September), the Art and Culture Festival in Mersin (September), the International Fair in Mersin (also September), and the Golden Orange Film and Arts Festival and the Mediterranean Song Concert both in Antalya in October.

Alternatively you could come in the low season when the resorts resume something like their pre-tourism lifestyles. Explore offers a special 'Winter Turkey' tour which involves walking in the Kas area and along the Koprulu Canyon. Explore and Exodus Expeditions also offer Lycian hikes where you follow mule tracks in the Taurus Mountains, stay in local village homes and get to know the families.

Discovering Places

One way to escape the milling crowds of the coastline is to travel inland to Turkey's very own Lake District, accessible via a loop that starts in Antalya and winds up in Manavgat. Popular with the French and Germans, this area is mysteriously overlooked by the British, despite its spectacular scenery, somehow evocative of the Scottish highlands.

Hiring a car is the quickest way to make the loop since buses are irregular beyond Egirdir. However, in Turkey that's an expensive luxury – quite apart from the environmental considerations. Instead it's better to reconcile yourself to taking several days over it, particularly since you're bound to want to stay once you get to the lakes.

From Antalya regular buses run to Burdur (for Burdur Golu) and Isparta, from whence there are connections to Egirdir (for Egirdir Golu). After that it gets tougher since buses to Beysehir (for Beysehir Golu) are infrequent. To get to Sugla Golu via Seydisehir is likely to be much harder and should only be attempted if you've got time to spare.

Of all the towns in this area Egirdir, with its islands, is the best-equipped for visitors. What's more, accommodation is usually in small family-run pensions where you'll have plenty of opportunity to talk to the locals. Some of the young men also organise lake fishing trips; those that do usually have a smattering of most European languages.

A completely different but increasingly popular way to discover the Mediterranean is aboard one of the many yachts or *gulets* that ply the coast offering one- or two-week cruises. Until recently these cruises were the only way to get to many of the Turquoise Coast's rocky coves. Sadly, however, this is no longer the case as the road brings more of them within comfortable reach of the resorts.

Several UK companies, including Turkish Delight, Explore and Temple World, and Trek Travel in Turkey, now offer small-group cruising holidays off the Mediterranean coast. Some of these concentrate on relaxed swimming and sunbathing, while others incorporate a full programme of excursions to the archaeological sites. To see the spring flowers at their best, you should pick a late April/early May cruise. However, if swimming is more important to you, then a later date will ensure that the sea is warm.

Trek Travel organise a number of walking holidays in the Taurus Mountains. Most originate in Istanbul although conceivably you could arrange to join locally. A typical trek takes in the Yedi Goller (Seven Lakes) Valley, Embler Dagi, the Hacer Valley, the Barazama waterfalls, the Seyhan river and Mersin. As an added extra some treks visit remote semi-nomadic villages where walkers can meet the locals and find out about their lives. In winter Trek Travel organise Taurus Mountain skiing trips.

Trek Travel also organise walking and camping tours of the Ak Daglari and Olympos Mountains, taking in Kizlarsivrisi Dagi (Maiden Peak), the highest peak in the Olympos Mountains at 3086 metres. Exodus Expeditions offers a trekking holiday which takes in the Koprulu Valley National Park, again with the opportunity to stay in village houses along the way.

Trekking and other activity holidays are also organised by Istanbul-based Travel Alternatif (see **Introduction** p. 50)

Communications

How to Get There

Until recently most charter **flights** to Mediterranean Turkey flew to Antalya. However, there is now a new and expanding airport at Dalaman which is far more convenient for the Turquoise Coast. Although flights average only a little over four hours, transfers to resorts like Kas can still involve a three-hour journey along a winding, motion-sickness-inducing road. Some of the organised tours taking in the south coast also choose to start and end with a few days in Istanbul. If you're heading for the Eastern Mediterranean, scheduled flights operate to Adana via Istanbul.

Independent travellers might prefer to travel by **boat** from Greece to Bodrum or Marmaris, although this is likely to work out more expensive than flying. Turkish Maritime Lines operates a summer-only ferry service from Venice to Antalya. There are also ferries from Northern Cyprus to Mersin and Tasucu.

Whether you fly to Istanbul, Dalaman or Antalya, you will have to continue to your chosen resort by **bus**. This is unlikely to be a problem since comfortable, air-conditioned buses ply up and down Highway 400 with great frequency.

When You're There

Bus – for getting around Mediterranean Turkey you will be dependent on the excellent bus network since there are no rail services. Between Fethiye and Alanya services are frequent during the day and the road is good enough to ensure smooth journeys provided you don't have to go too far. East of Alanya, however, the road deteriorates and its winding path may not suit those who suffer from motion sickness. Inland there are services to most towns and villages, but they may be infrequent and in buses so old you wonder they survive.

Boat – along the coast travelling by *gulet* is mainly an option for those booked on organised cruises. However, from Kas it's possible, and very pleasant, to visit the Kekova area by boat. Boats can also be hired to get from Kemer to Phaselis, although often the boatmen will only want to go if there is a group of you. From Antalya you can travel by boat to Kas. The islands ringing Fethiye are also best explored by boat. To get to Istuzu beach and Kaunos from Dalyan, boats are also the only option: to Istuzu there's a *dolmus* ferry service;

for Kaunos you need to assemble a group to make the price reasonable.

Walking – only the most determined cyclists would want to bring their bikes to such a mountainous area. However, for the same reason the Mediterranean hinterland is a paradise for walkers. Unfortunately, good hiking maps are almost impossible to come by in Turkey itself. Check with the Royal Geographical Society before you leave, or buy a copy of Lonely Planet's *Trekking in Turkey* which details hikes around the Turquoise Coast and in the Taurus Mountains. Alternatively you can join an organised trekking group (see **Discovering Places**).

Other Options – with the rapid expansion of tourism in the area, other possibilities are rapidly developing. You can, for example, hire a horse to explore the mountains north of Kemer from the Erendiz Ranch (Tel. (3214) 2504).

Geographical Breakdown of Region

The Turquoise Coast

The most westerly stretch of the Mediterranean coast from Dalyan to Antalya is rapidly becoming an extension of the Aegean coast, its beautiful shoreline and attractive villages vanishing beneath intensive tourism development. However, like the Aegean, the Turquoise Coast basks in its glorious historical legacy, this time mostly courtesy of the Lycian Federation. Life here has been dramatically transformed in the last ten years, and nowadays it would probably be true to say that most Turks living along this stretch of the coast depend to some extent on tourism for their livelihood.

The villages mainly cling to the thin coastline, in the shadow of the soaring Bey Mountains. Most retain attractive quays backed with shops and restaurants clustered round the village mosque, even as the villas and apartments spread out around them. Other than Fethiye, few of the settlements could really be called towns.

Fethiye

Fethiye itself has an attractive harbour lined with cafés, excursion boats and a promenade. Otherwise it's an uneasy mix of large-scale, and noisy, development alongside beautiful reminders of the original Lycian city of Termessos.

As you arrive, you can often glimpse the beautiful **Lycian tombs** cut into the rock-face above the town. Best known is the **Amyntas Tomb**, its fine pillared façade looking for all the world like a miniature temple. Sadly the tomb receives too many visitors for its own good; particularly at sunrise and sunset you can hardly get near it for photographers. However, just a short walk from Amyntas several similar tombs are fenced off so people can't climb all over them, making it easier to appreciate them as architecture.

Near the post office a solitary sarcophagus-style tomb is worth examining if you're unlikely to visit the other Lycian sites. The small **museum** is also of passing interest. If you're staying in Fethiye you might want to climb up to the ruined **medieval fortress** on the outskirts of town and explore the lively **market**; look out for 'Freddy's Place' where you'll be able to sample Turkish Delight and apple tea while you chat to its owner. Otherwise, the **harbour promenade** is the best place to while away your time in town.

From Fethiye you can either take a boat out to the islands in search of secluded beaches, or head to villages like **Calis** (by *dolmus*) or **Gemiler** (on foot). The best place to go used to be **Olu Deniz**, set on a nearby lagoon. However, large-scale development of the resort and noisy, disruptive road-building have destroyed most of its old appeal; if you do still want to visit, walk there from the abandoned Greek settlement of Kaya Koyu to take advantage of the beautiful coastal scenery, bearing in mind that the round trip will take up to four hours and is steep in places.

The government has decided that it would be insensitive to restore **Kaya Koyu** to provide homes for Turks while relations between Greece and Turkey remain so tense. However, at nearby **Ocakkoy** abandoned artisans' cottages have been restored as tasteful accommodation for holidaymakers in search of something quieter than the immediate coast offers, and with an authentically Turkish touch. From here you could visit the Lycian sites of **Tlos** and **Pinara**. Both are tricky to get to without private transport, and the ruins are scantier than at some other coastal sites. However, for that very reason, you have more chance of having them to yourself. In particular at Tlos look out for a striking tomb with carvings of Bellerophon riding Pegasus and a lion carved on it.

Accommodation

First Class

Hotel Likya, Gezi Yolu (Tel. (615) 12233). 40 rooms in a large hotel with all mod cons, including swimming pool and pool bar overlooking the sea. Choice of restaurants. Base for tours organised by Likya Tour.

Hotel Kemal, Kordon Boyu, Geziyolu (Tel. (615) 15009). Attractively situated at the quieter end of the promenade. Large modern rooms only let down by lack of fans or air-conditioning. Pleasant terrace restaurant.

Hotel Se-Sa Eine Rose, Akdeniz Caddesi 17 (Tel. (615) 4326). Out on Calis beach, with 36 rooms, overlooking the beach. Another appealing terrace restaurant with sea views.

Middle Range

Hotel Sema, Carsi Caddesi (Tel. (615) 1015). In town away from the beach, this is an old but comfortable hotel with 34 rooms, ideally positioned for exploring Fethiye's restaurant quarter.

Hotel Uzgun, Carsi Caddesi is also perfect for exploring the nightlife and has rooms with private bathrooms.

Economy

Hotel Kaya, Cumhuriyet Caddesi 6, is draped in vines and located in the market.

Ilkoz Aile Pansiyon, Carsi Caddesi is centrally-positioned and family-run.

Aygen Pansiyon, Karagozler Caddesi, a little further out, is quieter and offers breakfast to compensate for the walk.

Eating Out

First Class

The **Likya Hotel** offers a choice of Turkish, Chinese and Italian restaurants, all serving good food. The restaurant in the **Hotel Se-Sa** is also good.

Middle Range

The **Yacht Restaurant**, next to Hotel Likya, is worth visiting as much for its attractive harbour setting as for its tasty fish meals. The **Terrace**, in the town centre behind the *hamam*, serves a good selection of typical Turkish *mezes* and kebabs. Most of the restaurants along the promenade serve a similar range of dishes, many of them fish-based; take care to check the price before ordering. They're also excellent for after-dinner ice-creams.

Economy

Not surprisingly, Fethiye has lots of westernised fare to cater for its tourists. At **Pizza Pepino's** you can eat beneath a vine-draped trellis, although at night the noise from competing sound systems can be off-putting. Of the kebab and *pide* joints, **Doyum** on Ataturk Caddesi is particularly good. And if you want to dine al fresco with a view of the Amyntas Tomb, there's always **Café King** at the top of a steep flight of steps and just by the ticket gate.

Entertainments

If you want to dance the night away you should have no trouble at all . . . often it's just a question of following the noise. Particularly recommended are **Disco Marina** and **Entel**, the latter perhaps a little more downmarket. Most of the cafés along the promenade also play music in the evenings, so just going for a stroll along the quay can turn into something more lively.

Useful Addresses

Tourist Office: Iskele Meydani 1. **Post Office**: Ataturk Caddesi.

Transport Options

Within Fethiye itself you will probably want to walk everywhere. To get to Calis beach or Olu Deniz, however, you may need to take a *dolmus* from the rank beside the Hotel Kemal. The bus station is on the south-east side of town, close to the turning for the Amyntas Tomb.

West of Fethiye

Heading west from Fethiye, buses travel through Dalaman, an unexciting small town, to Ortaca, and from there to **Dalyan**, a much more interesting place to visit. Dalyan itself is little more than a village on a riverbank, and the jetty where the boats to Kaunos and Istuzu Beach tie up is very much its heart nowadays. Services to the beach are very organised and leave according to a schedule; it's an attractive three-quarters of an hour ride, along a reed-lined channel with impressive temple-type Lycian tombs looming up above you. Watch out for storks, reed-loving species of bird and colourful butterflies.

Once you get to Istuzu you'll find a 6-kilometre-long sandy beach, now supplied with toilets and two simple cafés. An information booth set up by the German *Aktionsgemeinschaft Artenschutz e.V* and the Turkish Nature Protection Organisation (with some financial backing from Thomas Cook) provides visitors with information about *Caretta caretta*, the loggerhead turtle, which lays its eggs on the beach between May and August each year. The female turtle digs a hole about fifty centimetres deep and lays roughly one hundred and twenty tennis-ball-sized eggs in it; these then take about fifty-five to seventy days to hatch, the male turtles hatching out at 28.4 degrees Celsius, the females at 32 degrees.

To protect the turtles there are rules about behaviour on the beach which apply right through from May to October when all the eggs should have hatched. The most obvious is that the nest area is marked out on the beach, and within that area people are asked not to set up beach umbrellas, play ball or dig in the sand. They are also asked to keep the beach clean so that baby turtles can't be harmed by anything carelessly thrown away. Camping is prohibited, and owners are asked to supervise dogs carefully. Simple rules you might think, and they are clearly displayed on the beach in Turkish and English. Sadly, in 1991 they were not being properly enforced. Even the ban on night-time visits to the beach is, apparently, more honoured in the breach than the observance. In 1991 all beach visitors were being handed a questionnaire asking their thoughts on the rules and whether they had been approached to go on a night trip to the beach. The battle for the Dalyan turtles goes on.

From Dalyan you can also take a boat northwards to the remains of the Carian city of **Kaunos** on marshy Koycegiz Golu. En route it's worth taking a swim in the warm mineral springs of **Sultaniye** which are supposed to be good for rheumatism and liver problems. At Kaunos itself are the remains of an amphitheatre, Roman baths and a medieval church and town walls.

If you want to stay in Dalyan village the river is lined with family-run pensions, their prices fixed by the local authorities. One of the best is **Aktas Pension** which has rooms overlooking the Lycian tombs. If you'd prefer to camp during the summer months when this is not permitted on the beach, try **Midas Camping**, right by the river. Atmospheric and aptly named is the **Caretta Caretta restaurant** where you can tuck into fish stews on a corner of the beach away from the turtle nests.

From Fethiye to Finike

East of Fethiye, Highway 400 cuts inland through pine forests and past the important archaeological sites at Xanthos, Letoon and Patara to Kalkan and Kas, both overgrown fishing villages and locked in frenzied competition for visitors. Past Kas there are yet more ruined Lycian sites, some of them offshore at Kekova. Just before Finike, a dreary resort but essential for bus connections, the Lycian site at Myra is probably too well-known for its own good.

Kas

Despite the rapid development that has overtaken it, **Kas** remains an extremely attractive base for exploring the surrounding area. Life still centres on the harbour where boats tie up in sight of a vast *cay bahcesi* (tea-garden) and the local mosque. The bus station is at the top of the hill leading down to the harbour, and shops along this street tout a pretty downmarket style of tourist goods. These vanish altogether to the east of town, where old wooden Ottoman houses have been converted into beautiful shops selling expensive designer items in lovely settings.

There's some sightseeing to be done in Kas itself. On the western outskirts is a fine, if plain, **ruined theatre**, very popular as a place to watch sunsets. And at the top of the Uzun Carsi Caddesi shopping street is a **Lycian sarcophagus-style tomb** with an inscription and lion-head carvings. It's also worth climbing up above the town to see an unusual rock-cut **Doric tomb**.

Really though, Kas is a place to use as a base for exploring the surrounding sites. Quayside tour operators will sell you boat trips to Kekova, Patara and Kastellorizo island. **Kekova** is particularly popular because you can look at ruins submerged beneath the gorgeous turquoise sea. A little less well-known but offering something similar is the site of **Aperlae**; here you can actually swim around the ruins, something not allowed at Kekova. **Kastellorizo** is not especially exciting in itself. However, if your three-month entry permit has expired, it's somewhere close at hand for re-entering Turkey and getting a new permit.

Patara is certainly worth visiting, whether you take an excursion or simply hop on a bus. For beach-lovers it offers sixteen kilometres of wonderful sand. For history-lovers the surrounding area is scattered with ruins, including a recently-excavated Lycian cemetery, a fine Roman triumphal arch and a superbly-sited theatre, gradually vanishing beneath baking hot sand. However, as at Dalyan, tourism development at Patara has been controversial, in part because a few loggerhead turtles also nest here. In March 1989 the Society of Nature had Patara designated a Specially Protected Area, where new developments must be two kilometres away from the beach and no more than two storeys high. Nevertheless one seven-storey building has still gone up, and local sewage and rubbish disposal systems are inadequate to deal with even those pensions already in place. Interestingly, when a petition aimed at getting support for protecting the turtles was organised, it was signed by many more overseas visitors than locals, evidence of the mixed feelings many Turks have when the needs of conservation come into direct conflict with individual opportunities to get rich quick.

The resort of **Kalkan** is very close to Patara, so you could drop in for lunch or an evening meal. Another ex-fishing village, it's a little more upmarket and pricey than Kas but has an attractive harbour and lots of bougainvillaea-draped white houses.

Using Kas as a base, you can also reach **Xanthos** easily by bus. The site here dates back to the eighth century BC, and the ruins are divided into two main areas: firstly, there's a fine theatre dominated by two striking monuments; then there's an area of Lycian tombs, round the back of a hill and overlooked by most visitors despite its peaceful beauty. For British visitors this is an uncomfortable place to visit: as you approach you see a board explaining that this was the original home of the delicate fourth-century BC Nereid Monument, removed by Charles Fellowes in 1842 and now housed in the British Museum. When you reach the theatre itself you find a second notice saying that the striking 'Harpy Tomb' is actually a copy; Fellowes removed this too in 1842 and once again the original is in the British Museum.

Not far from Xanthos, and within walking distance if it's not too hot, is the **Letoon**, site of a religious sanctuary where the Lycian Federation held their festivals. Together the Letoon and the site at Xanthos appear on UNESCO's list of World Heritage Sites in recognition of their importance.

Accommodation

Middle Range

Toros Hotel, Uzuncarsi Caddesi (Tel. (3226) 1923). Run by professional mountain guides, this 22-room hotel makes a great base if you want to plan a trip to the Taurus.

Hotel Mimosa, Elmali Caddesi (Tel. (3226) 1368). 26 rooms with *en suite* bathrooms and balconies. Within easy reach of the bus station for early morning departures.

Hotel Ekici, Hukumet Kpnagi Yani (Tel. (3226) 1823). 75 rooms in a comfortable modern hotel with swimming pool and Turkish bath.

Hotel Likya, Hastane Caddesi (Tel. (3226) 1270). Reasonably quiet hotel in hilly position offering fine sea views.

Hotel Korson Karakedi. Beside and above the ruined theatre, this is a quiet, modern hotel with a roof-top breakfast bar and fine views.

Economy

Ay Pension, Yeni Cami Caddesi (Tel. (3226) 1020). Reasonably-priced, centrally-positioned hotel with sea views.

Limyra Pansiyon, Meltem Sokak (Tel. (3226) 1080). Another good place for those wanting to catch early buses, with the bonus of hot showers too.

Andifli, Hastane Caddesi (Tel. (3226) 1042). This boasts excellent sea views and a flight of steps leading straight down to the water.

Lots of similar pensions are opening up all the time. Kas is a good place for camping too; try **Kas Camping** on Hastane Caddesi beyond the ruined theatre, which has its own swimming pool and restaurant.

If you'd rather stay in Kalkan, **La Bohème**, Yale Boyu Mali 40 (Tel. (3215) 1219) has five rooms in a lovely vine-draped building in the town centre, near the harbour. **Dionysia Pension**, Cumhuriyet Caddesi (Tel. (3215) 1681) has 25 comfortable rooms, some with sea views, and a terrace bar set amid begonias, geraniums and daisies. Equally comfortable and picturesque, the 17-roomed **Hotel Diva**, Eski Carikhan (Tel. (3215) 1175) also has a restaurant and terrace bar.

Eating Out

In Kas, the **Derya** and **Eris** restaurants, both in the square facing the harbour, are popular with locals and offer the usual Turkish cuisine as well as a range of fish dishes provided you're prepared to pay the prices. The Derya can get very crowded, the Eris rather noisy. The **Kalamar** in Sube Sokak (Tel. (3226) 1649) is an attractive alternative where a leafy garden makes up for losing the harbour view; again, the menu is strong on fish. Exactly opposite its entrance a nameless hole-in-the-wall café dispenses excellent pizzas and cake. For breakfast in a garden, try **Habesos**, a pension-cum-café in a converted Ottoman house at the top end of Uzuncarsi Caddesi.

Entertainments

Given its package holiday resort status, Kas has a livelier nightlife than many Turkish towns. The **Redpoint**, off Sube Sokak, is a good disco, while the **Nokta** on Uzuncarsi Caddesi features live music in a pub-style atmosphere. If you follow the harbour round as far as you can on the west side you'll find the **Sun Café**, where you can sit on Turkish cushions and drink in laid-back, almost hippyish surroundings, sometimes to a live music accompaniment. Several of the pensions have rooftop bars where music is usually played until late. The only problem with this, as with the music blaring from the east-side restaurants, is that it can get very noisy indeed in the evenings. To watch the world go by there's nowhere better than the *cay bahcesi* right in front of the harbour.

Useful Addresses

Tourist Office: Cumhuriyet Meydani 5. **Post Office**: Cukurbagli Caddesi.

Transport Options

Everywhere in Kas is within easy walking distance, including the bus terminal (for transport to surrounding villages) which is off Elmali Caddesi. If you want to take a boat to Kekova, Kalkan or Patara, ask at the *Kas Deniz Tasiycilari Kooperatifi* in the main square. They can also help with boats across to Meis island.

East of Kas to Antalya

From Kas, Highway 400 sweeps east towards Antalya, passing through the important transport interchanges at Demre and Finike. **Demre** has the ruins of a fifth-century Byzantine church where St Nicholas was originally buried. These are now protected by a metal superstructure, supposedly temporarily, but the delicate frescoes are rapidly fading away underneath it; look out particularly for the passageway under the *deesis* and for the beautiful mosaic marbled floors. The so-called Tomb of Saint Nicholas is probably that of a Byzantine couple to judge from the marble figures on the top. It's a two-kilometre walk from the church to **Myra** which has the well-preserved ruins of a theatre, with the covered passageways to the upper tiers of seats still intact. More interesting are the myriad Lycian tombs cut into the rock-face and visible from the theatre. You can examine these more closely by climbing up metal ladders, but inside you'll find nothing more exciting than bare shelves. However, it's worth examining the façades in more detail since some have carved figures on them, including what could be a funeral scene.

It's unlikely that you'd want to linger in **Finike**. However, this is where you come to pick up a bus to **Elmali**, in the hills to the north. The spectacular three-hour bus ride takes you past stands of cypresses and cedars and stretches of red rock-face sparsely sprinkled with pines. At **Gombe** there's a lively market and a couple of simple pensions if you want to break your journey. Elmali itself huddles in the shadow of Elmali Dagi. Its long thin main street passes the early seventeenth-century Omerpasa Cami, a huge Ottoman mosque with a blue-tiled portico facing a *medrese* across a wide, open platform. Plunge down the side-streets, however, and you'll discover Elmali's real joy, its surviving wooden Ottoman houses, some with upper storeys which jut out so far that their occupants could almost shake hands across the street. Take the eight o'clock bus from Kas and you can be in Elmali in time for lunch and a good look round, but check the times of return buses carefully since transport is infrequent.

East of Finike you come to **Olympos**, yet another ruined Lycian settlement but in a particularly beautiful setting on the banks of a river where you can spot birds and butterflies when the sightseeing gets too much. Once here you should certainly continue on to see the **Chimera**, a unique and mysterious site where flames shoot out of the bare rocks, apparently explaining why local Lycians worshipped the Greek fire-god Hephaestos in particular.

Antalya

In many ways Antalya, starting point for the Turkish Riviera, is the tourist capital of Mediterranean Turkey; apart from Alanya, the towns further east are larger but have much less to offer overseas visitors. Many people arrive in Antalya by air and their first view of the city is likely to be the not especially attractive outskirts. Nor is the bus station one of Turkey's more welcoming arrival points, an example of free market enterprise gone mad with chaotic competing bus companies and nowhere to get objective information.

That said, Antalya has more to offer than these initially bad impressions might suggest. In particular **Kaleici** is a wonderful old town centre district, enclosed between Cumhuriyet Caddesi, Ataturk Bulvari and the sea. Here three main streets, Hasepci Sok, Civelek Sok and Hidirlik Sok, are lined with wonderful old Ottoman houses, many of them meticulously restored and converted into pleasing pensions and restaurants. Just wandering these streets is a joy, and any grudging queries over the 'tweeness' of it should be silenced quickly by comparing the state of the few decaying, unrestored buildings with their glistening neighbours.

Of course there are specific sights as well. The **Old Harbour** is particularly pretty, placed as it is in front of a sheer cliff-face; **Mermerli Park**, at the top, offers the chance to sip tea in the shade with a fine overview of the harbour. Several mosques have particularly interesting minarets; the **Yivli Minare** is delicately fluted, while the **Kesik Minare**, in the heart of the old city, is curiously truncated. Also in the old town centre is the second century **Hadrian's Arch** set in a dip in the ground; watch out for shoe-shine lads on the make here.

If you're planning to take in the archaeological sites east of Antalya you will have to decide whether to head for the **Archaeological Museum** where the major finds from the sites are kept before or after your visits. In particular one room is full of statues brought from Perge, while another displays fine Phrygian griffon vases found in graves near Elmali. Elsewhere in the museum the ethnography section contains a fine reconstruction of a nomadic settlement, enabling you to see inside one of the black tents you may have glimpsed on bus rides. Take a bus or *dolmus* west along Kenan Evren Bulvari to get to the Museum.

Accommodation

First Class

Marina Hotel, Mermerli Sokak 15 (Tel. (31) 175490). Beautifully-sited in a Kaleici Ottoman mansion, with its own swimming pool and a restaurant in the courtyard.

Turban Adalya Oteli, Yat Limani (Tel. (31) 118066). 26 rooms in a harbourside hotel which previously served as a bank and a warehouse.

Middle Range

Hotel Yayla, Ali Cetinkaya Caddesi 14 (Tel. (31) 111913). 48 rooms in an old but comfortable hotel on the outskirts of the old town.

Dedekonak Pansiyon, Hidirlik Sok 11 (Tel. (31) 175170). Right in the heart of Kaleici, this converted Ottoman house is set round a garden.

Atelya Pansiyon, Civelek Sok 21 (Tel. (31) 116416). Like the Dedekonak but in a quieter street.

Economy

Garden Pansiyon, Kilicaslan Mah. Zafer Sok 16 (Tel. (31) 171930). Another converted Ottoman building, with a large and rambling garden café.

Pansiyon Hasbahce, Hesapci Sok 7–9 (Tel. (31) 185367). Similar conversion, again with garden, and boasting hot water.

Otel Sakin, 459 Sok 3, near Sarampol (Tel. (31) 111408). Although not as attractive as the Kaleici hotels, the Sakin is clean, cheap and minutes from the bus station if you need to make an early start.

Eating Out

Many Kaleici houses also contain pleasant cafés and restaurants, some in outdoor gardens and courtyards. **Oasis**, Barbaros Mah Imaret Sok 46, is one such café in a house filled with cats and antiques. Rather more upmarket is the **Marina** Hotel restaurant, where fish-eating in style is the order of the day. Cheaper, but still offering stunning views, is **Hisar Restaurant**, Cumhuriyet Meydani (Tel. (31) 115281), where good food is served in an attractive, kilim-decorated setting inside the castle ramparts.

Entertainments

If your tastes run to discos you'll really need to head out to the beach-side package holiday hotels, where daytime entertainment in the form of windsurfing and other watersports is also on offer. More sophisticated nightlife focuses on the upmarket bars around the harbour in the old town; try **Café Iskele**, one of the less pricey possibilities.

At the end of September/start of October Antalya hosts both a **Film** and a **Song Festival**. This could be a good time to visit, but rooms will be in short supply.

Useful Addresses

Tourist Office: Cumhuriyet Caddesi. **Post Office**: Ismet Pasa Caddesi. **Turkish Airlines Office**: Cumhuriyet Caddesi. **Turkish Maritime Lines**: Kenan Evren Bulvari 40/19.

Transport Options

Within Kaleici, everything is in easy walking distance. However, you will need to take a *dolmus* or bus to the Museum, the main bus terminal and the airport, which is ten kilometres from Kaleici. The once-weekly ferry to Venice goes from the harbour five kilometres along Kenan Evren Bulvari, linked to the town centre by regular *dolmus*.

East of Antalya

Antalya makes a good base for exploring many of the Mediterranean region's archaeological sites. To the east, for example, the Lycian site of **Phaselis**, with ruined harbours and the usual theatre, makes an easy day-trip. Afterwards you can lunch in the unremarkable resort of **Kemer**, where the beaches are man-made, before bussing back to Antalya again.

Getting to the Psidian site of **Termessos** is harder, although that much more rewarding as a result. Termessos is set in wonderful forested National Park which you can reach by *dolmus* from Antalya; it's still quite a walk from the Park entrance to the actual ruins though. Once there you'll find remains of another theatre, an *agora*, several temples, the old city walls and a hill-top necropolis scattered with first to third century AD sarcophagi. Conceivably you could get to Termessos in a loop from Finike through Elmali, but this would be tricky without your own car.

East of Antalya and heading for Alanya it's possible to bus-hop along the coast, stopping at the Pamphylian archaeological sites of **Perge**, **Aspendos** and **Side**, none of them more than an easy walk from the main road. Perge is perhaps the most impressive, a vast site in some ways reminiscent of Ephesus but less crowded. As usual the theatre is one of the most impressive remains, but this time you can also visit a stadium just across the road and then head on to the main site, entered through what is left of the later Roman walls. Inside you'll find extensive remains of Roman baths and of the Pamphylian agora. A paved and colonnaded street heads north to a ruined nymphaeum; on the way look out for pillars with tiny carvings of gods and goddesses on their tops.

Aspendos' theatre is particularly well-preserved and worth seeing even if you think you've overdosed on theatres. This one dates from the Roman period and so much of it was still intact when Ataturk visited it that he had it completely restored; consequently it can still be used for concerts. Even the stage buildings survive to give a good impression of what these theatres must have looked like in their heyday.

In contrast Side is a let-down. Once again there's a ruined theatre, and a paved and colonnaded street, but here the site is swamped by modern-day mass-market tourism which entails such horrors as Disney-style trucks pulled by tractors to convey visitors from the bus station to the village, and camels posed in the sand dunes ready for the snap-happy. The best thing to do is head straight on to **Manavgat**, more attractively sited on a river.

Antalya could also make a good base for a visit to the **Koprulu Kanyon National Park**, although without a private car you'll be lucky to reach the ruined city of **Selge** at its furthest end. En route to Selge you can eat in a tree-house in the pleasant **Kanyon Restaurant**, some consolation if you don't eventually get to the ruined temple, *agora* and Byzantine church there.

Alanya

Resembling a mini-Antalya, Alanya is even more swamped by mass tourism, the hang-gliders floating down from the Castle ensuring that even the sky is taken over by multi-coloured tackiness. It takes some determination to stay put in Alanya, although it's the obvious jump-off base for trips further east. Fortunately it does have some redeeming features, notably the **Castle** itself which towers above the paraphernalia of the beach and offers a pleasant morning's excursion.

Occasional buses run up to the **Castle** or Ic Kale, and, given the hill's steepness, you'd be well advised to take one and leave the walking for the return trip. The remains of the Seljuk castle are not actually that impressive, consisting mainly of sturdy walls. However, from them you do get spectacular views over the town, enabling you to appreciate its position on a rocky promontory between two beaches and the attractive harbour, normally with huge cruise ships moored in it. Halfway down from the Castle you come to the village of **Ehmediye** with the fine sixteenth-century Suleymaniye Cami and several attractive Ottoman houses, some draped with bougainvillaea. Once back at town level again you could pop into the **Museum** which contains the usual assortment of archaeological and ethnological bits and pieces. There are also the stalactite- and stalagmite-filled **Damlatas Caves**, although even if you haven't been to Cheddar, the horrendous development around the entrance, with camels in straw hats, may well be enough to put you off.

Accommodation

First Class

Bedesten Hotel, Ic Kale (Tel. (323) 21234). Beautifully-situated in the village of Ehmediye, the Bedesten was once a Seljuk market and inn, and has now been tastefully restored to provide Alanya's most appealing accommodation option. You may have to endure folklore and belly-dancing sessions here though.

Middle Range

Bayirli Hotel, Iskele Caddesi 66 (Tel. (323) 14320). 40 rooms in a centrally-positioned, modern hotel overlooking the Red Tower, part of Alanya's medieval walls.

Economy

Hotel Gunaydin, Kultur Caddesi 30 (Tel. (323) 11943). Reasonably quiet, clean hotel with solar-heated water supply.

Otherwise, try Iskele Caddesi where there are a succession of cheapie pensions, all of them much of a muchness.

Eating Out

The street behind West Beach is lined with reasonably-priced kebab and *pide* restaurants, most of them featuring fish dishes as well; try **Janus** or **Sultan Restaurant**. The **Bedesten** has its own restaurant, and you can also eat in the courtyard there on summer evenings. Also good is the **Moonlight Café** in Iskele Caddesi where you can dine on a roof-top terrace. For a quick fresh fruit juice try **The Vitamin Station** on Damlatas Caddesi.

Entertainments

Once again, nightlife is the province of the big hotels, who will also be able to help with windsurfing, waterskiing, hang-gliding and parasailing possibilities. However, Alanya really buzzes at night, with music blaring from most of the Iskele Caddesi restaurants and bars.

Useful Addresses

Tourist Office: Carsi Mahallesi, Kalearkasi. **Post Office**: Ataturk Caddesi.

Transport Options

Alanya is small enough to be explored on foot, although you'll need to take a *dolmus* out to the main beaches. Unless you're particularly energetic you'll also want to catch a bus up to the Ic Kale; check times in the tourist office which is opposite the bus stop.

Between June and September there are Friday night TML ferries to Girne in Northern Cyprus.

The Lake District

Instead of approaching Alanya from Antalya via the coast road, you could choose to head inland to Turkey's own 'Lake District' instead. The main bus interchange point is **Isparta**, otherwise an uninteresting town, but just half an hour from **Egirdir**, one of Turkey's forgotten gems as far as the British tourist market is concerned. Egirdir sits on a lake of the same name, completely surrounded by the Taurus Mountains and bringing the Scottish Highlands vividly to mind. From the mainland a causeway juts into the lake, passing first through a small island given over to swimmers, with changing cubicles and showers, and then to a bigger one, Yesilada, entirely ringed with small, family-run pensions and the odd restaurant. There's not a lot to do in Egirdir and no specific sights to explore. However, the setting is so spectacular you won't want to do much except relax and soak it up anyway. Pension-owners' sons organise swimming and fishing trips by boat on the lake. With a car you could also drive round some of the remote villages lining its shore.

Finding somewhere to stay in Egirdir isn't difficult since most buses are met by representatives of the pensions. Even without them you wouldn't have much trouble; just head out along the causeway and then start looking. Two possibilities with obvious attractions are the **Sunrise** and **Sunset** pensions, at opposite ends of the island. For fish suppers at reasonable prices, try the **Big Apple** restaurant where the causeway reaches Yesilada; on Sundays this is where the locals come to watch the sun set as they dine.

Beysehir, east of Egirdir, bestrides another lovely lake with many tiny islands that can be visited on boat trips. The town itself also has a few sights worth seeking out. Best is the Seljuk Esrefoglu Cami, much like other mosques from the outside but a sea of wooden pillars and fittings inside. The contemporary *turbesi* next to it is not normally open to the public but has a fine tiled interior. Another six-domed building close at hand was once a textile factory, and next to that stands a thirteenth-century *hamam*.

Although a road cuts south from Beysehir to Manavgat, bypassing the Sugla Golu, few buses run along it. Without your own transport you may have to backtrack through Egirdir to Antalya. Alternatively you could head straight for Central Anatolia on a Konya bus.

Alanya to Adana

East of Alanya you leave the well-trodden tourist path behind. The Taurus Mountains press more forcefully against the coastline here, leaving little space for a road. Consequently transport is slower and journeys rougher, although the situation is likely to change very rapidly now that developers have their eyes on Mersin. There are fewer really important historical monuments to detain you in this area; however, the smaller number of visitors does mean you have a better chance to get to know the Turks.

Mersin

The sudden desire to open up Mersin for tourism is in some ways odd, given that it has no major sights and isn't even a particularly attractive town. Even the beach is having to be created, together with a marina, by Hilton International who have recently built a 200-room hotel on the seafront. Nevertheless Mersin is a large port which cruise ships are expected to start using as a base soon. You can also get Turkish Maritime Line ferries to Northern Cyprus from here, and if you want to explore the further reaches of the Mediterranean, Mersin is as good a base as any town in the area.

Accommodation

First Class

Hotel Atlihan, Istiklal Caddesi 16 (Tel. (741) 24153). 93 rooms on the west side of town.

Middle Range

Sargin Hotel, Fasih Kayabali Caddesi 10 (Tel. (741) 35815). Comfortable, centrally-positioned hotel near the vegetable market.

Otel Ege, Istiklal Caddesi (Tel. (741) 21419). Attractively decorated in traditional Turkish style.

Economy

Emek Otel, Istiklal Caddesi 81 (Tel. (741) 25370). Cheap hotel down an alley which might put off some women travellers.

Hotel Ocak, Istiklal Caddesi 48 (Tel. (741) 15765). Slightly pricier choice, but on the main street, so perhaps more appealing.

Eating Out

The **Mersin Oteli** at Gumruk Meydani 112 has a roof-top restaurant with sea views and good food. Otherwise, there's the usual range of *pide* and kebab houses. If you can find it, the **Ali Baba Restaurant** in an alley off Silifke Caddesi has a good choice of food, including fish dishes.

Entertainments

For the time being Mersin is as much an entertainment desert as most of Eastern Turkey. Such nightlife as there is, is of the port-town variety and best avoided. No doubt the tourism push will bring the usual rash of discos in its wake.

Useful Addresses

Tourist Office: Inonu Bulvari. **Post Office**: Inonu Bulvari. **Hospital**: Hastane Caddesi. **Turkish Airlines Office**: Istiklal Caddesi. **Turkish Republic of Northern Cyprus Consulate**: Hamidiye Mahalle Karadeniz

Apt. **TML agent**: Turkiye Denizlik Isletmeleri Deniz Yollari Isletmesi, First Floor, Liman Giris Sahasi.

Transport Options

From Mersin there are ferries to Magosa in North Cyprus. Summer services leave on Mondays, Wednesdays and Fridays at 10 p.m., returning the next day. The crossing takes ten hours. On Fridays the ships continue to Syria from Magosa. You can also buy ferry tickets for the crossing from Tasucu to Girne in North Cyprus from Fergun Denizcilik Sinketi in Inonu Bulvari, Mersin. Services depart at 11.30 p.m. on Tuesdays, Thursdays and Saturdays and take eight hours. (Hydrofoil crossings from Tasucu take only three hours, but tickets must be bought in Tasucu.)

West of Mersin

West of Mersin, and a more attractive place to stay if a beach is what you're after, is **Kizkalesi** which is dominated by two huge thirteenth-century sea and land castles. A six-kilometre path leads north to a series of rock-cut Roman reliefs, well worth seeing. From Kizkalesi you can also head west to **Narlikuyu**. A five-kilometre walk north would bring you to the three so-called Caves of Heaven and Hell, one of them with stalactites and stalagmites.

Continuing west on the road to Silifke brings you to **Karadeli** where you can hire donkeys to explore the surrounding hill villages and ruins of Yalak Tas, Dilek Tas and Karakabakli. Most of the time you'll have these sites to yourself. The road then comes to sleepy **Silifke** (Seleucia) where the most interesting specific sight is the Byzantine fortress on the hills above the town. You may also enjoy strolling around streets which seem a world away from Side, before taking a *dolmus* north to **Uzuncaburc** where there are overgrown and forgotten remains of a Hittite and then Hellenistic site, complete with the usual theatre and temples. On the way there you could ask to be dropped off in **Demirciler** to inspect its Graeco-Roman tombs; transport onwards is likely to be a problem though. Just ten kilometres west of Silifke, **Tasucu** can be used as a base for getting to Northern Cyprus if you don't want to travel as far as Mersin; ferry and hydrofoil services leave for Girne three times a week.

From Silifke you can head inland for Central Anatolia, taking the road north which runs to Karaman and from there to Konya; taking this road you could break your journey at **Alahan**, just north of Mut, to visit a magnificently-sited abandoned and ruined monastery.

East of Mersin the obvious place to visit should be **Tarsus**, famous as the birthplace of St Paul. Sadly the only trace of the saint is St Paul's Well, supposedly on the site of his house. Otherwise, Cleopatra's Gate, a Roman triumphal arch, merits only passing attention, and that's it for Tarsus' sights. The country's fourth biggest city, **Adana** also lacks obvious attractions for visitors, although if you want to get the feel of ordinary life in Turkey at the end of the twentieth century this would be as good a place as any to do so. The Ulu Cami is worth a quick look, its black and white colouring calling Diyarbakir's mosques to mind. There's also the fine Tas Kopru, a rare surviving Roman bridge across the River Seyhan just south of the Provincial Museum, a fairly standard display of archaeological relics. If you fancy meeting Turkish weekend holidaymakers, take a bus east to **Yumurtalik** where you can camp in the shadow of a ruined Crusader castle.

5 Central Anatolia

Perhaps the most quintessentially Turkish part of the whole country, Central Anatolia occupies an elongated rectangular area right at the heart of Asiatic Turkey. It was across this bleak and largely desert-like region that first the Seljuk and then the Ottoman Turks poured to stamp their identities on the country. And when Mustafa Kemal Ataturk was looking for a new, more purely Turkish town to replace Istanbul as the capital in 1923, it was Ankara, in the middle of this region, that best fitted the bill.

As capital cities go, Ankara is not one of the world's most exciting, conceding the role of cultural pacemaker to its older and more western cousin, Istanbul. Nevertheless, as the hub of the transport network, it serves as a jumping-off point for tours of the area, especially for those to the Hittite sites in the north and east, and to Cappadocia in the south, one of the most exciting parts of Turkey to explore because of its rare combination of spectacular natural beauty and fascinating historical remains.

Although Ankara boasts its fair share of wealthy mansions, parts of Central Anatolia are still very poor and large sections of its population scrape a precarious living from the land. Areas like Cappadocia with plentiful tourist traffic wear their Islam lightly. However, Konya, once the centre of Turkish Sufism, is a thoroughly conservative, not to say fundamentalist, stronghold, and even in smaller towns like Afyon it is better to assume a conservative outlook. Lone women are likely to attract more attention than they may have bargained for even when dressed quite modestly.

Although much of Central Anatolia is well and truly on the beaten tourist trail, this is such a vast area that you can still get away from it all to traditional towns and villages without too much trouble. If Cappadocia sometimes seems to have sold its soul to tourism, other places like the nearby Ihlara Valley manage a much lower-key approach to their visitors.

Most people living in this region are ethnic Turks. However, don't be surprised to find a fair smattering of Kurds, often running the carpet shops and cafés. In Ankara and Cappadocia it's easy to find men with a working knowledge of most European languages. Elsewhere, however, it's worth brushing up on at least a few phrases of Turkish if you want to get the most out of your trip.

History

The twin tumuli at Catal Huyuk, to the south-east of Konya, are reminders of one of the world's oldest but least-known civilisations, dating back to roughly 7000 BC or the New Stone Age. The tumuli cover thirteen layers of houses, some with wall paintings, others apparently only accessible via holes in their roofs. Finds from this site, including many statuettes of big-breasted and -hipped fertility goddesses, are now in Ankara's Museum of Anatolian Civilisations where a house interior is also reconstructed.

During the Bronze Age the Hattis developed an important settlement, at Alacahoyuk, near Bogazkale; finds from the site, including striking bronze standards carved with deer and fine gold jewellery, are again on show in Ankara Museum. When the Indo-European Hittites moved into Anatolia, probably from northern Europe, in the third millenium BC, they adopted the Hattian culture. One of their most important early settlements was at Kultepe, near Kayseri; finds from this site can be seen in Kayseri's Archaeological Museum.

The Hittites went on to establish a powerful Central Anatolian empire with its capital at Hattusas, also near Bogazkale. At Yazilikaya nearby they created an important religious centre, impressive now for its fine carved figures of their gods. However, from about 1250 BC the Hittites were gradually forced further and further south by sea peoples pushing inland from their bases along the Aegean.

Their place in Western Anatolia was taken by the Phrygians, possibly from Thrace, who created a kingdom centred on Gordion, near Polatli, another site marked today by a huge tumulus, this time associated with the mythical King Midas. Like the Hittites the Phrygians were great metallurgists and reminders of their prowess are also displayed in Ankara. When Midas was defeated by invading Cimmerians in about 725 BC, the period of Phrygian influence came to an end. Meanwhile eastern Central Anatolia fell under the sway of the Urartians (see **Eastern Turkey** chapter).

Because of its geographical position Anatolia was fated to be overrun by successive waves of invaders from east and west. In the sixth century BC the Persians under Cyrus the Great swept across the region. Then in the fourth century BC it was the turn of Alexander the Great who is said to have sliced through the Gordian knot (an ingenious knot which yoked a beam to a wagon dedicated to Jupiter) with his sword when told that whoever untied it would become ruler of the East.

In the third century BC the Celtic Galatians seized Western Anatolia and established their capital in Ankara. In the East the Pontic king Mithridates extended his kingdom to take in most of Eastern Anatolia, until eventually the Pergamene kings swept Anatolia under their sway. When the last Pergamene king died without an heir in 133 BC he left his kingdom to Rome.

Under the Romans Christianity slowly took a hold in Anatolia, getting particular grip on the province of Cappadocia, where the centre of religious authority was Caesarea (modern Kayseri). Amongst prominent religious figures associated with the region were the Cappadocian Fathers, SS. Basil the Great, Gregory of Nazianzus and Gregory of Nyassa. The religious communities soon started to carve out distinctive churches and monasteries in the curious volcanic landscape. These often emulated normal building forms, with free-standing columns, altars and pulpits hewn out of the rock. In all, Cappadocia has more than a thousand churches and monasteries, most of them dating from the early Christian period through to the twelfth century. Their decoration reflects what was happening in the wider community; so some churches are elaborately painted with Bible stories, while others, more simply adorned with crosses, were presumably constructed during the Iconoclastic Period (726–843). From the mid-sixth century, as Muslims from the Arabian peninsula launched plundering raids on the north, the Christians also hollowed out unique underground cities where they could take refuge as much as seven storeys deep in the earth.

Turkey's modern character began to be forged in the eleventh century when the Seljuks emerged from Iran and overran Anatolia, stamping Islam on what had been Christian communities. The Great Seljuk Turkish Empire didn't survive long, but a rump of it lived on, with its capital at Iconium, now Konya; during the Seljuk Sultanate of Rum, Celalledin Rumi (Mevlana) founded the famous Sufic sect of Mevlevis, or Whirling Dervishes.

As the Byzantine Emperor in Constantinople grew weaker it was the Ottoman Turks who gradually gained authority in Anatolia. In 1453 they seized Constantinople and made it the capital of their own empire, of which Anatolia was very much a part. Past Ottoman suzerainty is apparent in almost every Anatolian town or village, most obviously in the classical mosques they built, but also in fine old wooden houses, like those in Afyon.

When the successful War of Independence drove the Greeks out of Turkey immediately after the First World War had finally put paid to the Ottoman Empire, Ataturk decided to move the country's capital to Ankara as part of a policy of Turkification which also saw all place names given Turkish forms and the modern alphabet introduced. Not surprisingly Ataturk is buried in Ankara, where his vast mausoleum is one of the city's most striking sights.

Geography

Most of Central Anatolia is a desolate high plateau roughly 1000 metres above sea-level, framed by the Pontic Alps to the north and the Taurus Mountains to the south, with occasional mountain ranges breaking up the monotony. One of the highest mountains is Erciyes Dagi, near Kayseri (3917 metres), which can be snow-capped even in summer. The Ala Daglari, a continuation of the Taurus Mountains south-east of Nigde, also has lofty peaks; Demirkazik reaches 3756 metres.

Extensive salt lakes add to the dreariness of much of the central plateau. The largest of them, **Tuz Golu** (Salt Lake), west of Kayseri and south of Ankara, is large enough to blight a considerable area around it; looked at through a summer heat haze the actual lake can seem deceptively near when in fact you'll need to walk a long way over the salt flats to find any water. Only desert plant species can survive in this area.

The Kizilirmak (Red River) drains south from Bafra through the centre of Anatolia, bypassing Ankara and flowing through Nevsehir. The Melendiz River flows through the Ihlara Valley and drains the area around Hasan Dag and Melendiz Dag to the south-west. To the south-east flows the Mavrucan Cay, draining the slopes of the Avla Dag and Kara Dag. Mountain streams flowing from these main rivers have added to the rain and snowfalls to erode the soft volcanic materials of the landscape, creating some of Turkey's most extraordinary scenery in the Cappadocia region.

Cappadocia centres on a triangular area with its angles at Nevsehir,

Avanos and Urgup. To the south-east runs a range of volcanoes with five main peaks: Erciyes Dag, Develi Dag, Melendiz Dag, Keciboydoran Dag and Hasan Dag. Eruption of the Erciyes and Hasan volcanoes in particular thirty million years ago threw mud and ash over an area of roughly 10,000 square kilometres. The compressed volcanic ash formed tufa, a soft rock form, gradually eroded by wind and water to create a unique landscape, characterised by cones of tufa, often with harder caps; these are dubbed *peribacalari* or fairy chimneys by the locals. The tufa's softness also enabled local people to hollow them out to serve as churches, monasteries, even complete underground cities; a few cones are still inhabited to this day, although many more are used for storage. Elsewhere, particularly in the south of the region, the same process of erosion created steep-sided gorges, as in the Ihlara Valley. Everywhere the effect of erosion on different types of rock resulted in multi-coloured scenery, with reds, browns, greys and honey colours predominating.

It's important to remember that the pattern of erosion is still very much an on-going affair in Cappadocia. To the work of wind and water must be added the efforts of mankind in carving out the cones to make them usable. As long as the cones retain their protective caps, the process of erosion is fairly slow. Once the caps are gone, however, everything speeds up and the cones gradually collapse. Conservation work is therefore vital if the landscape is to be preserved for the future.

Near Eskisehir there are important quarries for meerschaum, a soft white hydrated magnesium silicate which can be carved into ornate forms, most notably pipe bowls; look out for these on sale in the town.

Much of Anatolia is only suitable for sheep-rearing and wheat-growing, but orchards also flourish in the Cappadocia region; everywhere you go in this area you'll find apricot, pear and mulberry bushes laden with fruit in summer. Vines also flourish in the more fertile valleys. Around Afyon (Turkish for opium) extensive fields are given over to cultivating bright red opium poppies and more mundane sugar beet. Native forest still survives around Konya.

The barrenness of the Anatolian plateau means most of it is not blessed with bird or animal life, although it sometimes seems that every mosque roof has its resident pair of nesting storks. Montagu's harriers can be spotted occasionally around Tuz Golu. Near Kayseri the 500-acre freshwater Sultanazligi (Sultan Marshes) around the salty Yay Golu and Egri Golu provide an important breeding ground for birds. Of 250 species recorded in the area, some of the most interesting are the flamingoes, pelicans, spoonbills, cranes and golden eagles. The marshes are a Specially Protected Area, but hunting and draining for agriculture still continue.

The Hittite sites are also good for bird-watching, with crested larks, red-backed shrikes, black-eared wheatears and rock buntings common. Egyptian vultures also wheel in the sky overhead. At Yozgat, south of Bogazkale, rare king eagles can be seen in the Camlik National Park where unique Yozgat tulips also flower. Black kites can sometimes be seen near Sivas, while glossy ibises, bee-eaters and rosy-coloured starlings can be spotted around Divrigi.

There are thermal springs in Soguksu National Park, north-west of Ankara, off the E5 highway, and near Kangal, south of Sivas.

Climate

Although land-locked Central Anatolia has a severe climate with hot summers and cold winters, it doesn't experience quite the extremes of Eastern Turkey; summer temperatures in Ankara average only 24°C while winter temperatures rarely fall below zero. Nevertheless the dryness and generally desert-like terrain can make the heat seem less bearable than on the coast where higher temperatures can be alleviated by splashing in the sea. In particular in the salty atmosphere around Tuz Golu, strong, hot summer winds can make travelling very unpleasant.

Most snow falls between December and February and most rain between March and May.

Attractions

Central Anatolia is rich in historical monuments dating back to earliest times. Hittite remains are concentrated around Bogazkale, east of Ankara, with the best at Hattusas, Yazilikaya and Alacahoyuk. Amongst the much less visited Phrygian sites west of Ankara, the best known is Gordion.

Cappadocia is special because of its extensive reminders of early Christianity in Turkey; the open-air museums at Goreme and Zelve, with their wonderful frescoed churches, are especially important, although more cave-churches can be seen in the nearby Ihlara and Soganli Valleys, and there's a fine monastery near Nigde (at Gumushler). Cappadocia also offers the extraordinary underground cities of Kaymakli and Derinkuyu.

Seljuk remains can be found throughout the area, with Kayseri particularly well worth exploring. However, Konya's mosques and *medreses* are in a class of their own. Indeed the shrine of the Mevlana must be one of the most beautiful tombs in all Turkey. The remote mosque complex of Divrigi is also listed as a UNESCO World Heritage Site.

Reminders of the Ottomans also litter the area, with the old wooden houses in Afyon especially interesting. Ankara itself has a few relics of the Roman occupation, and the wonderful Museum of Anatolian Civilisations, but is most intriguing for the glimpse it offers of Ataturk's vision of Turkey; don't miss a trip to his stately Mausoleum.

This isn't the best area of Turkey for lovers of natural beauty, except in the curious Cappadocia region where the tufa cones, or 'fairy chimneys' are in a class of their own, rightly elevated to World Heritage Site status. Nevertheless there are beautiful National Parks at Yozgat, near Bogazkale, and at Cankiri and Soguksu, north of Ankara.

Anatolia is mainly a sightseer's paradise. However, in Cappadocia walking, cycling and horse-riding are possibilities, while Erciyes Dag offers facilities for skiers who don't mind roughing it. Skiing is also possible in the Cankiri National Park. Peaks in the Ala Daglari range near Nigde are also climbable without any special permits; Camardi village, where guides and donkeys can be hired, makes the best base.

Cuisine

Afyon is famous for its wonderfully rich milk; local cattle are said to feast on opium poppies along with the usual grass, with fantastic consequences for their milk. Be that as it may, it's well worth trying some of the thick local clotted cream (*kaymak*), sometimes served for breakfast with bread and jam. If you don't think you could face it neat, *kaymak* can also be eaten rolled up inside Turkish Delight. The poppy trade has been cut back since its heyday in the sixties, but much of Afyon's bread still comes scattered with poppy seeds.

Although you can get all the usual kebabs throughout the region, Konya boasts its own *firin kebap* made from roast mutton. Meat lovers may also want to try *sac kavurma*, a meat stew often served over a burner since the juices are meant to be kept piping hot. Kayseri offers a strongly-spiced, garlic-flavoured sausage called *pastirma*.

Fruit is a speciality of Cappadocia, and in all the villages you'll see apricots laid out on the roofs to dry. Pears, plums and mulberries all grow in profusion, and you would be unlucky not to be offered at least one handful of fruit during your stay.

Don't expect to find alcohol in conservative towns like Konya and Afyon. In contrast you'll be able to find even western dishes in 'tourist' areas like Goreme and Avanos. Avanos offers folkloric evenings which can sound pretty dreadful but which do offer the chance to sample a wider range of local dishes than in most restaurants.

Level of Tourism

The most popular part of Central Anatolia with visitors is undoubtedly Cappadocia. Back in the early 1970s tourists were a rare sight in villages like Goreme and Urgup. But in 1990 almost 300,000 international tourists visited the three provinces of Kayseri, Nevsehir and Aksaray, almost twice as many as in 1989. Goreme has been transformed by the creation of a hideous tourist centre, and Urgup has only been saved from similar devastation because it is more awkward to get to by public transport. Stalls selling tacky souvenirs (nutcrackers shaped like the lower part of a woman's body) now line many of the roads in the area, and some completely inappropriate hotels have been thrown up with no thought for their impact on the scenery – and despite planning regulations intended to prevent this happening.

Perhaps surprisingly it's the French, Italians, Spanish and Germans rather than the British who have 'discovered' Cappadocia; recommendation in *Le Guide du Routard* is the highest possible accolade as far as many hotels and restaurants are concerned. Particular regional bottlenecks are the Goreme and Zelve open-air musuems, and the narrow streets winding between the best of the 'fairy chimneys'. Both Derinkuyu and Kaymakli also get hopelessly busy in summer; about 40,000 people squeeze into Kaymakli every month between April and August, with the largest numbers in May when Turks are also on holiday.

Despite what could sound like a tourism horror story, Cappadocia is big enough to absorb most of its visitors without too much pain. It doesn't take much effort to get away from the herd, and there are still lots of outlying sites which receive hardly any visitors at all.

Ankara, too, receives a steady flow of travellers, almost 315,000 of them in 1990, even though it is not a particularly beautiful place. Most will head for the other regional honeypot sites around Bogazkoy which can get uncomfortably crowded in the middle of the day when coach parties descend en masse; Yazilikaya in particular is too confined a site to be comfortable when more than a few people visit it at once.

Konya also hosts huge numbers of visitors each year, although in this case its popularity owes more to the number of pilgrims pouring into the Mevlana's shrine than to tourism of the conventional sort. In 1990, the shrine received 1,200,000 visitors.

In contrast some parts of Central Cappadocia go virtually unvisited. Picturesque Afyon is just one off-centre town that is bypassed by most tourists; indeed Afyon province as a whole received only 3500 international visitors in 1990. Divrigi, with a mosque which features alongside Cappadocia in UNESCO's World Heritage Site list, is another forgotten gem.

Good Alternatives

Meeting People

Even in the most popular parts of Central Anatolia, the Turks remain friendly and welcoming. Venture into the **carpet shops** and you can still expect to be chatted up over a glass of *cay*, even though you may have been the hundredth person through the door that day. One noted exception is Kayseri where a line in hard-sell more usual in Morocco can be very off-putting.

However, the *hamams* are not quite as safe a bet in the more touristy areas. In Urgup and Avanos you'll find unisex arrangements that would be out of the question in more traditional areas; in such circumstances Turkish men may still come to the baths, but women certainly will not. In fact the baths at Avanos bear almost no relationship to the real thing; true, you can still get scrubbed in the steam and have a massage, but there's a swimming pool and sauna, and you're unlikely to find any Turks at all in here. For something more authentic try the baths attached to the Seljuk Hunat Hatun complex in Kayseri.

Discovering Places

Because Central Anatolia is such a large area with good transport networks, independent travellers should have no trouble finding corners of it to call their own. The Phrygian site at Gordion is little visited, as are the mosque at Divrigi and the fine Ottoman houses of Afyon.

Even in Cappadocia you can get away from the crowds if you head for Mustafapasa, the Soganli Valley, the Ihlara Valley or Eski Gumusler Monastery. There's even an 'alternative', if smaller, underground city to be found at Ozkonak, north of Avanos. Many of these areas are best explored on foot, by bike or on horseback. You can hire horses in Avanos, Urgup (Tel. 3890) and Ortahisar (Tel. 1763), and mountain bikes in Urgup (Tel. 3488). **Trek Travel** also offer organised cycling and horse-riding/camping tours of Cappadocia.

Although in general this is not an area you would want to explore by train, **Turkish Delight** does offer twice-yearly chances to see Anatolia by specially-scheduled steam trains. These run between Ankara and Kayseri, Sivas, Malatya, Adana, Konya, Afyon, Isparta, Burdur and Denizli, arriving on the Aegean coast at Selcuk, just outside Ephesus. The journey then continues up the coast via Izmir to Istanbul.

Communications

How to Get There

The quickest way to get to Central Anatolia is to **fly** to Ankara, although you will probably have to stop in Istanbul on the way. Since there are more flights to Istanbul than to Ankara, especially in summer, it may be cheaper to fly there and then travel on to Ankara by other means. If you don't want to start your journey in Ankara, there are flights from Istanbul to Kayseri, Konya and Malatya.

With time to spare, you might choose to take the Turkish Maritime Lines **ferry** to Samsun and then travel south by bus or train. However, it will be much quicker to use the first-class **Blue ('Mavi') Train** which takes about nine hours to reach Ankara. Trains leave Istanbul's Haydarpasa station daily at 1330 and 2300, and return from Ankara daily at 1330 and 2250. Tickets cost about £10 and advance reservations are advisable.

Alternatively you can, of course, take one of the frequent **buses** from Istanbul to Ankara which should take about seven hours and will cost slightly less than the train.

When You're There

Bus – you will probably want to use buses for most of your journeys. Services are generally efficient, comfortable and quick, although those south from Nigde may seem to take an eternity because the narrow mountain road suffers from a surfeit of old, slow-moving and carriageway-blocking lorries which can barely make it up the slopes.

Apart from Ankara the main transport hubs are Konya, Kayseri and Nevsehir.

Rail – there are a few railway lines, but trains are generally old, slow and unreliable. If you do want to try them, services run from Ankara to Kayseri, from Kayseri to Sivas and Malatya, and from Malatya to Konya, Afyon, Denizli and the Aegean coast.

Other Options – Cappadocia and the surrounding valleys lend themselves to exploration on foot, bike or horseback (see **Cappadocia** section p. 252).

Geographical Breakdown of Region

Ankara

When Ataturk was looking for somewhere to make the capital of the new Turkey in 1923, he chose Ankara (originally Angora) for its marvellously central position at the heart of the Anatolian plateau. At first sight an unattractive, sprawling modern city of two and a half million inhabitants, Ankara grows on you when you get to know it better.

As you approach the city, you can hardly fail to spot the vast **Anit Kabir**, the mausoleum built, after an international competition to come up with a design, to house the body of the Father of the Turks. You approach the Mausoleum along an avenue lined with Hittite statuary. Colonnaded porticoes surround a huge courtyard and house several rooms open to the public as museums displaying trophies like Ataturk's cars. Respectful behaviour is *de rigueur* inside the actual shrine, and guards watch over you as you walk round the tomb to ensure you don't do anything you shouldn't.

The other 'must' for visitors is the **Museum of Anatolian Civilisations**, a tastefully-converted *bedesten* or covered market, now housing finds from Catal Hoyuk, and the Hittite and Phrygian sites. From the Museum the old **citadel** or *hisar*, with its ninth-century walls, is only a short uphill walk away. In sharp contrast with Ankara's modern heart, all high-rise buildings and bustling traffic, the citadel encloses an older version of the city, where women in headscarves and baggy trousers still sit in doorways embroidering. Make sure you head for the Sark Kulesi or Eastern Tower which offers fine views of the city.

Ankara also retains a few reminders of the Romans, most notably the **Column of Julian**, a tall Corinthian column memorial to the

Emperor's fourth-century visit, on top of which storks habitually nest. Other remains include traces of the third-century **baths,** and ruins of the **Temple of Augustus and Rome**, now partly buried beneath the mosque of Haci Bayram Veli.

However, Ankara is primarily the place to come to get a feel for modern Turkey, something you can do while following an ad hoc Ataturk trail. Start your tour at the **Republic Museum** housed in the second headquarters of Ataturk's Grand National Assembly where interesting photographs are on display, and you can inspect the tiny original meeting room. For more reminders of Ataturk, visit the **Cankaya Kosku,** his original country residence, in the grounds of the Presidential Mansion; the interior is still furnished as it was in the great man's day. Then look for the **Opera House,** built at Ataturk's behest, beside the entrance to Genclik Park.

Like most capital cities Ankara boasts a variety of museums. Other than the Museum of Anatolian Civilisations, the most interesting is probably the **Ethnography Museum** on Ataturk Bulvari which houses Seljuk and Ottoman artefacts; there's also a room which Ataturk once used as an office. If you're planning on using the trains you may want to drop into the **Railway Museum** beside the station; the most prized exhibit is Ataturk's private white carriage.

Of the city's many mosques the best is the Seljuk **Aslanhane Cami** or Lion Mosque just south of the citadel, which has fine wooden columns and ceilings and a blue-tiled *mihrab*. The modern **Kocatepe Cami** might also be worth visiting since it's one of the world's largest mosques.

Accommodation

Unfortunately Ankara is for the most part an architecturally unattractive city of high-rise buildings. Few hotels, especially at the top end of the market, really fit the 'good tourist' ideal of small-scale, family-run accommodation. Those recommended below are, nevertheless, the best of what is on offer.

First Class

Buyuk Ankara Oteli, Ataturk Bulvari (Tel. (125) 6655). 194 air-conditioned rooms in a high-rise building very close to Turkey's Parliament. A full range of facilities includes a swimming pool, tennis court and sauna.

   Ankara Dedeman Oteli, Buklum Sokak 1, Akay (Tel. (117) 6200).

308 air-conditioned rooms and suites in a hotel with swimming pool and nightclub, and with a good restaurant.

First Apart-Hotel, Inkilap Sokak 29, Kizilay (Tel. (125) 7575). 15 apartments for rent if you're intending to stay a while in Ankara.

Hotel Bulvar Palas, Ataturk Bulvari 141 (Tel. (117) 5020). Reasonably priced, central hotel.

Middle Range

Otel Karyagdi, Sanayi Caddesi, Kurcesme Sokak 4, Ulus (Tel. (310) 2440). Comfortable, and fairly new hotel where some rooms have baths rather than showers.

Hotel Melodi, Karanfil Sokak 10, Kizilay (Tel. (117) 6414). 35 rooms with private facilities in a hotel with bar and patio café.

Hotel Yeni, Sanayi Caddesi 5/B, Ulus (Tel. (310) 4720). Popular centrally-positioned hotel with reasonable restaurant and foyer lounge. All rooms have private facilities but the décor is dark and old-fashioned.

Economy

Otel Sipahi, Itfaiye Meydani, Kosova Sok 1. **Hisar Oteli**, Hisarparki Caddesi 6, Ulus. Both with clean, comfortable rooms.

Babil Otel, Gazi Mustafa Kemal Bulvari 66, Maltepe. Reasonable hotel, although none of the rooms has private facilities.

Otel Devran, Opera Meydani Tvus Sokak 8. **Lale Palas**, Hukumet Meydani, Telgraf Sokak 5. Both retaining some attractive old fittings.

Terminal Oteli, Ankara Otobus Terminali. Handy if you're catching an early-morning bus.

Cumhuriyet Youth Hostel, Cebeci (Tel. (189) 916).

Campers will need to head for the **BP Mocamp** which has good facilities but is twenty-two kilometres away in Suzuzkoy on the Istanbul road.

Eating Out

First Class

The best food is usually to be found in the luxury hotel restaurants; apart from those listed above as possible places to stay, you could try the **Hilton International** in Tahran Caddesi, or either of the **Pullman Etap** hotels, one in Tandogan Meydani, the other in Ataturk Bulvari.

Middle Range

There's a slightly better choice of middle-range eating places, especially if you hunt around Sekanik Sokak or Karanfil Sokak in Kizilay. Try the **Akman Et Lokantasi** on Tavus Sokak 4 for a wider choice of meat dishes, or **Korfez Lokantasi** in Bayindir Sokak for fish dishes. Alternatively, the **Akman Boza ve Pasta Salonu** offers al fresco dining, with a good range of sandwiches, omelettes and pastries to wash down with the *boza*, a millet-based drink.

Economy

As elsewhere in Turkey, most of Ankara's restaurants offer cheap kebab and *pide* meals, and the Ulus area is as good a place as any to start looking. The **Kebabistan** in Ataturk Bulvari (second branch in Sanayi Caddesi) is a particularly popular choice. If you're visiting the Museum of Anatolian Civilisations, the **Yavuz Lokantasi**, in Konya Sokak, offers the same sort of food at very reasonable prices. **Rema Lokantasi**, Posta Caddesi, Ulus, offers bargain basement-priced food.

Entertainment

Ankara's essentially Turkish character is reflected in the absence of the flourishing nightlife you would expect in a capital city; after ten at night even most restaurants and *cay* shops close down and only the big hotels show signs of life. Still, if you're determined to hunt out some of the very few discothèques, Kavaklidere is the area to head for. Men (but never lone women) might also want to sample the *gazinos*, or bars, of Maltepe's Gazi Mustafa Kemal Bulvari. Finally if you can befriend a Turkish student you might get taken to some of the student watering-holes in Cebeci, not easy to track down on your own.

Useful Addresses

Tourist Office: Gaza Mustafa Kemal Bulvari 33 (Tel. (230) 1915). **Turkish Airlines Office**: Railway Station, Hipodrom Caddesi, Gar Yani (Tel. (312) 4900). **Post Office**: Ataturk Bulvari, Kizilay. **American Express**: Celikkale Sokak 12/B. **Central Bus Station**: Hipodrom Caddesi. **UK Embassy**: Sehit Ersan Caddesi 46/A, Cankaya (Tel. (274) 4310). **British Council**: Ingiliz Kultur Heyeti, Adakale Sok 27. **Hospital**: Hasilcilar Sokak, Sihhiye. **Turkish Maritime Lines Office**:

Sakaraya Caddesi, Inkilap Sokak, Deniz Apt 4/4, Kizilay.

Transport Options

Ankara is sufficiently large to make walking everywhere unrealistic. Fortunately there are plenty of buses, and you can catch many of the important ones along Ataturk Bulvari; number 63 goes to Ataturk's Mausoleum. The only snag is that you must remember to buy the flat-price tickets from a kiosk near the stop before boarding the bus. Still, most Turks are so friendly that someone is bound to help you if you're having trouble.

If you don't want the hassle of trying to use the buses, there are plenty of taxis, although you should take care to confirm the fare before starting out.

East of Ankara

From Ankara there are two ways to travel to Erzurum. One road heads due east via Kirikkale, Yozgat, Sorgun, Akdagmadeni, Yildizeli, Sivas, Erzincan and Askale. To take in the Hittite sites you would need to divert north at Yozgat along a very minor road. The second possibility is to take the same road as far as the turn-off to Delice and Sungurlu and then take in the great Hittite sites around Bogazkale. After that you can continue north to Corum, before turning east to Amasya. The road there forks again and you can either head south through Turhal to Tokat and Sivas, rejoining the main Erzurum road there, or head east through Erbaa and Susehri, rejoining the main road at Erzincan.

The easiest way to reach **Bogazkale**, the village which serves as a focus for exploring the Hittite sites, is to catch one of the hourly buses from Ankara to **Sungurlu** and then take an onward *dolmus*. Bogazkale itself is a small but attractive village with limited accommodation for tourists; the best of what's available is probably the **Hattusas Pansiyon**. If everything is full and you haven't got a tent with you, you may have to stay in **Sungurlu** instead, in which case the **Hittit Motel** (Tel. (42) 409) might be a good choice.

Biggest and best known of the sites is **Hattusas** which was the Hittites' capital from about 1375 BC to 1200 BC. What was once a walled city is now a World Heritage Site consisting of a number of separate sites strung out on top of a hill and offering fine views over the surrounding plains. Probably most interesting is the Lion Gate, with two huge carved stone lions guarding a gateway through the wall.

Passing through a second gateway, once guarded by two stone sphinxes, you come to a seventy-metre long tunnel. The area of the Great Temple is also interesting, and still contains the remains of amphorae used to hold liquids. Unfortunately Hattusas is so popular with coach parties that you are likely to be mobbed by men hawking Hittite pictures and inscriptions. They're handmade but certainly not original.

Only three kilometres to the east, **Yazilkaya** is a much smaller site where the remains of a temple pale into insignificance in comparison with the carvings on the adjacent rock faces. These show the Hittite deities, with hieroglyphs to identify them. However, since the carvings are inside a narrow defile, it pays to get to them early in the day, before the coach parties descend.

The third site, at **Alacahoyuk**, is less visited although in some ways easier for a non-archaeologist to understand. You approach the site via a gateway guarded by huge stone sphinxes; look out for the fine carvings on either side which show musicians, acrobats, etc. The main site consists of the foundations of a lot of buildings, attractively laid out in a garden. At the back don't miss another tunnel, this time with a bend in it, almost hidden in the long grass. There's also a small on-site museum, with archaeological finds on the ground floor, and carpets, costumes and other ethnographical bits and pieces upstairs.

If you're heading towards the Black Sea from the Hittite sites, you could stay in **Corum** which may not be beautiful but does have some good hotels, including a **Turban** (Tel. (42) 5311). Alternatively, if you're heading east towards Erzurum, **Amasya** (see **The Black Sea** chapter) would make a good stopover point.

Halfway between Amasya and Sivas, **Tokat** is worth visiting, if only to see the museum in the Seljuk **Gok Medrese**. With more time you could also inspect the two **turbesis**, one built by the Seljuks, one by the Mongols. Like so many off-the-beaten-track Anatolian towns, Tokat retains a few fine **Ottoman houses**; some have lovely interiors, should you be fortunate enough to get invited in.

At a crucial junction for roads to the east, **Sivas**, a town of a quarter of a million inhabitants, sounds more attractive than it actually is. However, it does have a fine assortment of **Seljuk buildings** clustered round the town centre which make it worth an overnight stop. The most important of these buildings are: the **Gok Medrese** (1271), the **Ulu Cami** (1179), the **Sifaiye Medresesi**, the **Cifte Minare Medrese** (1271) and the **Buruciye Medresesi** (1271). Best of them all is the Gok Medrese which has fine carvings and tiles. However, perhaps because Sivas isn't really on the overland 'milk run', not all the buildings are well maintained or even always accessible. If you do decide to stay the **Otel Kosk**, Ataturk Caddesi 11 (Tel. (477) 11150) is probably the best middle-range option. Ataturk Caddesi also has several cheaper hotels, none of them especially inspiring; perhaps the best is the **Otel Evin**.

South of Sivas, there are thermal baths near **Kangal**. In particular Balikli Cermik consists of a series of outdoor baths where small fish nibble flaking skin away while you bathe, a procedure which is said to be helpful to psoriasis sufferers.

From Sivas it's also possible to catch a train to **Divrigi**, site of Turkey's least-visited World Heritage Site, the **Ulu Cami** and the adjoining **Darussifa** hospital complex. These are Seljuk buildings put up by Emir Ahmet Sah in 1228, and the Ulu Cami in particular has one of the most incredibly elaborate entrances ever designed. Once you've admired this, you could go in search of the **kumbets**, or tombs, of local Seljuks, including Emir Ahmet Sah himself. The town itself is quiet and attractive. However, before rushing there you should bear in mind that accommodation is basic even by the standards of Eastern Turkey.

The railway line continues east to Erzincan, via **Kemah** where you can visit a ruined Byzantine castle and a few more tombs. Several earthquakes had already devastated **Erzincan** before the one which wreaked such havoc in 1992. Consequently it is not a very attractive place to linger and you'd do better to stay on the train through to Erzurum.

West of Ankara

West of Ankara are the best of Turkey's remaining Phrygian ruins. Trains run to Eskisehir, stopping in **Polatli** from whence it might be possible to find transport to **Yassihoyuk**, site of Gordion, one time Phrygian capital and the best known of the sites thanks to King Midas. However, only one huge tumulus and scant ruins of the city now remain. To reach the scene of a ruined temple to Cybele at **Ballihisar** you would need to take a bus from Polatli to Sivirhisar and then look for a *dolmus* or taxi on to the village.

Eskisehir has a ruined Seljuk castle and a small archaeological museum containing some of the finds from the Phrygian sites but is not, otherwise, an attractive town. Instead you could continue by bus or train to **Kutahya**, centre of Turkey's modern tile-making industry.

Traditional sixteenth-century Iznik patterns have been revived recently and you can buy vases or wall-plates decorated with them. *Dolmus* operate from Kutahya to **Aezani** where there are extensive remains of a Roman temple to Zeus and more limited remains of a stadium and *agora*. From Aezani you can continue to **Usak** for connections to either the Aegean or the Mediterranean.

Alternatively from Kutahya you can catch a train to **Afyon**, one of Anatolia's most attractive small towns, its streets lined with pastel-coloured wooden Ottoman houses in varying states of disrepair. The town is dominated by an enormous rocky crag, its summit adorned with the remains of a **fort** dating back to Hittite times (although most of what you see now is Byzantine or Ottoman). Seven hundred steep steps lead to the top, and along the way you'll see bits of rag with wishes written on them attached to the bushes. Afyon is a very religious town, and if you time your arrival at the summit for one of the prayer times, you'll be able to listen to all the town's imams intoning prayers at the same time, a deafening but impressive performance.

At the foot of the steps, the Ulu Cami is a thirteenth-century Seljuk building with magnificent wooden columns and ceilings. Even better is the Mevlevi Cami which has an adjoining ceremony hall where the Dervishes used to whirl before Ataturk banned their ceremonies; although in theory this is now a museum to the Dervishes it is frequently closed, perhaps because there are so few visitors. However, Afyon's real charm lies in its many old houses, some even retaining the latticed wooden windows that allowed household women to look out without outsiders being able to see them doing so.

Sadly, none of the old houses has been converted into a hotel. If you do want to stay, there are two reasonable but slightly over-priced economy hotels on Ambarayolu Caddesi: the rambling **Sinada**, and the more modern **Hocaoglu**. The best place to go to meet the locals is the large and lively *cay bahcesi* with a family section in Ordu Bulvari which sometimes has live music in the evenings.

Using Afyon as a base you could explore a few remote and barely-known Phrygian sites, although all are tricky to get to without private transport. At **Aslantas** and **Aslankaya**, which are very close together, ruined temples bear carved lion reliefs. At **Midas Sehri**, near the village of Kumb, temples and tombs are cut into the rock-face, while an underground tunnel to the valley below has recently been discovered.

From Afyon there are trains west to **Denizli** for Pamukkale (see **The Aegean** chapter) and east to Konya. If you're heading for Konya you could break the bus journey at **Sultandagi** to inspect the ruins of a Seljuk *kervansaray*, or inn. The road passes both Eber Golu and Aksehir Golu, and at Aksehir a fork south leads to Beysehir, Egridir and Isparta, the heart of the Turkish Lake District (see **The Mediterranean** chapter).

Konya

Konya was once the Roman city of Iconium and then capital of the Seljuk Sultanate of Rum. Now an industrial town of just over half a million inhabitants, it still holds a special place in Turkish architectural history, playing host to several of its finest Seljuk mosques and *medreses*. However, it is even more famous as the home of Celalledin Rumi, the *Mevlana* or Master, who is also buried in the city. It was the *Mevlana* who established the world-famous sect of Whirling Dervishes, Sufi mystics whose whirling was supposed to free them from earthly ties and help them achieve union with God. In 1925 Ataturk banned the Dervishes who had become increasingly powerful politically. Nevertheless, the *Mevlana* is still held in great affection by many Muslims and his shrine is popular with pilgrims who can be found praying beside his tomb from early in the morning. Over a million pilgrims now come to Konya every year.

It's worth staying several days in Konya to get to grips with all its sights. Logically, you should start at the **Mevlana Muzesi** which contains the turquoise-roofed, conical **Mevlana Turbesi** where the *Mevlana* is buried in a tomb, topped with a turban, which shows off the best of Seljuk embroidery, tilework and painting. Inevitably there will be people praying in front of it, so it's more than usually important to be appropriately dressed. Alongside the tomb are those of other Dervish worthies, including the *Mevlana*'s father.

Cases in this and the adjacent *semahane*, or ceremonial room, contain exhibits of costumes, books, carpets and lamps; perhaps most interesting is the thirteenth-century *Mathnawi* in which the *Mevlana* set out his ideas. In the courtyard in front of the *turbesi* stands a large ablutions fountain. Rooms around the courtyard contain further exhibits, and some rather unconvincing mannequin Dervishes. There's usually some slow and eerie music playing. This is typical of the music the Dervishes whirled to, and if you'd like to listen to it at your leisure cassettes are on sale in the courtyard kiosk.

Just inside the *turbesi* a large board facing the entrance summarises the *Mevlana*'s teachings as follows: 'Come, come whoever you are, whether you be fire-worshippers, idolators or pagans. Ours is not the dwelling-place of despair. All who enter will receive a welcome here.' However, this broad-minded approach to religion is not espoused by many latter-day Konyans. Just in front of the **Mevlana Musezi** is the Ottoman **Selimiye Cami**, liberally adorned with notices advising on suitable behaviour in and around the mosque. A blackboard on the platform outside also broadcasts a 'thought for the day' in Turkish. If you can find someone to translate it for you, you may well find that it offers such ironically illiberal sentiments as 'Christians are the worst animals to crawl on the earth because they don't believe in Allah'. Similar boards can be found outside many Konyan mosques.

From the Mevlana Musezi you can cross the overgrown **Ucler cemetery** (from where there are wonderful unimpeded views of the *turbesi*'s turquoise roof) to visit the **Koyunoglu Muzesi** in an unusually quiet part of Konya. The museum contains a fairly standard collection of archaeological, historical and ethnographical artefacts. More interesting is the vine-clad adjoining **house** where the museum's founder, a private collector, lived. This has been preserved as it would have been when he was alive, and enables you to see typical furniture and fittings from a Konyan house in situ.

The most important of the Seljuk monuments are clustered round the Alaettin hill at the end of Alaettin Caddesi in the town centre. Most striking is **Ince Minare** (Slender Minaret) **Medresesi** which has a spectacularly carved stalactite-style entrance; it now houses a museum of wood and stone carving. Also worth visiting is **Buyuk Karatay Medresesi** which has a wonderful blue-tiled dome; not surprisingly this is now a museum of tilework. On the hill itself is **Alaettin Keykubat Mosque**, an early thirteenth-century building undergoing extensive restoration.

To the south of Alaettin Tepesi, in a more run-down part of town, the thirteenth-century **Sircali Medrese** has an impressively-carved entrance, but is, once again, closed for restoration. Nearby is the **Archaeological Museum**, in the grounds of a Seljuk *kulliyesi* or monastery, which contains magnificent Pamphylian sarcophagi covered in lively carvings, some of them featuring the Twelve Labours of Hercules.

To see something of modern Konya, head for the lively all-day **bazaar** to the south of Alaettin Caddesi. You could try the *hamams*, although not all of them are very clean. On Alaettin Tepesi itself there are several pleasant *cay bahcesis*, while to the north there's a permanent **fairground**, an easy place to make friends with the less conservative locals.

If you're staying in Konya for a few days and find archaeology exciting, you might try getting to the site of **Catal Hoyuk**, regarded as the second-oldest known city, although you'd never guess that from what's left at the site now. *Dolmus* from Konya run to Cumra, but from there you'll probably need to hire a taxi unless you're prepared for a twenty-kilometre round-trip walk.

Accommodation

First Class

Dergah Hotel, Mevlana Caddesi 19 (Tel. (33) 111197). 100 rooms in Konya's best hotel, opposite the Mevlana Muzesi so that some rooms have wonderful views.

Hotel Seljuk, Alaettin Caddesi, Babalik Sokak (Tel. (33) 111259). 82 rooms with private facilities, recently renovated.

Middle Range

Ozkaymak Park Oteli, Hastahane Caddesi (Tel. (33) 133770). 90 rooms in a clean hotel, more convenient for the bus station than the town centre.

Hotel Konya, Mevlani Meydani (Tel. (33) 119212). Modern hotel, right behind the tourist information office.

Hotel Sema Two, Hastahane Caddesi (Tel. (33) 132557). 33 rooms, some with private facilities.

Economy

Otel Suat, Konak Meydani Kebabcilar Sokak 3. Basic hotel with some huge rooms. Right in the heart of the bazaar, so not always very quiet.

Hotel Ulusan, PTT Arkasi, Kursuncular Sokak 2. Clean, quiet and family-run.

Catal Aile Pansiyonu, Mevlana Caddesi, Nacifikret Sokak 4/2. Well-positioned, with access to roof, but limited washing facilities.

Despite the number of visitors, accommodation isn't really a problem; Konya is chock-a-block with cheap hotels, and boys often meet buses to 'guide' tourists to them.

Eating Out

The **Damak Et Lokantasi** in Aziziye Caddesi, off Mevlana Caddesi, is one of Konya's best places to eat, offering *firin kebab* and a surprising range of alcoholic beverages for such a conservative town. The **Dergah** and **Konya Hotels** also have excellent restaurants; the Dergah's is more fun since the dome of a *hamam* underneath protrudes into the room with a map of the world showing Konya at the centre drawn on it. Cheaper places to eat can be found all along Alaettin Caddesi; look out for bakeries selling Konya's speciality . . . long, flat pizzas with goats' cheese topping.

Entertainments

Inevitably nightlife in Konya is limited. However, the **fairground** off Alaettin Tepesi stays open quite late and is popular and lively, with the same mixture of rides and sideshows as you'd find at home.

Between 14 and 17 December each year Konya hosts a **Dervish Festival**, recalling its glorious past. However, the dancing is not performed in the Mevlana Muzesi but in a gymnasium, specially marked out for the occasion. Nor are the dancers real Dervishes, so the event lacks authenticity. Konya is always packed for the duration, so you may prefer to visit at another time. More genuine Dervish whirling can be seen, perhaps surprisingly, in Istanbul, at the Galata Mevlevihane where dancers live according to the original Sufic rites.

Useful Addresses

Tourist Office: Mevlana Caddesi 21. **Post Office**: Hukumet Alani. **Hospital**: Hastane Caddesi. **Turkish Airlines Office**: Alaeddin Caddesi 22, Kat 1/106.

Towards Cappadocia

From Konya it's possible to reach Cappadocia by taking a train to Kayseri. However, it's more fun to travel by bus, stopping off along the way. Between Konya and Aksaray the scenery is, for the most part, flat, dusty and uninspiring. However, at **Sultanhani** you may want to break your journey to inspect a *caravansaray* that has been restored, enabling you to envisage what these medieval roadside inns must have been like in their heyday. Huge walls and an elaborately carved entrance conceal a courtyard with a central mosque raised up on pillars, a stable for animals at the back and a series of rooms all around it.

Aksaray is not especially interesting in itself but is an important transport intersection. Buses from here head north for Ankara, skirting the vast **Tuz Golu** salt lake, an extraordinary phenomenon, more optical illusion than real lake in summer, with an unpleasantly hot, windy sub-climate all of its own. Regular buses also head due east for Nevsehir and Kayseri. Infrequent mini-buses head south-east towards the Ihlara, or Peristrema Valley, one of Turkey's best-kept secrets, which you can also reach by taking a Nevsehir-bound bus and asking to be dropped at the Guzelyurt turn-off; from there it should be possible to hitch a ride to Selime or Ihlara.

The **Ihlara Valley**, a steep-sided sixteen-kilometre-long gorge carved out by the Melendiz river, starts at the village of **Selime**, passes through **Belisirma** and continues to **Ihlara** itself. Although simple accommodation is available in all three villages, your best bet may be to head for Ihlara, attractively set around a square with the river flowing through it. There you can stay in the government-owned **Belediye Hotel**, surely one of the quietest places in Turkey, where you can wake to the sounds of nothing but the river flowing past the balcony, the imam calling from the minaret and the occasional cow-bell. Facilities are shared but this hardly matters when you can go to wash in a *hamam* built over a natural spring just behind the mosque. The friendly **Yesilkopru Restaurant** is right beside the river, and shops sell excellent tomatoes, bread, cheese and sausage for picnics.

Like Cappadocia, the Ihlara Valley is riddled with **caves**, some of them containing **painted churches** and **monasteries**. However, tourist development is much more low-key here. Halfway between Ihlara and Belisirma a flight of steps runs down from the rim of the gorge to the base, offering direct access to the best of the churches. A car park and hotel stand on the edge here, and there are a few postcard and souvenir stands, although hardly on the scale of Goreme or Avanos. You can dine on indifferent food but with a spectacular view in the **Valley Restaurant**, part of the hotel.

However, the Valley is much more than the handful of churches at the foot of the steps. To take full advantage of it, hitch to **Selime** and then walk back to Ihlara, taking care to carry as much food and water as you're likely to need with you since there are no shops on the valley floor. Although you'll have to scrabble over rocks in a few places, trainers should be adequate as footwear.

Near Selime itself there are a few simple cave-churches. The signposted path then follows the river bed through plum and apricot orchards to **Belisirma** where there is a **camp-site**. Here you can follow the path up to the tiny village and visit the **rock-church of St George** (it's also worth looking in adjacent caves where you'll find primitive agricultural equipment also carved out of the rock). After Belisirma the path gets a little tougher, and you have to climb over rocks to get to some of the churches; a few are difficult to identify (there are no signs), and men and boys will approach you offering their services as guides. Around the base of the steps you'll find the most important painted churches (which are signposted): Karagedik Kilise, Yilanli Kilise, Sumullu Kilise, Agacalti Kilise, Purenli Seki Kilise and Kokar Kilise. The path then continues on to Ihlara, still following the river and with fine views all the way. However, if you're tired you can escape the Valley by climbing the stairs to the gorge rim. Just before Ihlara village the river tumbles over rocks in a small waterfall, with a rock shelf where you can sit to watch it.

To reach Cappadocia proper you will need to return to the main Aksarary-Nevsehir road, bearing in mind that traffic between Ihlara and the junction is sparse. To get a seat on the bus it's probably best to go back to Aksaray and find one that's starting out from there.

Cappadocia

A Tourism Development Area since the 1970s, Cappadocia is now one of Turkey's most popular areas for visitors, which is not surprising given the spectacular landscape of gorges and tufa cones created by volcanic eruptions in prehistoric times. The scenery alone would be a crowd-puller, but when you add to that the marvellous painted churches and monasteries, and the staggering underground cities carved out of the rocks by early medieval Christians, it's hardly surprising that little villages which once subsisted on agriculture now rely very heavily on tourists for their livelihood.

Nevsehir is the real jumping-off point for Cappadocia although it is not, in itself, an inspiring town. You might want to examine the museum which contains artefacts from all Turkey's main historical periods. However, you are more likely to want to catch a bus or minibus straight on to Goreme, Urgup or Avanos, three villages that lie at the heart of the fantastic landscape which has made this such a popular area.

The main points of interest in Cappadocia lie within the triangular area enclosed by Goreme, Avanos and Urgup. Ten years ago all three were small, agricultural settlements. Now they have prostituted themselves to tourism in varying degrees, although Urgup is a little harder to get to and therefore perhaps a little quieter.

Arriving in **Goreme** can be a shock since the first thing you see is a hideous bus-station-cum-shopping-mall designed with no thought at all for its setting. Luckily once you escape down the back streets you'll find the old houses, with their wonderful carved stone doorways and colourful carts parked outside, still more or less intact. Many of the houses have been turned into simple pensions, and invitations to view the insides of houses should be seen as what they are: low-key commerce rather than simple friendliness. Still, it could be worse.

Goreme is home to one of the area's two **open-air museums**. The best of the painted rock-churches are now preserved inside the museum which has its good and bad points. The minus is that the churches are too small for the numbers of people wanting to view them, so that queues form and it's hard to stand back and appreciate the frescoes. However, at least they are protected, and restoration work is taking place on some of them. There's a clearly-labelled circuit inside the museum but the main churches to look out for are: **Elmali Kilise**, **Carikli Kilise**, **Yilanli Kilise** and the **Church of Saint Barbara**. Best of all are **Karanlik Kilise** (the 'Dark Church') which has just been restored, and **Tokali Kilise** (the 'Buckle Church'), a huge edifice just outside the main complex.

From Goreme you can visit **Uchisar**, a higgledy-piggledy village clustered around a huge tufa cone, itself once inhabited by troglodytes. This is an excellent place for getting your bearings and taking in an overall view of the area, although the souvenir stands and camels waiting at the bottom are rather off-putting. One of the village houses has also been converted into a **gallery** to show the work of local photographer, Irian Olmez. Olmez speaks English and also works as a guide.

You might also like to walk to **Cavusin** where an iron ladder set into the rock-face gives access to the painted **Church of St John the Baptist**. Or you could head for **Ortahisar** which, like Uchisar, is dominated by a huge cone offering fine views.

Avanos is another popular base for exploring the district. Much less picturesque than backstreet Goreme, it has a flourishing **pottery** industry; the high street is lined with shops selling the stuff where you can often see it being made as well. Avanos is perfect for visiting the second open-air museum, at **Zelve**. Here you'll find three interlocking valleys, their sides hollowed out with **monastic cave-dwellings**. However, this time carved crosses take the place of frescoes. Zelve offers some alarming walks through pitch-black tunnels and across sloping rock-faces . . . certainly not for the nervous or the vertigo-inclined. Leaving Zelve you can head back to the main Avanos-Urgup road via the **Peribacalar Vadisi** (Fairy Chimney Valley) where some of the most striking of the rock cones line the road; expect coach jams here in peak season.

From Avanos you can also take a *dolmus* to **Ozkonak** where there is a smaller version of the type of **underground city** to be found in Kaymakli and Derinkuyu (see below). This has the same entrance-sealing stones, air shafts and wine presses as its more famous fellows; however, fewer people come here, so you may enjoy a less claustrophobic experience.

Urgup is the most two-faced of the villages. On arrival at the bus station you think you're in a modern village, its wide high street lined with carpet shops. However, the whole place is dominated by a cone, so hollowed-out it resembles a chunk of Emmental, and once through an archway you'll soon find the old agricultural village still intact, its cobbled streets lined with fine stone houses, its headscarf-clad women eager to talk to anyone who ventures their way.

Urgup is a good base for getting to **Mustafapasa**, once a Greek village, with some more fine stone houses, and more lovely but less visited **frescoed churches** and **monasteries**. Tricky to get to without your own transport, the **Soganli Valley** lies beyond Mustafapasa; sites along the way include the **Keslik Monastery** at Cemil, a fourteenth-century **mosque** at Taskinpasa and yet more rock-cut frescoed churches in the beautifully-sited Soganli Valley itself. If you've been put off by the coach parties at Goreme and Zelve this might be the place to come; organised tours can be arranged in Urgup if the prospect of trying to hitch doesn't appeal. Alternatively try **Turtle Tours**, immediately opposite the bus station complex in Goreme, or **Efor Tour** right inside the complex.

Crossing Nevsehir it may be possible to get to **Hacibektas**, north of Avanos, where there's an interesting **museum** to Haci Bektas Veli, another thirteenth-century Sufi leader and Dervish. A Seljuk and Ottoman complex set around three attractive courtyards houses his tomb and is now the museum. However, like the Mevlana Musezi it is still a place of pilgrimage as well, so appropriate clothing is essential.

Accommodation

First Class

1001 Gece Bahcesi, 50240 Uchisar-Nevsehir road (Tel. 1293). Perfect if your idea of the best way to experience Cappadocia is from a hollowed-out tufa cone. Rooms are fitted out in Turkish style with plentiful kilims and cushioned divans arranged to offer fine views of the landscape.

Turban Urgup Moteli, Nevsehir road, Urgup (Tel. (4868) 1490). 240 rooms in tastefully-designed bungalows on the outskirts of Urgup.

Nevsehir-Dedeman Hotel, Nevsehir-Kayseri Yolu, Nevsehir (Tel. (4851) 5619). New luxury hotel with all mod cons.

Middle Range

Sofa Motel, Koprubasi, Avanos (Tel. (4861) 1489). A complex of 23 whitewashed rooms set round a courtyard, each individually designed, some cut into the rock-face.

Hotel Eyvan, Istiklal Caddesi, Urgup (Tel. (4868) 1822). Another hotel carved out of the rock-face, with tiny rooms but private facilities.

Hotel Zelve, Kenan Evren Caddesi, Avanos (Tel. (4861) 1524). Comfortable modern hotel right in the middle of.the action, decorated in traditional style.

Economy

Born Hotel, Ahmet Refik Caddesi, Urgup. In a fine old stone house, far enough from the high street to be pleasantly quiet but with a small bar on the premises.

Cappadoce Hotel, Istiklal Caddesi, Urgup. Reasonable rooms in attractive old stone building, close to the *hamam*. Idiosyncratic service though.

Kemer Pansiyon, Goreme. Cheap, cheerful and very friendly travellers' meeting place.

Eating Out

The better hotels all have their own restaurants serving good quality food at hefty (for Turkey) prices. For something with more character, try the **Sofa Restaurant** in Urgup's Cumhuriyet Meydani. Here you dine on a wonderful variety of Turkish dishes in the courtyard of a converted *han*, or bazaar, overlooked by a floodlit tufa cone and an astonishingly tame falcon. Across the road the **Somine Restaurant** is built around an ancient fireplace and serves good food in a comfortable setting. In Goreme's **Ataman Restaurant** you can eat well in rock-cut surroundings. All the local villages retain simple kebab and *pide* places frequented by locals as well as the restaurants more deliberately aimed at their visitors.

Entertainments

Entertainment options remain happily low-key despite all the tourists, and even things that might sound crass elsewhere can turn out to have their appealing side here. For example, Urgup has a rock-cut disco just off Cumhuriyet Meydani. Boasting an eclectic choice of music, from Cat Stevens to The Pet Shop Boys, this offers the chance to drink in little kilim-decorated alcoves which suggest privacy even amid the crowds. The 'pull' is supposed to be the belly-dancing. However, despite the hype about how traditional it is, expect something which panders more to western strip-tease tastes than the orient.

In Avanos it is possible to attend a 'folklore' evening at the Motif Restaurant. Once again belly-dancing is on offer, and the folk-dancing may not even be from the Anatolian region. However, the fairly steep entrance fee does cover a wide range of Turkish dishes and wines. Provided you don't expect anything too authentic you can have a very enjoyable evening here.

The **hamam** in Avanos should also be regarded as potential entertainment rather than as something authentically Turkish. Like the one in Urgup it admits men and women together, something which would never have been acceptable in the east, and women can expect to be ministered to by male masseurs, again a no-no outside the tourist areas. However, Avanos takes things one step further, charging tourist prices for a tourist experience, complete with swimming pool, sauna and apple tea.

If you visit in late August you may be able to join in the celebrations during the **Avanos Handicrafts Festival**; it helps if you like pottery. Also in August pilgrims head for Hacibektas to worship at Haci Bektas Veli's shrine; you may want to join them, but remember that this is a serious religious occasion and outsiders may not be terribly welcome.

Useful Addresses

Tourist Offices: Kayseri Caddesi, Urgup; Ataturk Bulvari, Nevsehir.

Post Office: Pastane Sokak, Urgup. **Hospital**: Ataturk Bulvari, Nevsehir.

Transport Options

Nevsehir is the main transport intersection for this area, so wherever you're staying you will probably find yourself crossing it frequently; getting direct from one village to the next can be difficult unless you're prepared to pay for a taxi. Once you've found a base it's well worth considering getting around on foot, by bike or on horseback; that way you escape the worst of the crowds and are best able to take in the breathtaking scenery. Mountain bikes can be hired from the **Bis Tour Company** in Urgup (Tel. 4868/3488), while horses and donkeys are available from **Ekita Tour** at Istiklal Caddesi 17, Urgup (Tel. (4868) 3890). Horses can also be hired from **Goreme Ranch** in Ortahisar (Tel. 1763) or from **Rainbow Ranch** in Goreme (Tel. 1463).

Around Cappadocia

The road south from Nevsehir to Nigde and Tarsus bypasses two of the most popular sights in the region: the **underground cities of Kaymakli** and **Derinkuyu**. Both were carved out of the soft tufa rock by early medieval Christians as places they could flee to whenever there were Arab raids. They descend through several layers of cave-like holes; in fact, Derinkuyu has eight separate levels. As you wander around, the various holes are hard to understand; however much you may usually dislike them, this is one occasion when a guide is well worth having; alternatively you could try tagging on to the end of one of the innumerable visiting groups who can make the cities feel uncomfortably crowded at times. The guide will point out huge round stones which could be rolled across the entrances to seal them off, vast ventilation shafts which brought air and light below ground and mangers for animals with poles to which they could be secured, and will identify bedrooms, kitchens and stables. Both cities now have electric lights and arrows to prevent you getting lost. Nevertheless they're not for those of claustrophobic disposition.

Of the cities Kaymakli is nearer to Nevsehir and therefore more visited than Derinkuyu. Its entrance is completely engulfed with stalls selling souvenirs. Derinkuyu is slightly, but not much, better. However, since it is the bigger and quieter of the two you might want to visit it, bearing in mind that if you make an early start you can catch a Nigde-bound bus, get off to look round Derinkuyu and then continue south in the same day.

In **Nigde** itself you might want to look at the **Sungur Bey Cami** near the market, a Seljuk mosque restored by the Mongols in the fourteenth century and revealing an interesting mixture of architectural styles. Better still you can catch a crowded minibus eastwards to Gumusler to visit the **Eski Gumusler Monastery**, an overlooked but perfectly preserved rock-cut building in an attractive garden. Until recently a farming family lived in the monastery and their bales of hay, etc. protected the frescoes in the church from damage; consequently the paint looks almost as good as new. However, here it's also easy to get a picture of monastic life in its entirety. The entrance leads to an open courtyard with rock walls rising up on all sides. Rock graves stand open in the centre of it, but these are much more recent than the medieval monastery. The guide will show you not just the church, but also the bedrooms complete with rock beds, the kitchen, a curious air vent and assorted other rooms. Finally he'll whistle up an owl nesting in a crevice above the church.

From Nigde frequent buses continue south on a dramatically beautiful but inadequate mountain road to Tarsus and the Mediterranean. You might want to break the journey at **Kemerhisar** where there are rarely-visited Hittite ruins and a Roman aqueduct. Forgotten Hittite reliefs can also be seen at **Ivriz**, a village south of Eregli which can be reached with more difficulty from Nigde.

Kayseri

East of Nevsehir buses head for Kayseri, once the Roman Caesarea, now a conservative town of roughly half a million inhabitants with a reputation for particularly hard-selling carpet dealers. A hotch-potch of a place, Kayseri sprawls in all directions from its massive central citadel, but the further south you go, the more it is dominated by the snow-clad peak of Erciyes Dag.

The **citadel**, or *hisar*, is something of a disappointment, its brooding black volcanic walls concealing a shopping bazaar rather than anything more ancient. More interesting is the **Hunat Hatun complex** across the road from it which consists of a fine thirteenth-century Seljuk mosque with a *medrese* and baths attached. The *medrese* houses an Ethnographical Museum; sadly, this has been closed for restoration for some time.

Beside the citadel is the town's main shopping area, with shady arcades and open courtyards full of sacks of wool. At its heart is an old **bedesten** where carpet-weavers are at work and where the hassle, such as it is, is at its strongest. Near here is the twelfth- and thirteenth-century **Ulu Cami**, but visitors are not especially welcome inside it.

Heading south from the citadel you'll pass the overgrown **Alaca Kumbet**, the first of a series of circular, conical-roofed Seljuk tombs for which Kayseri is famous. Better cared for is the **Doner** (or 'turning') **Kumbet** just before the turn-off east for the **Archaeological Museum**. In the museum you can see some of the finds from the nearby Hittite site of Kultepe amongst assorted other archaeological bits and bobs. **Kultepe** itself lies north-east of town, just off the road to Bunyan, but there's not much to see there.

If you're staying in Kayseri you might want to try climbing on **Erciyes Dag**, although you'll need proper equipment and plenty of water since there's none available on the mountainside. To get there take a bus to Hisarcik and then a taxi to Tekir Yaylasi and the Kayak Evi ski lodge where guides may be available. You can ski on Erciyes from December through to May although facilities are obviously rudimentary.

Bird-watchers might prefer to head for the **Sultan Marshes** by taking a bus to Yesilhisar on the Kayseri-Nigde road. From there you might be able to hitch the remaining eight kilometres to **Ovaciftlik** where there's a small museum and a watch-tower overlooking the marshes. You can camp in Ovaciftlik and hire boats to explore Yay Golu, the biggest of the lakes in the area.

Accommodation

Middle Range

Turan Oteli, 27 Mayis Caddesi, Turan Caddesi 8 (Tel. (351) 112506). Reasonably comfortable if elderly hotel with its own Turkish bath.

Kadioglu Oteli, Inonu Bulvari (Tel. (351) 116320).

Economy

None of Kayseri's budget hotels is particularly good, but the **Yeni**, **Meydan** and **Hisar** are at least conveniently placed for buses to Urgup, on Osman Kavuncu Caddesi.

Otel Beloz, Yesilhisar. Basic lodgings if you don't want to camp at the Sultan Marshes.

Eating Out

The best place to eat is certainly the **Turan Hotel**. However, the **Iskender Kebab Salonu**, opposite the Hunat Hatun complex, and the **Merkez Kebap ve Pide Salonu** near the citadel, also offer good, basic Turkish food. Around town you'll be able to buy sandwiches of *pastirma*, a dried beef flavoured with garlic and spices and something of an acquired taste.

Useful Addresses

Tourist Office: Kagni Pazari Honat Camii Yani 61. **Post Office**: Sivas Caddesi. **Turkish Airlines Office**: Sivas Caddesi.

6 The Black Sea

Turkey's Black Sea or *Kara Deniz* coast stretches from Igneada in Thrace to Hopa on the eastern border with Georgia. It's a region quite unlike the traditional image of Turkey; cool and misty rather than hot and dry, densely-forested rather than barren, and northward-looking rather than east or west-inclining. The Turks probably called the Sea black because its gloomy climate imbues the water, too, with a bleak hue.

In theory the Black Sea coastline, backed as it is by the lofty Pontic Alps, is one of the most scenically attractive areas of Turkey. Sadly, however, much of it is disfigured by ugly, utilitarian buildings that would look more at home in the suburbs of the old eastern bloc capitals. A good tarmac road runs alongside the coast east of Samsun, making it readily accessible, but detracting further from the area's natural beauty.

The further east you travel the better things get, particularly beyond Trabzon where the Kackar Daglari mountains provide wonderful trekking country, full of hidden valleys and rippling streams. Here, too, you're into tea country, the hillside plantations flourishing in the moist and misty climate.

Once in the north-eastern mountains you'll encounter a semi-nomadic lifestyle little touched by the modern world. In the Hemsin villages, inhabited by people who are thought to be descendants of the Armenians, women still wear colourful costumes, complete with turbans patterned like leopard-skin which are imported from India. The men, rather unexpectedly, play their own version of the bagpipes. From May to September the villagers move up from the valleys to the mountain slopes where they live in *yaylas*, communal dwellings built half of stone and half of timber. Hemsinli people are lightheartedly Muslim. In contrast the inhabitants of the Solakli valley are staunchly fundamentalist.

The far eastern region of the Black Sea is also home to the Laz people, believed to be descendants of the Colchians from whom Jason stole the Golden Fleece. They're Caucasian people, and the men in particular have a reputation for business acumen, often reflected in ownership of Turkish shipping lines. Like the Hemsin, they wear their religious affiliations lightly. However, you'll see fewer people in interesting local dress in the Laz villages.

Inland from Hopa the Coruh river leads to a Georgian enclave, its villages indicated by the place name prefix 'Ar-'. Historically an Orthodox Christian area, Turkish Georgia is now firmly Muslim.

For those more interested in meeting the Turks than in seeing sights, the Black Sea, like the Eastern Mediterranean coast, is relatively untouched by international tourism, except around Trabzon. If you're prepared to pack a tent and accept that camping facilities may be pretty basic, then this could be the perfect place to get to know the locals.

History

The Ancient Greeks knew the Black Sea as the Pontus Euxine, which featured in several important legends. The Greek historian Strabo claimed that Jason and the Argonauts had sailed to Colchis at the end of the Black Sea in search of the Golden Fleece, probably alluvial gold which villagers collected by laying fleeces on the river bed. The legend may have incorporated memories of a trading voyage in the thirteenth century BC. Certainly many Greek city states later used claims that Argonauts from their own state had gone on the trip to justify demands for trading rights in the Black Sea. Modern travellers can stop at Yason, a breezy headland with the remains of a chapel, where the Argonauts are said to have stopped on their way east. Those fearsome one-breasted female warriors, the Amazons, were also said to have come from Terme, near Samsun.

In the eighth century BC Ionian settlers from Miletus founded colonies at Sinop, Samsun, Giresun and Trebizond, all well-positioned to benefit from trading routes across the Pontic Alps. The colonies flourished until they eventually became the Kingdom of Pontus, with its capital in Trebizond. King Mithridates IV Eupator led the Pontic challenge to the Romans in 83-81 BC, and during his reign the Kingdom actually dominated an area extending as far inland as Cappadocia. In 64 BC the Romans eventually defeated Mithridates who committed suicide; they left a rump Pontic kingdom hanging on around Trebizond in the east.

However, in 47 BC Julius Caesar swept the Pontic Kingdom, as so much else, before him. When the Romans accepted Christianity, the Black Sea region also came under its influence. A Cappadocian saint travelled to the far eastern area and converted the Georgians, who had settled there in the Bronze Age, to Christianity. In the ninth century this Georgian enclave developed into the Bagratid kingdom, its rulers claiming descent from David and Bathsheba. In 1064 the Seljuks overran the area and destroyed many of its churches. However, in the twelfth century Queen Tamara led a Bagratid revival; many of the churches were restored, and the Georgian Valleys formed part of a political unit with modern Georgia, Armenia and Azerbaijan, with its capital in Tbilisi. This kingdom was gradually destroyed in the thirteenth and fourteenth centuries by Mongol and Persian raids and by Tamerlane's invasion.

In 1204 the Crusaders seized Constantinople and the deposed Byzantine Emperor fled to Trebizond where his son, Alexius Comnenus, set up a breakaway Empire of Trebizond, protected from much interference by the surrounding ring of mountains. During the Comnenian period many of the coastal settlements flourished, reaching the apogee of their wealth and culture during the reign of Alexius II (1297–1330). This backwoods state ultimately outlived the restored Byzantine Empire in Constantinople, struggling on until 1461 when it finally succumbed to Ottoman pressure. It was also during the later Middle Ages that Genoese traders gained a foothold in the Black Sea, extorting trading rights from the weakened Byzantine Emperors in return for helping them keep their enemies at bay.

The Turks renamed Trebizond Trabzon, and it was the coast's most important city throughout the Ottoman period. Given the easy access to Istanbul that it would offer them, the Russians eyed Trabzon greedily. As the Ottoman Empire crumbled they demanded the right to 'protect' the Orthodox Christians still resident in Turkey. Eventually this pressure led to the Crimean War, between 1853 and 1856, when Britain and France joined with Turkey to keep the Russians at bay. Even then the Russians continued to interfere, supporting the separatist groups who flourished in the remoter mountain valleys.

After the First World War Trebizond's Greek inhabitants tried to revive the old Comnenian state. However, in 1919 Mustafa Kemal Ataturk arrived in Samsun to use it as a base for organising resistance to the Greek invaders. The Turkish War of Independence (1920–22) led to the defeat of the Greeks. The monks of Sumela and the surrounding monasteries were forced to flee, and as Christianity passed into the realms of memory, the eastern Black Sea region suffered a period of economic collapse from which it has only recovered relatively recently.

Turkey's current borders with Armenia and Georgia date from treaties drawn up between Ataturk and the Soviet Union in 1921. The proximity of the Soviet Union to Black Sea Turkey partly explained American enthusiasm for keeping bases in the country. As the USSR collapsed in 1990 and individual states emerged once again, Georgian traders began to flood into the eastern Black Sea ports. In 1992 the Turks and Georgians started discussing a possible free trade area between the two countries.

Geography

The Black Sea is a huge inland sea encircled by Bulgaria, Romania, Georgia and Armenia, as well as Turkey. Via the Bosphorus, the Sea of Marmara and the Dardanelles, it is linked to the Mediterranean. The waters are surprisingly unsalty because of the quantity of fresh water poured into them from the Don, Dnieper and Danube rivers to the north. Unfortunately though, they are also badly polluted around areas of high population. Some of the world's most extensive uranium deposits lie beneath the Sea.

The Black Sea's southern coast belongs to Turkey and is backed for almost its entire length by the Pontic Alps, or Little Caucasus, which squeeze large settlements like Samsun and Trabzon into a thin strip of flat coastal land. In the far east the granite-diorite Kackar Daglari range contains some of Turkey's highest mountains and can be divided into four main massifs; the Altiparmak, the Bulut, the Kackar proper and the Vercenik. Mount Kackar, Turkey's fourth highest peak, reaches 3937 metres. This is an area of lakes and hanging valleys, scenery crafted by the Ice Age glaciers, and very popular with walkers and climbers.

Springtime scenery in the Kackar Daglari can be almost Swiss, with butterfly-attracting wild flowers dotting the lower slopes and pine trees clinging to the upper slopes. Cascading rivers give way to plateaux where barley can be harvested and where windmills still supply much of the power. The mountains offer homes for rare breeds of eagles and wolves, although bears and ibex are rare.

Beyond Rize, the slopes facing the Black Sea are planted with tea, hazelnut, cherry and tobacco plantations. The tea, first introduced into the area to perk up the economy after the expulsion of the Greeks, is planted on slopes between sea level and 600 metres, and is harvested in summer, mainly by women. This north-eastern part of the Black Sea lies on an important migration route for birds of prey.

Visitors to Sumela Monastery near Trabzon will find alpine-style vegetation, with snowflowers (a type of crocus) blooming on the slopes by the footpath each autumn. Beyond Trabzon valleys cut in from the coast to the mountains, following the trout-rich Solakli, Ikizdere and Firtina rivers; the triangular area drained by the Firtina and its tributaries is known as the Hemsin. At the furthest reaches of these valleys the wet climate has given rise to cloud-forest with fir trees and alders where bears and wolves still roam. Crocuses and gentian flower here in spring. The Coruh river and its tributaries, the Tortum and Kura, drain into valleys which were once part of medieval Georgia. The Coruh offers white water suitable for rafting.

Along the coast small beach resorts huddle in the shadow of the mountains; the best are between Amasra and Sinop. There are also overgrown fishing villages like Amasra, where anchovy are caught in winter. Many of the coastal villages depend on dairy farming for their livelihoods, and agriculture in general flourishes in the fertile soil and damp conditions of the coast. Samsun, on the floodplains of the Kizilirmak and Yesilirmak rivers, has boomed as an export centre for agricultural produce.

At the western end of the Black Sea, especially around Zonguldak, coal is mined, and in the east there are copper mines.

Climate

The Black Sea coast has a climate quite unlike the rest of the country. Even in August temperatures in Trabzon rarely rise above 22°C. Although sea temperatures average 25°C in August, rain can be expected even on the warmest days, as northerly and westerly winds fetch up against the mountains forcing the clouds to disgorge their contents on the seaward side. In the Hemsin area to the north-east as much as 500 centimetres of rain can fall in a year. The western reaches of the Black Sea are slightly drier than the eastern parts.

Mists are frequent; early-morning visitors to Sumela Monastery, even in summer, will find it shrouded in cloud. These mists can create problems for Kackar Daglari trekkers who must take care not to get stranded on the higher passes as the fog descends.

Winter temperatures along the coast are mild in comparison with those of East and Central Turkey. Nevertheless, they can still fall to 6°C in January and February (while sea temperatures average 9°C), and rain is again frequent. In the north-eastern mountains heavy snowfalls may close roads, especially around Artvin, for days at a time; in effect the climbing season is limited to June to October. Visit between November and February and you may even see Sumela Monastery buried beneath the snow in a scene of Christmas card-like beauty.

Attractions

Although the Sumela Monastery outside Trabzon is one of Turkey's best-known sites, most of the Black Sea coast is better visited for its scenery rather than for its historic monuments. In fact apart from Trabzon, the only other coastal town with significant monuments is Amasra which has two Byzantine churches and the remains of a Byzantine castle. Diverting inland from Samsun, however, you will find interesting reminders of the old Pontic kingdom in pretty Amasya.

The western reaches of the Black Sea are not particularly picturesque. However, once past Trabzon the scenery becomes increasingly spectacular and mountainous, especially if you travel inland away from the coast. The Kackar Daglari offers trekking and mountaineering opportunities, together with the chance to white-water raft on the Coruh river. Skiing is also possible in this area.

Walkers may want to visit the Hemsin valleys where villagers live a semi-nomadic lifestyle. It may be possible to visit or stay in one of their *yaylas*. The Georgian valleys, inland from Hopa, also offer walkers opportunities to visit a succession of little-known ruined medieval castles and churches.

In theory the Black Sea offers beach resorts for conventional summer sun holidays. However, the uncertain climate makes these less attractive places for foreign tan-seekers than the Aegean and Mediterranean coasts. In spite of this, many Turks flock to the resorts which offer good facilities for campers in particular.

Cuisine

Many of the Black Sea village restaurants feature fish dishes, including trout and anchovy in season. Otherwise, there is the usual range of kebabs and *pides*; chicken also features prominently in Trabzon dining places.

The Hemsin villagers are famous as pastry cooks. Even if you don't get to the villages themselves, you can still sample their handiwork in Trabzon restaurants. Look out for shops selling huge wedges of *helva* (a sesame-based sweet) and almond biscuits, in particular. You might also want to try *pestel*, a chewy sweet looking like a sheet of leather but flavoured with mulberries or nuts. *Suclak*, or rice pudding, is very popular and is sometimes eaten for breakfast.

Rize tea, produced by Caykur, a state monopoly, is omnipresent and usually served in tiny glasses to guarantee the liquid stays piping hot. Everywhere you go you'll see boys dashing across the street with metal trays of glasses suspended from a chain in their hands. Tea is served with rough-cut chunks of sugar; real aficionados grip the sugar between their teeth before draining the tea through it. In homes the tea is brewed up in a double pot which is constantly topped up. Although you will also be offered apple and orange tea, these are recent innovations, using chemicals rather than real leaves. They're pleasant enough for a change, but can't replace the real thing, without which you sometimes feel all social interchange would grind to a halt.

Level of Tourism

Since none of the big tour operators use Black Sea resorts as a base for holidays, international tourism along most of the coast is fairly low level; indeed in 1989, just 138,726 foreign tourists visited the region. Nevertheless, Turkish holidaymakers do flood there in summer, and some of the decidedly unattractive buildings marring the scenery are actually holiday homes for domestic tourists.

Trabzon is used as a base for many operators offering tours of Eastern Turkey. Consequently Sumela Monastery is the region's biggest 'honeypot' attraction, likely to be overrun with coach parties at the height of summer. In 1989 15,631 European tourists were recorded in Trabzon province, almost twice as many as in 1988. However, this compared with more than 1,930,000 European tourists recorded in Antalya. Samsun province received fewer than 10,000 European tourists in 1989, and Rize province less than 600. French and German holidaymakers are most enthusiastic about visiting this part of Turkey.

Recently, the Kackar Daglari have been receiving larger numbers of trekking parties, putting pressure on the limited accommodation available; it's wise to book the best places well ahead. The most accessible of the Georgian churches can also get swamped by day-tripping coach parties, and are best visited early in the day.

Good Alternatives

Meeting People

In some ways, although so little visited, the Black Sea coast offers the best opportunities to meet the Turks. This is because, without the pressure of large-scale tourism, people still respond to strangers with the age-old hospitality. Trabzon is obviously exceptional, although even there, out of season, you'll soon get chatting to locals in the vast outdoor café of the Taksim Meydani. Likewise if you venture into the *hamams* you are likely to find the Turks as chatty as anywhere else; the Fatih baths for women in Trabzon are especially welcoming.

Coastal camp-sites offer excellent opportunities for women in particular to meet holidaying Turkish families free of some of the 'pick-up' atmosphere of the cafés. Don't expect the level of facilities you would in most of Western Europe though.

The most interesting 'meeting people' opportunities are in the eastern valleys, especially in the easy-going Hemsin villages. Nevertheless, you should bear in mind that these communities are fragile and could easily be damaged if too many westerners start tramping through them flashing their cameras about. If you want to visit a *yayla* settlement, bear in mind that they offer very basic, not necessarily very clean living conditions; don't go unless you're ready to rough it. Also think carefully about how you will repay hospitality offered in these areas without disrupting the local economy or encouraging a begging mentality amongst the children.

Discovering Places

Because there are so few visitors to this area, your journey is bound to be a voyage of discovery. Actually, one of the hardest parts of the coast to explore is the section nearest to Istanbul which lacks the good road found east of Samsun. However, since this is the area most frequented by Turkish tourists you may well be able to hitch around here, making it even easier for you to meet people.

Few tour operators offer anything other than passing visits to the Black Sea using Trabzon as a base for getting to Sumela Monastery and from there to Erzurum. Nevertheless Exodus Expeditions does feature a walking and camping tour of the Kackar Daglari, ideal for those who wouldn't feel happy trekking in the valleys on their own. Trek Travel also offers mountain trips, with opportunities to climb Mount Kackar in company with others. They arrange skiing trips in the mountains too.

Independent exploration of the Hemsin and Georgian valleys is perfectly feasible if you have plenty of time and are happy to walk. There is public transport, but it's infrequent and often timed to get locals to markets, rather than tourists to sights. *Dolmus* and taxis are also available, if you're prepared to pay what can be fairly high prices because of the poor state of the roads.

Communications

How to Get There

It's possible to **fly** to Trabzon, changing planes in Istanbul and/or Ankara. There are also infrequent flights between Istanbul and Samsun. But it's much more fun and somehow more appropriate to approach the Black Sea by **ship**. Turkish Maritime Lines (TML) offers year-round, once-weekly sailings to Samsun and Trabzon from Istanbul, departing on Monday afternoons. From May to September boats also ply between Istanbul, Zonguldak, Sinop, Ordu and Giresun, departing on Thursday evenings. These boats are not luxurious, and the Black Sea can be rough, so it's wise to take precautions against seasickness.

Few train services serve the Black Sea coast, although conceivably you could use the daily **Blue Train** to get from Istanbul to Ankara, before taking a bus north to Samsun. This is a first-class night train with sleeping compartments; if you plan to use it it's advisable to book in advance. For Inter-Railers intent on using trains wherever possible, there's also a night service from Ankara to the coal town of Zonguldak.

If you don't want to boat-hop along the coast from Istanbul, the quickest way to travel will be by **bus**. Surprisingly it's the stretch of coast just east of Istanbul and extending as far as Samsun that causes the most problems. East of Samsun the road improves dramatically and progress will be that much faster.

When You're There

Bus – even more than in other parts of Turkey, you'll be dependent on the bus network to get you around the Black Sea area. Services along the main coastal road are good and frequent. Once you get to the eastern valleys, however, expect delays, especially in winter when snow can make travelling difficult. Buses run along spectacularly beautiful mountain roads to Ezurum from Trabzon and Rize. Provided there are no hold-ups these journeys take between seven and eight hours. However, in 1990 flooding wreaked havoc on the roads in this area.

Work to repair the damage is unlikely to be completed before 1993.

Private transport – to explore the Georgian valleys you will need your own transport since buses are few and far between; cars can be hired in Trabzon, or you could negotiate with taxi drivers in villages like Yusufeli and put together your own tour. Alternatively there's plenty of scope for walkers.

Rail – moving on from the Black Sea to Eastern Turkey there's a daily train service linking Samsun to Sivas.

Geographical Breakdown of Region

The Western Black Sea Area

The area closest to Istanbul is popular with holidaying Turks but lacks any large towns or major monuments to attract westerners. The coastal road as far as Karasu is poor, so most people heading east use the Istanbul-Izmir-Ankara road (E5) at least as far as Adapazari or Bolu, or bypass this stretch of coast altogether by ferry. Conceivably you might want to visit the resort at **Sile** which has a good beach and camping facilities in the shadow of a ruined Genoese castle. East of Sile, **Karasu** is being developed as a resort but is likely to suffer from its proximity to Istanbul. Alternatively, **Akcakoca** has decent beaches, camping facilities and its own ruined Genoese castle.

Following the main road through **Izmit** is not especially pleasant; the road is frantically busy and surrounded by unattractive industrial development and sprawling satellite towns. Even the vast **Sapanca Golu** is spoilt by evidence of quarrying right up to the water's edge; the camp-sites amongst the reed-beds are immediately overlooked by the E5. Just before Bolu a minor road heads inland towards **Abant Golu**. With your own transport it's worth diverting along this, since the lake, again well-equipped with camping and picnicking facilities, has a very attractive and very un-Turkish hill and forest setting. There's also a **Turban Hotel** if you're looking for more comfort. At **Yenicaga** an attractive road cuts north for the coast, forking at Devrek with one branch heading for **Eregli**, interesting only for its floating fish restaurants, and the other for **Zonguldak**, a coal-mining town best avoided except that it's an important transport interchange.

From Zonguldak you can pick up a bus to **Amasra**, the first really interesting port of call along the Black Sea coast.

Amasra

Once a fishing port, Amasra now welcomes tourists to its beaches. Unfortunately these are very polluted so swimming isn't really the wisest thing to do. Asmara is a place to relax and do very little, but there are a few sights: two **Byzantine-Genoese castles** guarding the headlands, and two **Byzantine churches** tucked away down the back streets. There's also a **museum** with archaeological collections.

Amasra is also a good base for visiting **Safranbolu**, almost two hours away by bus (you may have to change in Bartin). Don't be disheartened by the off-putting industrial outskirts; old Safranbolu is a wonderful hilly place of old Ottoman houses, one of them, the **Kaymakamlar Evi**, open to the public so you can find out what life in such a place would have been like. The seventeenth-century **Koprulu Mehmet Pasa Cami** and eighteenth-century **Izzet Pasa Cami** are also worth a look, as is the ruined **Cincihani Kervansaray**, soon to be converted into a hotel. Once again Safranbolu is a place for wandering; follow the grubby little stream out beyond the town for fine views of the mosques, or climb up the hill to the ruined castle for an overall panorama of the town. If there's time it's also worth dropping in on the *hamam* where you can get yourself thoroughly scrubbed in Ottoman splendour. Inevitably Safranbolu is a convenient place for summer coach trips; visit out of season to see it at its best.

The road east from Amasra is slow but attractive, and it's worth heading out to the beaches at **Boskoy** or to the boat-building village of **Kurucasile**. With your own transport you might also head for the beach at **Kapisuyu**, attractively sited where a mountain stream pours out to the sea.

Accommodation

First Class

Turban Abant Oteli, Lake Abant. Fairly luxurious bungalow-style rooms in lovely setting overlooking the lake.

Middle Range

Nur Turistik Pansiyon, Amasra. Family-run guest-house overlooking the western bay.

Hotel Uz, Misakl Mille, Mahallesi Kirankoy, Safranbolu (Tel. (464) 21086). Although in the new rather than the old town, this hotel offers comfortable rooms and breakfasts.

Economy

Nur Aile Pansiyonu, Camli Caddesi 63, Amasra (Tel. (3895) 1015). Clean, simple and overlooking the sea.

Camp-sites can be found in villages all along the coast and at Lake Abant.

Eating Out

The **Turban Hotel** provides good food. Otherwise, eating options are fairly limited along this stretch of coast. Good fish is available at the floating restaurants of Eregli. The **Canli Balik** restaurant in Amasra also serves excellent Black Sea mackerel.

Sinop to Trabzon

Since it is linked by ferry to Istanbul, Sinop is a possible starting point for exploring the eastern Black Sea region. However, the road east doesn't really improve until you get to Samsun.

Sinop

Sinop has an attractive setting on an isthmus jutting into the sea. However, its role as a NATO listening post and its large prison have not provided the best environment within which tourism could flourish; fishing remains an important source of income for many locals. Like Amasra, Sinop has the remains of a fine **Byzantine-Genoese castle**, this one with a history stretching back to the Pontic period and beyond. From the castle there are fine views of the **beaches** strung out on either side of the peninsula. Other sights include two thirteenth-century **mosques** and a small **museum** with an exhibition of nineteenth-century icons alongside the usual archaeological bits and pieces, and the remains of a Temple of Serapis in the grounds. The ruined seventh-century **Balatlar Kilise** has traces of frescoes.

West of Sinop, there are more beaches at **Helaldi** and **Inebolu**, although neither is particularly easy to get to without private transport; if you do manage it, this is a particularly scenic stretch of coastline. Alternatively **Kastamonu**, a sleepy inland town with more old Ottoman houses and a fortress rather surprisingly built by Tamerlane, is within day-trip distance.

East of Sinop, there is another reasonable beach at **Gerze**. The road then cuts inland to Bafra, across the floodplain of the Kizilirmak river, and then on to Samsun.

Accommodation

Middle Range

Melia Kazim Hotel, Dr. Riza Nur Caddesi (Tel. (3761) 163). 60 rooms in a comfortable, well-located city-centre hotel.

Hotel 117, Rihtim Caddesi 1 (Tel. (3761) 5117). Reasonable hotel with a few sea-view rooms.

Economy

Gul Palas Oteli, Cumhuriyet Caddesi 13 (Tel. (3761) 1737). Good position near the bus station, with a dormitory for those on shoestring budgets.

Otel Uzun Mehmet, Kurtulus Caddesi. Bargain basement option but with hot showers.

Karakum Holiday Village, on the eastern outskirts, also has camping facilities.

Eating Out

The usual range of kebab and *pide* houses is supplemented with a number of harbourside places featuring fish menus; try the **Saray Restoran** for tasty fish kebabs.

Useful Addresses

Tourist Office: Off Gazi Caddesi.

Samsun

Despite its promising name and attractive situation between the Kizilirmak and Yesilirmak rivers, Samsun is actually a dreary modern port town with little to show for its past, mainly because it was sacked by the Genoese in the fifteenth century. Consequently, although it makes a useful base for those using the Istanbul ferry link, it's not a place that many tourists hang around. The only sights are two fourteenth-century **mosques**, and they are not especially exciting. A **statue of Ataturk** in the park also serves as a reminder that it was here that he started rallying the forces to liberate Turkey in 1919. Nevertheless, the road east improves dramatically from now on, and people do sometimes need to spend the night in Samsun before heading east along it.

Samsun can also be used as a base for visiting the inland town of **Amasya**, two and a half hours away by bus, which makes up in sights what Samsun lacks. In particular Amasya has reminders of the Pontic kingdom; follow the path up above the Yesilirmak river and you'll come to the ruins of a **palace** and of fourteen **rock-cut tombs**. The **museum** in Ataturk Caddesi also contains finds from local Pontic sites. Even the ruined **castle** has some traces of the Pontic period. The streets along the river have more attractive **Ottoman houses**; Hazeranlar Konagli is open to the public as a museum. There are several interesting Seljuk and Ottoman **mosques**, foremost among them **Burmali Minare Cami**, a Seljuk building with spiral carving on its minaret. Every June Amasya hosts an **Arts and Culture Festival**; this could be a good time to visit provided you arrange accommodation well in advance.

Accommodation

Middle Range

Turban Buyuk Samsun Oteli, Sahil Caddesi (Tel. (36) 10750). 117 air-conditioned rooms in a comfortable hotel with swimming pool and restaurant.

Hotel Yafeya Cumhuriyet Meydani (Tel. (36) 51131). Newer but slightly cheaper than the Turban, this city-centre hotel has a good roof-top restaurant.

Turban Amasya Hotel, Helkis Mahallesi, Amasya (Tel. (3782) 4054). 34 rooms in a superb setting right by the river.

Ilk Pansiyon, Hittit Soyak 1, Amasya (Tel. (3782) 1689). A restored

eighteenth-century Armenian mansion with only five rooms to let . . .
book in advance.

Economy

Kristal Otel, Gaziler Meydani, Hastane Sokak 5. Simple but clean
rooms, some with showers.

Otel Terminal, Samsun Otogar. Useful if you're arriving or leaving
by bus. Some rooms with showers.

Apaydin Oteli, Ataturk Caddesi 58, Amasya. Probably the best
of an uninspiring bunch of cheap Amasya hotels.

Eating Out

In Samsun the **Turban** and **Yafeya hotels** have good restaurants. For
something cheaper you can try the harbour-front restaurants, some of
them selling good fish, or the *pide* and kebab places in the bazaar and in
Saathane Meydani. In Amasya there's a pleasant tea-garden, the **Belediye
Parki**.

Useful Addresses

Tourist Office: 19 Mayis Bulvari 2. **Turkish Maritime Lines**: Denizcilik
Kall Sti 19.

East of Samsun

East of Samsun the coastal road is good but busy and not as pretty
as you might expect because of the ugly, concrete buildings in various
stages of completion lining most of it as far as Trabzon. Heading
towards the erstwhile fishing village, now holiday resort of **Unye**,
you pass through **Terme**, supposedly the home of the Amazons. Unye
itself, surrounded by pine forests and hazelnut plantations, has good
beaches, lots of camp-sites and adequate pensions and motels. Neither
Fatsa nor **Ordu** is especially attractive, but it might be worth stopping
off at **Yason** on the way between them to examine the ruined church
and spot cormorants at a site where Jason is supposed to have stopped
en route to Colchis.

TML ferries also call at **Giresun**, another possible base for exploring
the coastal regions. There are few important sights here, although it's
worth visiting the museum in an old Greek church. Locals picnic in

the park in the grounds of the old castle at weekends, making this a good place for brushing up on your Turkish. The island of **Giresun Adasi** is only just offshore and is also claimed as one of Jason's stopover points; a boatman may be prepared to take you there to see the ruins of a Byzantine monastery. Don't forget to buy some locally-grown cherries; it was from Giresun that the Romans introduced the fruit to Europe in the first century BC.

Between Giresun and Trabzon the road cuts through some of Turkey's most dramatic coastal scenery, with fine coves and sweeping headlands all the way. You'll see tobacco leaves hanging out to dry on wooden frames by the roadside, and in summer the scenery is made even brighter by whole fields of radiant sunflowers. If you're looking for somewhere to stop, **Tirebolu**, an attractive fishing village in hazelnut-cultivating country, should fit the bill nicely; in the market look out for piles of watermelons, grapes and enormous tomatoes. There are beaches on the outskirts and a fine, intact fourteenth-century castle on the headland.

Accommodation

The middle range **Dolunay Motel**, Camlik Mevkii, PO Box 7, Fatsa/Ordu (Tel. (3721) 1247) has 15 comfortable rooms, all with facilities, and serves good food. Alternatively, the **Giresun Oteli**, Ataturk Bulvari, Giresun (Tel. 13017) has 29 reasonable rooms.

Trabzon

As far as international tourists are concerned the Black Sea effectively starts at Trabzon, described as 'like a green Eden at the foot of the Pontic mountains, a little Constantinople on the Black Sea coast' in Rose Macauley's *The Towers of Trebizond*. In fact at first glance you could be forgiven for wondering what all the fuss is about, since Trabzon is now a big (250,000 inhabitants) trading port with few apparent signs of its romantic past.

Although it turns out that the famed Sumela Monastery is some way out of town, Trabzon does have a few other sights of its own, most importantly the thirteenth-century **Aya Sofya church** with an attractive sea-facing site. This is now a museum, its walls adorned with wonderfully-preserved frescoes and mosaics; look out for vivid pictures of the Marriage at Cana and the Miracle of the Loaves and

Fishes in the narthex, and for the Miraculous Draught of Fishes and Doubting Thomas in the apse. The bell tower was built in the fifteenth century and stands apart from the main structure. Inspect the outside walls carefully and you'll also find ancient graffiti of sailing ships.

Also worth visiting for its beautiful setting and well-kept gardens is the **Ataturk Villa** on the south-western outskirts of town. Built between 1890 and 1903, it was given to Ataturk by the town's grateful citizens, although he only ever visited it three times. It, too, is a museum, filled with photos of Ataturk in plus-fours with the great and the good of his day.

Trabzon's old buildings are mainly concentrated in the **Ortahisar** or Middle Castle area, along the rim of a gorge. Here you'll find the thirteenth- and fourteenth-century **Ortahisar Cami**, once the church of Panayia Khrisokefalos where coronations took place during the period of the Kingdom of Trebizond. Of the medieval walls, the best-preserved fragment is the **Zagnos Tower**. On the gorge bottom you'll see allotments and down-at-heel housing. Here, and in the surrounding villages, look out for women wearing beautiful black, white and maroon-striped shawls and the golden jewellery of their dowries.

It's also worth exploring the **bazaar** where you may stumble upon such oddities as shops selling nothing but minaret loudspeakers. But of course Trabzon's real claim to contemporary fame is the spectacularly-sited **Sumela Monastery**, fifty-four kilometres south of the town and accessible by bus or *dolmus* along the spectacular gorge of the Degirmendere river which tumbles alongside striking basalt rock formations reminiscent of the Giant's Causeway. At the far side of the Zigana Pass, the monastery clings to a steep cliff-face and there are two approach routes, one a steep path winding up through the fir trees, the other a more gentle mud road.

As you climb the steep path, the building is invisible. Then all of a sudden it looms above your head. From a distance it looks intact; once you get inside, however, it's another matter. The monks were forced to flee in 1923, and since then the roofs have caved in and graffiti artists and souvenir-hunters have done their best to destroy the incredible frescoes caking the walls. Nevertheless you can still pick out such scenes as Adam and Eve, the Entry into Jerusalem, the Raising of Lazarus, and the Apparition of the Virgin. The monastery was actually cut into the rockface, and one room is effectively a cave where dampness has given the walls a patina almost as colourful as the frescoes. Here you can see a huge Black Virgin and Child, a tree of Jesse hung with grapes and a Nativity scene. One wall has later paintings, amongst them a conspicuous Jonah and the Whale.

In 1991, when Sumela was eerily deserted as a result of the Gulf War-inspired collapse of tourism, the monastery's custodians were carrying out a survey amongst site visitors. This was designed to discover what sort of 'improvements' they would like to see at the site, ranging from the mildly innocuous like more camping facilities to the just plain barmy like more shops.

In a normal year some of Sumela's mystique would be removed by the sheer number of tourists crawling over it, many of them in coach parties which tend to favour the mornings for visits. To see it at its best, come in the afternoon or out of season. Alternatively, seek out some of the other ruined monasteries in the area in the knowledge that you're likely to have them to yourself and that they are unlikely to see much preservation work without visitors to justify the cost. **Vazelon** and **Peristera** are probably the most interesting and are most easily reached with your own transport. Failing that, you might be able to negotiate with one of the Trabzon taxi drivers.

Overlooking Trabzon, **Boztepe** hill is also worth visiting, especially at weekends when it's a popular picnic area where you should be able to meet Turkish families. Also on the hill are the ruins of the Convent of the Panayia Theoshepastos, locked and awaiting restoration, and of Kapmakli, an Armenian monastery; remains of the latter belong to a farming family but are worth seeking out for their magnificent frescoes, which rival those of Sumela and Aya Sofya in quality.

The coast round Trabzon itself is too polluted to make swimming advisable. Instead you could catch a bus eastwards to either **Arakli** or **Surmene**, a pleasant ride through stunning scenery anyway.

Accommodation

First Class

Hotel Usta, Telegrafhane Sok 1 (Tel. (031) 12843). 72 rooms in hotel with modernised foyer and good rooms, but disappointing breakfasts and not especially welcoming staff.

Middle Range

Horon Oteli, Sira Magazalar Caddesi 125 (Tel. (031) 11199). 42 rooms with private facilities, conveniently close to the centre of the action.

Economy

Ezurum Oteli, Guzelhisar Caddesi 6. A nineteenth-century gardened building with big rooms, some with sea views.

Hotel Anil, Guzelhisar Caddesi 10. More modern, and can be a bit noisy.

Otel Konak, Iskele Caddesi 27. Rock-bottom option.

Eating Out

For the best choice of eating places, head straight for Taksim Meydani where you can start the evening with a *cay* or two in the hectically busy, sprawling centre-street café. The **Ozgur Restaurant** in Taksim Caddesi does Turkish specialities and is comfortable and expensive. The **Trabzon** opposite serves excellent fish in a pleasant atmosphere with good service. The **Hacibaba Iskembe Salonu** also has fish on its menu. **Derya Lokantasi** in Iskele Caddesi serves excellent spit-roasted chickens and milk puddings. Most other restaurants offer the standard fare, but at the **Sisman** in Uzun Yol you can at least eat your kebabs on the roof with views of the bustling activity far below you. For ice-cream and Hemsin-style sweets, try **Selale Pastanesi**, also on Iskele Caddesi.

Entertainments

Trabzon is as much a nightlife desert as anywhere else in Eastern Turkey. However, if you hunt around in the backstreets off Uzun Yol you can find the odd smoky bar, often in a basement, where beer will be the standard offering. It goes without saying that lone women should never venture into such places.

Useful Addresses

Tourist Office: Taksim Meydani. **Post Office**: Posthane Sokak, off Kahramanmaras Caddesi. **Turkish Maritime Lines**: Taksim Meydani.

Beyond Trabzon

South of Trabzon, the road to Sumela continues on towards Ezurum via **Gumushane**, a sleepy market town where anyone who can speak English will be falling over themselves to practise on you. At first the scenery is attractive with lovely rock formations lining the road.

The nearer you get to Erzurum the bleaker it gets, although clusters of bright blue beehives and flocks of brown-woolled sheep will break up any sense of monotony.

Beyond Trabzon the coastal scenery becomes even more dramatic, but tourist traffic falls away as most people strike off inland towards Erzurum on the 'milk run' tour of Eastern Turkey. There are even some good beaches after Surmene, although you have to pay to use some of them.

At **Of** a road cuts inland following the Solakli river. At weekends *dolmus* run to **Long Lake**, just outside **Uzungol** in the mountains above Caykara. From here it's possible to reach Ziyaret Dagi (3111 metres) or Halizden Dagi (3193 metres) where there are lovely glacial lakes if you're properly equipped. Alternatively you can camp at **Uzungol** and dine there on trout. Not far from Uzungol, the village of **Atakoy** preserves a few attractive old houses. The road eventually emerges at **Bayburt**, whose most striking monument is a vast castle dating back to the sixth century and rebuilt over the centuries by virtually all the peoples to have passed through this area.

Just before Iyidere another road inland follows the Iyidere river, emerging just before Ilica, west of Ezurum. The road crosses the highest pass in the Pontic Alps, the **Ovitdagi Gec** at 2800 metres. If you're planning to hike in the Kackar Daglari, **Baskoy** or **Saler** are suitable jumping-off points.

Towards **Rize** the lower mountain slopes are covered with tea plantations which flourish in the wettest part of a generally wet region. In 1987 the Chernobyl disaster contaminated tea in this area; leaves could only be sold when mixed with enough uncontaminated ones to bring the overall brew within permitted radioactivity levels. To find out more about the tea industry call in on the **Cay Enstitusu** on the outskirts of Rize, an otherwise disappointingly ugly modern town.

Beyond Rize the **Hemsin valleys**, cutting into the Kackar Daglari, will be time-consuming to explore unless you have your own transport. There are few sights as such; this is an area you come to for the spectacular scenery alone. However, if you can find your way to **Zilkale**, north of Camlihemsin, you'll find a ruined castle adding to the drama of the landscape. **Ayder**, a small town which is being developed as a spa, is the most popular base for exploring the Kackar Daglari, one of the preferred trekking routes out of it passing through Hazintak, Samistal and Asagi Kavron. This should not be undertaken without careful preparation; amongst other possible difficulties there's a risk of altitude sickness.

Heading on towards **Ardesen** you will find the road squeezed into a narrower and narrower space by the soaring mountains. It's worth stopping in **Cayeli**, especially on Wednesdays when it hosts a bustling market, to eat at the restaurant in the main square which has served such Turkish celebrities as President and ex-Prime Minister Turgut Ozal. **Hopa** is the last town and **Kemelpasa** the last village before the border with the ex-Soviet Union. Neither is an especially inspiring place so unless you're planning on a visit to Armenia or Georgia you'd do better to head inland instead of following the coast to the border.

Accommodation

The middle range seafront **Hotel Papila** in Orta Hopa Caddesi, Hopa, offers reasonably good food. The **Cihan**, also on Orta Hopa Caddesi, is a more modern alternative. The **Hotel-Restaurant Caykent** in Of's Cumhuriyet Caddesi has 27 rooms with facilities and a restaurant serving good fish dishes. The **Sisi Pansiyon ve Kamp** at Senyuva, near Camlihemsin, offers pleasant A-frame cabins. While not especially cheap, these are very popular. If you can't afford them there's camping space here too.

From Hopa to Erzurum and The Georgian Valleys

Heading along the valley of the Coruh river from Hopa, an astonishingly spectacular twisting, turning road heads south-west through the Kackar Daglari to Erzurum. **Artvin** is the first real town on the route although it's not an especially pretty one. If possible time your visit for June when the Kafkasor folk festival takes place here, attracting Georgians from across the border in large numbers. Alternatively organise a *dolmus* ride through **Hell's Gorge** to **Ardanuc** where you can explore a ruined Bagratid castle. If you're prepared to walk or chance it with infrequent public transport you can also explore several ruined tenth-century Georgian churches in the area; the best are in **Yeni Rabat** and **Hamamli**.

The road from Artvin bears east towards Savsat and Ardah, and there's another ruined church worth seeking out in **Cevizli**, near Velikoy. All these churches are in poor repair, but if you want a focus for exploring some of Turkey's remoter villages, they certainly provide it.

Bearing west from Artvin, the road zigzags south to Tortum. About halfway there, a westward turn-off follows the Coruh river to **Yusufeli**, a centre for white-water rafters, especially in June and July when other visitors might prefer to avoid it. A pleasant place in its own right, Yusufeli is also the best base for exploring the nearby Georgian valleys and their churches using local *dolmus*. The easiest to get to is **Dortkilise**, near Tekkale, where glimpses of fresco can just about be made out on the walls of the church. Requiring more of an expedition to reach it, there's a similar church at **Altiparmak**, although this is now in use as a mosque. Heading back to the main road, the church at **Ishan** is one of the oldest of the lot.

From Ishan a road leads east through dramatic desert landscape to Olur, Bana, Oltu and Narman, although you really need your own transport to get round this loop. All along it, however, ruined castles tower above the road and seventh-century churches crumble slowly away in the fields.

South from Yusufeli the road passes **Tortum Golu**, now used for electricity generation. The turn-off to **Camliyamac** will take you to one of the finest of all the Georgian churches, with frescoes and external wall carvings intact. Since this is the most accessible of all the churches it's also the most popular with coach tours, so try and visit early in the day or late in the afternoon. Another turn-off to **Haho** brings you to yet another church, again re-used as a mosque, with many of its monastery buildings still intact.

Accommodation

The middle-range, 57-room **Hotel Karahan** in Artvin (Inonu Caddesi 16. Tel. (0581) 1800), overlooking the Coruh river, has long been used as a base for exploring this area. It also serves excellent Turkish food. The management can help with all sorts of enquiries, and can also arrange a stay in **treehouse accommodation** in Altiparmak for you.

The Kackar Daglari

The highest range of the Pontic Alps, the Kackar Daglari are becoming increasingly popular with trekkers and climbers. They are accessible from **Cat** and **Ayder** to the north, and from **Barhal** and **Hevek** to the south. If you plan to explore the area you should make sure you have suitable camping and hiking equipment since accommodation may be impossible to find en route. The hiking season extends from June to October, with less danger of mists towards the end of the season. After

September, however, the upland *yaylas* will have been abandoned.

Few good maps of the area are available, so unless you're a very experienced hiker you should consider employing a guide; one possibility is to talk to Savas Guney who runs the **Sisi Pansiyon ve Kamp** in Senyuva (see above). The best guidebook remains Lonely Planet's *Trekking in Turkey* which includes a route taking in Bahal, Karagol, the Marsis Massif, Libler Golu, Ayder, Kara Deniz Golu, Dilber Duzu, the Nameless Lake, Tirevit, Cat and the Vercenik Massif. Organised tours of the area normally incorporate visits to some of the Georgian churches and may include climbing on Mount Kackar itself. In August it may even be possible to swim in some of the mountain lakes. Some tours also involve staying in *yaylas*.

7 Eastern Turkey

Eastern Turkey is where the West collides with and finally merges with the Middle East. For that reason it is, for many, the most interesting part of the country. A vast region, it stretches from Kayseri in the west to Dogubeyazit in the east and from Tokat and Ardahan in the north to Gaziantep and Hakkari in the south.

Borders play an especially important role in the East. Until recently the Cold War ensured that the north-eastern border was solidly sealed, and Russian influence is therefore slight. Nevertheless at Ani Soviet watchtowers dominate the site of the ruined city. The Iranian border is more elastic, and Dogubeyazit in particular is full of duty-free goods brought across it. There you'll also see Shi'ite Muslim women cloaked from head to toe in black chadors. In south-eastern towns close to the Iraqi border you'll find depressing evidence of recent political events; outside Mardin a vast, congested refugee camp still holds many of the Kurds who fled Iraq after poison gas was dropped on their villages in 1988. Diyarbakir, too, is full of sad men in boiler suits and cummerbunds who fled in 1988. Finally, in the very south close to the Syrian border, Turkish gives way to Arabic in villages like Harran.

Even away from the borders Eastern Turkey is an area of great cultural diversity. Eight million Kurds live in Turkey and much of the population of the south-east is Kurdish and intensely conscious of being so, despite the fact that until 1990 it was illegal even to speak Kurdish. Although this ban has now been lifted, the subject of Kurdish identity remains controversial. Curfews are frequently imposed in south-eastern towns, many of which are, in any case, under Emergency Rule. You won't be in Dogubeyazit, Van or Diyarbakir long before you hear uncomfortable stories about police activity in the area.

There are as many positions on the Kurdish question as there are people to ask. Not all Kurds support the demands of the PKK, or Kurdish Workers' Party, for an independent state. Some would be happy to settle for a degree of autonomy within the Turkish state, although few would accept Ataturk's description of them as 'mountain Turks'. The

Turks, too, have mixed views; in the west it's not uncommon to find people who believe granting the Kurds independence would result in a more cohesive Turkey and speed up the likelihood of its being admitted to the EC. Interestingly, Ataturk's dictum *Ne Mutlu Turkum Diyene* ('Happy is he who is a Turk') appears on bridges and hillsides with ever-greater frequency the further into Kurdish territory you go, as the Ankara government frantically tries to stamp its authority on the area.

It's a touchy subject and one where it pays to be careful what you say. Given that German tourists were briefly kidnapped in 1991 and that the political situation seemed to be worsening in 1992, it's also essential to check the current position carefully before venturing anywhere off the beaten track. It also makes sense to be aware of potential flashpoints, like Kurdish New Year celebrations which take place in March.

Of the vast Armenian population which also inhabited Eastern Turkey in the past, little trace now remains. In Diyarbakir you can visit churches used by the tiny surviving congregation, but surveying the ruins of Ani it's hard to credit that 200,000 Armenians once lived there. The question of the Armenians and their fate is as thorny as the Kurdish one. Museums in Kars and Ezurum present a thoroughly one-sided picture of the story, but in the absence of modern-day Armenians to argue their case it's hard to find Turks who have much sympathy for their viewpoint.

There are pockets of prosperity in Eastern Turkey (it's worth exploring the modern areas of the big towns which may reveal a different picture of life to the older, more touristically-interesting areas), but this is still by far the poorest part of the country. In Diyarbakir perhaps 50 per cent of the population is at least *under*employed, and around Ani you'll see housing more appropriate to the Middle Ages. The government is said to be ploughing money into building schools in the region, but more people in the west seem to believe this is actually happening than in the east. Perhaps not surprisingly then, you will find pockets of Kurds all over Turkey who have left in search of a better life.

What clearly is happening though is work on the South-East Anatolia (or GAP) Project, intended to provide irrigation and energy for 48,000 square kilometres around the Tigris and Euphrates rivers. The Project will consist of twenty-one dams, the biggest of them the huge Ataturk Dam which will be the world's fifth largest. When the Project is completed it is hoped that beet, corn, grapes, fruit, vegetables, rice, cotton and pistachios will grow in the area, with two annual harvests of some crops. The seventeen hydro-electric plants will also increase Turkey's generating power by roughly 70 per cent. If all goes according to plan, the Turkish government expects the GAP Project to halt the net outflow of population from south-east Turkey, allowing it to double to about ten million by 1995.

Eastern Turkey is the country's most conservative area. Nightlife is non-existent, even in the big towns. Accommodation exists on a take-it-or-leave-it basis, and restaurants, while plentiful, are much of a muchness, offering an unchanging menu of kebabs and *pide*. The one pleasing consequence of this is that it's very easy on the pocket; you'd be hard put to spend much money in the East. Even in the Kurdish areas Turkish remains the most widely-spoken language; fortunately English-speakers are also fairly easy to find.

History

Because of its geographical position, straddling Europe and the Middle East, Eastern Turkey has acted as a corridor for many invading armies. Consequently its history is a confusing one, with kingdom upon kingdom and empire upon empire following one another in quick succession.

One of the earliest identified settlements in Eastern Turkey is at Karatepe, in the foothills of the Taurus Mountains, about thirty kilometres north of the modern town of Osmaniye. The site here was originally settled by proto-Hittites, Old Bronze Age people, between 2600 and 1900 BC, although much of what you see nowadays is actually the remains of a later, neo-Hittite fortress. An inscription found at this site, partly in Phoenician, led to the translation of Hittite hieroglyphs which has eased the understanding of their history.

The Hittite Empire flourished from 1900 to 1300 BC and lingered in the south-east Taurus Mountains even after its overthrow by the Dorians in Central Anatolia. Eventually they too were defeated by another Anatolian tribe, the Hurri, who founded Sanliurfa, the city where the prophet Abraham was born in about 2100 BC. Abraham is believed to have spent the first ten years of his life hiding in a cave from the wrath of a local Assyrian tyrant, Nemrut, who had ordered that all new-born children should be killed. Later he is said to have visited the town of Harran on his way to Canaan.

By the middle of the ninth century BC the Urartians, possibly descendants of the Hurrians, had set up a kingdom in Eastern Turkey centred on Lake Van (Van Golu). There are important Urartian remains in Van itself, and at Cavustepe which boasts what may be the oldest known squat toilet. Much of the wonderful **metalwork** found at these sites is now in Ankara's Museum of Anatolian Civilisations.

The Urartian Kingdom was overthrown in the eighth century BC by the Assyrians encroaching from the south-east. Then in 547 BC the Persians, under Cyrus the Great, conquered a large part of Turkey; the south-eastern area became the province of Cilicia. In 334 BC Alexander the Great invaded Asia Minor from Greece and swept through Eastern Turkey on his way to India. After his death, the vast, unmanageable empire he had established quickly broke up. South-eastern Turkey fell to his general, Lysimachus, and then when he was killed, to Seleucus who set up a Seleucid Kingdom centred on Antioch (modern Antakya). Meanwhile the Armenians, a Phrygian tribe, had re-settled the old Urartian heartlands. Between 317 BC and 284 BC a Seleucid satrap, Ardvates, also established a Kingdom of Armenia around Lake Van. This gradually split into Greater and Lesser Armenia, was reunited in 94 BC by Tigranes I, and fell to the Romans shortly afterwards.

A footnote to the Seleucid Kingdom, the Commagene Kingdom around modern Adiyaman flourished most significantly under Antiochus I (64–38 BC) who was responsible for the incredible stone mausoleum at Nemrut Dagi. However, soon the Romans began absorbing Turkey from the west, seizing the eastern provinces of Cilicia and Armenia Minor in the first century AD.

The Roman occupation lasted for almost three centuries, during which time Antioch in particular flourished. In the Hatay St Peter preached against all sorts of moral excesses. However, the Christians too indulged in excesses; it was here that St Simeon Stylites started the fashion for sitting on top of pillars as a form of asceticism in the fifth century.

Roman rule was followed by Byzantine rule from Constantinople after the Roman Empire split in two. However, as the Byzantine emperors weakened, the Arabs and the emerging Turkish tribes of the Middle East began to encroach on Eastern Turkey, bringing Islam in place of Christianity. Edessa (modern Sanliurfa) was occupied by the Arabs until 1097–8 when Baldwin of Boulogne created a Christian city-state there during the First Crusade; it was snatched back again by the Arabs in 1144. In 1071 Alp Arslan beat the Byzantine Emperor Romanus Diogenes at Manzihert (modern Malazgirt), opening the way for the Seljuk Turks based in Persia to occupy Anatolia. Reminders of their occupation survive throughout Eastern Turkey, most strikingly in Erzurum, Divrigi and Kars in the form of finely-carved stone mosques and medresesi.

During the thirteenth century the Mongols poured into Turkey, overthrowing the Seljuk Turks and the Arabs. Gradually during the fourteenth and fifteenth centuries their place was taken by the Ottoman Turks who crushed what remained of the Byzantine Empire and established their rule throughout what is now modern Turkey.

Eastern Turkey's more recent history has been just as turbulent. Because of its chequered past it had become a bubbling cauldron of different races, amongst whom the Armenians and Kurds were lastingly important. At the end of the nineteenth century the Ottoman Sultan Abdulhamid developed a nationalist policy which led to the Armenians being repressed in the east. In 1895 an Armenian demonstration resulted in the massacre of about 50,000 Armenians; then in 1896 the Sultan encouraged the Kurds and Circassians to murder another 100,000. Although Abdulhamid was overthrown by the Young Turks in 1908, the Armenians' position did not improve. In 1915 their men were kicked out of the Turkish army and civilians in Anatolia were rounded up, most of the men being shot and many of the women and children dying on their way to concentration camps in the south-east. In all perhaps one million Armenians died between 1915 and 1923. However, the Turkish government claims that only 300,000 people died, most of them traitors who had allied with Russia or France during the war.

The Kurdish situation has not been a great deal better. Much of south-eastern Turkey is occupied by ethnic Kurds with their own language and traditionally Islamic culture. Since 1925 sporadic Kurdish revolts have aimed to achieve greater autonomy or even an independent Kurdish state with its own green, yellow and red flag. In 1984 the Marxist-Leninist Kurdish Workers' Party or PKK resumed small-scale guerrilla warfare in the east, although some of its extremist activities have alienated potential supporters. Until 1991 speaking Kurdish or playing Kurdish music was illegal. However, the lifting of these bans has done little to ease the tension, no doubt exacerbated by the temporary flood of Iraqi Kurds fleeing towards Turkey after the Gulf War. Indeed, in 1992, south-east Turkey sometimes seemed to be lurching towards civil war.

The Hatay only became part of Turkey in 1939 when France, which had administered it since the demise of the Ottoman Empire, handed it over in an effort to keep Turkey out of the Second World War. There are strong separatist tendencies here too.

Geography

Eastern Anatolia is a vast area, encompassing almost half of Turkey and extending to the Russian, Iranian, Iraqi and Syrian borders. In shape it is roughly rectangular, but with a thin southerly protrusion, the Hatay, which extends down alongside Syria and where Arabic is as widely spoken as Turkish. In theory there are beaches along the Hatay; in practice pollution from Iskenderun in particular makes these unsuitable for swimming.

North-eastern Turkey is drained by the Kura, Aras and Coruh rivers, while the Kekit river flows towards the north-west. The more historically significant Tigris and Euphrates rivers drain south-eastern Turkey, the Tigris continuing south into Iraq and the Euphrates passing into Syria. The Ataturk Dam, now nearing completion just south of Kahta, will harness the Euphrates' head-waters to bring prosperity to the desert. Not surprisingly, the Syrians view the project with suspicion, fearing it will dilute their own much-needed water supplies.

Much of Eastern Turkey is relentlessly mountainous which makes for long, slow journeys but spectacular scenery. The Kackar Daglari range, or Pontic Alps, soar to 3972 metres and separate the Black Sea from the Eastern Turkish hinterland. They offer excellent mountaineerng prospects, while the large number of small lakes also make them pleasant walking country (see **The Black Sea** chapter). Eastern Turkey's highest mountain, Ararat, very close to the Iranian border at Dogubeyazit, has two peaks, the higher of them reaching 5165 metres. In this wild countryside wolves and brown bears still roam. However, few trees grow, and the landscape is littered with pyramids of cow dung to be burnt as winter fuel. Wherever the mountains open out on to plateaux hay is also harvested in neat little stacks.

On the western side of the region the Munzur Daglari dominate the area between Erzincan and Tunceli, with the highest peaks in the Mercan Daglari area, north of Ovacik, ranging from 3300 to 3500 metres. In the heart of the mountains is the remote Munzur Vadisi National Park with natural springs and streams full of trout.

North of Lake Van, Suphan Dagi soars to 4048 metres and offers fine views of the lake. Nemrut Dagi (not to be confused with the identically-named site of Antiochus' mausoleum) reaches 2935 metres. At the summit you can climb into an extinct volcanic crater with a lake and hot and cold springs. (It was here that German tourists were kidnapped in 1991, so make enquiries before setting out.)

South-east of Hakkari and hard against the Iranian border, the Cilo Daglari have snow-capped peaks topping 4000 metres (Cilo Dagi itself reaches 4136 metres) which offer good mountaineering opportunities. Sadly, the border's proximity means you can only climb on set routes and with express official permission.

Lake Van, Turkey's largest lake at roughly 4000 square kilometres, is almost large enough to be called an inland sea. Van's water is very alkaline and feels soapy to the touch, but pollution makes swimming in it unwise although species of carp and grey mullet live in it. The lake area also boasts two breeds of rare cat, one adapted for swimming, the other with one green and one blue eye. Sadly, rarity has made them so valuable that most are now kept indoors to prevent them being stolen. You're unlikely to see a Van cat unless you ask around.

Lake Van plays host to flocks of white storks and a few flamingoes. Black-necked and great-crested grebes, pochards, shelducks, ruddy shelducks and white-headed ducks may also be spotted. Little ringed plovers, common sandpipers, lapwings, redshanks and corn and black-headed buntings can be seen along the water's edge, while reed warblers and black-winged stilts hide in the reed-beds surrounding it. On Arin Golu, a freshwater lake at the north-eastern edge, you may also see little egrets and avocets. Lake Van is at its prettiest in spring when thousands of poppies blossom around the lake's edge.

Alpine swifts and kestrels can be spotted in Van itself and at Hosap castle, while hoopoes, bee-eaters and rollers are resident around the Rock of Van. More exotic black and white Egyptian vultures can often be seen wheeling in the air, while Lammergeier's vultures can occasionally be spotted on the road south of Van to Hakkari.

Mesopotamia, the south-eastern region stretching from Kahramanmaras in the west to Siirt in the east and hemmed in by the Tigris and Euphrates, is relentlessly flat desert terrain. Ornithologists will want to visit the small town of Birecik, home to the few remaining bald ibises which the WWF is trying to protect. Rollers also nest in this area, and pied and white-breasted kingfishers can be seen along the banks of the Euphrates. Near the Syrian border, look out for Montagu's harriers, Saker falcons, warblers, short-toed larks and black-headed buntings. Harder to spot are the badgers, gazelles, jackals, deer, boars and ibexes which are hunted in the border areas.

Around Erzurum roads are lined with poplars, many of them planted to celebrate the birth of a son. These provide perfect nesting places for hooded crows, ravens and jackdaws. Near Gaziantep thousands of pistachio trees decorate the landscape. Olive trees and vines also flourish here, while apricot trees do especially well around Malatya.

Climate

Eastern Turkey has the country's most extreme climate. For much of the year it's freezing cold and thick snow, with drifts as much as three and a half metres deep, covers the ground, making access to smaller villages impossible. From December to April skiing is feasible near Kars and Erzurum, although temperatures as low as −30°C have been recorded.

However, in summer it is also the hottest area. In south-eastern towns like Diyarbakir, Sanliurfa and Mardin temperatures average 31°C in August, although they have been known to soar to a terrifying 43°C too. Further north temperatures are more moderate.

For tourists these climatic extremes are very important. It's only really realistic to explore Eastern Turkey from May through to September. Outside those months you need to be not only pretty hardy but also very lucky not to find blocked roads curtailing your schedule. Unless you love the sun it's also best to avoid July and August when the lack of air-conditioning or fans in all but the best hotels means there's no escape from the heat even at night. However, dawn trips to see the heads at Nemrut Dagi are likely to be extremely cold except in July and August.

Attractions

Reflecting its sometimes chaotic history, Eastern Turkey has a wealth of magnificent buildings from many different periods. Amongst the finest are the Urartian remains in Van and Cavustepe, the Byzantine walls of Diyarbakir, the Seljuk monuments in Divrigi, Erzurum and Kars and the Ottoman monuments of Sanliurfa. Then there are the off-beat buildings like the beehive-shaped houses of Harran. Better known are the incredible stone heads of the Commegnian mausoleum at Nemrut Dagi, and the romantically isolated ruins of seventeenth- and eighteenth-century Isak Pasa Sarayi near Dogubeyazit. Also popular are the Armenian churches surviving in ruinous state on Akhtamar Island and in greater quantity at Ani, only recently opened up to tourism.

Eastern Turkey boasts spectacular scenery, some of it with curious associations to make it all the more attractive. Mount Ararat is not only the highest mountain, but also the supposed last resting place of Noah's Ark. Lake Van is not just beautiful but is also home to unique swimming cats (see page 290).

Most visitors to Eastern Turkey will want to explore the specific attractions, but this is an area where the way of life is interesting in itself. The further east and south-east you travel the more exotic the costumes you will come across. And although many people are extremely poor, they are also very welcoming so that you'll be invited into their houses and asked to share their meals in a way that would be inconceivable in northern Europe.

Cuisine

If you want to stick to the standard *mezes* and kebab menus of Western Turkey it will be easy to do so in Eastern Turkey. In the modern quarters of big towns like Diyarbakir you can even buy American-style hamburgers and pizzas if that's your style.

However, Eastern Turkey also has its culinary quirks, some of them, like the raw meat kebabs of Sanliurfa, best admired from a distance. You'll also need a strong stomach for the stuffed stomach linings and goat's head soups of Mardin and the south-east. Erzurum's bazaar boasts a line in goat's cheeses that look, and smell, rather like socks.

Still, no one should miss the opportunity to sample some of the giant watermelons for which Diyarbakir is so famous that it actually holds a Watermelon Festival every September. The pistachios of Gaziantep are another must, as is the honey, sold in giant combs or spotlit jars in Kars.

Less healthy but just as delicious are the cheese-filled sweet pastries of Sanliurfa (pick them up in the bazaar), and the sticky, almost marshmallow-like ice-creams (*dondurma*) of Kahramanmaras. Vendors in a special costume and with a fine line in cone-whirling that will leave children goggle-eyed sell these all over Turkey but there's nowhere better to sample them than in their home town.

Another sweet delicacy no one should miss is *asure*, or Noah's Pudding, a syrupy confection traditionally made from forty different ingredients but nowadays more likely to be whipped up from grapes, figs, hazelnuts, raisins, pistachios, chickpeas, white beans, jelly and wheat. Again, this can be found elsewhere in Turkey, but is perhaps more popular in the east; the Iranian-owned Saray Lokantasi in Igdir on the road to Dogubeyazit is just one restaurant where it can be sampled.

Level of Tourism

Eastern Turkey is the country's least-visited region, receiving just 2.35 per cent of all foreign visitors to the country. In 1989, only 138,129 foreign tourists visited Eastern Anatolia, and 81,276 South-Eastern Anatolia, compared with four and a half million visitors to the Mediterranean region.

Those parts which do receive tourists form a 'milk run' popularised by the long-haul tour companies, outside which tourists are as rare as Van cats. Most visitors on this circuit approach either from Trabzon on the Black Sea or via Sivas, Malatya or Gaziantep in the west. A very popular route out of Trabzon runs through Erzurum, Kars (for Ani), Dogubeyazit (for Isakpasa Saray), Van, Diyarbakir, Sanliurfa and Kahta or Adiyaman (for Nemrut Dagi) to Kayseri, with many tourists concluding their tour in Ankara.

Within this circuit the most visited place is Nemrut Dagi which has become almost too popular for its own good because it's easy to get to from the Mediterranean or from Cappadocia as well as from the east. Certainly any hope of a solitary dawn or dusk visit in July or August is now out of the question. Even in 1991, when the number of tourists had fallen because of the Gulf War, noisy crowds were already assembled by six in the morning. What's more many of those tourists were happy to clamber all over the monuments regardless of signs telling them not to.

Ani, too, was reaching saturation point despite restrictions imposed because of its position on the Soviet border which prevented photography or note-taking. Glasnost has led to the lifting of these rules although visitors still require a special permit and coaches are not meant to stop on the road leading to the site, still carefully guarded and overlooked by watchtowers. Following the Gulf War tourism to Ani collapsed in 1991. It remains to be seen whether numbers will rise again and whether the turmoil in what used to be the Soviet Union will result in the re-imposition of tiresome restrictions.

Even when western tourists are scarce there are still plenty of visitors to Sanliurfa, reflecting its importance as a shrine. Muslims come here either on their way to Mecca, or as an alternative to making the longer pilgrimage. Most stop to pray at the site of the cave where Abraham was supposedly born. Non-Muslims are theoretically free to visit as well, but may feel uncomfortable and voyeuristic if they do so.

Away from this fixed circuit tourists are few and far between. If you want to discover the real Turkey the best way to do so would be to head for towns like Elazig and Malatya which lack significant historic monuments. However, you will need to be aware that few hotels are equipped for western tourists and that women, in particular, will attract a great deal of attention, not always of the friendliest kind.

Good Alternatives

Meeting People

Meeting people in Eastern Turkey is absurdly simple. In fact there are times when you may be more concerned to find ways *not* to meet them, particularly in Diyarbakir, a somewhat troublesome town where carpet-sellers, once they have discovered you, will haunt your footsteps with a dogged determination that must be experienced to be believed.

Eastern Turkey remains the best place to go for sampling the *hamams* which have, in many parts of the country, succumbed to the twin pressures of improved household plumbing and tourism. The *hamam*, or public bath, has a long and venerable tradition in Islam, which regards personal hygiene as enormously important, and has flourished in countries where individual families have not always had access to their own bathrooms. In the past every neighbourhood had its own bath, often attached to the mosque, with either separate sections for men and women or different times for them to use it. In Western Turkey it is now much less common for women in particular to use the baths since housing has improved enormously in the last twenty years. The bath buildings still exist, but in areas frequented by tourists they now offer a very different experience, with mixed bathing commonplace and male masseurs handling women as well as men.

In Eastern Turkey you can still head for the baths – easily identifiable by their rooflines of clustered domes – and experience the traditional Turkish bath. In doing so you will inevitably meet Turks, both those who work there and those who go there to make use of the facilities.

It's best to acquaint yourself with bath etiquette before you go. Basically you can choose between using them to give yourself a good scrub, or opting for the full works which will mean someone doing the scrubbing for you with a glove like sandpaper and then ruthlessly massaging you afterwards. It's cheaper to wash yourself and you'll still get to chat to other bathers. However, it's more fun to go for the massage which will enable you to talk to your masseur and leave the bath positively glowing with health and cleanliness.

Men will find it easier to avail themselves of the *hamam*, since all towns have baths for them, with longer opening hours too; Ezurum's male baths are especially well spoken of. But although it's harder for female travellers to use the baths, it's also more important since the segregation of Turkish society tends to mean that the only people they get to speak to otherwise are men.

As elsewhere in Turkey you're also guaranteed to meet Turks every time you venture into a carpet shop. The advantage of this is that the people who work in them often have an excellent grasp of several western European languages. Of course you may come under pressure to buy a carpet you don't want. But the Turks are naturally hospitable people; if you show an interest in their country, most will be more than happy to drop the sales pitch in favour of a chat over a cup of *cay*. Diyarbakir's Hasan Pasa Hani is just one place where conversation is taken as seriously as sales. Nevertheless, given the south-east's tense political climate it's vital to follow your host's lead over suitable conversational topics.

In some of the smaller villages like Harran and Hosap which are on the tourist 'milk run' you can expect to be pestered by groups of very persistent children, demanding sweets, pencils and even cash. At the very least they (and their parents) will want money to be photographed. The children present a real dilemma for the 'good tourist'. Refusing to give can seem niggardly when they are often dirty, barefoot and apparently malnourished. What's more you're unlikely to shake them off unless you do. On the other hand, by giving in you help create and perpetuate a begging mentality. If you go inside some of the Harran houses you'll find people are not perhaps as poor as you assumed anyway, since huge televisions and video recorders often have pride of place in their living rooms. Saying no to the children may seem harsh but is probably the best policy even if it does result in your getting stones or mud thrown at you. But you might want to consider carrying some small items which could be given as gifts to adults you have befriended; cassettes, baseball caps and toiletries are three obvious possibilities.

Discovering Places

Exploring Eastern Turkey can be tiring because the distances involved are so great, because roads are not always as well-maintained as in the west and because it's here most of all that laid-back eastern time scales come into play. However, the transport network remains surprisingly good, with efficient, modern buses for long-distance routes and plentiful *dolmus*, or shared taxis, for shorter journeys.

One of Eastern Turkey's most exciting excursions takes you up Mount Ararat. Unfortunately you're obliged to climb it as part of an organised group, but given the potential hazards, which range from wolves to terrorists, perhaps that's just as well. One way to do it is to join a group put together by Turkish operators, Trek Travel. Based in Istanbul but with a friendly, well-informed office in Dogubeyazit too (Emniyet Caddesi 53. Tel. (0278) 1981), they have been organising treks up Ararat since 1982 and really know the score.

Climbing the mountain requires considerable stamina; the top third is covered in snow and the final hundred metres in ice even in high summer. Experienced climbers may want to join a tour that simply takes in Ararat, but Trek Travel also run trips that start with a four-day warm-up in the Taurus Mountains. Alternatively they offer trips which combine climbing Ararat with trekking in the Pontic Alps or climbing Mount Suphan, near Nemrut Dagi. An even more exciting option involves crossing the Soviet border after ascending Ararat in order to climb Mount Elbrus, at 5642 metres the highest peak in Europe.

If mountaineering is not your forte, a trip up Nemrut Dagi may be more realistic. However, this too needs careful planning, particularly since its popularity has resulted in a proliferation of not always scrupulous tour operators in Kahta and Adiyaman. Given the difficulty of ensuring a trouble-free trip this could be one occasion when you might consider hiring a car, despite the generally prohibitive cost. If you do that you will need to ensure you have enough fuel to see you through the return trip and a reliable map in case the road signs have been removed, a popular trick to deter independent travellers.

Whether you drive yourself or risk an organised tour you should plan to take in more than just the stone heads on the summit of the mountain. Making a day of it, you can take in the Roman and Seljuk bridges, and Mameluk castle near Eski Kahta, and the impressive stelae and reliefs at Eski Kale (ancient Arsameia) as well. Given the dawn crowds, you may be better off visiting later in the day which also enables you to appreciate the stunning scenery en route to the mountain. Forgetting about sunrise also lets you use Sanliurfa, a much more attractive town than Kahta or Adiyaman, as a base for the trip.

Communications

How to Get There

You can reach Eastern Turkey by **air** by flying on Turkish Airlines to Diyarbakir, Erzurum, Gaziantep, Malatya, Sivas or Van, cutting out the long overland journey from Istanbul. However, most flights stop in Ankara so the overall journey time may still be quite long. Alternatively, you could fly or take the **ferry** from Istanbul to Trabzon and pick up the land route from there.

From Ankara or Samsun it's possible to head east by **rail**. The best trains to take would be the 'Blue' trains from Ankara to Erzurum or Gaziantep. Those to Erzurum leave daily at 9 p.m. and take eight hours. Those to Gaziantep leave at 7 p.m. on Mondays, Wednesdays, Fridays and Saturdays and take seventeen hours. Otherwise the trains are notoriously slow and unreliable and you'll need a flexible timetable to accommodate their whims. The rail route links up Sivas, Divrigi, Erzincan, Erzurum and Kars, with southern branches running from Sivas to Malatya, Kahramanmaras and Gaziantep; from Malatya to Mus and Bitlis; and from Malatya to Diyarbakir.

Travelling all the way from Istanbul by **coach** would be tiring. Even from Ankara it would test many travellers; from there, it's thirteen hours to Diyarbakir and twenty-two to Dogubeyazit. However, if you have time to divide up the journey, this would be the best way to break yourself into the east gently.

When You're There

Bus – the best method of travelling between towns is by bus. In general Turkish coaches are comfortable, with air-conditioning and free supplies of drinking water. Lone women travellers will also find that they shouldn't be seated next to an unknown man which may result in them having two seats to themselves because so few women travel unaccompanied.

Nevertheless, there are some snags. Turkish bus services are very competitive so you must set aside time to ask around in the *otogar* or terminal for the best times and prices. This isn't always easy given the touts waiting to snatch you into their own vehicle, and the willingness of ticket-sellers to stretch the truth to win your custom. Ideally you should go to the *otogar* the day before you intend to travel when you can sort everything out calmly.

Boat – you might want to explore Lake Van by boat in which case there are daily services from Van town to Tatvan and vice versa.

Car – travelling by car is prohibitively expensive unless you bring your own vehicle from Europe, in which case petrol is slightly cheaper than at home. The main problem then will be dealing with some of the terrifying mountain roads, and the drivers you'll find on them. In general it's not a good idea to drive in Eastern Turkey unless you have experience of mountain driving. This is particularly the case in remote border areas where banditry and kidnapping are additional hazards.

Geographical Breakdown of Region

North-East Anatolia

Stretching from Koyulhisar, Zara and Divrigi in the west to the borders of Georgia and Armenia in the east, and from the Black Sea hinterland in the north to Erzurum in the south, North-East Anatolia is a poor and mountainous area. There's spectacular scenery wherever you go, but perhaps most impressively in the Kackar Daglari to the north-east. However, away from the specific 'sights', the towns tend to be architecturally grim, ringed by eastern-bloc-style skyscrapers and dotted with half-built houses. Veiled older women wear an assortment of fantastic robes: completely black, or black gently printed with intricate green or dark brown patterns. Their younger sisters are much less covered up, suggesting that such clothing will vanish within a generation.

Erzurum

Whether you approach from Ankara or Trabzon, Erzurum, with a population of a quarter of a million and a flourishing university, is likely to be your first port of call. A brighter, airier town than others in the north-east, it has striking Seljuk architecture and a lively street market.

The **Cifte Minare Medrese** at the end of Cumhuriyet Caddesi is Erzurum's most striking monument, set back in a strip of parkland which lets you appreciate the twin minarets with their thin turquoise tiles flanking a typically elaborate thirteenth-century Seljuk portal. Inside, weeds are pushing up through the stonework and the caretaker seems more intent on molesting female visitors than in keeping out importunate shoeshine lads or doing anything about the neglect. Nevertheless, you can pop your head into the cells lining the courtyard where students once studied and climb the stairs to a stone gallery offering fine views. Behind the Medrese, side streets lead past souvenir shops to a group of three **kumbets,** or conical tombs, standing in a weed-grown enclosure. You'll need to be in a group to get them opened, but the insides are empty and of only passing interest anyway.

Across the road from the Medrese a road leads past the remains of a brick clock-tower to the **citadel** which dates from Byzantine times but has been added to over the centuries so that what you see now is of indeterminate date. The walls themselves are not very exciting, but do offer fine views over Erzurum's sprawling suburbs and the flat-topped surrounding mountains.

Returning to Cumhuriyet Caddesi and turning back towards the centre of town you'll come to the twelfth-century **Ulu Cami**, an attractive Seljuk mosque with fine arches and a tiny dome supported by stalactite carvings. Nearby is the sixteenth-century **Lala Mustafa Pasa Cami**, a stereotypical piece of Ottoman architecture but none the less pleasant for that; look out for the grandfather clock with a ship bobbing up and down on the pendulum. Opposite it stands the more imaginative fourteenth-century **Yakutiye Medrese**, due to become an ethnography museum but locked in the meantime. Its minaret has turquoise tiles, and lions and an eagle are carved on the façade, ideas perhaps imported from Persia.

Erzurum's **market** is across the road from Yakutiye Medrese. Alongside more mundane grocery stores you'll find lots of shops selling stringy white cheese, with sheep being herded on the pavements outside. Other areas of the market specialise in tin samovars and double-bowled tea pots, and leather shoes; styles for men are modern and attractive, those for women pre-date the War. Look out for **Rustem Pasha Hani**, a sixteenth-century covered bazaar, its tiny shops full of local black jet jewellery. These stay open until late, and shopkeepers are only too ready to chat over a glass of *cay* in the central courtyard.

Sadly, the Istasyon Caddesi *hamam* is for men only. However, this is the place to go to experience the full vigour of a real Turkish massage.

From December through to April it's possible to ski at **Palendoken**, four kilometres south-west of Erzurum, although there's only one chair-lift.

Accommodation

Middle Range

Hotel Sefer, Istasyon Caddesi (Tel. (011) 13615). 40 rooms within walking distance of the market and main attractions. Reasonably comfortable despite the unappealing façade.

Otel Oral, Terminal Caddesi 3 (Tel. (011) 19740). 90 more comfortable rooms, but further away from the attractions and on a noisy road junction.

Buyuk Erzurum Oteli, Ali Ravi Caddesi 5 (Tel. (011) 16528). 50 rooms in a rather old-fashioned hotel, but well positioned for visiting the monuments.

Economy

Hittit Otel, Kazim Kårabekir Caddesi 26 (Tel. (011) 11204). Used to foreigners and therefore a good bet for lone travellers for whom Erzurum is a first taste of the east.

Hotel Buhara, Kazim Karabekir Caddesi 9. A cheap and quiet alternative.

Otel Evin, Ayaz Pasa Caddesi, Bedendibi Sokak 12 (Tel. (011) 12349). Right in the old city and convenient for all the monuments.

Erzurum has many cheap hotels with little to choose between them; if the above options are full a little searching should turn up something else without much trouble.

Eating Out

Middle Range

The **Hotel Sefer**, **Otel Oral** and **Buyuk Erzurum Oteli** all have restaurants which, although not especially inspiring, are the most upmarket in town. The **Guzelyurt Restoran**, on Cumhuriyet Caddesi (Tel. (011) 11514) is the only place in town which serves alcohol with meals.

Economy

Lokanta Vatan, round the corner from Hotel Sefer, serves reasonably priced meals in light, airy premises. Good kebab shops are **Salon Cagin**

and **Salon Asya**, opposite each other on Cumhuriyet Caddesi.

Entertainments

In terms of nightlife Erzurum has nothing going for it. However, if you visit in spring or summer you might be able to catch a game of *cirit*, a type of jousting where the competitors try to push each other off their horses with javelins.

Useful Addresses

Tourist Office: Cemal Gursel Caddesi. **Post Office**: Cumhuriyet Caddesi. **Hospital**: Havuzbasi Bulvari. **Turkish Airlines Office**: Yuz Yil Caddesi, SSK Rant Tesisleri 24.

East of Erzurum

Heading east from Erzurum you come first to **Pasinler**, a sleepy small town dominated by the crumbling ruins of the **Hasankale citadel**. More impressive is the arched sixteenth-century **Cobandede bridge** across the Aras River, twenty kilometres further east. Attached to its side are tiny rooms, supposedly for travellers but with no obvious means of access. East of Cobandede the scenery becomes more interesting, at one point passing rocky landscape like a mini version of Goreme. Near **Karakurt** you'll also pass fields of sunflowers. Around here mountains of dung are piled up beside the rather mean housing, ready for the rigours of winter. Oxen still pull the ploughs, and huge wolf-like dogs guard flocks of brown-woolled sheep.

If you want to stop before Kars, **Sarikamis** would be the best place to do so, particularly if you'd like to sample the skiing. There isn't much choice about where to stay, but the middle-range **Sartur Motel** in the hills above the town is surrounded by pine trees and has a swimming pool. With private transport it's worth stopping to look at the great piles of obsidian right by the roadside on the outskirts of Sarikamis.

Extensive military bases lining the roadside indicate that you're nearing Kars.

Kars

At first sight **Kars** can look uninviting, with its grey streets of uninspiring breeze-block buildings. However, this initially bad impression is quickly dispelled when you set off to explore. Kars has a reputation for unfriendliness towards foreigners that seems uncalled for. Even the architecture bucks up once you find Ataturk Caddesi and the attractive neo-Classical Russian buildings lining it, and the cluster of ancient buildings flanking the river below the citadel.

Get your bearings by climbing up to the fifteenth/sixteenth-century **Citadel** which gives a fine view of the grid-plan streets below. Back at the bottom again you'll spot the circular **Church of the Apostles**, a tenth-century Armenian building with relief carvings on its dome. Sadly it's been left to decay and weeds are growing out of the roof. What's more the church is firmly locked so you can only view the outside. From its steps you can see the attractive **Tas Kopru bridge**, originally built in the fifteenth-century, but rebuilt in the eighteenth, and near it, the slight remains of an old mosque and palace, currently being restored. There is also an ancient *hamam* with interesting external carving. However, inside it is both filthy and unfriendly, so don't pick this for your first or only visit to the baths.

Out on a limb but worth the walk is the **Museum** at the east end of Cumhuriyet Caddesi. Here you'll find exhibits from all periods of Kars' history, together with some excellent photographs of the Ani churches. Upstairs are beautiful carpets and costumes and in the grounds stands a striking white train carriage adorned with black multilingual inscriptions where the Russian and Turkish governments signed a protocol ending the Russian occupation of Kars in the 1920s; get a curator to unlock it so you can see the plush interior fittings and complex heating system. The museum's only disagreeable feature is a case at the back devoted to the 'Armenian Question'. Turkish-only labelling makes it inaccessible to tourists although its general message, that the Armenians are not telling the truth about the genocide, comes across in the English titles of some of the pamphlets.

For most people, Kars is a base for trips to the abandoned Armenian city of **Ani**, 43 kilometres further east, just past Ocakli village. Driving there takes you past some of Turkey's poorest, bleakest homesteads: low, whitewashed buildings with turf roofs that somehow evoke the west coast of Ireland. Officially you're not supposed to stop in any of the villages in this 'restricted' border area. In practice, provided you're discreet, nothing worse is likely to happen than having children mob you.

At first sight Ani's solid curtain walls make it look like a medieval Welsh castle. Once you've double-tracked through the Alp Arslan gateway, though, you find yourself on a vast empty plateau hemmed in between the River Ahuryan and the Russian border, and a densely-farmed valley floor. On one side ugly watchtowers loom, on the other a honeycomb of caves, some of them occupied.

Hard though it is to believe now that nothing remains of the town but a scatter of ruined churches, Ani was once home to 200,000 people, many more than modern Kars. Its demise was the result of a lethal combination of Mongol raids and an earthquake in 1319. Despite the more relaxed, post-glasnost atmosphere you'll still have a military escort round the standard circuit which starts with the Chapel of the Redeemer, an eleventh-century circular building, now half collapsed. Not far away on the rim of the Ahuryan gorge is thirteenth-century St Gregory's Church, elaborately carved with peacocks, deer, dragons and foliage, and painted both on the inside and outside, mainly with scenes from the life of St Gregory. Heading away from the river again you come to the ruined tenth-century Cathedral, a huddled building more conservatively decorated with blind arcading, its dome only partially collapsed.

Back on the edge of the gorge you'll find the eleventh-century Ebul Menucer Cami which offers framed views of the Russian watchtowers from its windows. The minaret is technically off-limits but the soldiers will probably turn a blind eye if you attempt the hairy ascent. Ani's Citadel is out of bounds, but turning back towards the gateway you'll pass the ruins of the Church of St Gregory Abighamrets, the Church of the Holy Redeemer and the Church of St Gregory Gagik. It's worth walking right across the site to the ruins of a Seljuk palace offering a fine view of the densely-cultivated valley below. Returning to the gateway, look out for a swastika outlined in black brick in the sand-coloured walls.

Accommodation

Middle Range

Yilmaz, Kucuk Kazim Bey Caddesi 24 (Tel. (021) 11074). 30 rooms, conveniently positioned opposite the bus station, although the fittings and service are nothing to write home about.

The only real alternative if the Yilmaz is full is the 22-room **Temel**, Yeni Pazar Sokak 4 (Tel. (021) 11376).

Economy

Asya Oteli, Kucuk Kazim Bey Caddesi 48. **Nur Saray Oteli**, Faik Bey

Caddesi 26. None of Kars' budget hotels can really be recommended, but these two are the best of a bad lot.

Eating Out

Middle Range

The restaurant in the **Yilmaz** offers alcohol but sometimes slow and idiosyncratic service. Better is **Grand Manolya** in Ataturk Caddesi where the restaurant serves exquisite yoghurt upstairs and the coffee shop sells delicious cakes and puddings downstairs.

Economy

Ataturk Caddesi has several good, cheap kebab and *pide* restaurants, including **Antep Pide ve Lahmacun**. Also good is the **Baskent Lokantasi** near the bus station. Otherwise, once again it's take your pick, with Halit Pasa Caddesi a good place to start looking. For picnics to take to Ani, explore the shopping area for wonderful ripe cheeses with letters cut into their rinds, red-gold honey in illuminated jars and honeycomb sold in wooden frames.

Useful Addresses

Tourist Office: Ali Bey Caddesi. This is where you go to get permission to visit Ani. **Post Office**: Okul Caddesi. **Hospital**: Okul Caddesi.

Transport Options

Within Kars itself you can walk to all the sites. However, you'll need transport to get to Ani. There are a few buses, but their schedules won't necessarily coincide with yours. Provided you visit during the busier times of year, you should be able to arrange a private taxi or minibus tour with other travellers.

South of Kars

From Kars most people head south for Dogubeyazit, past mainly desolate scenery, with long stretches of unbroken flat land, cultivated in medieval-style strips. Huge purple thistles line the roads, and in summer the hills are tinged mauve with wild flowers. You'll pass beekeepers' makeshift camps, ringed with bright blue hives, and humble villages whose mud-brick houses have apricots laid out to dry on the roofs, most of them rarely visited by outsiders. Without private transport it will be hard to stop, but if you get the chance you're guaranteed a warm welcome. The difference between Ocakli, which sees frequent tourists en route to Ani, and a village like Kotek, through which they usually travel non-stop on buses, is enormous. At Ocakli you will be besieged with importunate demands for sweets. At Kotek you will be welcomed formally and the only requests will be polite ones for your address.

It's worth trying to stop at **Tuzluca** where salt-mines worked since Byzantine times are still in use and visitors are welcome to explore an eerie landscape of glass-like salt crystals, and huge caverns with paths sloping down to hidden lakes. From Tuzluca until Igdir you pass through a fertile area where most of the region's vegetables are grown. In **Igdir** itself the **Saray Lokantasi**, an Iranian-run restaurant, sells delicious Noah's Pudding.

Dogubeyazit

A small town of about 33,000 people, Dogubeyazit has a frontier feel to it. A vast indoor shopping mall positively overflows with cheap electrical goods imported from across the Iranian border, just forty kilometres away. If you're out of film this is the place to stock up again. Dogubeyazit is one of those places where everyone wants to talk; ask about the Kurdish situation over a glass of *cay* and you'll be there all night.

In the town itself there's nothing much to see. However, just outside is one of Turkey's truly great sights; the **Isak Pasa Sarayi**, famous from innumerable photographs which manage to suggest that it still stands in splendid isolation above the surrounding desert. Unfortunately this is one of the places where government claims to be protecting the environment ring most hollow. A line of pylons runs right beside the road up to the palace, terminating in a generator right against its walls. Also lining the road are a sequence of ugly advertising hoardings, mainly erected by hotels, but also by Trek Travel (who should know better) and by the local *hamam*. One of these signs actually welcomes visitors to 'Noah's Ark Country'! As if that wasn't bad enough the government has recently allowed a restaurant resembling a concrete bunker to be cut into the hillside immediately overlooking the palace.

The palace does its best to rise above all this, and certainly once you get inside the only question marks might be about safety precautions for visitors scrambling over the walls and about the damage that their scrambling must be causing to the structure. It's easy to assume the palace is ancient, but in fact work only started on it in 1685; it was completed almost a century later. You enter through a lofty gateway, its gold-plated gates long since carted away to the Hermitage Museum in St Petersburg. A huge empty courtyard gives way to a smaller one with the harem and the men's quarters opening off it. The harem contains bedrooms with fine views of the surrounding valley, while the men's quarters contain a delicately-decorated private mosque.

However, the palace's real claim to fame is more its setting than the details of the interior, making the cavalier way in which it is being treated all the sadder.

Dogubeyazit is also the base for visits to **Mount Ararat** which looms over the town, capped with snow even in the height of summer. Some believe this is where Noah's Ark came to rest although no convincing proof of this has ever been found. Because of its strategic position right by the Iranian border, visits are strictly controlled. The most straightforward way to climb the mountain is to join one of Trek Travel's organised trips (see **Discovering Places**). If you're determined to go it alone you'll have to apply for a trekking permit three months before leaving for Turkey and then persist in chasing up your application until something happens. Even then you'll have to take a guide with you and the compulsory cost of hiring mules, walkie-talkies and so on means you'll need to budget for a costly climb. The easiest ascent is from the Igdir side of the mountain. July and August are probably the best months for climbing since most of the snow will have melted. However, in June the skies are often clearer, offering better views.

Much simpler to visit is the site of a giant **meteor crater** on the road towards Iran, although again its sensitive position means you'll need to take one of the organised tours sold in Dogubeyazit.

Accommodation

Middle Range

Sim-Er Moteli, Kaya Burun PK 13 (Tel. (0278) 1601). 130-room hotel in its own grounds five kilometres out of town on the road to Iran. Light, airy rooms, some with magnificent views of Mount Ararat.

Hotel Isfahan, Emniyet Caddesi 26 (Tel. (0278) 1139). A comfortable 73-room trekkers' hotel right in the town centre.

Economy

Isak Pasa Hotel, Emniyet Caddesi 10 (Tel. (0278) 1245). Best of the cheaper hotels, right in the town centre.

Hotel Tahran, Buyuk Agri Caddesi 86 (Tel. (0278) 2223). Relatively clean and new with showers in the rooms.

Eating Out

Dogubeyazit is far from a gourmet's paradise. The best meals are to be had in the big hotels; the **Hotel Isfahan** has a particularly good restaurant. Otherwise, it's the usual kebab and *pide* places.

Transport Options

The town is very small and you'll be able to walk everywhere you want to. However, to get to Isak Pasa Sarayi you'll need to hire a taxi, obviously cheaper at the times of year when you can assemble a group.

South-East Anatolia

Once past Dogubeyazit you head towards South-East Anatolia which extends to Yuksekova, Hakkari, Diyarbakir and Kahramanmaras in the south, and Pinarbasi in the west, with the Hatay as a curious, semi-Syrian offshoot to the south-west. One of the poorest parts of Turkey, this is nevertheless the area that stands to gain most from completion of the GAP Project and the giant Ataturk Dam. The further south you go, the more you'll be penetrating the Kurdish heartlands. Given the tense political situation there, you should be particularly careful what you say and do and where you go outside the main 'milk run' tourist towns.

From Dogubeyazit the main road heads south, running close to the Iranian border, before turning inwards towards **Muradiye** and **Lake Van**. Just before Muradiye a yellow sign points you to a fine waterfall on the Bendimahi River approached across a stomach-churning swinging bridge; a tea shop with a pleasant verandah allows you to soak up the view in comfort. Muradiye itself is a dismal town with scant ruins of a castle. However, shortly after you pass through it you'll get your first glimpse of Lake Van.

Van

Van is a sprawling town of about 150,000 inhabitants with a somewhat makeshift air about it. Set back from the actual lake, it has a surprisingly enclosed feel. However, it's definitely livelier than other eastern towns; you may even find something to do at night.

The most important sight in Van itself is the **Rock of Van** to the west which overlooks the abandoned site of Old Van and the fringes of the lake. The Rock is actually a citadel dating back to Urartian times, containing the hollowed-out tomb of King Argistis at the base of a flight of steps that passes a wonderful rock-cut Urartian inscription. Cut into the base is a Muslim saint's shrine, visited each Thursday by unmarried women. On the summit are remains of a later Ottoman castle and mosque, complete with another barely climbable minaret. Scrambling up the Rock of Van can be tricky, so take sturdy footwear. A good time to visit is at sunset when you can watch the sun dropping behind the Lake.

You can get to the **Old Van** site direct from the Rock, but apart from remains of two Ottoman mosques, there's little to see except humps and hillocks covering the old buildings, destroyed in disputed circumstances (the Turks say the Armenians did it, the Armenians say the Turks did it) in 1915.

Back in New Van the fine **Museum** displays Urartian jewellery, pottery, glass, etc. Once again the upstairs section is devoted to ethnography, with good collections of carpets, kilims and clothing.

From Van you can visit the Urartian site of **Cavustepe**, twenty-five kilometres south off the road to Yuksekova. Cavustepe was once the Urartian capital and the hill is adorned with the remains of a fortress-cum-palace. It's a desolate spot and you may well share it with no one other than the custodian, who knows everything there is to know about the site and is keen to show people round. Most of what you see is the palace rooms, some with deep cisterns, but there is also a temple site, its gateway decorated with such sturdy basalt slabs you could be forgiven for thinking they were modern copies, and what must be one of the oldest known hole-in-the-ground-type toilets.

Thirty kilometres further south, **Hosap Castle** couldn't be more different. Built in the seventeenth century by a Kurdish chieftain it looks like something out of the Magic Kingdom cast in dusty desert colours and jutting up in the middle of nowhere. Hosap is less sleepy than Cavustepe and you'll be mobbed by sweets-seeking children, all wanting to clutch your hand in their own sweaty mitt. Inside, the castle is a haven of peace where you can, if you have enough energy in the debilitating heat, explore some of the hundreds of ruined rooms, including a *hamam* and mosque. From the castle's roof a fine view takes in the surrounding desert and hills topped with jagged-edged mud-brick walls, said, somewhat dubiously, to date back to Urartian times.

But one of Van's biggest attractions is its proximity to the **Lake** and its soapy-textured waters. Even if you don't fancy swimming, you'll probably want to take the ferry out to **Akdamar island** to visit one of the finest surviving Armenian churches. As you approach by boat it looks like any one of the many Seljuk *kumbets* you see in Kayseri. However, at closer quarters you find a ruined domed tenth-century church, its walls thickly encrusted with huge carved figures, mainly taken from Bible stories; in particular look for Daniel in the lion's den, Adam and Eve, David and Goliath, and Jonah and the whale. Inside are fast-fading murals of the Raising of Lazarus, the Presentation in the Temple, the Entry into Jerusalem and the Pantocrater.

The road to Akdamar passes through **Gevas** where it's worth stopping to compare the church's design with the later Seljuk *kumbet* in a cemetery. A *medrese* is being excavated there too, and the archaeologists will be keen for a chat. Despite one cluster of hideous concrete buildings, supposedly housing an orphanage, Lake Van seems to have escaped the worst of the ugly domestic tourism development that so mars the Marmara shoreline.

Accommodation

Middle Range

Buyuk Urartu Oteli, Cumhuriyet Caddesi 60 (Tel. (0611) 20660). A 75-room hotel in a conveniently central position; this hotel has some truly palatial rooms with bathrooms on a scale to match.

Hotel Akdamar, Kazim Karabekir Caddesi 56 (Tel. (0611) 18100). Another 75-room, centrally-placed hotel, but a little older and less spacious than the Buyuk Urartu.

Buyuk Asur Oteli, Cumhuriyet Caddesi 126 (Tel. (0611) 18792). Smaller and older, this hotel has slightly lower prices to match.

Economy

Hotel Van, off Sihke Caddesi. The place to go if you want to meet other travellers on a tight budget.

Hotel Caldiran, Sihke Caddesi. Should the Van be full, this is a handy, if slightly more expensive, alternative.

Luks Aslan Oteli, Eski Hal Civari. A family-run, cheap hotel with some good rooms; ask to look round before committing yourself.

Should these three be full, Van has lots of other budget rooms available, with little to choose between them. **Akdamar Camping Restaurant**, opposite the quay for boats to Akdamar island, has very basic camping facilities.

Eating Out

Middle Range

As usual, the best restaurants in town are in the big hotels, the **Buyuk Urartu** and **Akdamar**. However, despite the Lake's proximity don't expect to find much fish on offer. Service too can be lackadaisical. They do serve *otlu peynir*, or locally-produced herb cheese, though. If you'd rather eat in town, the **Kosk** in Maresal Cadmak Caddesi offers a choice between dining out of doors by a fountain where you'll be plagued by mosquitoes, or indoors where you'll pay more for the same food. Good choice of *mezes* though.

Economy

At the bottom end of the price range Van offers the usual range of kebab and *pide* restaurants. Amongst the best are: **Altin Sis Firinli** on Cumhuriyet Caddesi and **Solen Lokantasi**, Kazim Karabekir Caddesi. While on Akdamar island you can have a kebab and bulgar wheat barbecue at purpose-built picnic tables; place your orders at the **Akdamar Camping Restaurant** before catching the boat.

Entertainments

While in general Van is as much an entertainment desert as the rest of Eastern Turkey, the **Kosk Restaurant** does sometimes offer folk dancing and singing and belly-dancing sessions. These are very popular with the locals, and alcohol flows freely, so by the end of the evening you're bound to have made a friend or two.

Useful Addresses

Tourist Office: Cumhuriyet Caddesi 127. **Post Office**: Cumhuriyet Caddesi. **Turkish Airlines Office**: Cumhuriyet Caddesi 196.

Transport Options

To get to the Rock of Van you'll need to take a *dolmus* from Bes Yol, the square linking Cumhuriyet Caddesi and Sihke Caddesi. That's also where you'll pick up a *dolmus* to Gevas and the jetty for crossings to Akdamar Island. At the jetty you'll be able to get a boat across to the island, although unless you're in a group you may have to wait for enough people to assemble or pay a hefty fee to hire the whole boat.

Daily boats leave from the quay at the bottom of Iskele Caddesi (south of the Rock of Van) for Tatvan at the opposite end of the lake.

South of Van

From Van there are two possible routes on to Diyarbakir. The first heads south through Baskale and on to **Hakkari**. This route passes very close to the Iraqi border and is therefore crawling with soldiers. **Hakkari** itself is an uninspiring town, but the base for finding a suitable guide and exploring Cilo Dagi (4136 metres). If you do want to do that the best place to stay is the **Hotel Umit**, Altay Caddesi (Tel. (1408) 2467) which also has a handy restaurant.

Beyond Hakkari the road deteriorates and is frequently impassable in winter. You will probably have to hitch through Sirnak to **Cizre**, knowing that there is little proper accommodation before that. Once you get to **Cizre**, however, the situation improves and you'll be able to pick up a bus on to Mardin. However, in March 1992 there were serious disturbances between the Kurds and the police here, so check very carefully before visiting.

Mardin is one of Eastern Turkey's few architectural gems, staggering up a hillside, with winding, enclosed streets, hidden courtyards and gardens that bring Old Jerusalem forcefully to mind. The main sight is the fourteenth-century Sultan Isa Medrese right at the top of the town, with a finely-carved stalactite-style Seljuk doorway, but there's a particularly beautiful arched stone house in Birinci Caddesi too. Look out for spangled red and blue suits in shop windows, worn by small boys at their circumcision ceremonies. Nevertheless this is a town where sadness lurks just beneath the surface. The Iraqis you see strolling the town are mainly Kurds forced to flee in 1988 when Saddam Hussein dropped poisonous gas on their villages. The **Turistik Restoran** in Birinci Caddesi sells such local delicacies as *icli kofte* (meatballs with a crispy bulgar wheat coating) and *iskembe dolmasi* (stuffed stomach lining).

From Mardin you can walk the four and a half miles into the surrounding **Tur Abdin Plateau** to visit the **Deyr-az-Zaferan** (Saffron) Monastery, seat of the Syrian Orthodox patriarchate, now based in Damascus, from 1160 until the 1920s. However, in summer this would be a tough trek; taking a taxi would be wiser. The monastery dates back in part to the eighth century (an underground chamber is also said to have been used 4000 years ago by sun-worshippers), but most of what you see is later and bears some resemblance to St Katherine's in Sinai. Despite its considerable size, it's a sad place with only two monks and one nun still living there. They run a school for orphaned boys, some of whom you may see reading in the courtyard. In return for a small tip you'll be shown round the monastery on a tour that reveals the Patriarch's old reception hall, his throne and bedroom. From the roof, all but merging into the sandy scenery, you'll be able to make out the ruins of two neighbouring monasteries.

If you want to visit Mardin but would rather avoid the tense border route, another road heading due south from Diyarbakir will take you there too.

The road west from Van to Tatvan and then through Bitlis, Kozluk and Silvan to Diyarbakir is much easier. **Tatvan** is an ugly town where you won't want to linger. However, it makes a good kicking-off point for exploring the northern shores of Lake Van which see far fewer visitors than the southern ones. You might, for example, want to take a day tour up **Nemrut Dagi** (2935 metres), a dormant volcano with a pretty lake in its crater. A little further round Lake Van is **Ahlat**, home to a sprawling Seljuk cemetery full of elaborately-carved headstones sticking out at all angles. In surrounding fields stand several Seljuk *kumbets*, circular tombs, their shape probably inspired by nomadic tents; best of them are the Ulu Kumbet (Great Tomb), the Cifte Kumbet (Twin Tomb) and the fifteenth-century Bayinder Turbesi which has a distinctive porch and prayer room. A road north from Ahlat leads to **Malazgirt** (once Manzikert), site of the crucial Seljuk victory over the Byzantine forces in 1071, although there's nothing much to see there now. With longer to spare you could continue round the lake to Adilcevaz from whence it might be possible to climb **Suphan Dagi** (4058 metres) in July or August.

Bitlis, set in a rocky gorge and following a river bed, is much more attractive than Tatvan, its allegiance made plain in the name of the main road: NATO Street. Stepped-back alleys emerge on tea terraces above the shops, and there's a fine castle on a hill overlooking the town. Bitlis sees few tourists, and none of its three hotels is particularly good. However, if you want to experience life in a 'normal' East Turkish town, you could do a lot worse than stop here for a few days. On the outskirts, watch out for bright-green tobacco leaves hanging out to dry in the sun.

From Bitlis to Baykan the main road winds through attractive gorge scenery with rocks rising steeply on either side of it, small boys swimming in the river below and water cascading over occasional rocky outcrops. The surrounding vegetation grows scrubbily in gingery brown soil, although there are occasional poplar and olive groves. Halfway between Bitlis and Baykan two vine-shaded restaurants overlook the road. Popular with truck drivers, they serve excellent staples, like lentil soup and rice. Sadly, you only need to cross the road to find the rubbish carelessly discarded on the riverbank.

Beyond Baykan the scenery grows steadily more arid and desert-like. However, just before Silvan you'll pass the **Malabach Kaprusu**, a marvellous, high-arched twelfth-century bridge, much appreciated as a shelter from the blazing sun by passing sheep and goats. The town of **Batman** gained a certain notoriety during the Gulf War when many reports were filed from there. It's the site of one of a network of dams which should eventually 'green' this part of Turkey. South of Batman the Midyat road leads to **Hasankeyf**, capital first of the Artukid Turkomans and then of the Kurdish Ayyubids. The ruins of the old city perch on a cliff-top overlooking the river Tigris; look out for a twelfth-century palace with a fine view of the river, a mosque and houses with delicate decoration. The most substantial survival is the fifteenth-century, tile-clad Zeyn El-Abdin Turbesi, Turkey's finest piece of Ayyubid architecture.

Diyarbakir

A huge town of about 250,000 people, Diyarbakir, too, was very much caught up in the events of the Gulf War. Although most of what you'll want to see lies in and around the ancient walled city, Diyarbakir actually extends into modern suburbs where shops and restaurants pander to the tastes of the men from the American bases; if you're desperate for a pizza and ice-cream this could be the place to find it.

Old Diyarbakir is almost entirely ringed with huge, basalt **Byzantine walls**, dating from the fourth and fifth centuries. You can climb on to these at various points around the city to get your bearings. However, the most architecturally-striking parts of the walls are the huge **gateways**

(Harput Kapisi, Mardin Kapisi, Yenikapi and Urfa Kapisi) which bear fine **relief carvings**, and the remaining towers. The **Tower of Seven Brothers** (Yedi Kardes Burcu) has some of the best reliefs, of Seljuk lions and eagles.

Inside the town walls, the **Ulu Cami**, dating from 1091 and with a rectangular Arab-style courtyard, is a good place to start exploring; look out for old Roman capitals built into the stonework of the library. Just across the road is the **Hasan Pasa Hani**, a sixteenth-century *kervansaray* now filled with earnest carpet-sellers. Behind the mosque is the **Ziya Gokalp Muzesi**, erratically open but housed in a beautiful, peaceful courtyarded building. In the chaotic surrounding streets you'll spot several distinctive mosques, with black and white striped minarets built from basalt and white sandstone; the largest of these, the **Behram Pasa Cami**, dates from 1572.

Also in the backstreets, although hard to find without a guide, are a couple of Armenian **churches** and a Syrian Orthodox one. One of the Armenian churches is in ruins since its roof collapsed; funds are unlikely to be found for repairs, so take care when walking around inside. The building which has taken its place is of only passing interest. However, **Surp Giragos** is a fine, barn-like building, filled with icons framed in light bulbs like so many Hollywood film star posters.

The town **museum** is outside the walls, along Ziya Gokalp Caddesi to the north. This is the place to go if you'd like to find out more about the curiously-named White and Black Sheep Turkomans who ruled parts of Eastern Anatolia in the fifteenth century.

The specific sites apart, Diyarbakir repays exploration on foot, although it's sometimes tough getting rid of persistent and wily unofficial guides, many of them young boys speaking perfect English and very reluctant to confess their real aims in pursuing you. The side-streets off Gazi Caddesi are a good starting point where you'll find shops selling a fantastic assortment of animal innards for the pot. Many of the huge melons for which the city is famed will also be piled up beneath awnings in summer. This is also the place to look if you'd like a pair of baggy Kurdish trousers; be ready to haggle like mad.

With perhaps 50 per cent of its population un- or underemployed and 35 per cent unschooled, Diyarbakir is desperately poor, and if you explore the section of the old walls around the Yedi Kardes Burcu you will be unable to avoid seeing the reality of this; women clutching sick children with no recourse to treatment, ramshackle housing, market stalls bearing such inferior food that it couldn't be sold in the town centre. Here, too, you may bump into more of the refugees from Saddam Hussein's gas attacks.

Politics is never far from the surface in Diyarbakir; express an interest and you'll be regaled with stories of gruesome torture and ill-treatment by the police. As recently as July 1991 the crushing of a Kurdish street demonstration led to several deaths and many serious injuries in full view of people staying at the upmarket Otel Buyuk Kervansaray.

Accommodation

First Class

Otel Buyuk Kervansaray, Gazi Caddesi, Deliler Han (Tel. (831) 43003). Rooms set round the bougainvillaea-draped courtyard of a converted *kervansaray*, near the town walls. By far the best choice for comfort and atmosphere.

Middle Range

Demir Otel, Izzet Pasa Caddesi 8 (Tel. (831) 12315). 39-roomed hotel in a busy street in the centre of town. Comfortable lounge and swimming pool.

Buyuk Otel, Inonu Caddesi 4 (Tel. (831) 15832). Like the Demir but a bit cheaper and perhaps a little more secluded from the touts.

Turistik Oteli, Ziya Gokalp Bulvari 7 (Tel. (831) 12662). Just outside the old town, 39 rooms in a 1950s building, set round an attractive courtyard with a fountain.

Economy

Van Palas Oteli, Inonu Caddesi. The backpackers' favourite with rock-bottom prices and an attractive fountained courtyard.

Hotel Malkoc, Inonu Caddesi, Sutcu Sokak 6. Pricier but with more comforts.

Hotel Kenan, Izzet Pasa Caddesi 20 (Tel. (831) 16614). Budget prices and a private *hamam*.

Amid Otel, Gazi Caddesi, Suakar Sokak 7. Occasional local entertainment in the bar.

Eating Out

As elsewhere in the east, Diyarbakir's best food is to be found in the hotel restaurants. Particularly pleasant is the **Turistik Oteli** where tables are set round the courtyard fountain; this is a good place to sample some excellent local aubergine dishes. There are lots of good, cheap kebab shops along Inonu/Izzet Pasa and Gazi Caddesis, although they're a little inclined to hurry you out.

Entertainments

Once again, Diyarbakir is not the place to go for a wild nightlife. Your best bet will probably be to befriend someone in the town and go visiting, or to spin out a meal at one of the hotel restaurants where alcohol is sold. The **Amid Otel** bar has occasional Kurdish music sessions, so try there as well.

Useful Addresses

Tourist Office: Lise Caddesi 24, Onur Apartimani. **Post Office**: Inonu Caddesi/Yeni Kapi Caddesi. **Turkish Airlines Office**: Kultur Sarayi Sok 15.

West of Diyarbakir

From Diyarbakir you can head south to Mardin (see above), and from there due west through the desert to **Sanliurfa** via Kiziltepe and Viransehir, a long, hot and dusty road journey, unrelieved by many points of interest.

Sanliurfa/Urfa

Sanliurfa, the medieval Edessa, is one of Eastern Turkey's more attractive towns, the modern buildings designed to blend in well with the lovely honey-gold old ones. In summer this is a baking hot place, where you'd be well-advised to steer clear of the local delicacy: uncooked kebabs. Supposedly the birthplace of Abraham, Urfa is on the Muslim pilgrimage route to Mecca, and you will see people, many of them clearly Arabs, in all sorts of elaborate costumes around the main shrine. Urfa is a stronghold of fundamentalism, so this is not a place to expect much in the way of alcohol or organised entertainment.

Urfa's focal point is the so-called **Cave of Abraham**, enclosed inside a mosque complex, partly dating back to Ottoman times and partly brand new. The surroundings have a Lourdes-like feel about them, with stalls selling rosaries, *kefillayhs* and all sorts of religious artefacts.

You may well feel unwelcome inside the complex and there is, indeed, something voyeuristic about going in there at all since the architecture itself is unexciting and you wind up staring at people praying.

Further down the high street you come to a more attractive group of buildings sited round a rectangular pool full of supposedly sacred carp. High on the hillside above you'll see the ruins of the **citadel** and a **pair of pillars**, commemorating the legend that King Nemrut had Abraham catapulted from on high into flames below for smashing temple idols. The prophet was miraculously saved when God turned the flames into water and the firewood into the carp who now swim so placidly in the pool, waiting to be fed chickpeas by visiting tourists. Beside the pool a large tea-garden offers shelter from the sun which blazes relentlessly on the glistening stonework.

Urfa is another place best explored on foot. A huge **bazaar**, some of it under cover, spreads away from the high street. A few carpets are on offer, but you'll also find entire booths selling things like taps and makeshift barrows retailing cheap garlic crushers. At the heart of the bazaar a vast courtyard is filled with tea tables where men play backgammon in the shade of a giant plane tree. Pick up a cheese-filled pastry from one of the booths to eat with your tea.

On the outskirts of town you can watch goats and sheep being sold by men in an impressive array of local costumes at the **livestock market**. Women need to be alert for bottom-pinchers in the crush.

From Urfa it's an easy taxi ride south to **Harran**, a 6000-year-old settlement right in the desert which was, successively, the site of an Assyrian trading post, a Roman town and an Arab university, the **ruins** of which can be visited although there's not much to see. Perhaps more interesting are the curious beehive-shaped mud houses in which local people live, although it's hard to escape the feeling of voyeurism here, too. As soon as you get off the bus you'll be 'adopted' by local children, the girls in long, brightly-coloured dresses. Their 'friendship' comes at a price and you may find the attention overwhelming, especially in the heat. If you do go inside one of the houses you'll find an odd lifestyle, clearly poor by western standards (many of the children are barefoot and filthy) although televisions and videos have pride of place. Most of the families speak Arabic rather than Turkish, but the children know enough English to make their expectations clear. To get round the conflicts, a group of beehive houses are now enclosed in a compound and act as a kilim-draped tea-room.

Heading west, another place worth a stop is **Birecik**, home to some of the world's last breeding bald ibises, hideous relatives of the more common stork. From Birecik the road continues on to **Gaziantep**, an important pistachio-growing centre where you might want to stop to visit the mainly Seljuk citadel and the museum. It then heads on to **Kahramanmaras** en route to Kayseri and Central Anatolia.

It is possible, even advisable, to use Urfa as a base for visits to **Nemrut Dagi**, despite the greater distance you'll have to travel to the mountain. However, most people head north for **Kahta** or **Adiyaman**, both of them chock-a-block with agents selling excursions to the giant Commagenian heads. Neither Kahta nor Adiyaman has much to recommend it as a place to stay. **Adiyaman** is a one-horse town although friendly enough away from the main drag. If you want to stay, the **Hotel Bozdogan** (Ataturk Bulvari. Tel. (878) 13999) is the most upmarket option, complete with swimming pool but no air-conditioning, a serious drawback in summer. Given that, you might as well opt for something cheaper; the **Motel Sultan**, also on Ataturk Bulvari, is one possibility. In Kahta, the upmarket choice would be **Hotel Merhaba** in Carsi Caddesi (Tel. (8795) 1970). Again, you might prefer something cheaper, particularly since you'll have to get up at the crack of dawn to be on the mountain in time for sunrise. **Fortuna Camping Pansiyon**, on the outskirts of town, is as cheap as you'll get; if all the beds are full you can camp in the grounds.

Another possibility, particularly if you've hired a car for the trip, is to stay somewhere en route to the summit. In summer the best choice might be **Zeus Motel**, past the village of Karadut (Tel. (8781) 2180). In Karadut itself you could try the **Apollo Pansiyon**, **Restaurant ve Camping** (Tel. (8795) 1246) for a night under canvas or cover.

The colossal heads of Nemrut Dagi offer one of Eastern Turkey's best-known images although their purpose is less well known. In fact they were built to adorn the mausoleum of the second Commagenian ruler, Antiochus I Epiphanes (64–38 BC). The site was effectively forgotten until 1881 and then only properly excavated in 1953; it is now a National Park and a designated World Heritage Site. Sadly, it has become a 'must' on tour group itineraries with the result that much of the romance has vanished. Groups time their visits for sunrise and sunset which might be a good reason for you to do otherwise; it's hard to feel much excitement about sunrise when all it reveals is hordes of fellow travellers milling over the ruins. Even if you camp rough at the summit, as some people manage to do, you'll still have to share it with the dawn crowds. During the rest of the day you may be luckier. In fact immediately after sunrise most of the tourists miraculously vanish, apparently without even inspecting the site they got up so early to see.

Whether you're driving yourself or have opted for an organised tour you should try and take in some of the sites on the way up the mountain as well as those on the summit. From Kahta you come first to the burial mound of Antiochus' wife and then to a well-preserved Roman bridge. A turn-off to the west leads to **Arsameia**, the ancient Commagenian capital with some fine reliefs including one of Hercules shaking hands with Mithradates, the first Commagenian ruler. Other remains include a blocked tunnel, a cistern and column bases. The road is fairly smooth until near the top where it's been laid with bone-rattling cobblestones. These eventually run out at a restaurant-souvenir shop complex where you buy tickets for the final ascent. It can be icy cold on the summit in the morning so take socks, gloves and a woolly jumper even in summer. Although it's an easy climb along narrow paths and over loose scree, early starters should also take torches with them.

A twenty-minute walk brings you to a terrace which nowadays doubles as a helicopter pad. This is where most people wait for the dawn, with the headless statues of Apollo, a fertility goddess, Zeus, Antiochus and Hercules lined up behind them. The actual heads, fallen in front of them, have been righted again and are much smaller than you might expect but none the less impressive for all that. A path winds behind the tumulus to a western terrace where you'll find even more heads, amongst them a particularly fine one of Fortuna. Reliefs here show Antiochus shaking hands with Apollo, Zeus and Hercules, and an astronomical chart. If you come for the sunset this is where you should wait.

Accommodation

First Class

Koran Oteli, Ipekyolu 13/A-B, Urfa (Tel. (871) 31809). A short bus ride from the town centre. Comfortable, air-conditioned modern hotel.

Middle Range

Turban Hotel, Sarayonu Caddesi, Urfa (Tel. (871) 3520). 55 rooms.

Hotel Harran, Ataturk Bulvari, Urfa (Tel. (871) 34743). Brand new hotel with 54 rooms. Popular with groups and fills up quickly.

Economy

Hotel Istiklal, Sarayonu Caddesi, Urfa (Tel. (871) 11967). Rock-bottom-priced rooms set round attractive courtyard.

Hotel Kapakli, Sarayonu Caddesi, Urfa (Tel. (871) 15230). A little more pricey but rooms have bathrooms, an important consideration given the heat of summer.

Eating Out

In general, the best places to eat in Urfa are, once again, the hotel restaurants where alcohol is usually available. Otherwise there are pleasant kebab and *pide* places along the main street leading down to the sacred pool. Snacks can also be had in the tea-garden beside the pool.

Useful Addresses

Tourist Office: Asfalt Caddesi 3/B, Urfa. **Post Office:** Sarayonu Caddesi, Urfa.

Transport Options

Urfa itself is small enough to walk round. However, to get to Harran or Nemrut Dagi you'll need to sign up for an excursion run by the **As Urfa** bus company in Asfalt Caddesi. For the Tur Abdin Plateau you'll need a taxi.

The Hatay

Neglected by most tourists, the Hatay is where Turkey turns the corner of the Mediterranean and heads south towards Syria. In fact, until 1939 it belonged to the French Protectorate of Syria, and the present Syrian government would be happy to see it returned. This is a part of Eastern Turkey where there have been violent political disputes in the 1980s, and is consequently another bit which you should visit with one eye on the newspapers.

Iskenderun has a romantic name but is really just a modern industrial town. A better base for exploring the area would be Antakya, the ancient Antioch, which is easily accessible by bus from Adana or Gazientep.

Antakya

Modern Antakya sits in a valley pleasantly surrounded by hills. The River Asi serves to separate the neat modern town on the west bank from the higgledy-piggledy, Arab-type old town on the east one. Antakya grew to importance in Roman times, and the **Archaeological Museum** now houses some extremely fine Roman mosaics. The much-restored **Rana Koprusu bridge** dates from the third century AD, while the remains of the **Roman aqueduct** of Trajan also survive to the south of town.

St Peter is supposed to have preached from the **Sen Piyer Kilise**, a church built into a cave, with a twelfth-century façade added by the Crusaders.

North of Antakya you could try and visit **Bakras Kalesi**, an Arab fort rebuilt by the Knights Templar. Heading for the coast, you could also take in **Samandag**, a fading resort popular with Syrian visitors. Sea turtles nest on the beach here, but pollution makes swimming in the sea unwise. Instead you should visit what remains of Antioch's port, Seleucia, at nearby **Cevlik**; the most impressive relic is a channel built to divert mountain streams away from the town. Perhaps more enjoyable is the excursion south to **Harbiye**, a beautiful gorge with waterfalls where you can picnic in the shade of laurel and cypress trees. Even further south there's another ruined castle at **Qalat az Zaw**. By then you'll be well on your way to the Syrian border.

Accommodation

Middle Range

Buyuk Antakya Oteli, Ataturk Caddesi 8 (Tel. (891) 13426). 72 air-conditioned rooms, some with pleasant river views. Modern facilities include a nightclub and bar.

Economy

Atahan Oteli, Hurriye Caddesi 28 (Tel. (891) 11036). 28 rooms in a hotel which has probably passed its prime.

Divan Oteli, Istiklal Caddesi 62 (Tel. (891) 11518). 23 rooms in a reasonably comfortable hotel, conveniently positioned for the bus terminal.

Eating Out

Unless you eat in the **Buyuk Antakya Oteli**, you will be confronted with a range of simple eating places, the most interesting of them concentrated on the east bank of the river near the Rana Koprusu. Look out for Arab touches: mint and pimientos served with meals; *hummus* suddenly commonplace.

Useful Addresses

Tourist Office: Ataturk Caddesi 41. **Post Office**: Ataturk Caddesi.

Transport Options

Within Antakya you'll probably want to walk everywhere, although it's a five-kilometre round trip to Sen Piyer Kilise. *Dolmus* operate to Samandag and Harbiye.

There are daily bus services to Aleppo (four hours) and Damascus (eight hours) in Syria. Note, however, that there is no Syrian consulate in Antakya so you must sort out your paperwork in Great Britain or in Ankara before arriving at the border.

Regional & Local Tourist Information Offices

Tourist Information Office
Cinarh Mah Atatürk Caddesi 13
Adaha
Tel: (711) 111323

Tourist Information Office
Cumhuriyet Meydani
Akcakoca
Tel: 1354

Tourist Information Office
Kilicaslan Mah.
Otel Ihlara Yani 5
Aksaray
Tel: (811) 12474

Tourist Information Office
Edremit Caddesi Karabudak
Apt. 20 Zemin Kat
Akcay
Tel: 41113

Tourist Information Office
Carsi Mah. Calearkasi Caddesi
Alanya
Tel: 1240, 5436

Tourist Information Office
Saray Mah. Ataturk Bulvari 64
Anamur
Tel: 3529

Tourist Association of Turkey
Gazi Mustafa Kemat Bulvari 33
Demirtepe
Ankara
Tel: (41) 2317380, 2317395

Touring & Automobile Club
Dr. Mediha Adakale Sok. 4/11
Yenisehir
Ankara
Tel: (41) 1317648, 1317649

Tourist Information Office
Vali Urgen Meydani
Atatürk Bulvari 41
Antakya
Tel: (891) 2636

Tourist Information Office
Cumhuriyet Caddesi 91
Antalya
Tel: (311) 111747
Telex: 56121

Touring & Automobile Club
Mill Egemenlik Caddesi
Dallar Yildiz Carsisi No: 9
Antalya
Tel: (311) 17099

Tourist Information Office
Otel Vanessa Alti
Avanos
Tel: 1360

Tourist Information Office
Yeni Dörtyol Mevkii
Aydin
Tel: (6311) 14145

Tourist Information Office
Yat Limani Karsisi
Ayvalik
Tel: (633) 12122

Tourist Information Office
Terminal Ici
Balikesir
Tel: 31499

Tourist Information Office
Zafer Mah. Izmir Caddesi 54
Bergama
Tel: (5411) 11862

Tourist Information Office
Vilayet Binasi
Bilecik
Tel: (2291) 11588

Tourist Information Office
12 Eylüt Meydany
Bodrum
Tel: (6141) 1091

Tourist Information Office
Sumhuriyet Meydany 4
Cüitür Sarayikat 1
Burdur
Tel: 11078

Tourist Information Office
A Hamdi Tanpinar Caddesi
Saydam Is Merkezi 21 K 5
Bursa
Tel: (241) 228005, 227513

Tourist Information Office
Iskele Mey. 67
Canakkale
Tel: (1961) 1187

Tourist Information Office
100 Yil Kültür Merkezi Binasi
Cankiri

Tourist Information Office
Iskele Meyd. 8
Cesme
Tel: (5493) 26653

Touring & Automobile Club
Turkish/Syrian Transit Point
Cilvegözü
Tel: 11454

Tourist Information Office
Yeni Hükümet Konagi 8 Kat.
C Blok
Corum
Tel: 18502

Tourist Information Office
Dalaman Hava Limani
Dalaman
Tel: 1220

Tourist Information Office
Iskele Mah. Belediya Binasi
Datca
Tel: 1163, 1548

Tourist Information Office
Gar Istasyon Caddesi
Denizli
Tel: (621) 13393

Touring & Automobile Club
Turkish/Bulgarian Transit
Point
Dereköy

Tourist Information Office
Lise Caddesi 24/A
Diyarbakir
Tel: 12173, 17840

Tourist Information Office
Hürriyet Mey. 17
Edrine
Tel: (1811) 11518

Touring & Automobile Club
Kapikule
Edrine
Tel: (1811) 1034
Telex: 37173

Tourist Information Office
2 Sahil Yolu 13
Egridir
Tel: 1388, 2098

Tourist Information Office
Il Kalk kütüphansesi
Müdürlügü
Istasyon Caddesi 35
Elazig
Tel: (811) 11004

Tourist Information Office
Yali Mah. Hükümet Caddesi
54
Erdek
Tel: 1169

Tourist Information Office
Inönü Mah. Hükümet Caddesi
50
Erzincan

Tourist Information Office
Cemal Gürsel Caddesi 9/a
Erzurum
Tel: (011) 16882, 19127

Tourist Information Office
Iskela Meyd. 1
Fethiye
Tel: (6151) 11527

Tourist Information Office
Atatürk Mah. Foca Girisi
Foca
Tel: 1222

Touring & Automobile Club
Ali Fuat Cebesoy Bulvardi 5/D
Ganziantep
Tel: (851) 25224

Tourist Information Office
Özel Idare Ishani Kat: 2
Giresun
Tel: 13560

Tourist Information Office
Turkish/Iranian Transit Point
Hudur Kapisi
Gürbulak
Tel: 9

Touring & Automobile Club
Turkish/Iranian Transit Point
Gürbulak
Tel: 35

Touring & Automobile Club
Turkish/Iraqi Transit Point
Habur
Tel: 32

Tourist Information Office
Hacibektas Veli Müzesi Ici
Hacibektas
Tel: 1687

Tourist Information Office
Ipsala Hudut Kapisi
Ipsala
Tel: 1577

Touring & Automobile Club
Turkish/Greek Transit Point
Ipsala
Tel: 5

Tourist Information Office
Mimar Sinan Caddesi
Vakiflar Ishani Kat: 4
Isparta
Tel: 14438

Tourist Information Office
Atatürk Bulvardi 49/B
Iskenderun
Tel: (881) 11620

Touring & Automobile Club
Maresai Cakmak Cad. 8/2
Iskenderun
Tel: (881) 17462

Tourist Information Office
Mesrutiyet Caddesi 57/6-7
Galatasaray
Istanbul
Tel: (1) 1455693, 1456865,
1492782
Telex: 22224

Tourist Information Office
Hilton Oteli Girisi
Taksim
Istanbul
Tel: (1) 1330592

Tourist Information Office
Karaköy Limani Yolcu Salonu
Karaköy
Istanbul
Tel: (1) 1495776

Tourist Information Office
Sultanahmet Mey.
Sultanahmet
Istanbul
Tel: (1) 5224903

Tourist Information Office
Atatürk Hava Limani
Yesilköy
Istanbul
Tel: (1) 5737399, 5734136

Tourist Information Office
Iskele Meyd. 5
Yalova
Istanbul
Tel: (1) 12108

Touring & Automobile Club
Halaskargazi Caddesi 364
Sisli
Istanbul
Tel: (1) 1314631/-7
Telex: 27800

Touring & Automobile Club
Topkapi
Istanbul
Tel: (1) 5216588
Telex: 23841

Tourist Information Office
1 Atatürk Caddesi 418
Izmir
Tel: (51) 220207/8, 224409
Telex: 53451
Fax: (51) 216841

Tourist Information Office
2 Gaziosmanpasa Bulvari 1/C
Izmir
Tel: (51) 142147, 199278
Telex: 53451 tbiz tr

Tourist Information Office
Tourist Police
Liman
Izmir
Tel: (51) 255320

Touring & Automobile Club
Atatürk Bulvardi 370
Alsancak
Izmir
Tel: (51) 217149
Telex: 52565

Tourist Information Office
Kilicasla Caddesi 71
Iznik
Tel: 1933

Tourist Information Office
12 Eytul Bulvan Ataturk Parki
Ici
Sabanci Kültür Merkezi
Kahramanmaras
Tel: 15247

Tourist Information Office
Kapikule Hudut Kapisi
Giris Üniteleri Turing Terisleri
Kapikule
Tel: 1019

Touring & Automobile Club
Kapikule Gümrügü
Kapikule
Tel: 1034, 1327
Telex: 37173

Tourist Information Office
Lise Sokak
Kültür Merkezi Binasi
Kars
Tel: (0211) 12300

Tourist Information Office
Cumhuriyet Meydani 6
Kas
Tel: 1238

Tourist Information Office
Beled ye Binasi
Kemer
Tel: 1536/7

Tourist Information Office
Cumhuriyet Meydani
Asik Pasa Caddesi
Kirsehir
Tel: (4871) 11416

Tourist Information Office
Cumhuriyet Caddesi Kizilay
Ishani
Zemin Kat: 16
Kirklareli
Tel: 11662

Tourist Information Office
Mevlana Caddesi 21

Konya
Tel: (331) 111074, 120926

Tourist Information Office
Kordon Gölpark 1
Köycegiz
Tel: 1703

Tourist Information Office
Iskele Meydani
Kusadasi
Tel: (6361) 11103, 16295

Tourist Information Office
Ozel dare Sitesi Kat: 4
Kütahya
Tel: 36213, 35535

Tourist Information Office
Izzetiye Mah. Atmali Sok
Esnaf Sarayi Kat: 5
Malatya
Tel: (821) 17733

Tourist Information Office
Side Yolu Uzeri
Manavgat
Tel: (3211) 1265

Tourist Information Office
Iskele Meydani 39
Marmaris
Tel: 11035

Tourist Information Office
Yarhasanlar Mah. Dogu 8

Eylül Ishani 14/3
Manisa
Tel: 3685, 2541

Tourist Information Office
Inönü Bulvardi 5/1
Liman Giris Ünitesi
Mersin
Tel: (741) 16358, 11265, 12710

Touring & Automobile Club
Mücahitler Caddesi 55 K:2/10
Karadag Ishani 10
Mersin
Tel: (741) 20492

Tourist Information Office
Cumhuriyet Meydani
Belediye Atapark Sitesi
Mugla
Tel: (6111) 3127

Tourist Information Office
Atatürk Caddesi
Hastane Yani
Nevsehir
Tel: 1137, 2712

Tourist Information Office
Örenyeri
Pamukkale
Tel: 1077

Tourist Information Office
Il Halk Kütüphanesi
Cumhuriyet Mah. Dr. Kamil
Sok. 42

Sakarya
Tel: 21593

Tourist Information Office
1-19 Mayis Bulvari
Bestas Is Hani Kat: 7
Samsun
Tel: (361) 10014

Tourist Information Office
Atatürk Mak. 23
Agora Carsisi 35
Selcuk
Tel: 1328, 1945

Tourist Information Office
Side Yolu Üzeri
Side
Tel: 1004

Tourist Information Office
Gazi Mah. Atatürk Caddesi 1/2
Silifke
Tel: 1151

Tourist Information Office
Hükümet Konagi
Sivas
Tel: 13535

Touring & Automobile Club
Abdi Ipekci Caddesi 27/B
Tasucu
Tel: 1463

Tourist Information Office
Belediye Yani Kütüphane

Talvan
Tel: 2106, 2108

Tourist Information Office
Vilayet Binasi Kat: 3
Tokat
Tel: (4751) 13753

Tourist Information Office
Vilayet Binasi Kat: 4
Trabzon
Tel: 35833, 35818

Touring & Automobile Club
Iskender Pasa Mh.

Cami Sok. 17/11
Trabzon
Tel: 17158

Tourist Information Office
Kayseri Caddesi 37
Ürgüp
Tel: 1059

Tourist Information Office
Il Halk Kütüphane Binasi
Kurtulus Mah. Enstitü
Caddesi
Okul Sok.
Usak

A Selected List of Non-Fiction Titles Available from Mandarin

While every effort is made to keep prices low, it is sometimes necessary to increase prices at short notice. Mandarin Paperbacks reserves the right to show new retail prices on covers which may differ from those previously advertised in the text or elsewhere.

The prices shown below were correct at the time of going to press.

☐ 7493 0961 X	**Stick it up Your Punter**	Chippendale & Horrib	£4.99
☐ 7493 0988 1	**Desert Island Discussions**	Sue Lawley	£4.99
☐ 7493 0938 5	**The Courage to Heal**	Ellen Bass and Laura Davis	£7.99
☐ 7493 0637 8	**The Hollywood Story**	Joel Finler	£9.99
☐ 7493 1032 4	**How to Meet Interesting Men**	Gizelle Howard	£5.99
☐ 7493 0586 X	**The New Small Garden**	C. E. Lucas-Phillips	£5.99
☐ 7493 1172 X	**You'll Never Eat Lunch in This Town Again**	Julia Phillips	£5.99

All these books are available at your bookshop or newsagent, or can be ordered direct from the publisher. Just tick the titles you want and fill in the form below.

Mandarin Paperbacks, Cash Sales Department, PO Box 11, Falmouth, Cornwall TR10 9EN.

Please send cheque or postal order, no currency, for purchase price quoted and allow the following for postage and packing:

UK including BFPO £1.00 for the first book, 50p for the second and 30p for each additional book ordered to a maximum charge of £3.00.

Overseas including Eire £2 for the first book, £1.00 for the second and 50p for each additional book thereafter.

NAME (Block letters) ....

ADDRESS..

....

☐ I enclose my remittance for ....

☐ I wish to pay by Access/Visa Card Number

Expiry Date